Stone Age Religion at Göbekli Tepe

From Hunting to Domestication, Warfare and Civilization

Karl W. Luckert

Foreword by Klaus Schmidt

www.triplehood.com

Library of Congress Cataloging-in-Publication Data

Luckert, Karl W., 1934 —

Stone Age Religion at Göbekli Tepe:
from Hunting to Domestication, Warfare and Civilization

Foreword by Klaus Schmidt.
Includes bibliographical references and index.

ISBN 978-0-9839072-2-0 paperback

1. Archaeology of Göbekli Tepe, a personal interpretation from the perspective of ethnology and the history of religions; pre-historic religion, pre-biblical religion.
2. Religion and Culture in evolution, theory and overview.
3. Religion in Evolution: (a) from gathering and hunting to domestication, Wemale, Ainu, Navajo, LBK Europe, the missing Scapegoat; (b) from domestication to hyper-domestication, Egypt, Greece, China.

Foreword by Klaus Schmidt

Director of Excavations at Göbekli Tepe
The German Archaeological Institute, Berlin

From his research in history of religions and ethnography, Karl W. Luckert presents in this book a refreshing personal interpretation. I will not hide the fact that I cannot without hesitation *(nicht durchgängig)* share his thoughts about the meaning of the T-pillars *(T-Pfeiler)* at Göbekli Tepe. But in this Foreword, such points shall not be judged from the perspective of a petty shopkeeper *(soll nicht mit Krämerseele geurteilt werden)*—not by itemizing and commenting on details that anyhow would not affect the sum total. I have gladly accepted the author's invitation to contribute some lines of introduction to his work. I thank Karl W. Luckert for his efforts to visit Göbekli Tepe on several days and to scrutinize the site with his own eyes. I thank him for our personal encounter that was thereby possible, and for this book where he has brought together a rich collection of materials toward an interpretation of the place.

—Compared to some decades ago, archaeology today can give more definitive answers to the important question of why humans—who were hunters and gatherers over the course of tens of thousands of years—have turned into food-producing farmers during the Holocene (beginning roughly 10,000 years ago). It was not as Gordon Childe, one of the leading archaeologists of the twentieth century, formulated, a shortage of resources that led humankind to a new relationship with nature and in this manner brought food production and sedentary living. What brought the new ways were not shortages caused by nature—not as far as the beginnings of new subsistence strategies were concerned.

—Of course, at the end of the Ice Age a basic global change of climate occurred. In North America and Europe, gigantic stretches of glaciation disappeared. With more than a hundred-meter rise in global sea levels, coast lines ran in entirely different directions. The fact that the stretch of *Beringia* was submerged and became the Bering

Sea—thereby separating Asia and America—is well known. Less well known is that large stretches of land were also flooded in the Near East. For example, the present Gulf of Persia took shape when once-dry land was flooded west of the Strait of Hormuz. In a similar and more complicated manner, the Black Sea was formed.

—In Asia Minor, in spite of the abrupt change of climate at the beginning of the Holocene, there was no decline in the amount of available foods—no decrease that would have forced humankind to adopt new strategies of survival. As we know today, the situation was the opposite. After a distinct dry phase, during the Pleistocene (1.6 million to 10 thousand years ago), came a rainier and more favorable climate for humankind and animals. To the environmental and climatic factors were added social changes that remained not without consequences for cultural development. The phenomena of large feasts and monumental sacred sites we have only come to recognize recently. Both are factors that have played an important and enlarged role in Asia Minor—as we find there for the first time people in transition between hunting and planting.

—How did this worldwide earliest Neolithic process get underway? After the last phase of cold climate subsided, what used to be huge stretches of tundra during the Ice Age turned into permanent forests which extended over large parts of Europe and Asia. With sufficient winter rains, the vegetation along the Euphrates and Tigris rivers blossomed exuberantly. Thick forests spread along the valleys, interspersed with lush meadows. Along the heights of mountain ranges, some savannah-like park landscapes took shape. Spread wide before the high Taurus and Zagros mountain ranges, the so-called "Fertile Crescent" was greening. In the form of a crescent moon, it embraced the deserts of the Arabic peninsula and offered ideal living conditions for animals and humankind.

—In this landscape, not only wild animals were at the disposal of Stone Age hunters and gatherers. Also available were many plant foods such as almonds, pistachios and other nuts, lentils and peas, chickpeas and wild grains. Of course, the wild forms of these varieties were still less productive than the bred and tested varieties we have today. Nevertheless, these rich resources, combined with improved harvesting strategies, enabled the gatherers to settle in suitable places and villages.

—Alongside sedentary dwellings was soon added a phenomenon that provided the basis for Neolithic living: food production. The gathering of wild plants was replaced with harvesting on fields that had been intentionally seeded. Wild wheat *(Triticum mono-coccum)* and barley became leading cultivars. Yields were increased by selecting the best seeds. For the first time in human history, there was domestication of selected species of plants, and of animals that were added soon after. Antecedent hunters were already used to taming individual young animals. Their practice transformed into a strategy for keeping domestic animals in groups. This process, which in light of its far-reaching consequences was designated "Neolithic Revolution" by Gordon Childe, eventually turned hunters and gatherers into planters and agriculturists. It happened toward the end of the 10th and 9th millennium BC in the Fertile Crescent—and it happened not only with regard to the domestication of plants and animals. Many more innovations were added soon afterward in architecture, in the manufacture of stone and bone utensils, and with artistic symbolic representations. At this point, the "package of culture" was tied, and the possession of this bundle guaranteed the superiority of those who owned it over those who did not. From that point on occurred the quick spread of Neolithic culture: its character was defined in Asia Minor, and from there it spread to Europe, Northern Africa and Middle Asia.

–But why did this bundle of innovations first appear in the Fertile Crescent along the Euphrates and Tigris rivers? Why during the Early Holocene did similar developments not come at the Danube, the Nile and Congo rivers? Here the monumental sanctuaries of Göbekli Tepe fit into the overall sketch. In no other mega-region, at the beginning of the Holocene, do we encounter such monuments.

–The interpretation of Stone Age monuments at Göbekli Tepe presents a challenge not only for excavators. At Göbekli Tepe, we step into new territory. It is therefore proper that our researches not be limited to the spheres of subsistence and ecology. We are being led far beyond the world of *Homo necans* (Man the killer). The maxim, "Power and Aggression are the Message of Stone Age Art," as formulated by Joachim Hahn, applies not only to the Aurignacian but, surely, also to societies of the Early Holocene. Thanks to the iconic finds from this period we may now, for the first time, penetrate the mental world of hunters who were transitioning to agriculture. These finds lead us into the world of *Homo pictor*. They supply precious data for a history of Stone Age images, as for instance Hans Belting's requested "New Science of Imagery," or materials for a "History of Remembrances" *(Gedächtnisgeschichte)* according to Jan Assmann. A primary goal of our excavations has been, and will continue to be, access to these imaged resources and their evaluation. And in this task we still have a long way to go.

—In any case, the systems of symbolic art and of architecture pertaining to the Göbekli Tepe monuments reveal a Stone Age society quite different from what we formerly thought about humans of some twelve millennia ago. This society was able to erect major edifices and embellish them artistically. A greater knowledge of technology and logistics, and a greater organization of man-power were required. But these innovations, in the meantime, could be attained more easily. The "feast" or "feasting"—as motor of social systems and as impetus for the accomplishment of collective works—are increasingly being moved to the center of our research. They help inform our explanations of ancient surprise achievements that simple-structured societies have accomplished. "Legendary feasts" *(Sagenhafte Feste)*; with this catchphrase a setting may be named that, like a conductor's baton, has regulated the rhythms of people's lives, not only in historical times but also during the era of gathering and hunting.

—As was the case with Ice Age artistic images, at Göbekli Tepe, too, we lack correspondences that might help reach beyond the monuments themselves. It is quite obvious that every attempt to reach further generates its own set of problems—such as focusing on surviving mythological themes from written sources of later periods, or trying to derive such themes from the still obscure world of images of Early Holocene hunter-gatherers—as from the depth and well-spring of bygone times. It is clear that now and in the future many interpretational threads will need to be traced and uncovered.

Berlin, August 2012, Klaus Schmidt

Author's Preface

The so-called "Neolithic Revolution" was probably the grandest cultural upheaval in which the Homo sapiens species has ever participated throughout its last six million years of becoming. Being viewed in hindsight, at least from this writer's perspective, it involved three major modes of human involvement—probably more. Firstly, it was an era of industrial innovation. Then the results of that innovation required large biological adjustments, and thirdly, major revisions in rational and religious orientation became necessary for balance.

—Between twelve and nine thousand years ago Göbekli Tepe was an industrial center where flint nodules were mined. The industrial teeth, claws, and talons of the Neolithic Revolution were artificial, and made of flint. Flint was flaked to provide "knives" with edges that would cut. Flint weapon points were knapped to pierce deeper. The same advanced weaponry which Neolithic hunters used to reduce fauna populations was still good enough several thousand years later, to kill and to chase domesticator folk behind fortified city walls, for safety first, and then to make virtue of necessity—to organize something that later would be named "civilization."

—With his improved Neolithic flint weapons Homo sapiens won his arms race against all the natural predators which, until then, had ranked solidly as totemic deities. Human populations grew while the fauna was being slaughtered. But then, having so reduced the resources for their own nourishment, the eventual domestication of plants and animals became unavoidable necessities. And indeed, emmer wheat, goats, sheep, and cattle were domesticated within easy reach of the Göbekli Tepe flint industry.

—The excavation of Göbekli Tepe led to the discovery of a hitherto unknown Neolithic religion—a Neolithic Cult of Atonement. A little after twelve thousand years ago, this cult established itself at the southeastern Anatolian hill-sanctuary complex that is now known as Göbekli Tepe. In all likelihood, the cult was organized by the same flint-workers who at that place made weapons—thus by shamans, hunters, miners, knappers, and sculptors. From the limestone "ovaries" of the Earth Mother, the Stone Age miners extracted quartzite flint "eggs," to flake, to knap, and to inflict death on animals more easily. For recompense and reconciliation, in appreciation for the Earth Mother, these industrial penitents quarried and sculpted the Earth Mother's own limestone ovaries into abstract shapes of monumental phalluses.

—Göbekli Tepe shows this religion of Stone Age hunters in a state of transition. After six million years of evolving into an artificial predator, an intellectualized killer, the humanoid hunter began to use his mind, finally, to think more about the processes of life. This is the path along which atonement with Mother Earth has motivated the Neolithic Revolution. The new religious attitude prepared hunters for conversion to the domestication of plants and animals. For hunters who did not convert, the Neolithic Revolution meant sliding into warfare and "hyper-domestication," sometimes called "civilization."

—Aside from introducing fascinating archaic subject matter, this book also intends to introduce an interdisciplinary theoretical perspective for archaeology, ethnology (anthropology) and the history of religions. It is high time to introduce scholars of these contiguous areas to theoretical bridges that transcend our traditional gaps of academic separation. To that end, our book offers a compilation of methodology, data, and theory, interspersed here and there with simpler, down-to-earth "predispositions." The rewards for this expanded approach will become obvious. Coherences among primitive archaeological data help us focus on the larger mysteries of human existence. They will help define facts of human evolution and help illuminate, perhaps, even our own destiny a little ways into the future. It has been said that those who ignore history must repeat it —I dare to extend this maxim to also include prehistory.

—Inasmuch as religion represents an inverse attitudinal mode to "culture," both these orientations must be approached together and contrastingly. The dimension of culture includes all the material artifacts that can be brought to the surface by the techniques of archaeology—everything that humankind has managed to inflict on prior natural conditions. The dimension of religion can be understood as multiple human responses that have been provoked by culture. Thus, to the extent that culture can be explained archaeologically, religion also can be surmised from those same archaeological data.

This insight affects then how culture and religion may together be detected as parallel phenomena in evolutionary strata, and how these became embedded in later historical processes. Culture and religion can be identified even more precisely among human activities and habits, at the surface—along the living stratum observed by ethnology.

—All this needs to be said, at the outset, to orient readers who might have prematurely concluded that for their general education "irrational religious" aspects should summarily be discounted. Different words mean different things to different groups of people. Modern societies, generally, do know a few things about religious habits that are less than three thousand years old—about how time-worn solutions, at seminal moments in history, were introduced to cure problems that were generated by civilization. Some of these religious saving "solutions" are still being summarized today under broad labels like Judaism, Christianity, Islam and such in the West, or Hinduism, Sikhism, Buddhism, Taoism, Confucian-ism and such in the East. Still older modes of religiosity, here and there, go under labels of shamanism and folk religion. Modern secular ideologies, such as democracy, communism, scientism, or philosophies a few centuries older, though they may still be endowed with a multitude of religious facets from ancient times, nevertheless do try to present themselves today as "nonreligious." Regardless of their claims of proximity to modernity, I intend to suggest in the course of this volume that remnants of Stone Age culture and religion—scientific experimental methods, theological meanings, and rituals—are still with us today.

—Seen through the lenses of this writer, there exist no non-scientific *homines sapientes*—and the only nonreligious people are imaginary ones, whose existence can therefore not be verified. Cultural aggression and religious retreats, and associated habits of thought, are universal aspects in all human modes of existence. They are vital processes, as essential to human beings as are inhaling oxygen and exhaling carbon dioxide—or as are taking in food and excretion. Our approach to the evolution of religion, at the scope of six million years of hominid attempts at culture-building, is therefore well suited to sketch historical profiles of meaning, to help edify human introspection.

—The virtual order of my son Martin, to the effect that indeed I "must" write this book—moods of finitude notwithstanding—is greatly appreciated in hindsight. For venturing into unknown territory it is easier to lean on someone else's convictions than to dare step into the dark with having only one's own hesitations as a guide. I thank Erika for having done a double round of adjusting my style to the sensitivities of native readers of English. Arne Hassing has read portions of the manuscript and has provided valuable suggestions. But none of these people have seen the manuscript as it now has taken shape. This means that the responsibility for all mistakes is truly mine. Ravi has given me once again some much appreciated advice on photography, before I traveled to southeastern Anatolia. Jens Notroff has supplied me with DAI photographs, while Klaus Schmidt has smiled benevolently on my efforts and, in the end, has agreed to write a "Vorwort." His perspective, from his vantage point as archaeological discoverer of Göbekli Tepe and director of excavations, remains very important to me. Then during the finishing stages of publication, Robert Hamerton-Kelly has provided friendly advice and strategic assistance. Thanks to each and every one—and to countless others who also should have been mentioned here!

—I dedicate this book to the memory of Li Shujiang, a Chinese colleague and research partner. Our cooperation in China and America has provided fresh depth to our understanding of the history and culture of his homeland. In addition to Li Zengjiang, Wei Cuiyi, and Yu Zongqi, five of Li Shujiang's Ningxia colleagues, English interpretors and students, have supported our mutual publishing efforts in the United States—as graduate assistants at Missouri State University. Zhang Zuotang and Du Xiaoyu have helped my personal efforts to become better oriented in Chinese ethnology and prehistory, with linguistic aid, as well as with field assistance.

Portland Oregon, Spring 2013, Karl W. Luckert

Contents

List of Illustrations

Fig. 1. Global Temperature Variations after the Last Glacial Maximum. Based on Steven Mithen, *After the Ice,* 2004, p. 12.
Fig. 2. Göbekli Tepe: One of many work sites, with flint chip debris. Insert: Image of a flint nodule. Photos by author, courtesy of DAI.
Fig. 3. Limestone slabs at the Southwest "knee" of Göbekli Tepe, looking northeast. Suspected point of the miners' first approach. Photo by author—courtesy of DAI.
Fig. 4. Simplified topographical map of Göbekli Tepe. Archaeological information is here reduced, and topography is highlighted to illustrate the suggestions presented in this book. The original is in Klaus Schmidt, 2008, p. 101. By Courtesy of DAI.
Fig. 5. The two orifices between which the first temple enclosure was laid out, marking the northern perimeter of the enclosure. On the left, please note the elevated lip. Photos by author—by courtesy of DAI.
Fig. 6. Enclosure E—*Felsentempel.* Southwest Promontory of the Göbekli Tepe plateau. See Schmidt, 2008, p. 107. Photograph—Courtesy of DAI.
Fig. 7. Backing off a few steps, north of the preceding photograph, one finds a pair of larger ceremonial pits. The stub of a broken-off pillar, in the left pit (east), still sits encased by supportive rocks. Photos by the author—courtesy of DAI.
Fig. 8. Pillar 18, Enclosure D, showing Fox totem and a twisted ribbon. Photo courtesy of DAI.
Fig. 9. Nevah Cori Totem Pole—tentative reconstruction by Klaus Schmidt. Courtesy of DAI.
Fig. 10. "Lion-Man" totem-pole from the Southwest Hill at Göbekli Tepe. Author photo—Courtesy of Sanliurfa Museum.
Fig. 11. A somewhat later statue from Sanliurfa may represent a priest or an anthropomorphic deity. Author photo—Courtesy of the Sanliurfa Museum.
Fig. 12. The central pair of *menhirs* 18 and 31, at Enclosure D. Author composite photo—courtesy of DAI.
Fig. 13. Pillar 33, Enclosure D, Author photo—courtesy of DAI. The composite author's sketch is based on four photos in Schmidt, 2008, 182ff.
Fig. 14. Blanket woven of snakes. On pillar 1, Enclosure A. Courtesy of DAI.
Fig. 15. Fourth Sandpainting in the Navajo Coyoteway Ceremonial. Anthropoid Coyote gods carrying stuffed "Coyote" skins and baskets. Photo by the author.
Fig. 16. Scene from the Navajo Coyoteway Healing Ceremonial. From left to right: 1. Patient. 2. Talking-god. 3. Masked Coyote girl impersonated by a woman. 4. Masked Coyote, a man carrying stuffed Gray-Fox skin. Photo by the author.
Fig. 17. Pillar 31 in Enclosure D. Photo by courtesy of DAI.
Fig. 18. *Menhirs* that were too slow to get out of the way. Young animals on Pillars 43 and 27—photos by courtesy of DAI.
Fig. 19-a. Southeast Promontory—"the left knee." Author photo by courtesy of DAI.
Fig. 19-b. Southwest Promontory—"the right knee." Author photo, by courtesy of DAI.
Fig. 20. The Lions Enclosure, View from the east. A limestone engraving of the Göbekli Tepe Earth Mother (Fig. 23, below) was found at the foot of the Northeast *menhir*, in the lower middle of the picture and seen as darker rectangle, partly hidden by that *menhir*. Photo by courtesy of DAI.

Fig. 21. New Excavation Area in the western crotch between the Southwest and the Northwest Hills. Author photo—by courtesy of DAI.
Fig. 22. Early significant finds at the new West Excavation Area, 2011. Author photos—by courtesy of DAI.
Fig. 23. The Göbekli Tepe Earth Mother, found in the Lions Lodge on a bench that connected and braced the eastern pair of freestanding pillars. Photo by Dieter Johannes—courtesy of DAI.
Fig. 24. Path of the Dead for initiates used by Temes Savsap, underworld Guardian at Malekula. Drawn after A. B. Deacon, 1934, pp. 127ff.
Fig. 25. Top view of Enclosure C, excavated to bottom level. Courtesy of DAI. Fig. 26. Enclosure C— DAI reconstruction, at http:/ /www.urgeschichte.org/Die Beweise/ GobekliTepe/gobeklitepe.htm.
Fig. 27. Enclosure C—Author drawing based on a DAI reconstruction, at http:/ /www. urgeschichte.org/DieBeweise/GobekliTepe/gobeklitepe.htm.
Fig. 28. The Holy Barnyard. A recently found "porthole-stone" sculpture at Göbekli Tepe. Northwest Hilltop. A similar photo image was first published in Klaus Schmidt, 2010, p. 252. Courtesy of DAI.
Fig. 29. Rock carving of a cow, near a natural outflow, resembling a bovine vagina. Photo by courtesy of DAI.
Fig. 30. *Menhirs* with hollows scraped into the top. Enclosure B. Source: Klaus Schmidt, 2010, Photo by Irmgard Wagner, courtesy of DAI.
Fig. 31. The Accumulation of Five Levels of Cultural Adaptation.
Fig. 32. The Teeter Totter Scale of Experiences and Responses.
Fig. 33. Stick figurine—Navajo Indian replacement sacrifice for a fellow predator. Author photo, by courtesy of Claus Chee Sonny.
Fig. 34. Wild Boar with Coconut. Adapted to "Ameta and Hainuwele" by the author. Based on Richard Bartz, Munich, habitat photo.
Fig. 35. Ainu *iomante.* Japanese hand-scroll painting. Courtesy, Trustees of the British Museum.
Fig. 36. The Narmer Palette. Courtesy: Trustees of the British Museum.
Fig. 37. Chamber One of Burial M45 of Yangshao grave at Xishuipo, Puyang Source: Pictures 6, Page 5, Plate One, in *Cultural Relics of Central China*, 1988. Courtesy of Du Xiaoyu. Redrawn and composition by the author.
Fig. 38. Dragon Rider. Burial 45, Chamber Three of a Yangshao grave at Xishuipo, Puyang. *Archaeology*, 1989, 12, p.1069, 4. Courtesy of Du Xiaoyu; Excerpted by author.
Fig. 39. Anyang, China: A Shang Dynasty excavation pit in a field of human sacrifices. Author photo, courtesy of Anyang Museum.
Fig. 40. Chariot and charioteer sacrifices. Author photo by courtesy of Anyang Museum.
Fig. 41. The third-year anniversary of the funeral of Zhang Jucai, in the summer of 2002, at Fanmagou, Ningxia. The invitation to this event was given by courtesy of Zhang Zuotang, nephew of Zhang Jucai. He can be seen, slightly bent forward to tend the fire, at the lower right. The man with the hat, standing behind him, is Zuotang's father—brother of the deceased. Photos are extracted from author videos.
Fig. 42. The Scapegoat, painting by William Holman Hunt (1827-1910). Courtesy of Wikimedia Commons.

PART ONE: ATONEMENT EMPOWERED THE NEOLITHIC REVOLUTION

Six Million Years to Göbekli Tepe

Over the course of six million years our hominid and
humanoid ancestors developed a predator's appetite and hunter
culture. In that time, while hunter culture became successful,
it also became religiously problematic for them. Human
intellect evolved while our ancestors were experimentally
reshaping sticks, bones, and stones into artificial teeth
and claws. Artificially augmented
aggression and science needed to be balanced by conscience,
feelings of guilt, and religious retreat.
The human species divided along gender lines,
into female scavengers and gatherers
and male predators.

1. Six Million Years to Göbekli Tepe

On the Romping Grounds of Primates

Glimpses of Prehistory: The first sanctuaries, built of limestone by flint miners some twelve thousand years ago, are found along the River of Time situated approximately six million years downstream from the romping grounds of our primate antecedents. At the man-made hillock named "Göbekli Tepe," in eastern Anatolia, these sanctuaries heralded a climax in the evolution of human hunting and gathering. They belong to a period that is now designated Pre-Pottery Neolithic (PPN). As a cult place Göbekli Tepe marks the beginning of a transition from gathering and hunting to domestication and hyper-domestication. Over the past ten thousand years, while visitors at the ancient cult place became less frequent, this process of transition has continued among hunter and gatherer cultures all around the planet. To this day, the shifting has not been fully completed anywhere in the world. Any domesticator or hyper-domesticator who occasionally reverts to hunting or who uses rock-derived minerals in constructions still draws from inventions and religious legitimizations that were first attained by Stone Age precursors.

—Those groups of artisans that built the ceremonial sites at Göbekli Tepe, and created ritual paraphernalia, were imitating and modifying knowledge that was learned as far back as the time when hominids were still indistinguishable from apes—or at least farther back than this author can safely imagine. But in spite of a writer's shortfalls in perception, an attempt of stepping back in time still seems called for to satisfy formal logic. We are being challenged by the archaeologists' data to sketch an approximate prehistory of

Göbekli Tepe culture, to catch glimpses of what must have happened in the past six million years to get us to where we are today.

—From which direction might one expect to obtain such evolutionary glimpses? As a historian of religions, I have been searching for them at many places around the globe, over more than five decades. I do not have as many spectacular discoveries to show as I would like to have. But then, if I fail to reveal the few things that I have noticed, or concluded, I would be sharing less than I should to fulfill my human duty.

Chimpanzee relatives: This introductory section about chimpanzees is only a very sketchy approximation of the religion of our hominid ancestors. The early hominids have all gone extinct. I suspect that along their path of evolution some of their younger cousins were too successful in fighting them. Nonetheless, as reflective members of the only surviving humanoid species, we owe it to ourselves to remain interested in the fate of our relatives. There are good reasons to suspect that our closer ancestors had something to do with the disappearance of related ancestral lineages. Could their difficulties have been caused by some of the same maladaptations with which *Homo sapiens* groups are still upsetting each other today? This question probably will never be completely answered by the descendants of guilty ones. But we can, tentatively, infer a few things about distant relatives by observing our nearest extant cousins—even though these cousins surely differ from us a little more than our own hominid ancestors did.

—When our adventurous Australopithecine or Ardipithecine ancestors left the forest, chimpanzees stayed behind, apprehensive, and probably watching with some feeling of relief when those proud progressives walked away and left them finally alone. Chimpanzees stayed at home in the relative safety among their trees. I appreciate their conservatism that today provides us with a sample of what life might have been like in remote ancestral days. It is even possible that our distant ape relatives learned reactionary survival skills while watching runaway relatives from a distance—watching those progressives struggle, and invent new experimental difficulties and misssteps for themselves.

—In any case, the story of those who remained behind among the trees can be read and contemplated as an analogy, as referring to groups of animals that apparently have not yet become introspective about their sins of eating. However, up to the present point in their evolution, these apes already trespassed occasionally against the lives and status of their own kind. Chimpanzees use all kinds of objects as tools, but they have not yet gone so far as to strike hard rock against another hard rock in order to make substitutionary teeth, or claws to be mounted on sticks and held in hands. This implies that they have not yet left any hard evidence of wanting to commit long-premeditated murder. Nor have they needed, in storytelling, to diminish a Stone Age sin of modifying quartzite "tooth-rock" in a quarry, and to diminish their story by daring to eat, instead, a forbidden soft tree-fruit in a garden owned by God.

—Not many decades ago, we discovered that our chimpanzee cousins, though quite capable of going on impulsive cannibalistic raids, are far from the brutes that they have been made out to be. They share their food far beyond the simple parent/child radius of care. The chimpanzee alpha male does not always keep the largest portion for himself, and special assistance on the part of some inferiors is acknowledged and rewarded about as frequently as in human society. It appears as though meat, in particular, is shared among chimpanzees in accordance with prior rights of ownership—meaning ownership by hunting, capture, and killing. Large animals have been seen begging from smaller owners.[1]

—The size difference between male chimpanzees and females is almost negligible. At the same time, the life-protecting authority of females is prominent. On one occasion, Frans de Waal counted no less than six confiscations of stones from the hands of an aggressive male by a peacemaker female. But restrictions in male chimpanzee ethics are not only imposed by active female interference. The typical male chimpanzee also harbors inhibitions of his own. When he gets into a fight with a female, he does not use his large canine teeth. Rather, he pinches with his regulars. He could not have learned this from a typical female, because when she defends herself or her young, she holds no qualms about which teeth she uses to make her points.

—Jane Goodall's pioneering work among chimpanzees has given us excellent insights into how our closest primate cousins interact

[1]Frans de Waal, *Chimpanzee Politics*. New York, 1982, pp. 200ff.

in the wild.[2] Students of primates and of human evolution will forever appreciate her efforts and observations. Frans de Waal, with a little more distance, managed to observe the overall process of "political" interactions among these animals.

—But what can we know about chimpanzee religion? Could the violent outbreak of cannibalistic warfare among estranged males at the Gombe Range have had something to do with a human misunderstanding of chimpanzee culture and religion? I suspect this might have been the case.

—Put yourself in the place of one of the juvenile chimpanzee males, who without outside interference would quietly and without embarrassment have been able to cultivate personal friendships with the leading matriarchs. Is it possible that the presence of an ever-silent and observant *Homo sapiens* goddess—Jane Goodall—could have had something to do with keeping young adult males away? Under the circumstances, with her presence she honored the slower moving inner circle, comprised of matriarchs and younger animals. Might not the pubescent males, whom mothers would have tolerated to play with their youngest while they were watching, have become frustrated because they no longer were able to do so? Could the deprivation of gentler "home experiences" have driven adolescents into estrangement and frustration and into a situation where they would erupt in violence? If nothing else, then at least the relatively divine (i.e. greater-than-chimpanzee) presence of Jane Goodall may have prevented juveniles from attending "babysitting school" and could so have created a generation gap—between pubescent males and the still younger members of the troop. Of course, at this stage in our quest for understanding we cannot know for sure the answer to all these questions. Nonetheless, questions about elementary "religion," per se, will be approached more systematically in Part Two of this book. Some readers may wish to leap ahead for a while.

—For a general overview on the evolution of hominid religion, it is helpful to approach the subject matter as an ongoing process of intellectualization—that is, as a gradual trickle of learning that began even earlier than the ape level. The phenomena of dominance and hierarchy formation are basic for an understanding of both culture and religion. These factors prevail among all the social species of the

---

[2]Jane Goodall. *Reason for Hope: The Spiritual Journey*. New York, 1999.

animal kingdom, alongside the more basic fact of being caught up in a food chain and in ecological niches. Implied also is a struggle for survival. These issues were not actually transcended when an ape raised her first *Ardipithecus* offspring. They were not abolished in favor of cerebral features when a *Homo erectus* pair engendered some *Homo sapiens* types. The intelligence of *Homo sapiens* needed to prove its worth. But then, mothers had no choice but to love what they got.

—The quest for survival within a food chain, as well as competition and mobility in social hierarchies, has not become more rational over time. It has only become more complex. The basic perceptions of what was up and down or high and low were at best, among later generations, sublimated and rationalized in terms of choices and greater detail. What at the animal level began as sharing, and what hominid "artificial" predators evolved into pursuit, trickery, robbery, murder, and eventually into atonement sacrifices to greater-than-humanoid predators, all this was learnt gradually and, as such, it had to be balanced with all other aspirations, abilities, and limitations.

—Shining some light at the opposite side of this issue at the greater-than-human dimension—and at corresponding human limitations—one can say that the outcomes of human activities have always been checked by natural or divine limitations that were being encountered. The outcomes have consistently been modulated by fear, caution, retreat, and religious common sense.[3]

Three styles of adaptation: In the quest for food, three styles together represent our oldest discernible stratum of hominid existence and of early culture in Africa. These styles are gathering, scavenging, and hunting. The first two of these eventually led to improvements for the third, which was self-initiated hunting. Our hunter ancestors from ape to human levels, when successful, took control of their victims, plants or animals, in order to terminate lives. Like all living beings on this planet, they "borrowed" or "took" remains of other life to sustain their own. They ended the lives of plants and animals on land, in water, and in the air, primarily to win food, but sometimes also to take—i.e. to rob—materials for clothing and shelter.

---

[3]Readers unaccustomed to thinking about "culture," "religion," and "science" as interrelated categories are encouraged to read for a while in Chapter Ten.

—As gatherers, scavengers, and hunters, our ancestors did not yet plant, breed, or nurture any offspring other than their own kind; nor did they master many tricks of taming and domesticating fellow animals—with the possible exception of the dog. They gathered wild fruits, foliage, vegetables, roots, nuts and seeds. They caught small and young animals and robbed eggs laid by birds and reptiles. They scavenged what they could from cadavers and overkill left by other predators. And they developed a taste for meat. Eventually, with improvements in their tool kit, they devised strategies for killing prey animals at their own hands, fresh "off the hoof." By utilizing flint chips and inventing knives, our hunter ancestors learnt how to butcher their victims more efficiently.

—For several million years the weapons of our ancestors were poor and almost indistinguishable from what could be found scattered naturally in the environment. Their hunting abilities were limited and they "harvested," so to speak, from the fringes of a still mostly mysterious domain. When they were desperate and when they dared, they trespassed into the domains of greater-than-hominid competitors that ordinarily surrounded and confined their space.

—A special type of animal, the mutant offspring of a breed of apes, has wavered in its evolution between being a forager and becoming a predator. When it was possible, humanoid females opted for a gentler lifestyle so as to nurture their young in peace. They tended to remain foragers. By contrast, the human males existed by and large in open competition with natural predators, which also meant that by and large they respected the abilities of their adversaries. They became envious of what those more able predators could do. They felt challenged to imitate and to hunt the same prey that those exemplary predators killed and ate.

—When males began to pick up bones and stones, and to utilize these more intensively by fashioning weapons, biological genders of the human species began sorting themselves out in cultural opposition. Occupationally polar, men became predators while women tended to remain gatherers and foragers. They came together as families for feeding, and they cooperated to protect and to raise their offspring. Basically, it can be said that tool and weapon manufacture drove the genders apart, and that the yields of hunting brought them together for intervals of sharing food. The children were raised by their mothers, and when the younger males grew old enough to become fulltime killers, as were their fathers, a traumatic ritual of initiation—a kind of second birth of training to become predators—became necessary.

Artificial Predators: Zoologically and anthropocentrically speaking, a new era began on Planet Earth when our ancestors of several million years ago used their fingers and thumbs to pick up rocks, no longer merely to throw a tantrum and to let rocks fly at random, but to take aim at specific targets—to throw rocks farther and harder, and more precisely than they could spit. In the course of time, by way of manufacturing artificial "teeth" and "claws" which they fashioned from wood, bone, and stone, the males of our lineage reinvented themselves as artificial predators. The method of scientific daring and experimentation became primary at that stage of development. They learned how to "bite" and even how to kill over significant distances. They did so progressively and sometimes just to prove to themselves that they could. Their sport became their profession as hunters, and their profession defined their identity as artificial predators. Altogether, and with a few additional cultural refinements, they eventually recognized themselves as *homines sapientes.*

—Culture is what man superimposes on the natural order, and the natural order is here defined to include everything and everyone except the role consciously played by the "artificial" *Homo sapiens* predator himself. By naming and by thinking about names, and by artificially assigning different categories and purposes of things, humankind has estranged itself from the natural world. Scientific and technological progress is part of the weaponry—similar to smell—that this artificial predator species exudes to inflict stings, teeth, claws, blades of flint and other causes of pain. Most human technologies, to this day, remain extensions of that archaic arms race which has been waged by artificial predators against "nature" peoples, and against each other.

—The contest began with modifications of sticks of wood, bones, and stones, and continued with the modification of harder quartzite nodules, such as flint and obsidian. Still later, this weapon technology was enhanced with the addition of fire, and more recently still, with the introduction of metals and explosive chemicals as substitutes for flint and muscle power. Perhaps the invention of striking fire was a natural and logical continuation from learning to work with flint—from striking sparks accidently.

—Stashes of rocks, compiled more than three million years ago and sorted by size, have been found near watering holes in Africa. None of the animals who came there to drink, and for whom these stashes of weights were intended, could tolerate barrages of stone hailing down on them. Of course, the rocks were meant for safe-distance aggression. For close defensive encounters, one can assume that sticks and thorny branches would have been used. Even lions would try to avoid thorny switches on their snouts, as long as their own tempers still permitted them to consider caution.

—On the steppes of Africa, a wildebeest may be taken down by a lucky lioness. The predator begins tearing and gulping her fill. But three strong hyenas could drive her away. A single hyena could be dislodged by five dogs. Today, this arrangement of competitors can still determine the order by which "chow circles" are formed on the African savannah—and the order in which the predators will get to eat.

—Of course, this scenario is rather hypothetical. Most lionesses are backed by prides of hungry kin and cubs, and this would thwart any easy takeover by scavenging hyenas. And hyenas, as well, tend to roam and hunt in groups. So, by the time scavenging dogs can have their turn, most carcasses would be reduced to bones. But then, there always exists a chance that, at an opportune time, fewer predators compete in a particular area. Our theoretical "chow circles" therefore remain mostly sketches of possibilities for estimating a variety of different outcomes.

—During their early episodes of hunting, our ancestral hominids had to wait their turn far out along the periphery of these chow circles. But armed with stones, sticks, and intelligent strategies, with torches later, they could eventually snatch portions of cadavers straight from the middle of the melee. Tool-using humanoids had an immediate advantage. While other predators needed to tear into the felled carcasses head first, quickly gulping down what they could, humanoids with weapons and knives could begin cutting with their hands. Heads and eyes could remain aloft and above the gore, where they remained aware of any approaching danger. And even after all the meat was gone, a tool-wielding hominid could still find some marrow to eat by smashing bones between an anvil and a hammer stone, and all the while they were also learning how to shape raw bones into pointed weapons.

—In their exuberance, our ancestral humanoids evolved their work-sport into a play-sport, eventually even to the point of turning it against their own kind. The boundary between games and serious competition disappeared when inter-clan and intertribal rivalries deteriorated into warfare. Sports evolved into something that we have now learned to praise as heroism and as part of "orderly civilization." However, in the course of this book, civilization itself will be redefined less ideally, as "hyper-domestication"—as domestication that eventually was overdone. Sports we consider to be the social equivalent of "serum" that may help weaken the inherited "venom" of cultural violence and predation.

Sin and Guilt: In the course of six million years, hominid gatherers, scavengers, and hunters have cultivated the sort of rudimentary inventiveness that began with the apes. For the delineation of culture and religion in evolution we therefore need not worry about assigning precisely dated thresholds, as to when a certain subspecies of the genus *Homo* could have appeared or might have vanished. Tool use predates *Homo sapiens* by a considerable span of time. Here we classify religious behavior under the category of fear- and guilt-induced retreat behavior. A causal link that was established in *Homo sapiens* minds by intentional weapon manufacture, by killing and a rising awareness of the hunters' general guilt, may safely be postulated. Apes and dogs can mind the fact of guilt. Dogs do fear and respect strict greater-than-canine human masters, and such fear is the point at which canine religious understanding begins.

—During the recent Western period of philosophical "Enlightenment," feelings of sin and guilt have been generally discounted as irrational inconveniences—as disabling phobia or lingering paranoia. I argue however, that our distant progenitors—over the span of millions of years—have consistently encountered better endowed greater-than-hominid predators. Without a good measure of rational, life-saving religious fear, they would not have survived long enough to produce *Homo sapiens* offspring. A socially complex species could hope to survive only to the extent that its members could sense, and realistically communicate, moments at which emotional reactions alone might have led to disaster.

—It is the combined rationality and strategies, by which our ancient progenitors have come to terms with their greatest fears, that I consider to be an important aspect of their rationality and religion. At some point in their evolution, our ancestors felt the need to communicate about the limits of their powers, and their fears. They needed to find words and names to symbolize and to objectify the greater-than-human realities that intimidated and restricted them.

—For our inquiry into religion we are willing not only to consider the case of *Homo sapiens*, but also to include other mammalian species toward which *homines sapientes* have shown themselves empathetic. At a minimum, I am prepared to consider all the animals with which we have become acquainted while trying to domesticate them or to adopt them as pets. The number of animals that some of us deem capable of understanding or expressing human emotions, or which are able to learn guilt- and fear-induced manners, is large indeed. From among the animals that I have come in contact with, dogs have generally been the most religious. Many of them accepted humankind as their greater-than-canine masters and gods. For perhaps fifteen thousand years some dogs have been submitting to humankind. Their domestication can be understood as a type of conversion on their part, in accordance with the standards of "dog religion."

—Unbeknownst to men, man-made weaponry could not be increased beneficially beyond a point of ecological balance. As a direct result of improved hunting tools, prey animals became rarer, and impending shortages of meat forced the adaptation of substitute styles of harvesting and finding nourishment. Wood, bone, and stone-technologies, wielded in the hands of artificial predators who were striving to surpass wolves, lions, and more, helped the human population prosper. And such technology sufficed, already during Neolithic times, to erase what food surpluses may still have existed on hooves, in the wild.

—I suspect that before ten thousand years ago, along the upper edge of the Fertile Crescent, a man-caused shortage of wild animals began to be felt increasingly by sedentary hunters. Apparently some wolves and dogs sensed the approaching crisis three to five thousand years before humans noticed anything; they made friends with humankind in hope of a better survival. They made necessary religious adjustments toward their New Age human competitors.

—Late Neolithic men, finally well enough equipped to be the best hunters on the planet, struggled to increase their food yields in two ways: first by improving their weapon technology and strategies, and second by maximizing the number of trained hunters. Technological and strategic improvements, for a while, helped grow larger human populations and, accordingly, contributed to a speedier demise of hunting. We suspect that along the northern arc of the Fertile Crescent, before ten thousand years ago, a "Crisis of Opulence" began to develop among growing human populations—spearheaded by the Göbekli Tepe flint industry. It led to overhunting and resulted in a shortage of prey animals. For their shortfall of meat, humans needed to compensate by gathering more wild grains, vegetables, nuts and fruits.

—Rank-and-file hunters found themselves obliged to "hunt" substitutes for meat. By about ten thousand years ago they had reached a point where they needed to think about propagating and protecting their cultivars. They also learnt that they needed to stoop to the level of becoming "nannies" to wild young animals, and become "servants" to the mature animals that they themselves tamed and raised. They needed to devise strategies of nurture, to save remnant herd animals from extinction—to save as many as still could be found wandering in the wild. Some farsighted hunters understood the signs of their time—while others, surely, insisted on continuing to hunt in accordance with old-fashioned egos, customs, and faith in unlimited supplies. Ever since human intelligence found itself starving among limited supplies, pious orthodoxy was challenged to help conceal short-sighted foolishness and greed.

Hunting with a Shaman's Help

The totems of most ancient hunters were greater-than-human predators which our ancestors recognized as exemplary models and gods. Totemic gods were acknowledged as masters of animals as well as sponsors of the hunt.

Once befriended by male hunters, these master-sponsors could be inherited within maternal clans as some variety of "honorary ancestors." They co-existed with humankind as animals and gods in a state of transformational "prehuman flux" mysticism and interdependence. Shamans were intellectual elites in hunter-gatherer societies; ordinarily, they maintained relations with multiple gods or totems. Shamanic mediation with the gods was sought for problems of health as much as for assistance in the hunters' quest for food.

2. Hunting with a Shaman's Help

Shamans are a class of intellectuals: The Göbekli Tepe cult today exists in scholarship mostly as an archaeological marvel. In hope of bringing our subject matter into some kind of human context, and historical focus, it may be necessary to adjust our mental antennas toward extant similar subject matter, elsewhere in the world. We must elsewhere have recourse to what within the larger context of human evolution we can learn about hunter-gatherers in transition.

—Before the bas-reliefs on the sculpted limestone menhirs at Göbekli Tepe can begin to speak to us, we need to understand the totemic, social, and religious backgrounds that could have informed the sculptors.[4] It is quite obvious that the totemic images could not have dropped into the minds of Stone Age workmen out of thin air. There had to have been a prior cultural and religious tradition in ancient eastern Anatolia—thus a social and religious tradition, from the angle of which the shapes that were chiseled in stone could have been derived and understood.

Predisposition: *How may I explain "totemic" and "totems" for a starter? I remember well a short time span during my early childhood when, while running, I imitated the sounds of an automobile engine. My brother and a neighbor boy started doing the same thing three years later when I had already abandoned the habit. We all were running as cars, and empowered by some mighty automobile, we could indeed outrun some of our age-mates. It was a temporary childhood totemism. Then, during my college years in Kansas I was a Jayhawk—a mythological cross between a Bluejay and a Hawk. In the evolutionary scheme of things, collegiate totems represent a gamey form of archaic religious submission. While modern students learn to split Uranium and fuse Hydrogen, they also retreat "religiously" to a time when their ancestors were still less lethal Neolithic hunters who answered to predator gods and divine sponsors that now seem harmless—but still mighty enough to help win ball games.*

---

[4]"Menhir" in this book is used in the sense of Celtic megalithic studies as an "elongated stone that is stood up."

—My first exposure to a Stone-Age hunter tradition, in its evening twilight, happened in 1971 on the Diné Native American (Navajo Indian) Reservation. It happened in the context of a field study that required comparable information from hunter traditions elsewhere. More encounters regarding the subjects of hunting, gathering, domestication and healing in Native American traditions followed.[5]

—Obviously, with comparative data drawn from half a world away, and from ten millennia later, certain divergences from Göbekli Tepe must be assumed. But the Diné Native American encounters, which helped me understand the Göbekli Tepe cult, happened under analogous circumstances, still evolving in the same whirl of transition—that is, on the slide from hunting and gathering into domestication. Any comparative study that links up with recent cultures utilizes data from ethnology—and one does encounter thereby as well the ambiguities of later modern intrusions. It is true that historically detached modernisms can obscure and disfigure earlier situations. However, most of my estimates regarding the Göbekli Tepe backgrounds, expressed here, are derived from what I believe I have learned in interaction with actual Stone Age hunter mentality—with shamans who themselves were still trying to cope with similar issues of transitioning.

—A typical active shaman in a Stone Age hunter-gatherer society used to be an intellectual leader. He had the same totemic memberships in maternal clans and in situational hunter associations as had any of his fellow huntsmen. But he enjoyed friendly relations with additional totems and divine helpers. He had extra religious "connections" with the greater-than-human dimension.

—Our explanations here are intended for general readers who might never get closer to a Stone Age clan or tribe than this page. Getting closer would require, then, consideration of specific local situations and differences. Nowhere in the world are living societies and religions run by mechanically predictable laws. In real life, and in most situations, fluidity and exceptions are the rule. The minds of

[5]See Karl W. Luckert. *The Navajo Hunter Tradition,* University of Arizona Press, 1975; also *Coyoteway...,* 1979, and my entire twelve-volume edited "American Tribal Religions" series (1977-1987)—published by the Museum of Northern Arizona and the University of Nebraska presses.

homines sapientes, to function effectively, require a great amount of experimental tolerance and latitude. Averaged estimates often end up being oversimplified abbreviations—useful only occasionally, as entry assumptions.

—Generally speaking, two types of activities were expected of traditional hunter shamans. Firstly, a certain amount of assistance was expected of them by people who suffered from illness or who were in danger of dying; secondly, shamans also were expected to be able to divine the whereabouts of prey animals.

—Help in healing was needed regardless of whether prey animals were plentiful or not. Hunters with a general keen geographical orientation expected their shamans to know where one might find the agents or sources of health—whether in the form of herbs nearby, or under the jurisdiction of gods who lived farther away. Strategic methods for hunting animals, and finding the means for health, both needed to be intuited during revelatory ecstatic quest-journeys—seemingly as though the mastery of the chase, and of travel, provided not only skills for obtaining nourishment but also for finding the medicines and agents of health.

—It is customary in some Western scientific cultures to credit shamans with dealing in "supernatural" affairs. However, we have no reasons to suspect that shamans ten thousand years ago had any concept akin to our secular concept of "nature." Thus, one should not distort, knowingly, the ancient hunters' worldview by attributing to them a mostly denigrating label of a "faith in something supernatural." While trying to explain distant concepts, we should try to avoid notions that distant people could not possibly have understood. There are hunter societies around the globe that have survived into our times, which still came under the scrutiny of modern Western historians and scientific observers. When we revisit remnant hunter peoples in transition, with the help of such observers—as we will do in Part Three of this book—and when we concentrate on moments at which native peoples actually were encouraged to speak for themselves, in their own words, it is then that we come closer to the minds of Göbekli Tepe Neolithic hunters, by quantum leaps.

—Shamanism is an integral part of the communal dimension of hunter existence—just as higher levels of education are integral aspects of modern societies. Confronted with gigantic animals, the early hunters needed to pull together and work in larger groups to win their battles, both for safety and to obtain food. When prey animals were plentiful, the shaman's help was not actually necessary for scouting. Still, it was always a good idea to include in a hunting party some man who had additional experience as a healer, just in case an injury might happen.

—And then, when animals became scarce, when hunters had to stalk them over great distances, enlisting the best available human minds made sense as well. In that case the brightest, or sometimes the most eccentric, males were approached and invited to function as shamans. Every hunter could perform some shamanic rites, but not everyone could perform them equally well, or enough of them. The shaman who had a nice singing-voice would more easily become popular. But when animals in the Göbekli Tepe area were thinning out and dispersing northward through the mountains, a shaman's task of divining their whereabouts became increasingly difficult.

—There really was nothing spooky about shamans who functioned in the context of a hunter society. They were rational people, and their strangeness usually pertained to eccentricities that people within the culture expected. Moreover, any wise man who answers questions from within his own culture will, by outsiders, be judged as someone who gives strange answers. Understanding the worldview and logical context of another culture requires an understanding of whatever data some well-stocked human minds in such environments have available.

Toward a Western understanding of shamanism: During the 1950's Mircea Eliade was working to make sense of Siberian shamanism by way of scrutinizing Western European, Indic, and Russian ethnological sources. What he found he explained in his classic volume as "archaic techniques of ecstasy." His was a rational exposition by which readers, oriented toward Western psychology, could relate to the subject matter.[6] But then, the metaphor of "techniques" of Eliade's exposition was eventually pre-empted by Mark Levy and others, who restyled archaic shamans into "technicians of ecstasy," who then, together with all their arctic idiosyncrasies, could be posited to vouch comparatively for the normalcy of modern artistic geniuses. While it appears legitimate to highlight the activity of

---

[6]Mircea Eliade, *Shamanism: Archaic Techniques of Ecstasy*. New York. Bollingen Foundation, 1964.

shamans based on their own habits and techniques, in the sense that any speaker may utilize the techniques of a native rhetoric, it does seem somewhat hackneyed to refer to all technique-habituated archaic shamans as technicians.[7]

—When in the course of my Diné fieldwork I personally tried to relate Eliade's characterization of Siberian shamanism to the world-view of Native American ceremonialists, I ran into a related problem. The English word "ecstasy," while it continues to serve a useful purpose for superficially explaining Siberian shamanic behavior, turned out to be a hopeless exaggeration for the sentiments that I found expressed by serious Diné (Navajo Indian) priestly singers and shamanic practitioners.

—Meanwhile I also had a chance to make contact with Asian shamanism by way of China. And there, again, the work of shamans displayed quite reasonable demeanor. Chinese shamanism shows itself as a logical and straightforward style of behavior—as logical as any academic discipline can afford to be when it engages in mental gymnastics—ruminating among ontology, theology, cosmography, climate, and geography.

—To begin with, in older Navajo shamanism there is, strictly speaking, no concept of a "soul." Diné persons in "prehuman flux" (see Chapters 14 and 15) do transform their appearances at whichever places they happen to be. Thus, persons do not normally get penetrated, possessed, or abandoned by transient souls or spirits. There were no lost or wandering souls that needed to get retrieved from faraway places—other than perhaps some "ghosts of the newly dead" who needed to be hurried away quickly, northward.

—For an Asian baseline let me share my encounter, with a rural Chinese mother in Ningxia, who revealed how she would retrieve the soul of a sick child or of a family member. She did it with a paper cut-out in the form of a child—representing the estranged human soul—and a fishing stick to the top of which a fuzzy string of sheep wool was tied. No frantic tricks or dangerous hooks were utilized—only maternal patience and gentle love to entangle the paper image that represented the soul, lying on the floor. She fished it back and

[7]Compare Mark Levy, *Technicians of Ecstasy: Shamanism and the Modern Artist.* Ruth-Inge Heinze Books, 1993.

landed it on the patient who, supposedly at this demonstration, was resting there on the "kang"—a heatable clay bed. The non-ecstatic shamanically active mother never left the edge of that bed on which her patient lay.

—Of course, the pathology that a professional shaman utilizes as reference may not be as simple as what this mother was up against in her demonstration, attending a hypothetical child. In the greater Asia there are large spaces and frigid climate zones; accordingly, cosmology and psychology have become rather complex. With three souls and seven spirits per individual person—one spirit to occupy each window "opening" in the human skull—the task of shepherding and keeping them all together as a single personality bundle, could become a true challenge. Anyone who ever in life had a desire to run away from home, he or she will understand the agonies of those souls and spirits, predestined to be together and to get along. At some point in time, when space in Chinese cosmology got partitioned into terrestrial and subterranean realms, more places became available to get lost in. The origin of such problems probably should be traced back to a time when people still lived in caves—a time which here and there in China still reaches into the present.

—Therefore, calling on the help of an experienced professional retriever, a super-hunter and super-shaman, made a lot of sense. In Siberia an effective shaman had to be able to travel across frigid distances and spaces, over which Siberian multiple souls could get lost. While trying to achieve a cure across frigid spaces, one should not be surprised if such cures are ceremonially staged with some visible shivering. Moreover, long distances were most easily traversed by symbolic ecstatic, or by simple mental flight.

—The Siberian shaman should not be explained in terms of Western psychological categories that were formulated under shady trees in gentle lukewarm breezes. It would be more authentic to meet up with shamans in the service of their people, in their own geographies, climates, and quests for survival. There probably never was a typical pathology of "arctic madness"—not any more than there is a distinctive pathology for American or European academics. Some eccentricities were being cherished for emphasis, indeed. But these were no more peculiar than the eccentricities that some of my university professors cultivated to retain the attention of their students—with some success, I might say.

Shamans at Göbekli Tepe: One may assume that shamans at Göbekli Tepe divined the whereabouts of prey animals as hunters have tried to do elsewhere and all around the world. They drew from their general knowledge about geography, landscape, and the seasons, about regional vegetation, animal tracks and grazing habits, and by relying on patterns established over time. Most ungulate herds are territorial and move in large cirles. Some of this general knowledge included memories of long ago—memories recalled with divine help, and preserved by individuals that were intellectually gifted.

—Most latter-day shamans who I met did not become shamans because they wanted to, but rather because, when approached to render help one day, they could not refuse the people's neighborly pleas. They consented to carry the additional and often thankless burden of assuming responsibility for someone else's existential worries. To refuse help to someone in need was almost unthinkable —it could be construed as though a potentially able shaman would intentionally wish to see a needy person suffer or perish.

—Down to a certain level of density among wild animal populations, the shamanic method of giving advice to hunters by divine inspiration worked well enough. If after a round of ecstatic singing, and careful thinking, the shaman missed his first prediction, no real harm was done. No-one else would sing as nicely as the deity who empowered the voice of a divinely graced person. Nevertheless, to assure both, the shaman's non-liability and his personal credibility, all eventual outcomes needed to be credited to the gods that were addressed in the songs. The shaman's next attempt at divination was made easier by the simple fact that one possible geographical direction had already been tried and eliminated. And at any point along a deep valley there are usually only two favorable directions to choose from—upstream and downstream.

—The shaman can chant again and ask his divine helpers where the prey animals might have escaped to—perhaps at that time the gods would pay closer attention when their own personal contact songs are chanted. Then the hunters would adjust their path according to some fresh insights. Sooner or later a hunting party found fresh tracks—or no tracks. If a shaman failed repeatedly, the group might next time quietly find another leader—someone else who, like his predecessor, could not refuse the requests of his neighbors.

—Ancient shamans may have philosophized privately about where the essences of animals originate or might be going eventually. But in working for the people, they needed to face up to the prior and more immediate question of where specific animals might have escaped to. This preliminary question became important at the very moment when shamans in the vicinity of Göbekli Tepe first realized that indeed the animals were getting fewer. The temple lodges at the flint mining camp thrived during the last two millennia of fulltime hunting, while the populations of wild animals were declining. The Neolithic hunter associations gave both industrial and religious responses when the dangers of "emptiness" were growing and threatening to overtake them.

—It was probably at unavoidable moments of failure when a shaman would begin to wonder about the "life essences" of wild animals, of those that he hunted to butcher and eat. Thinking about essences immediately opens a question of conscience. Which people's or animals' essences were entitled to absorb which other essences? The question is easier to deal with if it is reversed materially. Which bodies exist to nourish others? At least this second formulation begins by affirming nourishment.

—At a point where reason collapses, songs and prayers can usually carry on a little further. Sometimes the movements of dance and chant are added to mask uncertainties and doubts that lurk within, or that bother the human soul. Most people know something about how to whistle in the dark. Most shamanic actors do not really understand what gives power to their songs. If pushed for more specific answers they will need to invoke faith in the existence of indefinable greater gods.

—It is conceivable that on this broad philosophical path, of reasoning about the origin of essences, some ancient hunters decided to build their first open-air sanctuary at Göbekli Tepe—for the general purpose of exciting the Earth's fecundity and goodwill. Their ceremonial repertoire needed to be in touch with reality—to the effect that animals needed to be born, to die for human hunters to eat, and to live. Because these men wished for more fertility in the animal world, at a time when hunters themselves reduced animal populations, they would also have reasoned more generally about the collective ovaries that bestowed all life on Earth. This thought advances our discussion to the general level at which the Göbekli Tepe builders might have begun building their sanctuaries. But almost certainly, much of what they built, and subsequently believed, was resolved while they explained and improved on what they were doing. Human theology and philosophy are at their beginnings mostly *a posteriori*—stimulated by existing conditions and needs.

—It goes without saying that the rounded ceremonial platforms, in this hunters' world at Göbekli Tepe were set up by and for the men. Children and their mothers had no reasons to come to such places. This is not the statement of a historian of religions who might have been bitten by his patriarchal upbringing or by some type of theological sexism. No. It is of a historian who has searched far and wide for religions that might have been founded by females. But no! With only few exceptions, religions were founded as answers to problems that stemmed from hunting, domestication, and hyper-domestication. They were founded mostly by males who, over the course of six million years, had a hand in contriving the violent excesses that made religious corrections necessary in the first place. Even the least chauvinistic religions among them, those who come closest to acknowledging equality between the genders, were either founded or eventually managed by men—adjusted for effectiveness, to prevail in a world predefined by masculine violence.

—The great conflicts that have been engulfing cultures, tribes, and civilizations, were generated predominantly by men. While writing "by men" I specifically refer to "huntsmen, domesticators, butcher-priests, hyper-domesticators, executioners, kings, warriors, craftsmen, manufacturers, merchants, scientists and technicians." Indeed, what a latter-day holy book confirms may be read gender-specific in English, to the effect that "by man came death" (1 *Cor.* 15:21). By males was amplified the art of killing, and consequently life and salvation needed to be brought back, or at least be permitted to return, by men who had become obstacles to life.

—And so at Göbekli Tepe, between the founding moment of sculpting their first *menhirs*, and the periodic decisions to cover up some of their twenty-or-so sanctuaries with overhead and tailings fill, there dawned on these people a broader realization. Not only did they need to better understand the essences of lesser prey animals, they needed to better understand their own human essences as well—and also their totemic inter-relatedness with greater-than-human sponsors.

—The totemic animals (divine crest animals and sponsors) that these miners and sculptors depicted on their monuments can generally be identified as being male—just as were the miners and the quarry-men who did the sculpting. Most of their totemic models functioned for them as some type of greater-than-human predators. They were perfectly suited to inspire and to empower human hunters who invented weapons and improved their tools to kill. As intelligent artificial predators and butchers, our ancestors knew anatomy, and they understood how most animals and especially mammalians reproduced. But how could a rationally evolving and artificially trained predator begin to make sense of the sexual dichotomy of "food-killing" and "people-growing" mysteries? He did what he thought he needed to do first, by way of improving his arsenal of weapons. He postponed unanswerable questions until later. He prepared for hunting, and by doing so he got his predator totems involved and excited—just as on the lower hunting path itself his dogs would get excited.

—But all the contradictions of hunter-gatherer culture came home to roost among the weapon-makers at Göbekli Tepe. Within their industrial complex rankled impenetrable ambiguities that weighed on the consciences of all the active artificers. The bodies and souls of quarry-men and toolmakers felt the pain when, occasionally, they struck their own fingers with a hammer stone and drew their own blood. Their blood was of the same color as the blood that their weapons drew from animals. And in response they could think of nothing better to do than to make better weapon points and sharper cutting knives. In earnest they sought the approval of the Great Mother for what they were doing—so that she might willingly continue to supply them with more and better nodules of flint, as well as give birth to more prey animals to hunt. This goddess will come into better focus as we proceed. But she will reveal herself rather slowly, as most of those ancient Stone Age deities are in the habit of doing, nowadays.

—The men improved their hunting about as nicely as any murderous activity can be improved. They improved their weapons industry and skills of predation, so much so that the prey animals could not keep pace with procreating and replenishing their numbers. Such are the blessings of human industries and sciences. They reduce the world to "resources" and "raw materials." Most human artificialities are based on the logic of utilitarian demand and unlimited supplies. But as the Buddha, looking at it from a different angle, so wisely has noticed: "all suffering is caused by craving"—thus not by the economics factor of "supply shortages" but by the presence of "demand." Among predators, there will never be enough supplies or lives to prey upon. Thus, the world's first industrial ethical battle was fought, and lost, in the sanctuaries of these miners and quarry-men, on that holy pile of mining debris called Göbekli Tepe. We detect there not merely a concern for fertility of the fauna, but also the hunters' and weapon makers' own sense of guilt, and their dawning sense of responsibility toward the Earth Mother.

—Expanded responsibilities and guilt are not sentiments that very intimately belong to our present-day understanding of hunting—an activity of sports undertaken out there in the green realm of nature. This issue will be examined more systematically in Part Two of this volume. But here I must serve advance notice that, in all my years of examining archaic hunter traditions, I have not yet found one for which sin and guilt were not serious issues.

—Of course, questions concerning sin and guilt, among any peoples, always appear either in conjunction with some scientific theoretical fix or some religious justification—just as bandages are applied quickly to hide and to protect serious wounds. In this manner the primary function of primitive hunter religion, as of a number of scientific theories, appears to have been balancing and soothing disturbed killer consciences.

—If a religious balancing system or our modern shortcuts of scientific rationalization could really justify, then the issues of sin and guilt would never need to be mentioned again. However, the "justification" of killing and eating has remained worldwide one of the deepest and most hidden problems in the behavior of sensitive *homines sapientes*. The function of religion, worldwide, has been prefigured by agonies about sin and guilt—or, in Western psychological paraphrasing, about "illusions" regarding such—to enable humankind to continue eating—or rather, to continue killing and butchering in order to eat with a minimum of repentance or abstinence.

—We may survey any society on our planet—primitive or modern, theistic or atheistic—and we find among them peculiar styles of behavior or patterns of reasoning, regarding the issues of spilling blood, killing and eating, and of mitigations thereunto. We may investigate food sources that are deemed taboo and the reasons that these are considered taboo. We may examine prior ownerships, sacred calendars by which certain foods are restricted for certain days or weeks, alongside table manners and dress codes judged appropriate for class status or caste levels. Acts of killing may be blessed and sanctified. "Living flesh" may be rendered kosher, halal, or hygienically pure "meat." Without the initial mediation by some greater-than-human agency, rational humanoids would never have found a way to own "meat." There are ritualized prayer, thanksgiving, chant, sacramental eating, sacrifices for atonement, all-out fasting—or reckless feasting—all in addition to prescribed table manners, the proper use of utensils, designed to ascertain a hungry eater's appropriate distance from the questionable prior acts of offensive or unclean killing, butchering, or the routinized preparation of food.

3. A Hill Compiled by Industrial Hunters

Göbekli Tepe means "Abdomen Hill." Between 12,000 and 9,500 years ago, the hill was heaped up by flint miners and weapon makers from shavings, debris, and overhead loads. Hunting and the weapon industry flourished until animals became scarce. During the Late Glacial Interstadial, animals and hunters were slowed in their northward dispersion across the glaciated Taurus and Zagros ranges. When the glaciers melted, the animals dispersed more freely. Hunters and weapon makers followed them.

The Place and its Name: Professor Klaus Schmidt is an archaeologist of the German Archaeological Institute in Berlin (DAI), and he is excavating a man-made hill that sits on a limestone plateau near the city of Sanliurfa, in southeastern Anatolia (Turkey). The place is called Göbekli Tepe. The Professor has translated its name into German as *Bauch Berg* or *Gebauchter Berg.*[8] In English the name means "Abdomen Hill, Tummy Hill, or Belly Hill."[9] I prefer the inclusive German translation over the English alternatives, but I am writing my book first in English. And in this situation, recognizing myself as just another "earth-born son," it does seem more respectful to refer to

---

[8]Klaus Schmidt. *Sie bauten die ersten Tempel. Das rätselhafte Heiligtum der Steinzeit Jäger.* Sachbuch—Verlag C. H. Beck, München, 2008 (2006). Professor Klaus Schmidt's excavation report has, all along, not been available in English. It would have helped to know the Professor's preferred English catalog designations.

[9]The aforementioned "Sachbuch" about Göbekli Tepe, by Klaus Schmidt, will appear in English under the title *Göbekli Tepe—A Stone Age Sanctuary in Southeastern Anatolia.* It is scheduled to be published in December of 2012, by Exoriente (www.exoriente.org).

the bulge on our pregnant Earth Mother as her Abdomen—rather than as her Tummy or as a frivolous Belly. I am convinced that "Göbekli Tepe" was never meant to represent something like a Daddy's Beer Belly. For the latter to be a possibility, the pre-pottery Stone Age builders on this hill would have needed to establish a brewery of sorts, with lots of carved limestone containers.[10] But instead, they built temple platforms and set up limestone *menhirs.* Onto the surfaces of the *menhirs* they sculpted bas-reliefs that portray a variety of totem animals.[11]

–The alternate German rendition of the Turkish name "Göbekli Tepe," as *Nabel Berg,* which some journalists have preferred, seems to introduce a serious error in communication. In light of all the "incense" that Western academicians have been burning to the euphemistic altar-words of "navel" and "omphalos," as a central category for the history of religions, to name Göbekli Tepe a "Navel Hill" would definitely corrupt the meaning of what those who piled it into existence had in mind. In fact, calling this place *Nabel Berg* would even amount to an insult to the intelligence and profession of its builders. Just because some Western academicians are tempted to confound wombs, vaginas, phalluses, navels, cranes and storks, does not mean that Stone Age hunters at Göbekli Tepe, twelve to ten thousand years ago, knew not where baby animals came from. As hunters and butchers they were life-long students of anatomy. They surely could tell the difference between a tummy and a navel on any creature—and when they looked close enough, even on a mountain. I suspect that they had precise names for all these things.

–That someday archaeologists would excavate a complex of twenty-plus megalithic "temple enclosures" that embody the last two millennia of religious quests of hunter-gatherer culture would have been unthinkable as recently as 1995, when Professor Klaus Schmidt first surveyed Göbekli Tepe. Twenty-plus temples or, perhaps, as I prefer to think of them, "exclusive cult-lodges for huntsmen and flint-knappers," were built at that place by men who were among our

---

[10]My conclusion on this matter is based on rudimentary Göbekli Tepe data; not on what my answer to Professor Josef H. Reichholf would need to be. Compare the latter's *Warum die Menschen sesshaft wurden—Das größte Rätsel unserer Geschichte.* Fischer Taschenbuch Verlag. Frankfurt a/M, 2010.

[11]"*Menhir*" in our book is used in the sense of Celtic megalithic studies, as a "stone which is stood up."

planet's earliest industrialists. They were hunters who gathered there to work as miners of flint nodules. From the quartzite nodules they chipped cutting tools and knapped weapon points. To get at flint nodules they quarried and broke up the stratified beds of lenticular slabs of limestone.

The Survival of Meaning: My preliminary marvel question for this essay concerns the very name "Göbekli Tepe." After having surveyed the iconography that distinguishes this place, the marvel of its name becomes noteworthy. How could the ceremonial intent of this temple complex have outlived the actual cult by ten millennia? And how in 1995 could Kurdish farmers still have named this hill accurately as "Göbekli Tepe" in Turkish—as *Bauch* or Abdomen? How could the original meaning have endured the linguistic onslaughts of ten millennia? Only the continuous core of a domesticator population, since domestication began, could render this happenstance somewhat possible.

—So, why am I persisting in creating a linguistic whirlwind about translating a geographical field-name that, until a few years ago only local Turkish-Kurdish farmers knew? The answer to this question has shocked me—even me—someone who already has experienced a number of similar shocks while approaching megalithic iconography. The top portion of this mountain is manmade. It was heaped on the limestone plateau and has come to represent the abdomen of Mother Earth.

—How can a twenty-first century commentator know anything about this? He can, because the builders of Göbekli Tepe acted toward this artificial hill *as if it actually was* the abdomen of the Earth Mother.[12] Every *menhir* that was stood up represents an endorsement of that faith. The builders expressed their thinking pictorially, in the exuberant Boy-Man language of Stone Age hunters. They came as human "artificial predators" in search of atonement with their Mother. My exegesis of the excavation records will in the end substantiate the meaning of the name "Abdomen Hill," which I am affirming here.

---

[12]At this point I am not in a position to trace the linguistics of the Kurdish name "*Xerawreşk.*" See K. A. Kent, *Göbekli Tepe (Xerawreşk) Uyugarligi*, Istanbul 2012—suggestion by courtesy of Jens Notroff.

—It now is possible to reconstruct the Göbekli Tepe cult story beginning at the Southwest promontory of the plateau (see the start of illustrations, below), at a place where two "rim-pedestals" of bedrock have been left standing above the adjusted bedrock level of an enclosure (Figure 6). These base formations appear to have been designed to accommodate an early pair of T-shaped *menhirs*. It is possible that the hillock that has come down to us as "Göbekli Tepe" could have been recognized as Abdomen Hill already on the first day when a few miners engaged upon it to mine flint—thus, when the virgin plateau still was untouched by human hammers and adzes.

—In contrast to Professor Schmidt's actual work in physical archaeology, my discovery of Göbekli Tepe is prosaic and almost simplistic. But because the explanations communicated by the present book may be far-reaching, I owe to the reader at least some explanation of why someone as distant to the site as I would dare to express himself at all. The credit for all our awareness goes, as has already been said, to Professor Klaus Schmidt who lives in Sanliurfa and Berlin. He has shortened the stretch of "prehistory" by some millennia, and in compensation he has effectively expanded the span of temple builders' history.

—In 1995, while the professor started working on his exploit at Göbekli Tepe in eastern Anatolia, I was still engaged in doing sporadic field research on Native American religions and on similar subject matter in Middle America, Africa, and in China. My broader category of academic interests involved the same evolutionary episode—namely, the Homo sapiens transition from gathering and hunting to domestication. All the while I was oblivious to Klaus Schmidt's work until January 11, in 2011. I never will forget that date. It was the day when I discovered the title of his book, *Sie bauten die ersten Tempel*, printed in 2008. My academic field, the "history of religions" or *Religionswissenschaft* has, thanks to his work, suddenly swelled in the middle and taken on a new shape.

—My discovery of the Professor's book happened while I was writing on a related subject matter, tentatively titled "Religion in Evolution." In light of the Göbekli Tepe discovery, most of what I had written prior to reading the Professor's data needed to be pushed farther back in the volume and converted into Parts Two and Three. Göbekli Tepe and what it can teach us deserves to be placed up front as the new geographical and chronological point of orientation.

For the duration of this volume my "Religion in Evolution" theme needs to begin at a fresh focal point in prehistory, at Göbekli Tepe.

—But then, inasmuch as the archaeological finds at this site have recently been hailed by *National Geographic* as the "Birth of Religion" (June 2011), I must begin with disassociating myself from this hyperbole by way of a personal demarcation. An assortment of temples, lodges, and sculpted *menhirs* does not add up to a seed of everything there is to the religion of humankind—and even less to the "origin of religion" as such. This is a basic point on which I must insist, in order to be able to maintain the integrity of the "history of religions" as my academic field.

—In Chapter One I have volunteered some glimpses of my shorter evolutionary view, regarding the prehistory of hominid religion over the past six million years or so. However—as for some time I have presumed—in my longer view the beginning, the "origin and prehistory" of religion in our universe took on form already with the simplest submissive behavior enacted amongst sub-atomic particles, electrons, molecules, viruses, and amoebas. There is no room in this volume for such a detailed introduction to religious phenomena and behavior. But after this protestation it is nonetheless possible to concede certain "innovations" regarding the creation of religious symbolism. These men at Göbekli Tepe sculpted "original" ceremonial paraphernalia of limestone, using skills acquired for smaller artifacts, carved on different materials many thousands of years earlier. So, there are still plenty original things to get excited about at Göbekli Tepe.

—It should be assumed that for the length of Part One of this volume I will regard the data published by Professor Schmidt as primary. The reader is therefore advised to read my exposition in consultation with the 2012 scheduled English edition of his 2008 German book, *Sie bauten die ersten Tempel.* Anyone in the fields of archaeology and history knows how to maintain a distinction between data and interpretation. It is humanly impossible for two people, with different minds and different academic orientations and questions, to come up with identical hypotheses and interpretations.

—After reading *Sie bauten die ersten Tempel* the first time, two puzzles remained for me—the significance of the *Bauch Berg* and the meaning of the *menhirs,* recorded as *T-Pfeiler* (T-shaped pillars). During my second reading, the historical process surrounding the

Abdomen Hill was partially clarified. And while no illumination came during a third reading, all the core pieces of the puzzle that initially evoked my curiosity assembled during a fourth reading. Real archaeologists might call my approach to the data "armchair archaeology." Their judgment is indeed accurate. At my age I really appreciate the padded arm supports on my work chair.

—The pieces came together for me against the background of fifty years of exposure to contemporary remnants of transitional Stone Age hunter religions in America, and exposure to adaptation struggles exhibited by various domestication cultures around the globe. It turned out that nothing I had written for the initial volume, or had concluded about the worldwide transition from gathering-and-hunting to domestication, needed to be discarded on account of the new Göbekli Tepe data. The evolution of human culture and religion still appears to be of one piece. Göbekli Tepe fits right in.

—The evolutionary transformative process, or the transition from gathering and hunting to domestication and beyond, has been unfolding around the globe—and now we know where in the world, and when in human history, it began rolling. It began sometime after twelve thousand years ago at Göbekli Tepe, and it has been spilling beyond the Fertile Crescent for almost as many years. To this day it has not finished spreading, nor has it achieved a point of rest on any of the planet's continents. Remnants of Stone Age mentality are still with us, stubbornly embedded in all branches and advances of modern civilization. The only thing that really has changed for history of religions studies is the fact that some additional categories, such as "Flintstone Culture" and "Limestone Religion," need to be contrasted and brought into focus.

—Professor Schmidt was impressed by the fact that in human history the "cathedral turned out to be older than the city." But neither cities nor cathedrals rank foremost in my mind. Both of these amenities—cathedral and the city—will need to be thought about later in this book, far beyond the points of hunting and gathering and even far beyond the simple world view of ordinary domestication. Together these added achievements bear witness to an era beyond commonplace domestication—with another progeny of problems. To recast some of these insights into larger evolutionary categories and contexts, and to add the benefits of hindsight, I will need to travel the path of this book all the way through Parts Two and Three.

Predisposition: *Professor Schmidt's general conclusion, that the cathedral was older than the city is undoubtedly correct, if by "cathedral" we mean some type of architectural edifice that appears to have served a societal religious function. But people who are barely emerging from their era of hunting do not ordinarily live in houses, and where wild animal populations are migratory, hunters and fishermen may live in camps, but not yet in villages. The obsolescent hunters on Ceram built a men's club-house which, from the point of view of desperate men, was their place of religious justification and ego-salvation—see Chapter Thirteen. But the fact that their men's lodge also was the place where headhunting and human sacrifice were being plotted makes me hesitate twice before generalizing the metaphor of a "cathedral" quite that far. Likewise, the pyramids of Middle America do represent megalithic ceremonial centers where obsolescent hunters organized themselves as warrior-priests. For the most part these pyramids represent hungry Dragon heads, or coils. In the Serpent's mouth atop these platforms human victims were killed by hundreds and thousands. These pyramids were pedestals for sacred altars—butchering blocks on which to sacrifice humankind. Indeed, while even the most numinous cathedral in Christendom could harbor an element of beastly mysterium tremendum, I consider a cathedral somewhat differently balanced for the well-being of an organized citizenry; at least different from these pyramids on which human hearts were being fed to the solar Serpent. These pyramids were power centers for warriors and butcher-priests, and as cult places they seem closer to the function of Twentieth Century extermination chambers. By contrast, I believe that the temenoi at Göbekli Tepe represented the vagina of the Earth Mother. They were places of atonement and improvement of the human condition. These sites apparently preceded the construction of cities. Miners and weapon-makers were periodically sedentary. Thus, while Professor Schmidt is quite correct with his metaphorical formulation, the temenoi at Göbekli Tepe were neither Ceramese "baileo" nor Middle American pyramids or altars of terror. They compare more favorably with the kiva lodges of Hopi Indian men's societies with which I happen to be familiar—though possibly not entirely free of terror either.*

Taurus-Zagros Mountains were a Wall of Ice. Professor Steven Mithen is another scholar upon whose work I rely.[13] While the excavations of Klaus Schmidt do provide us with fresh data in the dimension of space and historical time, Steven Mithen has attained a broader perspective on the evolutionary flow of time, relative to the last Ice Age. The Late Glacial Interstadial represents the end phase of the Ice Age (ca. 12,700 - 10,800 BC). At that time global temperatures dropped again significantly, and accordingly, the glaciers in the

---

[13]Steven Mithen. *After the Ice, a Global History, 20,000 to 5,000 BC.* Cambridge: Harvard University Press, 2004, pp. 10f.

Taurus and Zagros ranges began building up and separating the northlands from southlands with a barrier of ice. During the Younger Dryas that followed, 10,800 BC to about 9,600 BC, average temperatures in the region rose to where they have been hovering since.[14]

—Where prey animals cannot go, predators do not need to follow. Archaeological research along the Fertile Crescent, in our decades, has gradually revealed how during the final millennium of the Ice Age, life for hunters was improving. Along the southern edge of the aforementioned latitudinal ice barrier, animal populations of many now familiar varieties multiplied and accumulated in the wild—bear, wild ox, deer, reindeer, antelope, goats, sheep, cattle, pigs, donkeys, fishes, and a great variety of birds.

—Among these prey animals also roamed their natural predators—lions, tigers, leopards, wolves, foxes, eagles, vultures, serpents, and more. Among these predators, trying to keep an aloof distance from the others, roamed the latest intruder into the ranks of hunters—a creature of the Homo variety. He was a self-made artificial predator and the topmost ape, imitator and trickster that had thus far been seen on the planet. Some 500,000 years ago, perhaps still alongside an older humanoid species, *homines sapientes* have been practicing their enhanced predator skills in Africa.[15] Older humanoid relatives arrived in Europe and Asia 250,000 years or possibly twice as long ago. Some sources estimate the global *Homo sapiens* population, of 250,000 years ago, as low as ten thousand. We do not really know.

—During the past Ice Age, *homines sapientes* hunted and tracked animals as they moved from Africa northward into Europe and Asia. Many of them got held up when they ran up against the icy Taurus and Zagros Mountain barriers. Professor Mithen estimated about a million humans for that time. Prey animals have accumulated there to a considerable density along the southern edge of these mountains, along the upper arc of the Fertile Crescent.

---

[14]A note about the acronym "BC"—in order to avoid the narrow Christian formulation of B.C. (Before Christ), scholars in history of religions and biblical studies sometimes prefer to write B.C.E. (Before the Common Era). Here I prefer to use the simpler BC (meaning Backward Count). In practical terms, to maintain our calendars, all three options are arithmetically identical.

[15]The oldest evidence of hafted spear points is from Kathu Pan 1, South Africa, 500,000 years old. Jayne Wilkins et. al. www.sciencemag.org, 16 Nov. 2012.

—Our ancestors learnt how to compete with other hunter species, with predators that many of us still respect today. To our aspiring hominid ancestors, in Africa, these natural hunters were superior models and de facto gods. Some of their images are still hoisted today by aristocracies, as totemic crests. Predators such as eagles, lions, bears, and dragons, are used today, still, as national emblems even in democratized lands where offspring of proud aristocratic hunters and royals have been relegated to the background.

—The lineage that mutated into *homines sapientes* changed during the past six million years at a considerable speed. They evolved from the level of apes into scavengers and successful artificial predators. Along the northern arch of the so-called "Fertile Crescent," amongst an abundance of fauna, some of them managed to stabilize themselves as hunters, enough to become more or less sedentary. The males of this species became predators, and predators generally do follow potential prey animals wherever these go. While the prey animals were slowed for a time by glaciated mountain ranges, the hunters camped behind them and went only as close as they needed to go, to assure regular access to supplies of meat and to keep competitors at bay. Human hunters learned from foxes, badgers and beavers. Together with these predators they knew themselves to be "people who go forth from their homes to hunt."[16]

—Our ancestors would watch birds nesting, one breeding season at a time. Whenever food supplies held out, humankind could afford to make their shelters more permanent. Eventually, along the Fertile Crescent, they managed to establish larger camping sites and to transform these sites into villages and even into some semblances of towns. Human hunters imitated sedentary animals and began investing more time and effort in constructing their dwellings. We may assume that this adjustment increased their numbers and improved the cohesion of their ecologically divided species.

—When the sizes of families were no longer determined by how many babies or toddlers a woman dared to carry on her wanderings, a sedentary population of hunters could increase and possibly even double or triple within a century. No one could foresee the outcome of this development. But a number of problems awaited

[16]"Men who go forth from their homes to hunt" was an ancient category of Diné Native American Stone Age hunters who also aspired to become sedentary.

these successfully settled hunter families just a few generations down their happy path. Would their populations increase in a reasonable ratio to the prey animals that were left available to future generations? In what manner have Malthusian and Darwinian food- and population ratios overtaken those ancestors? This is a question that at the time no-one knew how to ask—nor would have known how to answer if it had been asked. And even if they had known what lay ahead, and if they had practiced prudent family planning, they still could not have adjusted to the changes of climate and demographics that lay ahead. When animals became scarce nearby, the men banded together and roamed to follow herds of animals that wandered farther from the camps—just as the lions and wolves were doing. Being able to compete with, to outsmart and defeat, natural predators, *homines sapientes* began controlling and owning the hunting ranges, and in the regions that they claimed, other predators were restrained.

—Humankind with all the animals, predators and prey, fell into the rhythms determined by weather and topography. In hindsight we recognize that human fortunes depended on external climate and geography, and on how well the fauna prospered in their environs. Their fortunes also depended on how well they could balance their social ambitions among themselves, and on how well they could prevent competitors from reaching the prey.

—To keep the upper hand on natural predators and to maintain their own effectiveness against their victims, human hunters needed to invent and manufacture a supply of reliable tools. Their weapons needed to outperform the teeth, claws, beaks, and talons of natural predators. They needed to defeat lions, bears, wolves, and anything else that had to be taught, now and then, to keep a respectful distance from humankind. In addition, to defeat larger animals like wild ox and bear, or compete successfully with lions and tigers, they needed to enhance the effectiveness of their artificial "flint teeth" with some type of poison.

—While it has not been proven, and possibly cannot be proven anymore, the general familiarity with serpents that we see reflected in the stone reliefs at Göbekli Tepe could suggest that these hunters knew how to capture, handle, and "milk" vipers, spiders, scorpions, or other venomous creatures—and that they possibly also understood how to utilize poisonous plants. Poisoning spear-points and arrowheads with fatal venom would have significantly reduced the time it took to track wounded animals.

When the Ice was melting: During the Younger Dryas, approximately between 10,800 and 9,600 years ago, a relatively rapid warming trend set in. The Taurus and Zagros mountain ranges began to open up their glaciated valleys. Seasonally the snow and ice would melt from some of the lower saddles between high and permanently icy peaks. All of this meant that more prey animals would wander northward into the mountains, would skirt the shrunken Black Sea, and reach northern grasslands that were recovering from prolonged cold and drought.[17]

—For the sedentary hunters along the upper Fertile Crescent this change of climate presented a dilemma. As a result of increased hunting, the animal populations that roamed south of the mountain ranges had thinned. Increasingly more animals ended up north of the mountains. The settled hunters may not have been well prepared to respond to this new situation. "When will the animals return?" many probably wondered.

—Certainly, the mere fact that for a time animals tended to bunch up south of the icy mountains did not mean that some hunters would not continue to move onward into Asia or Europe. The Fertile Crescent touched on Mediterranean shore lines in the west and offered rivers and a rising gulf-lake in the east. Mountains and surveyable waters did not prevent Homo sapiens from moving on. Detours meant nothing to roaming hunters who followed the orbital trails of territorial prey. Whoever wanted to leave the area could find ways.

—At some point in time some hunters followed the animals northward, deeper into the mountains and noticed that they were not returning but continued moving toward Black Sea shores and onto the inner continental grassy plains. Some of these hunters returned to their villages in the southern Hilly Flanks and told the news. Some surely picked up their families and clans and followed the animals to the other side. But, no matter how many hunters emigrated and followed prey animals, those who stayed behind multiplied according to established opportunities. They hunted the animals that remained, and they stayed trapped in the downward spiral for their livelihood.

---

[17]Compare: Milutin Milankovitch's Glacial and Interglacial Scale, *NOAA Paleo-climatology, http://www.ncdc.noaagov/paleo, & Steven Mithen. After the Ice, a Global History, 20,000 to 5,000 BC. Cambridge: Harvard U. Press. 2004, pp. 12f.*

—Whenever sizeable hunter populations experienced shortages in other parts of the world, whether for reasons of overhunting or environmental changes, the men tended to respond with "unionizing." We will observe this process in greater detail in Chapter Thirteen, where we consider the Wemale history of decadent hunting on the island of Ceram. Forming secret men's associations was a typical response when Stone Age hunters experienced food shortages. As disappointed losers on the hunting range, the men needed each other for assurance and moral support. One man alone could be dismissed as a failure, or a fool—and no man was immune to this danger—but all men united could not be chided for being bad providers. The men needed to defend their status against the stressed foragers in their households, the women, who had good reasons to complain that the men no longer were carrying their weight in the family's quest for survival. Cohesion among the Göbekli Tepe brotherhoods, one may assume, was negatively affected over the longer run by the natural environmental trends and crises.

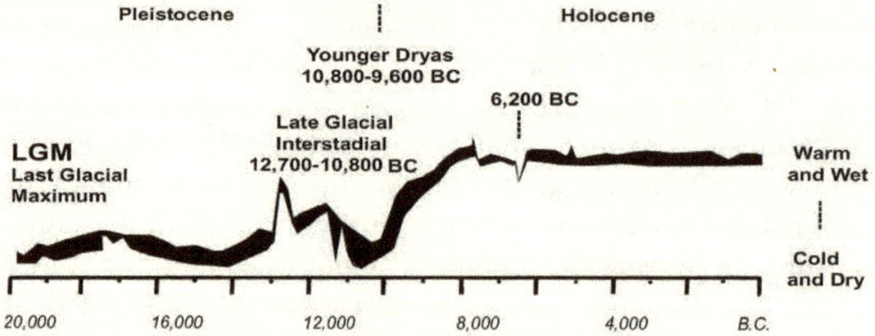

Fig. 1. Global Temperature Variations after the Last Glacial Maximum. Information based on Steven Mithen, *After the Ice*, 2004, p. 12.

—Fortunately, along the northern loop of the Fertile Crescent wild cereal grains were growing, which the women had been gathering all along. To compensate for the shortage of meat, to feed their children, the women needed to gather more grains. And while the latter intensified foraging, and in the process invented seeding, the men with likeminded brothers wandered off to hunt farther away. They were trying to be more effective, collectively. Together they were probably commiserating about their destiny of being hunters.

But as of yet, no one knew of any alternatives to fulltime hunting. Such alternatives needed to be discovered and invented. Being obliged to make do with the grain that the women gathered, the men experienced serious feelings of insecurity creeping up on them—i.e. doubts about their hunter identity and selfworth. This has been the perennial problem among clans of obsolescent Stone Age hunters.

The Neolithic Revolution, a crisis of opulence? With great appreciation I acknowledge the "Foreword" that Professor Klaus Schmidt has contributed to this volume. I concur with his reasoning, that a positive climate was added to the Neolithic culture panorama at the end of the Ice Age. Klaus Schmidt objected to Gordon Childe's theory, which espoused that pressures in the direction of domestication culture were, along the Fertile Crescent, generated by crises of climate and economics. Schmidt insists that at the end of the Ice Age environmental conditions have actually gotten better there, for animals as well as for humankind.

—A small point at which I dare to venture beyond this safe observation is the possibility, that there still could have been a "crisis of sorts" that necessitated domestication—a crisis of culture, signaled not by economics but by religion. Seen from the perspective of a historian of religions, crises can result from any condition by which existential equilibrium is getting lost. It is possible, in this instance, that ecological balance was lost as the result of extraordinary human prosperity and opulence—resulting in overconsumption and overpopulation. Indeed, good climatic conditions could have boosted the fauna and increased the hunters' supply of meat. This directly could have increased the human numbers. And thereby prey animal populations would have been decimated all the more.

—Homo sapiens toolmakers at Göbekli Tepe aggravated their own problems. They were successful manufacturers of flint weapons. Seen from their perspective, weapons surely served only positive functions. Their innovative hunting methods enabled the men to harvest meat in larger quantities. As a result, the human artificial predators prospered and multiplied. Half of all babies born were males and were potential hunters. Weapon-enabled killers multiplied faster than the prey animals could regenerate.

—Ironically, even the people who switched to plant-cultivation and herding added their weights to amplify the general problem. They, too, contributed to human overpopulation, to increase the number of potential hunters who then helped hasten the decline of the fauna. In addition, cultivators of plants turned themselves into competitors with the wild animals who also lived on vegetation. No improvements in climate or environment are immune to exuberant populations of *homines sapientes*. At Göbekli Tepe the consciously guilty predators tried to repent and to atone. But their efforts of atonement in return for ever greater divine blessings were self-defeating. With sentiments of stimulating the Earth-powers for more life, they overpopulated and thereby created a potential for episodic famines.

—Inasmuch as studies of climate history in the Göbekli Tepe area will sooner or later be attempted, to correlate ancient events climatologically, an increase in precision will be required. Wherever prey animals were depleted, domestication strategies became vulnerable as well. One or two seasons of drought could uproot a population of planters. Herders would move away first, and then the planters, all sent adrift amidst dunes of sand. We do not have the ability to plot in detail such short catastrophic intervals on our time scales.

—As a first step toward a Göbekli Tepe climate history one will need to differentiate among (1) periods of Ice Age glaciation and spells of drought during which water would scarcely flow, (2) glaciers melting with water flowing, and (3) periods when glacial water reserves were exhausted. Then onto this elementary periodization, annual tree ring variations or similar precision measurements would need to be superimposed. From such data might estimates regarding the feasibility of permanent domestication ventures be obtained. For sketching the effects of glaciation and its aftermath I recommend, as a starting point, something like the paradigm study of talus slopes and Uighur villages, along the northern edge of the Tarim Basin—which I have visited.

4. LIMESTONE RELIGION AT ABDOMEN HILL

At Abdomen Hill, shifting attention from Flint-tool manufacture to Limestone sculpting signified a softening of culture by religion. Recognizing Flint nodules as embryos of the Mountain-and-Earth Mother offers a break-through hypothesis for decoding the remainder of the Göbekli Tepe atonement cult. The temenoi sanctuaries may be understood as exclusive club lodges for archaic hunters who have begun ruminating beyond flint-tool manufacture and hunting. These enclosures may be understood as entrance sanctuaries to the Great Mother's womb. The T-Pillars —herein named menhirs—may be limestone representations of phalluses. They are ceremonially positioned to impregnate the Earth Mother. Göbekli Tepe as a growing hill demonstrates thereby the Earth Mother's pregnancy.

Temples to appease the Earth: The men at Göbekli Tepe were miners and toolmakers; they worked for themselves and served a hunter-gatherer society in transition. They were huntsmen—that is, confessed killers, butchers, weapon-makers, and quarry-men who thereupon evolved into sculptors. Their hunger for rational understanding required openness toward the larger Earth which they knew to be an immensely greater-than-human, living Mother.

—To ravage the Mother's ovaries, to extract flint nodules—her embryos—for the manufacture of projectile-points and cutting tools, and to hone such tools for chiseling away at that selfsame Mother, for all this the men needed to make amends. Trying to summarize here the complexity of all technological and religious problems would be premature. There are many archaeological data that need to be examined individually before one can begin to understand the Göbekli Tepe cult in its entirety.

—The first thing that comes to the minds of researchers when they become interested in the prehistory of religions is to find some formal funerary evidence. The next question to be asked would then be about "burial gifts," with the assumption that people that are willing to invest in material gifts would thereby, indeed, be serious about their faith in an afterlife. This is an unnecessarily minimalistic view or approach to religion, notably tainted by latter-day archaeological materialism.

—Indeed, it is true that all creatures eventually do reach the peak of their religious surrenders in death, at the moment when they fall off the "teeter-totter plank" at the right end of the scale (this metaphor is explained in Chapter Ten). Indeed, it is always interesting to know "how" someone faces death or succumbs in the process of dying. But then, we can learn much more about the religions of living people when we first acknowledge the presence of real-life opposites—that is, the limits of cultural aggressiveness. Even while people enthusiastically expand their culture, they make religious concessions to greater-than-human boundaries by which they are surrounded. The miners at Göbekli Tepe marked their advances against the surrounding greater-than-human reality especially at moments when they flaunted their growing confidence as sculptors and builders.

—The first question of a historian of religions, at a place like Göbekli Tepe, may therefore be about the miners' reasoning at the moment when they "drove their first stake"—when they raised their first *menhir.* This was a moment when they positioned their self-willed conceptual boundary against the presence of greater-than-human reality. The *menhir*'s shape was imposed by human minds and hands, and it symbolized the outer limit of their collective cultural darings. At the same time, however, this outer limit also signified the nearest edge of the greater-than-human dimension that they dared to push up against.

—The cultural gains that the men at Göbekli Tepe achieved were obtained, literally, at the expense of the Earth Mother's flint and limestone. Their progress further happened at the expense of the totemic animal deities that they sculpted. To a point that a sculptor can flatten and "petrify" a deity in stone, he establishes himself as its de facto master. Moreover, at Göbekli Tepe the sculptors' gains also came at the cost of rendering irrelevant the role that a Sky Father might have played beforehand. This last-mentioned implication will become clearer in relation to Hesiod's *Theogony*, in Chapter Eight.

—So, how have these hunters and miners of flint, from their perspective, expressed what they were doing by carving and setting up their first *menhirs*? A timid scholar will know, dogmatically, and will declare that ten thousand years later an answer to this question is no longer possible. The truth is that on the basis of that same timidity, limited to the aforementioned minimal scope of religion, the miners' thoughts would also have been impossible to understand twelve to ten thousand years ago. But we can safely assume that those who built Göbekli Tepe were able to communicate with each other and express their intimate ontology (theory of being) by means of common symbolic images—some of which have retained meaning into our time.

—In today's great world, which is explained to us mostly by scientific minds that tend to subscribe to unlimited experimental solutions, we further know that religious subject matter will either be discarded without a second thought, or will never be understood well enough to become a question. For scientists who think only along the left half of their existential Teeter Totter scale (see again Chapter Ten), religious understanding is removed from consideration *a priori*. But rational religion is as rational as is rational science. Each operates along its own proportional dimensions and existential foci.

Hill, Limestone, and Flint: In the religious perspective of the men at Göbekli Tepe, what *was* the plateau to which they came? What *were* the hill, the limestone slabs, and the flint materials that they mined for the manufacture of better tools? Twelve thousand years ago none of these miners had yet seen one of our geology study manuals. This means that the definitions we derive from such books—in terms of chemicals, atoms, and molecules—are inadmissible to the present discussion. These Stone Age men understood their work on their own terms. They knew their tools and learned about materials unto which they inflicted their wills. They knew when they were successful, and they knew when they failed to comprehend or needed to back off. In other words, they understood when they needed to be more cautious—more religious.

—The quarry-men and sculptors knew how to replicate the rounded shapes of living animals that represented the greater-than-human realm of hunter totems. In order to move from that world of personal totems into the wider social order, and into a still larger cosmic divine order, they carved large rectangular *menhirs* (T-shaped pillars). They sculpted abstract shapes.

—Contemplating the bas-relief and the high-relief sculptures, the scientifically oriented analyst is prepared to recognize animals that supposedly represent totems. But what are totems? They are deities that reigned during an era when the ancestors of humankind still felt inferior to, or were awed by, certain types of animals. Some of these totems, back then, included animals that still are swimming, flying, or running about today. In our modern times, most of these ancient totems have depreciated and have now become a subject matter categorized by scientific zoology. Correspondingly, eleven or twelve thousand years ago, at an early level of artistic abstraction, totemic animals were being flattened to bas-relief images—packed down onto angular slabs of limestone.

—Facing the Göbekli Tepe level of abstraction, a scientific zoologist is left with few clues concerning the added meaning that angular T-shaped limestone *menhirs* might have held. Had those ancient sculptors rounded off the corners and edges of their *menhirs,* in a more naturalistic manner, a modern observer could more easily guess the elementary shapes and their biological prototypes. But had the sculptors rounded those edges, they would have expressed their own wills toward the limestone subject matter to a lesser extent. To interpret the *menhirs* only as symbols, without sensing their original overlap with reality and life, as such life was being challenged by greater-than-human reality, is to look at the aesthetics of clothing and imagine only skeletons underneath. It is the difference between scraping at inert bones and touching anatomy that still pulses in the service of softer life.

Material realities that ghosts cannot see: In his book, *After the Ice,* Steven Mithen presents a wonderful archaeological overview of the last fifteen thousand years of human prehistory. His literary device of sending the ghost of John Lubbock to visit a variety of ancient archaeological sites, when these sites were still teeming with life, enabled him to dramatize hypothetical encounters, that could in all probability have happened. But, frequently, for such events concrete proof could no longer be had. However, the invisible ghost of a historical figure would visit dangerous and otherwise inaccessible places. He would hide in the shadows and then slip away from cannibals and other threats. When the two—Professor Mithen and his befriended ghost—came to Göbekli Tepe, their double presence there was of little help. They were looking at the remains of an ancient cult with two sets of similar modern eyes between them. Both together saw only what would pass through their school-defined archaeological filters. Here is what we are told:

> "what the animal and symbolic images mean, and what kind of ritual activities took place at Göbekli, we are unlikely to discover. The images may have been clan totems or depictions of Neolithic gods—but there had been no 'mother goddess' at Göbekli. All of the animals are male, and there is a limestone carving from the site of a human figure with an erect penis. Indeed, rather than notions of wholesome fertility and reproduction, the emerging religious themes from both Jerf el Ahmar and Göbekli are about fear and danger of the wild."[18]

—Professor Mithen's assessment is quite remarkable. It senses correctly the present danger and fear of the wild. But then, what else can one expect in sanctuaries built by hunters? Hunters are professional killers and butchers, and their totems therefore needed to be superior predators—as well as superior males. Moreover, should not the presence of multitudes of excited males hint at the nearness of some female? Of course, totems are not alternatives to gods; they themselves *are* the gods. In addition, any archaic hunter deity could choose to be visible as well as to be camouflaged and somewhat invisible—almost like John Lubbock the ghost, except more substantial and somewhat less "spiritual." In Neolithic hunter religions no category is needed to vouch for something that is always invisible, such as "spirituality." The concepts of "visibility, transformation, and shades of visibility or invisibility" suffice.

—The presence of predator gods produced fear and danger for all potential victims, including humankind. But then for contrast, just as men were expected to wield the powers of death, women in hunter

---

[18] Steven Mithen, *After the Ice…. 2003,* pp. 66f.

cultures were traditionally endowed with the powers of life. For millions of years hominid male hunters have formed physical unions with females for the propagation of offspring. But they sought mystic bonds with the types of predators whom they most respected—thus with exemplary predator divinities—for shared physical prowess, as well as for the moral justification of wielding death, as hunters.

—In the distant past, when the ancestors of humans themselves still lived at the animal level, totemic animals were their gods. They had the ability to sponsor, to influence, and to make those hunters successful as well as to withdraw their help. Men were owned and "possessed" by those gods in the same way that human domesticators, later on, began to utilize and to own animals. While they hunted, the men deemed these totemic gods to be great enough to be obeyed. The gods operated the muscles and weapons of their human protégés and, thereupon, took responsibility for felling prey animals. By the time their totemic images could safely be sculpted in bas-relief, circa 11,500 years ago at Göbekli Tepe, not all of these divine animals were still greater than human. With sufficient planning, men were able to kill any of these gods—also to borrow their skins and faces (i.e. masks). But nonetheless, our hunter ancestors continued to respect them as divine authorities and as partners who thereby could be honored for taking responsibility for whatever objectionable deeds those human devotees wrought under the influence of these gods. Here, at Göbekli Tepe, their death-wielding temperaments were becoming seriously entangled with libido and life. The Göbekli Tepe cultural and religious reform meant repentance, and atonement for millions of years of artificers' progress, and killer sins.

—The ghost of John Lubbock was unable to recognize the "mother goddess" at Göbekli Tepe. He could not recognize her for the simple reason that the Göbekli Hill, herself, was a material goddess. How much of her would have needed to be exposed to trigger recognition? How correctly could a latter-day British "spiritual" ghost have identified material deities?

—Labels such as "totemism," "animism," "polytheism," and "monotheism" were invented to assist modern minds who were already trying to avoid encountering actual greater-than-human personages. Naming the gods is the first human gesture of affecting them. Counting them in numbers is the next step of taking control. Counting is a gesture of ownership.

—We know that John Lubbock's friend has seen at least some of the exposed portions of the Göbekli Tepe Mother's abdomen—in the process of being laid bare archaeologically. Had he been initiated into one or two remnant Stone Age traditions—had he been aware of the fact that no "nature objects" or "nature features" really existed in Neolithic religion—his chances of recognizing the goddess would have improved by some ninety-nine percent. Eyesight and recognition are two different things.

—The gods of humankind are, effectively, whatever humans encounter as being greater—or as one co-founder of one of our Western religions has suggested—"the One in whom we live and move and have our being." Of course, there was a sprawling Earth and an overarching Sky twelve thousand years ago—between which the men at Göbekli Tepe had their being. These two greater-than-human realities, Earth and Sky, revealed themselves to budding sculptors accordingly, in southeastern Anatolia, once these men began formulating their fresh Neolithic questions.

—What Stone Age artist could have chiseled full images of either Earth or Sky in limestone in some recognizable form? There always was more to a Mother Goddess cult than dignified sculptors were able, or would have dared, to show—though at Göbekli Tepe the sculptors could not have been much more explicit than they were. Their mysteries now lie there, concealed only by the clear air we breathe, excavated, and in full view.

Mining embryos of Flint: The builders of the Göbekli Tepe sanctuaries initially came as hunters and butchers to the limestone plateau. They went to work there as miners and toolmakers while their minds were set on finding the best possible nodules of flint; this much we can infer now from the cleared limestone terraces, and from the flint and limestone tailings that these men left behind at their work places. They also left behind a sufficient number of flint tool stashes to verify their profession.

—Our primary question at Göbekli Tepe pertains to the cult platforms that the Stone Men built there. What was it that these hunters, toolmakers, and miners thought they were up to? How might they have explained to their younger apprentices what they were doing? What did the hill that they created signify to them? How did flint nodules and flint tools fit into the context of their worldview? How were all these matters related to their hopes and goals of hunting? What did all this mean for what these men were trying to accomplish at their hill?

—I am convinced that I have sufficient answers to these questions; but I also know that neither the German nor the English language has the vocabulary to describe the fundamentals of the Göbekli Tepe cult in a straightforward manner without reducing some intended meanings to banalities. For that reason I cannot simply write a quick essay and be done. My explanations require a larger archaic context, and the space of a book.

—All of the above questions are central to understanding the religious vision by which those temple-lodges were constructed and for which, in the end, they also needed to be covered up again. In the early days, the hunters who came to Göbekli Tepe could probably find quartzite flint nodules strewn about, exposed to rain and sunshine, all over these Hilly Flanks, especially in eroded ravines below limestone escarpments. Harvesting these raw materials initially required little cultural aggression—and correspondingly, the activities of these men required little religious retreat or other serious mental balancing. But their readily available resource of flint nodules could have been exhausted in a single decade of intensive collecting. Thus, in order to obtain more flint the miners needed to accomplish the work of Weather and Time more speedily, and more violently. They needed to dislodge the limestone slabs for crashing and removal and to harvest the embedded flint nodules fresh from the Mother.

—So, what might flint nodules and limestone slabs have meant to these miners? An answer to this question is essential. It is needed to explain the meaning of everything that these people ever inflicted on limestone, on flint, or on anything else by way of using flint tools or flint weapons subsequently.

—Traditional hunters around the world often have blamed the deaths of prey animals on the makers of their weapons. This was a handy ruse if a hunter did not manufacture his own weapon from scratch. For example, some traditional Diné Indians—practitioners of the Navajo Coyoteway ceremonial—would blame the lethal accuracy of their arrows on "bird people" who "contributed" the guiding tail feathers that had been attached at the rear of the arrow shafts. It is conceivable that hunters at Göbekli Tepe who traded venison for arrowheads would, out at the open range or at the "holy place of a killer's success," have blamed the distant workmen who mined the flint and who chipped and knapped the successful arrow point. Or, they might have blamed the vipers who "contributed" the venom that might have been smeared on the arrowheads. In order to shift the guilt for their deadly deeds, human artificer-predators probably spoke such false excuses as early as any of them mastered the art of speech. They probably learned to speak lies and denials like "I did not do it" before they ever attempted to speak a word of truth. Anyone could see the truth. If there had been no intended lie there would have been no need to manufacture words just to speak "truth" differently.

—During times of early metallurgy that overlapped with the beginnings of writing, nodules and nuggets of ore were recognized by miners and smiths as being the embryos of the Earth Mother. The miners probably found their first nuggets of ore while looking for flint or obsidian.

Mircea Eliade about the Earth Mother: In this context I will quote a summary statement about early metallurgy that Mircea Eliade, my honored teacher of five years, was articulating in his Chicago lectures while I was in attendance, during the Nineteen-Sixties.

> "Mineral substances shared in the sacredness attaching to the Earth-Mother. Very early on we are confronted with the notion that ores "grow" in the belly of the earth after the manner of embryos. Metallurgy thus takes on the character of obstetrics. Miner and metal-worker intervene in the unfolding of subterranean embryology: they accelerate the rhythm of the growth of ores, they collaborate in the work of Nature and assist it to give birth more rapidly. In a word, man with his various techniques, gradually takes the place of Time: his labors replace the work of Time."[19]

—Though Professor Eliade was not specifically writing about the mining of flint, what he says about ores is nevertheless relevant to our questions. Flint nodules, themselves, have been mined and worked into tools by a technique of cold chipping and knapping. If

---

[19]Mircea Eliade. *The Forge and the Crucible.* Univ. of Chicago Press, 1962, p. 8.

early metallurgists came to understand ore nuggets as the Earth Mother's embryos, then certainly the flint miners, before they advanced to mining ores, must already have thought about their quartzite nodules of flint and obsidian in a similar manner. Flint nodules resemble eggs more closely than did those metallic nuggets that they mined later. Moreover, the striking of flint against another flint occasionally produced sparks of fire, suitable to ignite the fires that made metallurgy possible. By this line of reasoning, the use of chipped flint tools—of "splintered" or forcefully "hatched" flint eggs —which the somewhat tortoise-like and crusty Earth-and-Mountain Mother had laid, might have preceded mining and smelting of metallic ore by possibly as much as a million years.

Fig. 2. Göbekli Tepe: One of many work sites, with flint chip debris. Insert: Image of a flint nodule. Photos by author, courtesy of DAI.

—While we are arriving here at the concepts of flint "embryos" and limestone "ovaries" by analogous evolutionary inferences, we shall be using this imagery only for general context. Recognizing flint nodules as having probably been embryos in the minds of Göbekli Tepe miners is only one of the matching thoughts suggested at this archaeological site. It helps us see the *menhirs*, and reliefs of freshly hatched chicks, in a more meaningful context. And certainly, assertions of meaning by these miners have found their most emphatic and explicit mode of expression in the general pattern of those standing *menhirs*. The overall probability of our interpretation increases with the number of pieces that will fit the larger puzzle. We do not have literary documentation proving that flint nodules were, in fact, thought of as embryos, for the simple reason that Neolithic monuments from that period carry no decipherable textual inscriptions.

—But if flint nodules were indeed the Earth Mother's embryos, then the limestone layers in which such embryos had been growing were, for Neolithic people, the encrusted "ovaries" of the Earth Mother. This means that Göbekli Tepe miners would probably have described, and justified, their work as an act of intrusive obstetrics. They helped the Earth Mother lay her flint eggs more speedily, for the obvious purpose of enabling miners to "hatch" her offspring—those divine eggs and weapon points—more quickly. Or as Eliade said it: "their labors replaced the work of Time." In any case, with hypothetical assumptions such as these, the function and meaning of the T-shaped *menhirs* can be brought into focus with a reasonable degree of probability.

Limestone Religion along the Moh Scale: For a translation of the total archaic mining metaphor into concise scientific jargon, the reader is here invited to contemplate animal ovaries. These would "scratch" nothing and would score Zero on Moh's Hardness Scale which geologists use to classify minerals. From there, one may conceptualize an increase to relative hardness level Three, which is the hardness of average limestone. One would thereby have adjusted our analogy as high as the hardness level of the Earth Mother's ovary tissues.

—Among the limestone strata that cover the plateau of Göbekli Tepe, the hunter-butcher-miners dug flint embryos from within the ovaries of the Earth Mother. Making tools for their own use and for barter, the men chipped and knapped the hard flint nodules with angular hammer strikes and pressure flaking. While fashioning flint arrowheads, spear-points, axes, adzes, daggers and picks, these tool-makers operated at an approximate hardness level of Seven on the Moh Scale. Such hardness, we may postulate, bestowed now and then some bloody fingers on those toolmakers.

Predisposition: *The Moh Scale is easily accommodated by the graduated Teeter-Totter Scale below, in Chapter Ten. It happens to apply a small step farther in the material direction. But then, primitive religions were not "spiritual" ideologies that concern never-never lands; they include retreats from "harder," greater-than-human realities—from realities which seldom showed any less than the hardness of claw and tooth. So, rather than only paying attention to hardness and resistances in the material world, a historian of religions may estimate "aggressiveness" and "retreat" intensities in a variety of human contexts and responses. Man is not merely a manipulator of hammer stones and flint chisels, nor is he only aware of muscle tensions that deliver projectiles. He also senses resistance and reciprocal forces in the larger external world. His reflective mind is aware of impacts on his conscience, as on his body. Differences in hardness can be noted between flint, limestone, among tailings fill, blood, a friend's touch, as well as escapist cosmologies that ignore human existential problems altogether. Without sensing such existential Moh Scale differentials concretely, the real-life experiences and struggles of miners, twelve millennia ago, would shrivel to stale theories—to tales without active verbs or living people.*

—In order to mine flint, these men needed to develop the necessary skills for quarrying limestone. The miners needed strength to crash slabs of limestone into rubble, to free flint nodules from within or from under the limestone strata. Their playful skill of sculpting seemed almost like a reward for their labor. It is likely that their pictorial sculpting techniques were introduced a little later during their Göbekli Tepe occupation—perhaps by 11,500 years ago. This means that at hardness level Seven—the level of flint—these men struggled to expand their culture and to make a living. But by working at hardness level (or "softness level") Three, the level of limestone, they found recreation and a style of devout and practical religious symbolizing, atonement, and sensible retreat.

Göbekli Tepe, the Pregnant Hill: When Professor Schmidt first eyed the Göbekli Tepe site, he could not think of a natural force that would have put such a hill on that limestone plateau. This makes sense. When I, a former experimental tree farmer on land underlain by limestone and flint, was contemplating his photographs of the bare limestone plateau surrounding the hill, I also could not think of a natural force that would have scraped specifically these portions of the plateau down to bare bedrock while sparing an earthen hill. And when I added my cultivator's experience to the Professor's geological estimate, and then envisioned people who came to the area in hope of finding flint nodules I, too, realized that this artificial hill must have been heaped up from miners' tailings and from scoops of overhead.

—The essential idea that Göbekli Tepe began with flint mining is clearly implied in the writing of Professor Schmidt.[20] I am elaborating on the mining fact only in order to continue explanation of the cult that still begs to be exposed. Because my essay is mostly a response to the Professor's data, I presume that his book will need to be considered first to understand my contribution.

A Faltering Predisposition: *The thought, that hunter-gatherers had come to this plateau just to build a hill that would accommodate stone-pillars and a temple cult, something which before their time was nonexistent, seems quite unlikely. Great things sometimes may happen by chance. Or, if a greater-than-human reality is to be given credit, they happen by divine degree and societal expectations. Revelations generally do come from a direction in which people are looking: they come from where human curiosity is already manufacturing questions. This hill—so I thought—could have been a necessary byproduct of flint-mining operations. The men needed to clear away the overhead dirt and loosen and smash the limestone strata. They needed to clear away their debris from the plateau. And so the tailings hill grew over time. It might have grown regardless of whether the miners were going to build temples on it or not. Moreover, this hill probably would have turned out to be a more uniform cone if sanctuaries had not claimed a streak up the slope and required, for the duration of cult activities, that selectively a "No Dumping" zone be declared. Explaining the existence of the hill as a byproduct of their weapons and tool industry as well, would have thrown some light on the eventual construction of "temples" which I, personally, still prefer to think of as "exclusive hunter lodges." The construction and maintenance of these lodges needed not have come about as the result of a great religious vision. It could as well have been inspired while some quarry-men did some recreational doodling and thereby invented "sculpting." But then, these temples certainly filled a religious deficit along the existential "teeter-totters" of these people (compare Chapter Ten). But then, such a large number of "temples," built continuously over two millennia, cannot be explained away as "doodling." A central religious vision must have been present.*

—The faltering predisposition to which I have confessed here seemed reasonable until September 27, 2011, the morning on which I first set foot on Göbekli Tepe. I repeated my visit to the mountain

[20]Cf. Klaus Schmidt, 2008, pp. 15-17, photographs on p. 14.

on October 2 and 6. Having all along tried to be a cautious religionist, careful so as not to assume too much religion *a priori*, it became obvious that I had been postulating too little of it. Upon walking some rounds at this archaeological site, and hobbling along the quarry stretches, it became quite apparent that from any point on this star-shaped plateau any amount of overhead dirt, or limestone tailings, could far more easily have been dumped into ravines over the edges than be carried uphill to grow a mountain. The convenience of the compilation of this mountain, which I had assumed from the distance of half a globe away, could have been a valid factor if the plateau had been continuous and larger.

Fig. 3. Limestone slabs at the Southwest "knee" of Göbekli Tepe, looking northeast. Suspected point of the miners' first approach. Photo by author—courtesy of DAI.

—But nonetheless, the men came to this mountain to mine flint. Under escarpment ledges of irregular limestone slabs they probably dug with backward-forked hardwood picks. Later flint miners in Europe used deer antlers. They dug to search after quartzite "flint-eggs." And even though the flint nodules that they found under that ledge may have been small, there still are plenty of flint chips lying on the unbroken rock slabs to explain the men's activity (Figure 2).

In any case, at the Southwest "knee" of the mountain they broke off, and then abandoned, a series of large limestone splinters (Figure 3; Figure 6-A). Had these miners not been sidetracked by other features on this interesting mountain, they could easily have dressed up some of these large slabs into respectable *menhirs,* had they wished.

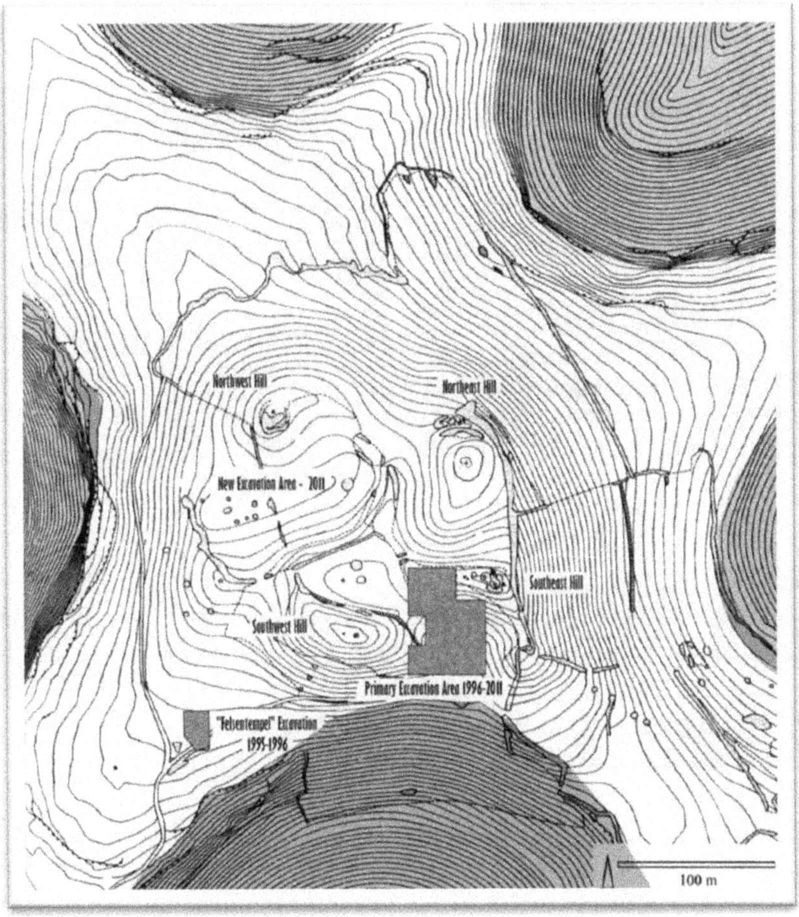

Fig. 4. Simplified topographical map of Göbekli Tepe. Archaeological information is reduced, and topography is highlighted to illustrate the suggestions presented in this book. The original is in Klaus Schmidt, 2008, p. 101. By Courtesy of DAI.

—A little farther uphill from the "knee" they found several unique round holes leading down through the bedrock (Figure 5; Figure 6-B1, B2), apparently pre-shaped by soft Jurassic or Cretaceous tree stems. These were about the size of flint nodules and could have suggested that "flint eggs" formerly were "laid" through holes of that size. As hunters and butchers these miners knew that all eggs and living things come from holes. Professor Schmidt has called my attention to the fact that the top-most hole, along the northern edge of the temple perimeter, had a low relief "lip" spared out, facing the site (Figure 5, left). The temple site was aligned with it.

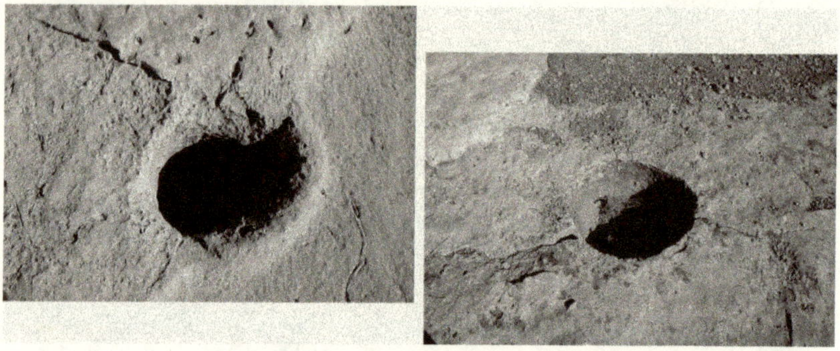

Fig. 5. The two orifices between which the first temple enclosure was laid out, marking the northern perimeter of the enclosure. On the left, please note the elevated lip. Photos by author—by courtesy of DAI.

—So, adjacent to that specially rimmed natural orifice, on the bedrock, they built their first rock temple with two feminine base pedestals ("C" on Figure 6) spared out on the floor surface. But then, perhaps even before they began working at the layout of their sanctuary, they might also have dug two larger holes, perhaps to contain the entire group of men of a dozen or so. One of these holes held an upright stone pillar, stabilized by a surrounding pile of double-fist-sized rocks.

—Thus, the "duality" principle—of orienting oneself by two orifices, of having two larger cavities for ceremonial huddles (Figures 6 & 7), plus the practice of sparing two central stone "pedestals" on a rock-hewn platform (probably for two semi-moveable *menhirs*, which are no longer present)—was already established at this first temple site. This duality principle remained valid throughout two thousand years of sanctuary architecture, here, on this mountain. However, as the miners became more familiar with the topography of the mountain, they began to reorient themselves in the larger landscape.

—At some point in time the bedazzled celebrant miners discovered that they were nestled in at the perforated upper right thigh of a mountain-sized manifestation of the Earth Mother. In contrast to the much later archaeologists these mining pioneers, back then, saw no five-pronged star-shaped plateau (Figure 4). Instead, this mountain revealed herself to them as a woman, reclining spread-eagled. Her two legs pointed and splayed southward, and her two arms were pointing northwest and northeast. Her head was pointing north. They decided therefore that their cult activities should be relocated eastward—that they should establish themselves more intimately in the Mountain Mother's crotch.

—Twelve millennia after the miners came to Göbekli Tepe, a team of modern archaeologists followed almost precisely in their tracks. In 1995 they excavated the early Rock Temple *(Felsentempel)* area that, as readers of this book, we have just stepped on to. In 1996 they moved east along the ledge. The archaeologists were not lured by the Mountain Woman's more distinctive crotch there, but by the protruding cubic head of a large "T-pillar." They excavated, and over time they found there the greatest mother-lode of pre-pottery Neolithic limestone *menhirs* that, as far as we know, has ever been implanted into this planet.

Predisposition: *This was not the first time in his life that this writer looked at a landscape and learnt that he was looking at a living being. Looking at Black Mesa in Arizona, from east across the Chinle Valley, he was told by some of his Diné Stone Age teachers that there lies a Serpent. Further west, beyond the northwest corner of Arizona, he was shown two Rainbows of stone that were united in marital union—known together as "Rainbow Bridge." Nearby sits Navajo Mountain which turned out to be the Head of Earth—at least of Earth as the early Diné Indians there knew her.* [21]

—It was at the time when miners at Göbekli Tepe quarried and sculpted their first *menhirs,* that the outlines and concerns of their hunter and miner religion became visible. The most conspicuous symbolic presences at Göbekli Tepe are the *menhirs* themselves. It is the creation and use of these T-shaped monuments that in time will identify, as well as certify, the meaning and function of all the ceremonial enclosures. *Menhirs* are sculpted slabs of limestone. On their surfaces many of them bear the images of animals which, aside

---

[21] Karl W. Luckert. *Navajo Mountain and Rainbow Bridge Religion.* Museum of Northern Arizona Press, Flagstaff, 1977.

from totemic clan and lodge affiliations, would also suggest totemic attributes for self-promotion. Among the living prototypes of these images, in all likelihood, lingered still some roaming gods.

—Each man who joined such a group was either already associated with one of those totems by his clan membership, or he received his new totemic identity when he joined. No matter where these hunters came from to mine flint, they were likely to find either totemic maternal clan brothers or totemic hunting-association brothers at Göbekli Tepe. All came to replenish their tool and weapon kits. This meant that all of them, as hunters and killers, shared similar culture-defined ambitions and corresponding shades of guilt complexes. Specific styles of cultural aggression call for matching styles of atonement. Paths of religious retreat must correspond logically and proportionately, to counter-balance the ways of cultural aggression.

—The hunters' guilt over killing animal people was compounded at Göbekli Tepe by the special fact that those men there also were attacking the very rock layers that were the Earth Mother's encrusted ovaries. Both of these cultural sins of aggression, the hunting and the mining, taken together or separately, required ceremonial atonement and making amends. By building sanctuaries, the miners found a way to atone and to forgive themselves—to reconcile with the Earth-and-Mountain Woman. Consequently they could assume that if she did not fully endorse, she at least pardoned some of their violent behavior by her presence and participation in their rituals, (e.g. "her" rituals).

A Mountain of Riddles: In all the major lodges that miners built during the earliest phase at Göbekli Tepe, which so far have been excavated, stood two *menhirs* that straddled the center line of the floors. It is conceivable that two such *menhirs* were quarried and sculpted before any sanctuary was envisioned, and before plans were made for those *menhirs* to be stood up. In other words, the principle of using two central *menhirs* could have been established because two of them had been sculpted and two sculptors agreed to stand them up together. But such a causal explanation would almost certainly be too simple.

—I have followed the lead of the excavators and have acknowledged their designated *Felsentempel,* Enclosure E, at the edge of the

Fig. 6. Enclosure E—*Felsentempel*. Southwest Promontory of the Göbekli Tepe Plateau, looking south. See Schmidt, 2008, p. 107. Photograph—Courtesy of DAI.

Southwest Plateau, as having possibly been the first *temenos* (see Klaus Schmidt, *Sie bauten...*, p. 107). The oval space that features two base pedestals to accommodate two *menhirs* (Figure 6) would then derive from a time when the Abdomen Hill had not yet been heaped as a bulge onto the virgin plateau. The original two *menhirs*, in all likelihood, would then have been moved eastward to the actual crotch when that place became the geographic focus of the cult. But we do not yet know which among the known or still hidden *menhirs* those first two could have been.

—At the moment we must base our interpretations on incomplete data. If the present pattern holds for the excavation of future platforms at Göbekli Tepe, we can expect that two hundred *menhirs* might eventually come to light. But there have been indications that later enclosures, farther north and west, might turn out to be less embellished.[22] A room up north does not contain any *menhirs.*

—The intended significance of dual *menhirs* must, therefore and meanwhile, be surmised from additional context. All *menhirs* taken together, with numerous bas-reliefs and a few high-reliefs, are our primary clues to understanding totemic attributions within these lodges. But we do not yet know the sequence in which all the lodges were established and abandoned.

Fig. 7. Backing off a few steps, north of the preceding photograph, one finds a pair of larger ceremonial pits. The stub of a broken-off pillar, in the left pit (east), still sits encased by supportive rocks. Photos by the author—courtesy of DAI.

[22]If pushed to make a premature estimate from half a world away, I would suspect that Enclosure C (Figure 25), frequently remodeled, could have been the first. However, without being able to see all enclosures fully excavated, and in context, such an estimate is superfluous. We have no idea what central "origin point" might still lie hidden under the Southeast Hill. Might it ever be wise to dig to the bottom, or to tunnel from behind and beneath the Lions lodges?

—Perhaps it would have been better for this entire chapter to have been written after all the excavations are completed. But then again, no harm will be done if we proceed carefully and anticipate in years to come a certain number of surprises. Perhaps an opportunity will be given to update these chapters at some future time. Meanwhile, I intend to comment on some of the *T-Pfeiler* as they have already been introduced by the archaeologists. In English dialogue I prefer to allude to these monuments not as T-pillars, but as *menhirs*, which is a neutral term that stems from the domain of Celtic studies. "*Menhir*" simply refers to a "stood-up stone."

—A moiety relationship of two clans may have existed between the first sculptors. The possibility of a Fox and Crane moiety recommends itself tentatively. But because we do not know what the first two *menhirs* looked like, we cannot even begin guessing. If we could identify those two with certainty, and if there were distinct totemic affiliations, then such a hypothesis would stand on firmer ground. But be that as it may, I am inclined to assume that each generation of hunter and miner brotherhoods at Göbekli Tepe produced its own leaders and organizers. These would then have recruited members into their respective totemic associations. I also suspect that such organizers exuded charisma as competent explainers, as master flint knappers and limestone sculptors.

—A lodge sanctuary had only limited space for seating members and for setting up *menhirs*. When a lodge became overfilled, space for expansion or a branch site was needed. The membership ratios among multi-totemic affiliations probably shifted over time. With the glaciers melting in the mountains, some clans were inclined to move north. And then, especially during the early years at Göbekli Tepe, there was prestige to be gained from sitting next to a stately *menhir* that had been sculpted by the man who proudly enjoyed sitting in prominent proximity.

—Having two large *menhirs* erected at the center may suggest that from the start there were two leaders, each having a group of supporters who helped in the heavy lifting and moving. In multi-totemic associations, each new member with a different totemic affiliation may have had his totemic animal-deity sculpted on one of the *menhirs*. From this possibility would follow that, if a member left the fraternity, or was expelled, his totemic emblem could be erased to make room for another entry. But considering the fact that with each erasure the limestone slab would have gotten thinner, erasures and substitutions probably did not happen very often. Vacant spaces could have been created by combining groups of totems and by expanding the fraternities. I personally doubt whether an artist's aesthetic predilections were much of a factor when it came to erasures. One cannot expel totemic gods just because one does not like their looks. On the other hand, totemic sponsors tended to hover over places where their own images and human protégés assembled.

What are these Menhirs? At the moment that I am writing these lines, the June 2011 edition of *National Geographic* is still the latest Göbekli Tepe summary that has been published. The author Charles C. Mann, on page 44, rhetorically asks: "Carvings mark the pillars as stylized human figures, but did they represent powerful people or super-natural beings?" Our answer has to be "probably none of these." Before long I trust that I will be able to lead my readers on to a better answer. But why are there usually two standing as a pair, at the center?

—My first quick answer was that in this assembly of two abstract anthropomorphic beings, one would have been a male and the other female. But which of these would be which? It turned out to be an unnecessary question. Indeed, this question and my first answer occurred while I was still unfocused on what I was looking at. I took for granted, as everyone else did, that we were looking at pillars that actually represented some kind of human shapes with squared heads. From my work on Diné Indian sand-paintings I was already accustomed to seeing square-headed deities—and Diné squared heads usually indicated female deities (see Figure 15). At Göbekli Tepe there also are hands and stoles shown on some of these *menhirs*, which would seem to indicate the directions of right and left, up and down.

Predisposition: *During my first year in grade school our teacher used a limerick to teach us pronunciation and control of the tongue. It began like this: "In Ulm und um Ulm und um Ulm herum..." I am quite certain that the famous Ulm student, Albert Einstein, was subjected to this exercise as well. We can save ourselves the remainder of this tongue twister. The formula, as it stands, provides us with the perfect archaeological re-orientation that I once applied to decode the famous "mosaic masks" at the ancient Olmec site of La Venta, in the present-day*

Mexican state of Tabasco. The key words translate into English as "around," and "round-about." In relation to the La Venta archaeological reports, I "walked around" the mosaics and quickly saw that my predecessors had looked at them, and interpreted them, backward and upside down. They so mistook rattlesnake faces for jaguar masks.[23]

Six Millennia later, a theological Roll-over in Egypt: There existed on this planet another famous symbolic system that must also be read with the somersault method of orientation. Now that we are close to decoding the *menhirs* (T-pillars) at Göbekli Tepe, the challenge to understand the shapes of ancient Egyptian obelisks, of pyramids and the rising Hill named "Atum" in Heliopolitan theology, awaits us for comparison. Far south from these very ancient Göbekli Tepe *menhirs* we must learn to view the world while doing a headstand. In Egypt, five or six millennia after Göbekli Tepe, we must picture the obelisks, the pyramids, and the rising hill of Atum against the ancient Egyptian cosmos in the background. And why is this necessary? Because for the ancient Egyptians the Earth was Father Geb, and the Sky was Mother Nut. She was born of Tefnut and gave birth to Isis beneath her. To understand the general Heliopolitan theology one must, of course, first give up fantasizing about builders visiting from outer space, and one must read for orientation the Egyptians' own underworld Pyramid- and Coffin-texts.

—The beginnings and history of ancient Egyptian obelisks are somewhat unclear, because most of them have been dragged to foreign places as souvenirs, by foreign conquerors. The oldest hieroglyphic depiction of an obelisk may be found in a pictogram of *Pyramid Text* 1652. There the primordial deity Atum is shown as a slender obelisk-like shaft of which its tip still appears somewhat rounded—not yet abstractly pointed. And this still rounded "pyramidion" tip is pointing skyward.[24]

---

[23]See Karl W. Luckert. *Olmec Religion, a Key to Middle America and Beyond.* University of Oklahoma Press, Civilization of the American Indian Series 137, Norman, 1976.

[24]Hans Bonnet. *Reallexikon der Ägyptischen Religionsgeschichte*, Berlin 1952, pp. 539-542.

—It may well be that the geometry of obelisks and pyramids evolved together. Their symbolic meanings appear to have been convertible. The God Atum, rising from Nun—the primordial sea of chaos—was primordial Hill, royal pyramid, as well as the *pyramidion* tip of obelisks. The pioneer builder and developer of pyramids, the Pharaoh Sneferu (ca. 2613-2589 BC—father of Kufu who was the builder of the Great Pyramid), he left us three vastly different prototypes to scrutinize. He thereby enabled us to track the development of his ideas. The first extraordinary burial place that he built for himself was the Pyramid at Meidum. There he tried to build something in seven stages, too steep and too high. Much of the top section collapsed. But judging by the contours that are still standing, his upper stage probably was meant to have the shape of a shortened obelisk, perhaps with a *pyramidion* tip at the top.

—Fortunately we know what was on the builder's mind, because the next mausoleum he built—now called Bent Pyramid—had in fact in its entirety been given the squeezed shape of a stubby obelisk. We therefore know that the Pharaoh Sneferu would have preferred to be buried inside a gigantic obelisk—inside the Godhead Atum. But looking at the finished shape of this "Bent Pyramid," Sneferu still was not satisfied. Its shape was far less elegant than was his first attempt at Meidum, and he probably feared another disastrous collapse. He thereupon built a third structure, the Red Pyramid, for which he imagined his obelisk shaft to be completely out of sight, hidden underground, and he only bothered to build an enlarged version of the *pyramidion* tip. The "Red Pyramid" thereby became the first sturdy standard model for subsequent Egyptian pyramids. In clear-script this means that those ancient pharaohs adjusted their burial edifices to where at death they could return to the Godhead of Atum, in order to issue from there again as rising Sun and Horus Falcon, to impregnate the divine Tefnut/Nut/Isis femininity with light—thereafter to be reborn upon (from) Isis the divine "Throne."

Ceremonial Paraphernalia: At Göbekli Tepe the "Earth Beneath" was the Mother, and this arrangement left the Sky on High completely free to be Father. So it is quite obvious, now, why in Egypt the phallic Atum was rising as a hill and why Egyptian obelisks and pyramid tips point toward Nut? If one were to turn a very ancient

Göbekli Tepe *menhir* downside-up, one would anticipate the essence and direction of subsequent Egyptian obelisks, adjusted for access to the Egyptian feminine upperworld.[25]

—The ancient Egyptian Falcon-pharaohs loved to arrive "trailing clouds of glory" (as William Wordsworth did) as if truly born from on high. It is possible that this relatively late original ancient Egyptian cosmology was still a subconscious reaction against the earth-oriented Mother cult, spiked with *menhirs* at Göbekli Tepe.

—I am now convinced that the hands and stoles on a few of the *menhirs* at Göbekli Tepe were part of the ceremonial paraphernalia, and that they represented the cult mystery of this place. And they were arrayed to be intentionally riddle-some. Look more closely! None of these "pillar heads" has a face—and not even a nose. The heads are either shown empty, or they are loaded with more of the same totemic animal presences as are on the shafts. Whether these animals were sculpted on the surmised "heads," or only along the shafts, they all were protruding from the rock surface as true bas-reliefs. Positive reliefs on stone were far more difficult to sculpt than simple negative engravings would have been. This suggests that as protrusions these figures were part of the "naturalistic" essence of the menhir. Like protruding arteries and veins on an old man's hands, these bas-reliefs reveal primary characteristics of a substratum.

—All the explicitly positioned animals, in bas-relief, seem to be of the male gender—and they are prominently so depicted. This feature must have been important to the sculptors and to their quarry-men partners. And then, many of these male totemic animals, one should notice, are shown assuming some kind of ready-to-mount posture. This mounting posture is depicted also at some of the round-sculpted totem pole remainders (see Schmidt pp. 100, 110, 159). Those bird totems are holding on to heads or to whatever else in this mythical world of the hunters' pre-human flux they may have been impregnating. Even the crouching canine or boar, and other higher-relief animals at Göbekli Tepe, are raised in a manner that suggests a readiness to mount. With all that male excitement, a female being cannot be far away. This ornamentation opens up the possibility that

---

[25]See Karl W. Luckert. *Egyptian Light and Hebrew Fire...*, SUNY Press, 1991. Also Karl W. Luckert, "Out of Egypt an Other Son," a downloadable videoscript, 2002, www.historyofreligions.com/outofe.htm.

the faceless and cubic tops of the T-shaped *menhirs* have, all along, not been abstract square heads but squared testicles instead—that is, squared just enough to keep the uninitiated out of the loop. With all these *menhirs* the Göbekli Tepe Mountain Woman became pregnant and, subsequently, her abdomen needed to grow.

—While intentional "abstraction" initially might seem to be an attractive academic designation for the squared shapes of Göbekli Tepe *menhirs,* we must not overrate it. "Abstraction" may have happened here unintentionally. The thicknesses and sizes of the *menhirs* seem to vary in proportion to the available dimensions of lenticular limestone slabs that the quarry-men were able to loosen. This means that a quarry-man, as a potential sculptor, would at the outset have admired his block as a nice coherent stone surface. Rather than smashing it to rubble, he drew an outline of the most important thing that came to his mind. It is even possible that some portion of its first outline was pre-cracked naturally—and that this omen might have given him the outline of what was contained in the block of limestone. The resulting contour resembled a T-shaped phallus, and the men kept chiseling to improve on its geometry. The better they could square those lenticular raw blocks of limestone, the more their skills and their power over the Earth-Mother's ovaries would be demonstrated. From the smooth surface and the improvised outline might have resulted their simple technique of squaring which, twelve millennia later, can be explained as artistic abstraction. It seems quite possible that the word here should be "simplification," or rather, was meant as a "dare" or a "challenge" by which an ancient sculptor could behave as a culture hero.

5. Stoles, Hands, and Totem Poles

The menhirs at Göbekli Tepe feature numerous totemic male animal figures in bas-relief. Some are active as adults while others linger at infant stages. The two largest menhirs feature stoles and hands. They may be discussed together with totem pole statuary, a bird column from Nevalı Çori, a local Lion totem pole, and a later human statue found in Sanliurfa. Images and contexts support the hypothesis that limestone menhirs represent phalluses, operated jointly by various totemic associations.

Stoles or hands? Intentional "abstracting" or unintentional "squaring" notwithstanding—what are those stoles and hands? We observe first that these features represent moveable subject matter. In their objective condition stoles and hands could be placed anywhere one wished them to be. Moreover, "hands" on those central *menhirs* in Enclosure D are things attached to ever-so-slender arms that seem to be originating nowhere. These "arms" certainly did not grow forth from the broadest "shoulder" dimensions of these *menhirs.* One wonders whether "arms" are flimsier than even the formal stoles. Or are they stoles? On the Göbekli Tepe version one of these flimsy arms appears even twisted like a stole, at what is supposed to be the "elbow" (Figure 8). The twist looks like an afterthought at the wrong place; the sculptor apparently did not have a piece of stole on hand to twist and to observe. I remember when I drew twists like this in grade school, straight from faulty memory and imagination.

Predisposition: *At some time during the year 1965 I was reading about megalithic menhirs in Europe. At that time I was alerted to several situations where the symbol of a hand was shown engraved. It was said to signify the Mother Goddess in shorthand. Where was the other hand of that Mother? Then, in 1991 I published a book titled* "Egyptian Light and Hebrew Fire," *during the writing* *of which I learned all there could be squeezed from Pyramid and Coffin Texts about the hand of Atum in Heliopolis—extending the story to explain Tefnut, Nut, and Isis. I even animated this creative Heliopolitan theology for a video. And now at Göbekli Tepe and at Nevah Çori we are being shown pairs of hands on some of these famous and older T-shaped menhirs. My forty-seven year-old question, concerning that second hand, is on its way to being answered here.*

—The excavation of the *menhir* hands, on Pillar 18 in Enclosure D (Figure 8), had to be delayed over concerns about structural stability. Alleged limestone-anthropomorphs could not be depended on to have steady flat feet. The delay in excavation gave some of us the needed years to think about alternative meanings. Or is it conceivable that these limp arms, or stoles, were intended to represent some kind of moveable features? The more one envisages or compares, the more one gets the impression that they may be leftovers from an initiation ritual, possibly a mating ritual of sorts, which novices were meant to remember, or to imagine on account of those stoles. The comparative approach is our only path forward.

Fig. 8. Pillar 18, Enclosure D, showing Fox totem and a twisted ribbon. Photo by courtesy of DAI.

The Nevah Çori Totem Pole: An obvious clue to the totemic mating connotation, of the symbolic stole-and-hand combination, can be found in the tentative reconstruction, by Professor Schmidt (Figure 9), of a Nevah Çori totem pole. This limestone totem pole, seems to advertise a hunter's totemic "Raven-ness." It sports five-fingered stoles, associated with three alternate levels of humanoid and raptor personages. Extending this concept to the stole/arm on the primary Pillar 18, of Enclosure D, could mean there more or less the same. For similar such instances it seems safe to postulate that, where stoles and fingers do occur together, they might indicate a "verb" of sorts—one that signifies the most central sacramental activity that was contemplated in these lodges.

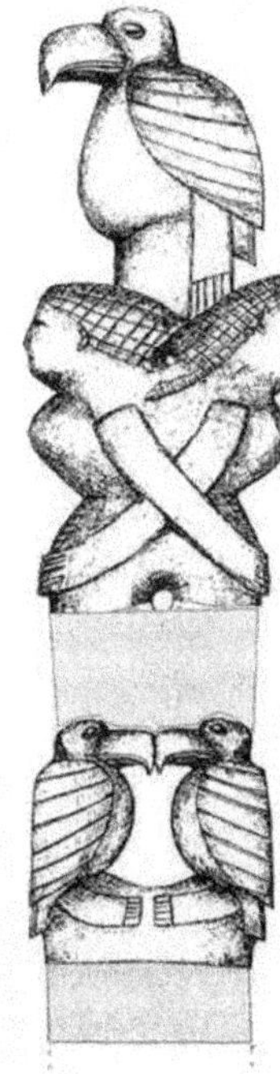

Fig. 9. Nevah Çori Totem Pole—tentative reconstruction by Klaus Schmidt. Courtesy of DAI.

—We might postulate that, metaphorically, these were the "holy hands" that, as stole tassels, have bound together generations of members of totemic faith of these sedentary hunters. They are are a ceremonial corollary to prehumen flux mythology (cf. Chapters 14 and 15, below). From bottom to top this totem pole declares, "I am a Raptor! (a Raven-Eagle) Once upon a time two such birds mated. The union of two humans was dysfunctional; they turned away from each other. A perforation indicates their point of vulnerability. The emerging hunter at the top is thereupon quite proud of his Raptor ancestry."

—Transcribed into the dramatic syntax owned by the inimitable Shakespeare—assuming that someone of that stature carved the Nevah Çori totem pole—it would read: "Some are hatched Raven. Some are born Raven. And both types have Raven-ness thrust upon them." Hatched, born, or conquered by the deity as a possession—the result was the same. The offspring had no choice in the matter. But his descendants would, nevertheless, have tried to inherit his totemic-divine status. The two modes of getting a totemic sponsor were (1) being possessed and joined to a group of initiates possessed likewise, and (2) inheriting such status from parents and clan.

—I have seen a variety of such "Raven" totem poles along the Northwest Coast of North America. Obviously, I will not be too disappointed if someone, someday, convinces me that these majestic birds were meant to represent some other raptor—or possibly even a "Raven-Eagle" hybrid—a hybrid like the Kansas University Jayhawk that I was in my college days . The carver knew what these birds were —and the iconoclast who destroyed the totem pole apparently also thought he knew.

Totem Pole for an aristocratic Lion: The somewhat deviant totem pole from the eastern slope of the Göbekli Tepe Southwest Hill stands now in the Sanliurfa Museum and is shown here from three angles (Figure 10). It features three sets of arms and hands. There are the larger hands of an active Lion Man who, while procreating, is holding on to what used to be the head of his spouse. The hands of the female seem to be bracing her own back, while her buttocks and legs appear to entwine the legs of the male in serpentine fashion. The

Fig.10. "Lion Man" totem-pole from the Southwest Hill at Göbekli Tepe.
Author photo—Courtesy of Sanliurfa Museum.

two serpents in this configuration are dual-feminine buttocks. This fact begs a question. Do her dual serpentine endowments represent a "flux" transition toward a phallic serpentine world? All the same, a human Lion-cub is being born while procreation is still in progress —born from the crotch of the female unto the head of what appears to be a crouching ancestral lioness. In the process the "cub" holds on with its small hands and covers those ancestral feline eyes. The face of the Lion man and the head of his spouse were removed by anti-Lion iconoclasts. The head of the older Feline matriarch was spared by the rebels probably because it was hidden in the ground.

—Just look at this ancient matriarch and listen! You can still hear this aristocratic Grandmother Feline purring, today. The composite "procreation and birth" scene here features three sets of stole-hands similar to those at the Nevah Çori bird-totempole which, together, confirm a man's aristocratic and totemic lineage. It seems certain that the face of the Lion Man has been split off to punish him for that very same aristocratic arrogance. Moreover, it also appears as though the iconoclast was a master sculptor himself. He knew exactly how to apply his chisel to remove a face.

—Before and while this Lion aristocrat and sculptor chiseled his image onto his totem pole, he probably participated in ceremonial life as some kind of a Lion shaman or chief, fully masked and garbed in a skin which he "borrowed" from a real Lion partner—from his totem in the divine animal realm. For all the dancers of any group at Göbekle Tepe some kind of a mask cult may be assumed. The small limestone masks which Professor Schmidt has replicated seem to point in the direction of a mask cult as well (see Schmidt, 2008, p. 81). These may pertain to some type of Flint-egg hatchlings—totemic faces for human apprentices.

—I am reasonably certain that no direct cultural or literary link exists between what has been found so far at Göbekli Tepe and biblical texts of seven millennia later—with the possible exception of some Lion of Judah or the beginnings of an Egyptian sphinx, perhaps. But, having nevertheless learnt much of what I know about religions from the Abrahamic family of faiths I may be forgiven, if at this rare point I summarize the general sentiment of the Göbekli Tepe totem pole statues with a sentence from Hebrew Scripture. Beyond Shakespeare, it happens to fit better than anything else I can think of. What all totemic statues and *menhirs* on these *temenoi* platforms are shouting out loud is a chorus that I hear resonating through all the ages of men. Whoever wrote Psalms 2:7 for the Hebrew Bible, as words spoken by a sole Almighty Deity, probably was supporting Solomonic priests who huddled under the influence of Egyptian pharaonic hyper-domestication theology. Their influence has haunted the religious offspring of Abraham incessantly with a typical messianic formula: "You are my Son, this day I have begotten you!" On Figure 10, above, this exclamation continues then with an anticipation of Isaiah 6:9, "for unto us a Child is born, unto us a Son is given…" (...continue reading: "and he will be for us a Lion Chief, a successful Hunter"). The continuation in Isaiah, about "government shall be upon His shoulder…," needed to wait for a time when hyper-domesticators would create hardships which an alleged royal savior eventually could relieve.

Fig. 11. A somewhat later statue from Sanliurfa may represent a priest or an anthropomorphic deity. It is the oldest known full-size statue on this Planet. Author photo—Courtesy of the Sanliurfa Museum.

Priest or anthropomorphic Deity? So then, to top all of this, it seems as though we already know what a stole-wearing priest and owner of real human hands used to look like (Figure 11). The oldest full-size statue in the world, from post-Göbekli Tepe times, at the Sanliurfa Museum, might be such a priestly celebrant. Or, it could be the statue of an anthropomorphic deity—a first Father-god—who at Göbekli Tepe began to empower his humanoid priestly celebrants. Anthropomorphs can be suspected to have intruded into the ranks of older animal totems during the closing phase of fulltime hunting. The proximity of the man's hands to his genitals endorses the sacramental association of five-tassel embellished stoles with five-fingered human hands at totem poles—as well as on the central *menhirs* in Enclosure D, and also on a fragment set into the wall of the Lion's Lodge.

—These stoles represent killer arms and hands, sacramentally thinned—softened into appendages of atonement, for gentle embrace and caress, signifying support and procreation of softer new life.

Tubs and Pedestals: Another hint for our revised interpretation of Göbekli Tepe "menhirs" is provided by the tub-shaped female bases, or sleeves, into which masculine *menhirs* have been set. Not enough *menhirs* have been excavated to their full depth to reveal all the base receptacles that have been chiseled into bedrock or set on fill materials. When sometime in the future more excavations can proceed deeper, in all likelihood more of those female foundation sleeves will be found. I have seen them exposed in Enclosures C and D. One need not expect total uniformity regarding this matter for the full two millennia. The overall setup at Göbekli Tepe, to the extent that it now has been laid open, is symbolically coherent. It is consistent even without any more of these corresponding "tubs" being laid bare.

Fig. 12. The central pair of *menhirs* 18 and 31, at Enclosure D.
Author composite photo—courtesy of DAI.

—The author of the aforementioned *National Geographic* essay has asked the preservation architect at the site, Eduard Knoll, regarding the design of the mounting systems for the central pillars (June 2011, page 41). The architect's answer—perhaps given tongue in cheek—was that there were none. He suggested that the "pillars may have been propped up… by wooden posts (cf. Figure 12)." I am inclined to accept the suggestion that wooden posts were used, but I must discount the allusion that these ancients hadn't mastered engineering sufficiently to stand up pillars. I suspect that those quarry-men could easily have made functional foundation pedestals or castings. They had no trouble pouring or compacting terrazzo floors.

Dancing menhirs? Perhaps these *menhirs* never were intended to be anchored on the ground totally still, as if they were actual "pillars." Simply naming them *T-Pfeiler* does not make them rigid pillars by virtue of their excavation. The builders may indeed have used some support posts as the architect has suggested. Perhaps they even used poles and ropes together for controlling sway and movement. Or perhaps, during a ritual, some of the men may have gestured with their stoles to help keep the *menhirs* in balanced motion, symbolically swaying. Why not? On a stage such as this, where male totemic animals are shown mounting, and where men entered narrow passage-ways in rhythmic steps, some movement on the part of the sanctuary's chief actors, those central *menhirs*, would not have been impossible to imagine.

—In Figure 27, below, I am offering a ceremonial scene for Enclosure C which seemed simple enough to draw. But perhaps the two central pillars were indeed linked with wooden beams for mutual support and movement, possibly as the letter *"H"* would be able to sway—to incline parallel—if it were so constructed. The reader is free to imagine rhythms and sounds, while this writer continues to remember the chthonic hum and harmonies of Hopi *katsina* chants. Dancing in the company of a brotherhood of real flint miners and weapon makers, next to a pair of swaying sixteen-ton limestone members, could indeed have been a genuine thrill—if not just pleasurably scary. What are the chances of finding grooves and scars of a rocking motion at the rounded tips of some of those "pillars," or in those receptacles? I agree, these pediments do not measure up to the architectural standards of being ordinary "pedestals for pillars."

—From an evolutionary perspective, it is possible to surmise that these ancient flint-mine operators have already been staging some kind of advance birthday celebration for humanoid military-industrial complexes which, back then, still lingered in infancy. The great Mother Earth surely noticed some of this mega-commotion upon her —upon her own rocky Göbekli Tepe self. Had M.I.T. been in existence back then, I wonder what enhancements one of those famous engineering fraternities could have contributed to improve the dexterity of sixteen-ton dancing members.[26]

Fox Skins: There are fox-skins depicted as loincloths around the tips of these *menhirs* (Figure 12). Do these not prove the anthropomorphism of stoles and fingered hands? Indeed, the presence of loincloths suggests that Göbekli Tepe miners would have been capable of conceptualizing their mega-sized members as anthropomorphs, as people in many languages still do so jokingly, at smaller scales. They certainly could also conceptualize phalluses as representatives of the male essence. But let us stay with the facts. How much could a life-size fox skin conceal on one of these giants, fastened around its tip? This loincloth served no Puritan scruples—not any more than the frayed lobes of a legendary "fig leaf" were ever able to conceal. On the contrary, the fox skin was added here for at least three purposes —first to add a life-size measure for estimating the true size of those sculpted limestone immensities, and second, to perpetuate the most ancient clothing joke in the evolution of humankind. Fox skins and lobed fig leaves, as covers, have always drawn attention to what they pretended to conceal. What was there to conceal, this close to the tip? Thirdly, these loincloths reveal that the men were in the habit of killing foxes and to use their skins—those very same foxes that they impersonated as totems. They would not hesitate to use divine skins as protective clothing for running in high grass or brush.

In the Cathedral: Professor Schmidt occasionally has explained Göbekli Tepe, as well as historical sequencing, by referring to the archetype of a "cathedral." I shared a precious moment with the Professor at which he referred to his tallest *menhirs* in Enclosure D (Figure 12) as *himmlische Wesen* (heavenly beings), having just descended unto earth. Indeed, when he struck one of these angelic tuning

---

26"MIT"—the acronym for Massachusetts Institute of Technology, Cambridge.

forks with his bare hand, I heard its heavenly overtones with my own ears. My aging ears, enhanced by a would-be composer's imagination, could perceive only a slight difference between the song of this annunciating heavenly being at Göbekli Tepe and a *Magnificat* number sung elsewhere in a cathedral by an almost-angelic choir.

—The heavenly stone angels, heavily descended at Göbekli Tepe, indeed resounded and quivered in ritual as might the colorful winged figure of an angel in a late Renaissance "annunciation" painting. Meanwhile in the cathedral the mixed choir of male and female voices eventually burst forth with the Virgin's song of jubilation. I make it a point to hear J. S. Bach's *Magnificat* at least once a year, during the Advent season.

Operated jointly by Foxes, Cranes, and Geese: Indeed, there was a fourth meaning to those fox skins in Enclosure D—something of a more serious nature. It signified that these phalluses, dressed in fox skins, were actually operated by Foxes. One of these two central *menhirs*, "Pillar 18" in Enclosure D, shows the relief of a male fox protruding from the side of its shaft—conspicuously it appears to pulsate and to shiver: "Fox inside!" (Figure 8). And it is surrounded and legitimated properly with stoles of matrimony. Altogether these features suggest that the two gigantic limestone *menhirs* were being operated by an association of totemic human Foxes. And yet, the broods of chicks that had just been hatched beneath them were cranes. Of all things! But please be patient. There is some rationality to all of this, and it will be explained.

—So how is this possible? How can Foxes procreate geese or cranes? Before we permit our rational doubts to deny the paternity of Foxes, we do well to examine Pillar 33, set in the south wall of the same Enclosure D (Figure 13). There is no question about the identities chiseled unto the broad sides of this *menhir*. This phallic *menhir* is jointly operated by Fox and Crane. In addition, Geese are present up at the testicle level. The collaboration of Fox and Crane expresses the ecumenism that seems to have prevailed at Level One enclosures. Along the bottoms of the two central *menhirs* (Pillars 18 & 31) we see the results (Figures 12 & 17). Together these menhirs have procreated two gaggles of chicks. From the outset I suspected crane chicks; the archaeologists wrote "ducks *(Enten)*." A chance author

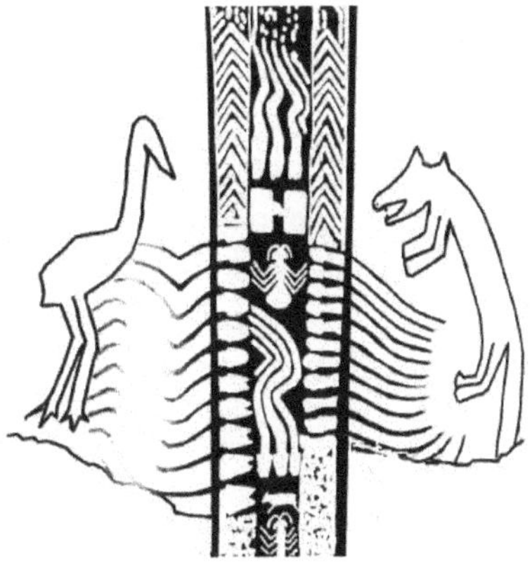

Fig. 13. Pillar 33, Enclosure D. Composite author's sketch, based on four photos in Schmidt, 2008, 182ff. Right: Author photo—courtesy of DAI.

photograph, taken later, indicates the presence of geese at the testicle level of "Pillar 33." Thus, before I would recognize them as ducklings, I might recognize here two gaggles of goslings. But be that as it may, the existential implications are the same. Foxes are the "natural" hunters of cranes as well as of geese and ducks.

—Inasmuch as many years ago an aunt of mine enlightened me, then a three-year-old toddler who was starting to wonder about human life, that "The Stork" brought my baby brother, it is nice to discover now, finally, the evidence that twelve thousand years ago Göbekli Tepe Crane Men anticipated the role of those later baby-bringing European storks—here duly documented in the largest possible context of sanctuary gender polarity! In this sacred lodge, Cranes and Foxes ended up being totemic siblings!

—"To procreate and to hunt cranes"—so the sculptors seem to have been assuring themselves here—"are the rightful sports and occupations of Crane Men and of Fox Men." Of course the Crane, Goose, and Fox societies that were cooperating at this lodge were also human hunters. So, if Fox totems can resolve their differences with Cranes and Geese, then their human devotees should be able to do so as well.

—On the "face" of *Pillar 33* (Figure 13) the snakes are moving downward. It almost seems as though these Stone Age sculptors anticipated what a spermatozoon might someday be discovered to look like under a microscope. But then, those multiple relief serpents at either side on this menhir do represent phalluses, and their multiplication simply expresses intensified passion, quantity and movement. The "female" spiders nonetheless move upward against the downward current of those phallic serpents.

—It may well be that Spider-Woman was the only sculpted totemic female present at Göbekli Tepe—as she also seems to have survived so among the Hopi Indians.[27] It may also be the case that animals with stings and bites, including scorpions, were somehow classified together with other stinging "males" and hunters. These creatures are ambiguous, indeed—just as were those ancient human hunters who with their arrow-snakes could sting and kill from considerable distances, even the largest animals.

—As the miners danced, surely they also chanted and generated rhythm. To the extent that certain lodges celebrated contemporaneously, the different groups could have danced and chanted concurrently in adjacent temples. As men and *menhirs* danced together, Abdomen Hill and those visiting "heavenly beings" trembled in unison. The massive *menhirs* resounded like tuning forks, struck by as little as bare human hands. The men alternated between moving about like Foxes and dancing like Cranes. Both totemic mascots, together, knew everything that a man needed to know about rhythmic movements and showmanship.

—Totems and their human devotees danced mystically at such occasions, together as two-in-ones. There is no point in asking who was doing the actual dancing then, the men or their totems. A predator totem that could possess a man and affect his hunting style could also possess and dance him—by his own free will, of course. Both, the totemic deity and his human aspect moved together as if they were a single person. The sculptor of *Pillar 33* knew how to make

---

[27]If one compares the head shape of Spiderwoman, here, with the Mother Earth engraving in the Lions Lodge, Figure 23, one is rewarded with a hint for extended studies in comparative ethnology.

his chiseled serpents multiply and appear as though they were dancing. Quite likely, Foxes and Cranes were major totemic sponsors in these events. Nevertheless, a direct totemic relationship cannot be postulated for all the snake bas-reliefs. Some of the serpents may indeed have been totemic sponsors, while others could have symbolized phalluses on the loose.

—With their technique of depicting serpentine phalluses, these Stone Age sculptors invented a pre-cinematic technique of multiple exposures. Those phallic serpents that issue from a Fox, on the right (Figure 13), bounce on the limestone menhir, joining up and invigorating the downward moving snakes which come face to face with upward crawling specimens of Spider Woman, inclined to pinch. From the other side of the menhir, the Crane totem conjures up his complimentary magic of movement and multiplication. Of course, the downward moving serpents, up front, represent the animated phallic limestone menhir itself. We know the direction it was intended to move.

—A crane's general status may also have had something to do with its "natural" style of courtship dances. The shape of its head and neck resemble serpents in relief—as Professor Schmidt has already observed. The primitive shapes of serpents morph easily into parts of other bodies. On Figure 10, above, we have noticed how even the legs of a human female mutate into serpents. But I personally would hesitate to classify all totemic bird images that show forward bent knees as anthropomorphs—such as one seen on Figure 13—even though the operators of all those *menhirs* are obviously human. A novice sculptor should be forgiven for getting the shape of those knees wrong if this was his first challenge of carving a crane. Hunters who shoot a crane do not take time to examine the actual bend of a living bird's legs; they aim at the body and try to penetrate feathers with their flints. Moreover, by extrapolating from the lowered gait of crane chicks, their thighs and "knees" are anyhow often overlooked.

Predisposition: *Western minds may be puzzled by any still-picture technique of multiplication. But let us consider how things in Taoism and in Mahayana Buddhism are not just "smaller" or "bigger." Both of these religions play on both number and size—such as the number of heavenly generals in Taoism and the mindboggling multiplicity of bodhisattvas in Mahayana Buddhism. They also have produced larger than life statues of Taoist deities, and downright gigantic statues of the Buddha. At Göbekli Tepe both size and multiplicity were being imaged with these menhirs—to excite lethargic masculinity or perhaps even Father Sky himself, to move and to swoon in the presence of totemic activists and dignitaries.*

In a broader evolutionary context I see the temenoi at Göbekli Tepe as exclusive men's lodges for obsolescent hunters. I do acknowledge the obvious fact, that the typical Hopi kivas, as men's lodges and feminine Earth sanctuaries, are quite similar. The Hopi kivas are on average structural matches to these "temples" at Neva Çori and Göbekli Tepe—minus the menhirs of course. But with all the masked katsinas that dance in Hopi kivas, adding menhirs would have seemed redundant. And then, Hopi men are not very into limestone. While Hopi men still go into their kivas to weave ritual sashes—similar to stoles—the ancient miners of flint, at Göbekli Tepe, initially may have used their lodges as eateries, to store and to eat their carry-in lunches. I suspect that some of them bedded down there regularly for a night of sleep. Perhaps they went there for a night of dancing, on special days.

From Hopi clan mythology we learn that a conspicuous spider generally was conceptualized as Spider Woman—typically a female deity. She also is the kind of woman that in some contexts represents the Earth Mother. She also is the Spinning- or Weaving-woman which means, the divine patroness of the male Hopi weavers. At Göbekli Tepe the weavers of nets may have been the first hunters associated with a Spider clan; all this is speculation. But of course, someone had to weave their ceremonial stoles. And while speaking about nets, I suspect that not all suspected nets, engraved on menhirs at Göbekli Tepe, are what they seem to be. Some probably were depth indicator grooves for lowering the background level that surrounds protruding bas-reliefs. The task of leveling was not always finished.

Snake, Fox, and Others: Most of the totemic animal emblems on the Göbekli Tepe *menhirs* can be identified as predator beings with whom at one time or other the men could have competed or identified as fellow hunters. And this assembly includes canines, serpents, felines, raptors, spiders and scorpions. And then, as far as we can decipher the Göbekli Tepe index, there also were the bull, the ram, boar, and the donkey. These may have been inducted into the hunters' Hall of Fame as totemic ancestors on account of their ability to hurt, for being male, or for having been masters of herds of their respective species. Snake and Fox are thus far the most numerous totemic animals found depicted at Göbekli Tepe. But the totemic individuals that are represented may not reflect the actual totemic clan distribution in human demography. The number of sculpted snakes probably was inflated by the fact that snakes as well represented phalluses on the loose.

—Moreover, every male of any species carries with him a snake, whereas male serpents in the animal kingdom carry two—and the religion that we find at Göbekli Tepe, quite obviously, was ancient hunter ceremonialism for men only. By the same token, snakes are convenient symbols with which to manage *mysterium tremendum* effects (fear and trembling), so as to scare audiences and to elicit much-needed respect. On top of that, they are the simplest animals to draw, to carve, and to sculpt.

A Blanket woven of living snakes: Figure 14 could represent an actual handicraft idea that aspired to ultimate coordination of hands and minds among a brotherhood of Snake Men. How many human hands would it take to weave such a blanket and to keep all the living strands in place? And should a novice be required to lie on it during an initiation ritual? For this fraternity no challenge appears to have been too great or too dangerous. Nevertheless, a serious practical need may have inspired this training. Hunters who were taught how to weave such lively blankets also learned how to "milk" vipers and secure the venom. The toxic saliva could be smeared on arrow heads for serious hunting. Hunting in those days was not yet a "sport."

Fig. 14. A Blanket woven of snakes. On Pillar 1, Enclosure A. Courtesy of DAI.

Gates and Rings: Limestone rings *(Kalkstein Ringe)* found at Göbekli Tepe, appear to be kindred objects to the symbolic female "tubs." Professor Schmidt has catalogued the rings as *Türlochsteine* (porthole stones, Schmidt 2008, pp. 93f, 126). My first suggestion toward an interpretation, from the distance, would be this—if the inside diameter of such a stone ring can accommodate the body of a man then it probably was made to accommodate the body of a man. Some form of ritual of a miner's second birth, of being born not of a woman but of stone, or being laid after the manner of flint eggs, comes to mind as a possible motif. I would submit, hypothetically of course, that the natural orifices in the rock floors at the first Rock Temple (Figure 5), naturally vacated by decaying tree trunks, would have been large enough that the Earth Mother could lay flint eggs through them, or even that they might have facilitated the symbolic birth-ritual for a human baby. For smaller holes in ceremonial floors I am reminded of the *sipapu* holes (symbolic holes of emergence) that one finds in Anasazi and Hopi Indian kivas. A similar Earth Mother cult, presumably, can inspire similar ceremonial symbols. Some holes at Göbekli Tepe may have been anchor points for posts and ropes.

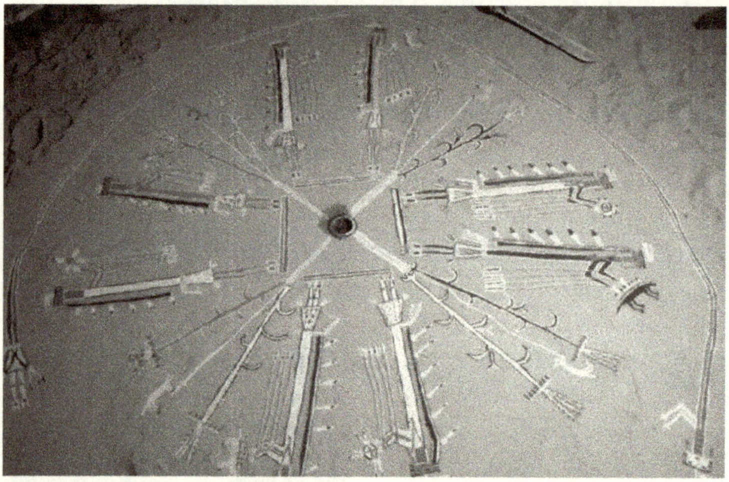

Fig. 15. Fourth Sandpainting in the Navajo Coyoteway Ceremonial. Anthropoid Coyote gods carrying stuffed "Coyote" skins and baskets. Photo by the author.

Foxes, Dogs, and Wolves: There are ethnological parallels for counting foxes, coyotes, dogs, and wolves as members of a single species. In 1974 I recorded the nine-night Diné (Navajo) "Coyote-way" healing ceremonial. In one of the sand-paintings (Figure 15) eight such fox-dog-coyote-wolf figures are shown.[28]

[28]Karl W. Luckert, Johnny C. Cooke Navajo Interpreter, *Coyoteway, a Navajo Holyway Healing Ceremonial.* Museum of Northern Arizona Press, and University of Arizona Press, 1979.

—The stuffed Coyote that was used by a Coyote impersonator was actually a blue-gray fox skin "of the south." One could find those same "blue" fox-coyote-wolves running about in other cardinal directions, of course. The officiating shamanic practitioner and two dancers wearing masks were all Coyotes. During this Diné ceremony the patient became a Coyote-person as well (Figure 16).

Fig. 16. Scene from the Navajo Coyoteway Healing Ceremonial. From left to right: 1. Patient. 2. The Talking-god. 3. Masked Coyote girl impersonated by a woman. 4. Masked Coyote, a man carrying stuffed Gray-Fox skin. Photo by the author.

—It may be the case that totemic Foxes at Göbekli Tepe were a generic variety of the *Canidae* family, which included fox, wolf, and any kind of dog. Together these animals may have been seen as a single species. The large number of foxes among the relief images at Göbekli Tepe may reflect the symbolic relevance of these burrowing animals for the mining occupation. Snakes and foxes are both earth-dwelling animals, and this may explain the fact that many of their human devotees engaged in mining and in the manufacture of flint tools.

Children Born of One Mother

Cranes and Foxes are numerous among Göbekli Tepe totems. After having identified some paternal totems, we go looking for hints regarding their offspring. Predators and prey animals are hatched, or born, together as siblings. In the wider world of hunting this happenstance produces conflicts. With help from comparative ethnology it is possible, hypothetically, to consider solutions by which such inherent conflicts might have been resolved at Göbekli Tepe.

6. Children Born of One Mother

The edges of the Earth Mother's "pedestals" in Enclosure D bear the bas-relief images of birds which at a first glimpse appear to represent gaggles of crane chicks. Their presence in this vicinity means that eggs were laid to be hatched right there, by the Earth Mother herself. They have been fathered by the *menhirs* that can still be seen sitting in place. Procreation and the emergence of life are frequently imaged together at Göbekli Tepe—after the manner in which time was shown collapsed on the Raven-Eagle and Lion totem poles, featured in the preceding chapter. The long period of gestation, between procreation, laying and hatching, or birthing, is thereby frozen to a single moment in sculpted space. Anyone unaccustomed to this mode of artistic compaction of time, dictated to the sculptor mostly by limitations inherent in his medium of limestone, may find the resultant display somewhat puzzling.

—One can also find crane chicks sculpted along the sides of some standing *menhirs* (Figure 18). In context it becomes clear that these hatchlings—including the young snake—were not sculpted there as active totems, but as totemic offspring and representatives of a next generation. Once the entire inventory of *menhir* images has been excavated and recorded, they may be differentiated into "adult operators of *menhirs*" and "offspring." The offspring is seen running all over their mother and her place—and sometimes over those sluggish limestone phalluses as well—over all those that did not know when it was time to get out of the way.

—There are several of these *menhirs* at Göbekli Tepe that, apparently, have dallied too long. For example, on *menhir* 43 we find our familiar baby cranes, and *menhir* 27 has been overtaken by a predator puppy and a piglet (Figure 18-b). Judging by the size of the puppy's tail, we may presume that it was the fox variety. The possibility of humor in Göbekli Tepe's sanctuaries should not be discounted.

Without recognizing the story plot, photographers, to their chagrin, may hitherto have published what must have been extremely embarrassing personal moments for these *menhirs*.

—On Pillar 33 (Figure 13) we have seen Fox and Crane totems procreating in unison, by way of jointly operating a limestone *menhir*. At Enclosure D, one may consider a combination of associated presences: the fox-skin loincloths at the central *menhirs* (Pillars 18 and 31) representing Fox, the low relief of a male Fox at the side of Pillar 18, along with the hatched gaggle of crane chicks surrounding the Mother. They all appear related to those paternal Crane and Fox "operators." But then, bones found at the site do indicate that cranes were regularly hunted and eaten. Thus, the combined evidence suggests that some type of a fraternal and sacrificial solution had been found to resolve the problems of Crane and Fox Men who were partnering at Göbekli Tepe. Their ceremonialism apparently was informed by transformational "prehuman flux" totemic religion, and it involved the entire polarity of life and death.

Fig. 17. Pillar 31 in Enclosure D. Photo by courtesy of DAI.

—Obviously there is a problem when hunter offspring and prey animals are born from the same mother. The children will meet each other sooner or later on the hunting range, pitted against each other in struggles of life and death. Some of them will become martyrs and food; the others will end up being guilty hunters in dire need of atonement.

Fig. 18. *Menhirs* that were too slow to get out of the way. Young animals on Pillars 43 and 27—photos by courtesy of DAI.

Predicament and Atonement: Some recent retainers of Stone Age hunter tradition have been able to resolve this conflict of sibling-killing religiously, with rites of fraternal self-sacrifice. An example is the story of Zuni Indian Deer Clan members who used to live by hunting deer. Their activity of hunting juvenile male Deer from the underworld was sport. These underworld boys ran about in the surface world in speedy deer clothes.[29] Properly hunted, and ceremonially butchered by Zuni hunters of the Deer clan, who lived in the surface-world, those victimized relatives could be back in the underworld before sunset, fully resurrected to their original condition.

—Some faith similar to the Zuni sacrificial kinship arrangement, a kind of voluntary self-sacrifice by way of transforming physical

---

[29]For leads to Zuni mythology see the works of Steward Culin and Frank H. Cushing—also Luckert, The Navajo Hunter Tradition, pp. 134, 140n, 221. See also the files of Father Berard Haile, at the Museum of Northern Arizona archives.

appearances on behalf of starving kinfolk, may have been anticipated by Crane and Fox fraternities at Göbekli Tepe. Human totemic Foxes and Cranes—linked together by joint *menhirs* and ceremonial vestments, in joint ritual and artistry—were procreating Crane and Fox offspring together.[30] Later on, at the open range, both types of initiated human hunters, Cranes and Foxes, would turn against their own animal offspring and hunt both for meat and clothing. Along their entire ceremonial path, from procreation to killing and eating, they would ritually atone for identical meat and clothing.

—Foxes in animal form are the natural hunters of cranes. Both of these animal prototypes participated in the Göbekli Tepe cult with their divine-totemic and their human-initiate identities, together. The totemic animals lent their skins and feathers as paraphernalia. Thereby they naturalized the inducted human Cranes and Foxes. Both types could henceforth hunt cranes and foxes together, in friendship. Most likely they wore each other's feathers and skins in rituals as signs of respect, as well as for camouflage and ambush whenever they stalked their totemic relatives to kill on the open range.

—Sounds complicated? Indeed, it is! But so are the religions and philosophies of all predators and killers. Totemic religion was a revelation, especially intuited and evolved for the atonement and justification of humanoid artificial predators—to shift the blame for hunting to what we now call "natural" predators or to appreciate the voluntary participation of the victims themselves.

The Convoluted Religion of Hunters: Along with the problematic habit of hunting siblings, one's own Mother's children, and along with using the quartzite embryos of Earth as raw materials for the manufacture of weapon "hatchlings"—to be used against both the Mother's ovaries and her wild offspring—there also existed, back home in the hunter families, a matching ambiguity regarding the natural status of the human female—concerning her menstruation. In the eyes of practicing hunters the human female appeared to impersonate the essence of a natural bleeding wound in synchronization with lunar cycles. Whether the hunters at Göbekli Tepe atoned for their role by practicing circumcision or sub-incision, we do not know.

---

[30]The Fox and Crane combination, at Pillar 33, also brings to mind a contemporary predator-and-prey totemic alliance: the "Snake and Antelope" societies of the Hopi Indians are still cooperating ceremonially today, in Arizona.

—This cosmic ambiguity of human females used to fit almost perfectly the identity crisis of the male hunters. To the extent that a vagina was seen to be a bleeding wound, the phallus became a hunter's natural spear and weapon. The unfortunate result of this strained analogy, on the part of the male, was that his woman by virtue of her natural condition would become his victim. To this awareness one must add the fact that already in Paleolithic times, males and females have become culturally segregated into predators and foragers. Each has become a culturally distinct "subspecies." And we should further keep in mind that, still more anciently, foragers and grazing animals have fallen prey to all the larger totemic predators that humanoid males have come to admire and to imitate.

—In light of these considerations one can sense how the divided *Homo sapiens* species has gotten itself deeply entangled in conflicting modes of reasoning. At the side of the male hunter, the circle of ambiguity is completed by the fact that phalluses, lightning, and flint-tipped arrows were all explained as similar kinds of weapon-like "snakes." Some bowmen almost certainly used the venom of phallic looking serpents to poison the tips of their arrows and spears. Snakes and flint points were both naturally and procedurally affiliated. Both were "hatched" from eggs. And having been regarded akin to snake venom, how much "dirtier" or more dangerous could semen be still imagined? No distinction of "pure spirit" from "dirty matter" has so far been able to expunge this predator-axiology of our Stone Age legacy.

—And this is not all that could go wrong during an artificial predator's biology lessons. While a snake, seen from above, looks like a freely roaming phallus, the mouth of snakes, stretched open, has in some older Native American cultures given rise to the notion of a "toothed vagina"—something that clearly surpasses the severity of a Spider's bite on Pillar 33, at Göbekli Tepe. This snake-mouth caricature still survives as an underground joke of sorts among men in at least a few Native American tribes.

—It seems obvious, then, that *Homo sapiens* communication between the genders was mired ever more deeply, steeped in contradictions and in emotional conflict. Had Sigmund Freud known some of this prehistory, I suspect that our psychology books today would read a little different. And considering the religious traditions, indeed, there never was the chance of a paradise that could be opened to a human soul—certainly not for members of a species that had chosen for itself the "sin" of wanting to be artificial, pre-meditating, and supreme predators.

—With an eye looking back along the path of evolution, one can see how a simple material adaptation, such as the domestication of plants and animals, could never have been enough. A simple change in livelihood could never balance all the paradoxes that the last few million years of hunting had bequeathed on the evolving minds of male artificial predators—or on their female partners who had slipped into playing the roles of gatherer-victims. All the while, both genders developed a taste for meat. Here at Abdomen Hill, at the hands of progressive miners and weapon makers, at a place where people were pitting their wits against the shapes and weights of stone, the paradoxes became increasingly more symbolic and complex. Today, twelve millennia later, both genders have finally achieved a semblance of equality; both have at last entitled themselves to have equal rights militarily, as hunters of people.

Two Paths to the Atonement for Hunters: For artificial predators —*homines sapientes*—there have basically existed two paths of orientation which could lead to emotional balance and to some measure of rational justification. Firstly, there was atonement by prehuman flux mysticism according to which all animals were regarded as persons of the same essence. All could transform their shapes and appearances, and all transactions between hunters and victims, including killing and eating, required rituals of egalitarian consent. This mode of elementary food-mysticism will come into better focus in chapters Fourteen and Fifteen.

—The second path of rational atonement was sustained by special divine favors—that is, by favors or conditions granted by greater-than-human personages, thus, originally by totemic deities who are now classified as "natural predators." In their ancient divine roles, totems used to accept full responsibility for the actions of human hunters whom they possessed, owned, adopted, and spon-sored. Thus, divinely sponsored human hunters saw their own status rise while the value of their victims was being depreciated. Both paths to atonement were rationally inconsistent and ontologically dishonest. In actual practice, the axioms and solutions from these two paths frequently do run parallel, collide, or support each other in piecemeal fashion. But then, neither path can be said to be wrong in an absolute judicial or ethical sense. If for the sake of human nourishment and survival we grant the fact that killing living beings is a necessity, then there are no real alternatives.

—Please note as well the inconsistency with which I am writing about these alternative paths to atonement. Participating in our common linguistic predicament, I am wavering between designations like hunting, killing, and harvesting—choosing and rejecting terminology as I write.

—All those who are committed to walk the path of mystic "oneness" on this planet—i.e. the mythic "prehuman flux" option—are trying to show utmost reverence for all living beings. Any pain they inflict returns to them, hurts their consciences by virtue of the Golden Rule. As siblings they end up suckling on their eternal Mother forever, pretending to be innocent grazers which, of course, their species has long ago ceased to be. Their paradisiac hopes eventually will get bogged down by sibling rivalry, envy, martyrdom, and in extreme cases even by ritualized cannibalism. Gatherers and foragers, who try to remain on the pure abdomen-oriented path of procreation, pure love, and maternal self-sacrifice, set themselves up in weakness, to be hunted down eventually. They become entangled in hunting campaigns against their own siblings, both as hunters and as the hunted.

—It should not come as a great surprise when, in the course of human evolution, a less intimate ethical road was sought and found that would allow hunting without the constant burden of fratricide or cannibalism. This rational outlook, while encouraging valorization of the hunters' own egos, and essences, allowed for the devaluation of victims. Eventually that second path permitted the devaluation and domestication of plants and animals, along with a new style of economy. It allowed for lives to be paid with sacrificial shares or portions, and to be reimbursed with lives or goods of lesser value—with hard and shiny valuables extracted from the realm of minerals or supplemented with the added value of human labor. To justify this new economy, Neolithic hunters needed to find greater-than-human authorities—divine predators whose presence justified their own participation in predation. Those authorities also needed to be creators and owners of living beings that could be purchased for food. Divine creators and owners would then introduce new scales of valuation, gauged in favor of humankind. These would authorize methods of killing and butchering by which "flesh" could legitimately be converted into "meat," and that helped reintroduce plant-food substitutions as these were then needed. New divine authorities would introduce new deals and covenants.

—By extension the second path, with its goal of securing adequate resources, also led to the legitimization of warfare. It allowed for the devaluation of living "souls" not only of the hunters' victims, but among competing huntsmen as well. Uneven ontological rationalizations justify uneven status and privileges.

—Bio-chemistry is the modern scientific method (i.e. ritual) that facilitates the devaluation of food organisms—their conceptual reduction to chemical substances which, for moral legitimization, are marketed as non-personal chemical compounds. Implicitly this "applied science" legitimizes the production, acquisition, and labeling of abundant supplies, of depersonalized food beings.

—A little over three half-centuries ago, the Western sciences were blessed with ideas that grew into an almost unified Theory of Evolution. This theory has revolutionized biology and proceeded to rearrange all the natural sciences. In the shorter historical view, this theory sprung from biology as a dynamic corrective to mechanistic Newtonian physics. In the longer prehistoric view it grew forth from the much older style of Stone Age "prehuman flux" mythology and mysticism—where it still underlies our first mentioned "path to atonement." Like its mythological predecessor, so too does the modern Theory of Evolution assume the continuity and unity of all life. Ancient mythic "transformations" were thereby reformatted into "mutations." It goes without saying that evolutionary thinking is therefore not especially helpful for establishing a practical ethic that justifies the exploitation of food victims. But thanks to basic materialistic presuppositions in bio-chemical theory, modern humans no longer need to worry about devouring the corpses of "animal persons" or confess to eating milled "wheat babies." Our modern science-oriented culture has found its own soteriology—i.e. formulas and labels that can be utilized to avoid ancient bites of conscience. With bio-chemistry we attain our modern existential atonement.

7. A Victory over Death

An alternate geographical orientation, initiated by the Lions Lodge, provides hints of political discord among the totemic brotherhoods of hunters and miners. A most fortunate find at the Lions Lodge was an engraving that depicts the Earth Mother anthropomorphically. The image also features a pair of menhirs that can be recognized to interpret such central pairs in general. A comparison with ethnological data from Malekula introduces helpful suggestions. The general religious struggle for atonement at Göbekli Tepe appears to have been resolved with a symbolic victory of Life over Death.

Whether and how Adam and Eve acquired navels is an enduring theme for entertainment in Semitic and Christian mythology. Whether the Mountain Woman, whose abdomen became known as Göbekli Tepe was ever blessed with a navel we best leave to journalists who already have started writing about this delicate subject matter. But indeed, there is an obvious high point on this Abdomen Hill which archaeologists have selected as their point of orientation—and which historians should probably also consider. Precisely at this apex we might need to continue our evolutionary reorientation and comparisons. Differences might be found between the lodges at the south slope and lodges that are oriented from that hilltop toward the west.

Fig. 19-a. Southeast Promontory—"the left knee." Author photo by courtesy of DAI.

—We observe that in the sanctuaries below us, in the southern crotch area, the pairs of central *menhirs* are aligned so as to invite entry between them from the ravine to the south. In order to cover most of her southern spread I have split a photograph into halves (Figures 19-a, and 19-b). The promontory on the left shows the Mountain Woman's left knee, and the promontory on the right half of the photograph shows her right knee. Enclosure C is primarily at the left half of the image, but it extends a little ways over into the right half.

—Enclosure A is on the right half of the image, top left and back. Then follows Enclosure B, where two central *menhirs* are prominently showing. *Menhirs* of Enclosure D are at the center of the right

Fig. 19-b. Southwest Promontory—"the right knee." Author photo by courtesy of DAI.

picture, including two with props, in line with but here mostly hidden by the roof that protects the Lions Lodge. The last small enclosure seen partly at the upper far right, fenced separately, is the place where the Lion totem pole, Figure 10, was found.

The Lion Aristocracy at the Apex

Still standing atop the pregnant abdomen of the Göbekli Tepe Woman, we turn ninety degrees to the right and peer into the now sealed and protected Lions Lodge. The *menhirs* there are set up differently. The orientation of these stones (Figure 20) became relevant some weeks later when I finally noticed what I should have learnt at the outset from Professor Schmidt's book (2008—pp. 228-239), that the central *menhirs* in the Lions Lodge are aligned not southward, but westward. Even the totemic Lions iconography, as it is sculpted on their *menhirs* and illustrated in the Professor's book, suggests that this Lions fraternity had little in common with the totemic ecumenism that prevailed at the mountain's southern crotch, below the Lions outpost. Among the bas-reliefs on central *menhirs,* excavated at the Lions' Enclosure, mostly profiles of large felines have been found. I suspect that members of this Lions Lodge were hunting with a mental perspective that, in the cause of self-justification, systematically devalued the lives of their victims. Not much prehuman flux mysticism seems to be implied here.

—So, why might Lion *menhirs* be aligned west-and-east up here? Alongside this oddity, what might a Lion fraternity have been up to at the top of Abdomen Hill? Was it to spite all the others who approached from the south and celebrated life down below? Or was it simply the fact that Foxes, Cranes, and Lions are totemic deities of different sizes, temperaments, habits, and of course status? Not all gods of humankind could ever be deemed equal, and certainly none of the religions in human history were intuited as solutions to exactly identical human ambitions or problems, or questions. But among all religions are found resemblances and similar counsels to common existential problems.

—The southernmost walls of Enclosure C do seem to feature an ambiguous entryway, showing the remains of a gate that appears to have been formerly guarded by sculpted lions. At some point in time this Lion's Gate seems to have been intentionally destroyed, and walls leading up from there, to the core of Enclosure C, seemed problematic enough for excavations to have been suspended indefinitely. At the very least, this situation suggests that at one time Lions might have been gatekeepers down there. It also appears as though at some point in time the political fortunes of the Lions down there changed. We noted the severe deprivations that were inflicted on the face of a Lion aristocrat and on the head of his spouse in Figure 10, above. Such a treatment suggests impacts caused by some sort of rebellion. This is another reason why the Lions outpost, at the top of Abdomen Hill, arouses our curiosity.

Fig. 20. The Lions Enclosure, view from the east. A limestone engraving of the Göbekli Tepe Earth Mother (Fig. 23, below) was found at the foot of the Northeast *menhir*, in the lower middle of the picture and seen as darker rectangle, partly hidden by that *menhir*. Photo by courtesy of DAI.

Ninety Degrees West: From the apex of Göbekli Tepe we descend westward, and there in the new excavation area we find some promising clues. But as the excavations have barely begun there, it may be too early to attempt enduring conclusions. Nevertheless, it seems remarkable that the two largest *menhirs* there bear the familiar large feline iconography of the Lions fraternity. In fact, one Lion bas-relief (Figure 22, left) is strikingly similar to some that were found in the Lion's Lodge, on the hill.

Fig. 21. New Excavation Area in the western crotch between the Southwest and Northwest Hills. Author photo—by courtesy of DAI.

—Another *menhir* shows a hunting scene in which cranes appear to be the prey (Figure 22, right). Whether the vulture (or eagle) at the center represents an ally to the Lions fraternity, I am unable to infer from this singular bas-relief. A pride of lions, depicted, appears to be quite self-sufficient while they are in pursuit. The very presence of this singular hunting scene is astonishing by itself, but it tentatively supports my general suspicions regarding elitism in the Lions fraternity. So far I see no hint of any interspecies mysticism in this fraternity of Feline hunters, nor a desire for atonement. Until additional excavations prove otherwise, the aristocratic Lions do seem to have hunted with the justification of being superior to other living beings. I will be very surprised if, near the floor of this Lodge, it turns out that managers of these Lion menhirs thought of themselves as progenitors of crane or goose chicks. But then, of course, if the excavators' spades should bare such a surprise, I will gladly re-examine, in context, any piece of Lions evidence that Göbekli Tepe has to offer. Whether my present suspicions are confirmed or whether other data will later sway my mind, it will all add up to positive learning. Our next question will simply be —"Why?"

Fig. 22. Early significant finds at the new West Excavation Area, 2011. Author photos—by courtesy of DAI.

—To return to our initial question on the hill, then, "What colonial stunt were those Lions trying to perform when they built their exclusive lodge right above the Foxes, Cranes, and the remaining menagerie of totems?" Apparently the Lion totem, as king of beasts, already ranked higher than other predators back then. Perhaps aristocratic high-mindedness and monarchic arrogance left their first monumental imprints already up there on Abdomen Hill. While we now know, by historical hindsight, that the option of domestication for the Göbekli Tepe area was just around the corner, the problem at the time seems to have been which group of hunters would first concede to become domesticators. Who would retire his weapons first and volunteer to become a lowly friend, a servant and step-kin, of domestic animals?

—Meanwhile in 2010, excavations at the Southwest Hill have uncovered evidence of a trend toward a more individualistic or "aristocratic" style of totemic poise. This trend may have begun under the sponsorship or influence of the Lions. The Lion totem-pole (Figure 10) was found at the Southwest Hill's eastern slope.

The Anthropomorphic Earth Mother

At least during the later days of Göbekli Tepe, some questions and uncertainties appear to have been murmured among initiates regarding the meaning of those central pairs of *menhirs*. As typically happens in the evolution of a religion, when the original vision fades, later explanations of ideas must be more forthcoming and more explicit. So, in answer to the basic query, "what is the meaning of those pairs of freestanding *menhirs* in Göbekli Tepe lodges?" an unknown Lions elder, an engraver has carved a response, and apparently it was to his own and to his Lions brothers' satisfaction. His engraving was prominently displayed at the eastern half of their lodge, on a stone bench between the two most prominent Lion *menhirs*. It sat openly on that platform for all initiates to see, to contemplate, and possibly to take turns sitting upon. Apparently they all understood, tolerated, and even appreciated the commentary and the clarification that they were given there.

—This engraving is not graffiti. It is anthropographic theology that gave a precise answer to the most central question of the miners' cult, as it had been asked at Göbekli Tepe. Any average member at those lodges would expect that his lodge elder be able to answer such a fundamental question. And thanks to their question, we can now see how this engraver in the Lions Lodge visualized the Göbekli Tepe Earth Mother. He has shown what those pairs of limestone *menhirs* would have looked like together, reduced to human propor- tions. This engraving represents a view of the Göbekli Tepe Earth Mother, seen from the perspective of the Lions fraternity. Their rectangle lodge had been aligned from west to east—implying that they probably entered the enclosure from the west, over the wall.

—The original engraving is now on display at the Sanliurfa Museum. Our image here is the *in situ* photograph that was published by Klaus Schmidt in 2008, p. 238. Cardinal directions are not indicated at either exhibit as these probably seemed insignificant for a piece that initially appeared to be graffiti—but at the DAI picture library these can be verified easily enough if needed someday.

—I am left to my own devices to infer from the circumstances the directionality that appears most probable. The engraving was made on an elevated bench immediately south of the northeast *menhir*

(Figure 20). This means that the engraver was probably kneeling, facing east. This line of reasoning would situate the woman's splayed legs to the west, and it would provide additional support for my hypothesis that the Lions fraternity was orienting itself by the Mountain's alternate "true crotch" in the west. For a conclusion to this query we must await the full excavation of additional central *menhirs* in the new excavation area, to the west.

Fig. 23. The Göbekli Tepe Earth Mother, found in the Lions Lodge on a bench that connected and braced the eastern pair of freestanding pillars. Photo by Dieter Johannes—Courtesy of DAI.

—The notion that someone can create a magic phallus to impregnate a divine lady was known in the mythology of ancient Egypt later on, concerning Isis and Osiris. Quarry-men at Göbekli

Tepe knew how to accomplish this feat many millennia before an Egyptian storyteller got around to telling what he knew.[31]

—It is time to recapture some of the primary points. Beginning with Figure 5 we have traced the duality of the central *menhirs* to two natural round orifices, two female "pedestals," and two larger pits which were all associated with the Rock Temple site named Enclosure E. We also have come to believe that the limbs of the Earth Mother can be recognized in the topography of Göbekli Tepe itself (Figure 4). And now we have found an anthropomorphic engraving of the Earth Mother showing two *menhir*-like objects. In a little while, we will be ready to add to this list of data a hypothesis concerning "pelvic architecture" at Enclosure C. But before we revisit this fascinating *temenos*, and face up to the possibility of looking at a megalithic "labyrinth" as well, I consider it wise to go on a brief ethnological excursion to the New Hebrides, in the Pacific. There we can find something megalithic that has remained alive and functioning until very recently.

Ethnological Excursion to the New Hebrides

The rounded head portion of the engraved female figure at Göbekli Tepe, and her dual orifice points, are reminiscent of similar sketches that were drawn of the Earth Goddess at the entrance to a Stone Age underworld. A megalithic men's cult has survived on the island of Malekula, in the New Hebrides, clear into the twentieth century. According to their drawings, the entrance to the underworld was the place from which humankind was born in the beginning. For homeward-bound ghosts there were provided designs of mazes that show varying degrees of complexity. These mazes are associated with the shape of Temes Savsap, the female Underworld Guardian who controls the entryway. While Temes Savsap was drawing her own design, she also represented the Earth Mother by her own shape. Her outline was drawn on the ground at the place of the underworld entrance.

---

[31]Only a later version by Plutarch has survived: Plutarch, *Isis and Osiris,* Vol. V of the Loeb Classical Library edition, 1936.

—Like megalithic labyrinths in general, so too do the Malekula drawings represent the maze of the Earth's own innards—perhaps as it was conceptualized by hunters and butchers. When a departing ghost approached Temes Savsap she wiped out half of the design that had been drawn on the ground. A duly initiated man would have memorized the correct path through her maze in advance—especially the crucial intersections inside. On Malekula the maze was taught at various levels of complexity, as the drawings of A. B. Deacon show.[32] A well informed ghost, having practiced on half-erased drawings while alive, will know how to continue and to complete the design—how to continue along the correct path that will lead to life.

Fig. 24. Path of the Dead for initiates, used byTemes Savsap, underworld Guardian at Malekula. Drawn after A. B. Deacon, 1934, pp. 127ff.

—In clear language this likely means that the wandering ghost enters at one of the Earth Lady's dual openings. If he knows how to complete the path through her inner maze, without getting lost by ending up in the wrong passage, he will be reborn and continues to exist. Those who do not know the path through her maze will be lost inside. "She will devour those who get lost," it is said. But clearer still, those who get lost inside this goddess at the intersections of her mysterious digestive or reproductive tracts can assume that they have been devoured while becoming lost, apparently predestined to exit at the second orifice as excrement. The contrast is life versus death.

---

[32]One may note here the manner in which this account oscillates between mythological narrative and imagery from memorized ritual practice. Compare A. B. Deacon. *Malekula, a Vanishing People in the New Hebrides*, ed. Camilla H. Wedgwood. London: G. Routledge and Sons, 1934, pp. 552-556. Also A. B. Deacon, "Geometrical Drawings from Malekula and other Islands of the New Hebrides," ed. Camilla H. Wedgwood. *Journal of the Royal Anthropological Institute, LXIV*. London, 1934, pp. 129-147.

The Victory over Death

—Some such soteriology, of salvation by knowing the divine anatomy, similar to the one on Malekula, may have informed the men at the Göbekli Tepe lodges. Such or similar mysteries were probably whisp- ered in the Earth Mother's sanctuaries.

—Two is the number of the great existential mysteries. There is Life and there is Death. These are anatomically represented by two nether or rearmost orifices in all mammalians, including humankind. One orifice discharges dead waste. Males and females are both endowed with such a cavity of death. As for the other mysterious endowment, for males their phallus was a weapon of life; the vagina of the females was the wound to be pierced and planted. And the latter was then seen to bring forth new life. Thus, one orifice meant the end of the road for living food beings, and the other signified a new beginning, the continuity of life and offspring.

—The Mountain Woman engraving (Figure 23) has clarified that during Göbekli Tepe cult days both orifices were dealt with as being somehow comparable. In addition, it has become clear that a symbolic parallelism existed in relation to all the central pairs of sculpted *menhirs* that spiked the various sanctuary enclosures. In each sanctuary at least two phallic *menhirs* created life. Their number was two-some to occupy both orifices—thus, the one that naturally presented life as well as the one that ordinarily brought forth the produce of death. By placing phalluses at both orifices, the abominable pit was miracu-lously transformed into its natural opposite—to function as a source of life as much as the other. Life thereby was winning out over death.

—How can a writer twelve to ten millennia later still know this? The notion of phalluses implanting seeds into vaginas, which are like fields, has survived in Western civilization and is still understood in our days. At Enclosure D we find a clear testimonial regarding the meaning of those mysteries at Göbekli Tepe. Similar types of limestone phalluses implanted similar types of seed into each of the two orifices. Both central *menhirs* and their female pediments in Enclosure D are surrounded by gaggles of identical crane chicks. From both orifices—out from the wellspring of Life as well as from the pit of Death—have been laid the same type of fertile eggs. And from these same eggs were hatched the same type of birds.

—Who are we, modern archaeologists or historians of religions, to tell ancient men at Göbekli Tepe how they should or should not have celebrated their Easter? They were huntsmen, imitators of totemic models, killers and butchers of animals, miners, makers of weapons while plotting murder—burdened with existential contradictions and bad consciences. They lived, they killed, they ate and died. But at the Göbekli Tepe sanctuaries, for a time, they succeeded in ritually discounting and defeating death. With the skills they had they could not win immortality for themselves. But then, not all was lost. The education and enthusiasm for life, which they perpetuated in their rites, eventually enabled some of them to convert to a strategy of nurturing living things. Learning thus, they invented domestication and helped themselves and their offspring prosper. We have here, for a brief moment in evolutionary time, the glimpse of a religious intuition that enabled human minds, and hands, to begin resolving the self-inflicted crisis of the Neolithic.

—Specifically, by way of accepting the Göbekli Tepe two-orifice mysteries, all subsequent handlings of barnyard manure on the part of start-out domesticators has been rationalized and naturalized in favor of hands-on animal husbandry and agriculture.

Revisiting Enclosure C for Comparison

The dual entranceway to the complex stonework design of Enclosure C may be a place to pursue our questions a little further. Additional excavations, and re-examinations of the archaeological record, will become necessary in future years as a result of these fresh questions and hypotheses.

—At a website of the German Archaeological Institute one can find a three-dimensional computer reconstruction of Enclosures B, C, and D. For our present considerations I shall replicate here only the portion that was made available of Enclosure C.

—The maze-like double and triple walls of Enclosure C present a real challenge. Indeed, theater was being staged there on a large scale, as Professor Schmidt has rightly commented. As of now, I suspect that the central circle outlines, as do all the lodges, a vaginal sanctuary with implanted phallic *menhirs*. But then, the DAI photograph, and the published DAI reconstruction, both stop at the most crucial spot for our interpretation—at the apparent dual entrance to Enclosure C (Figures 25, 26).

—The excavation data themselves are still ambiguous. Some intentional destruction appears to have been wrought during intertotemic conflicts at Göbekli Tepe. On the original excavation map projection two entry "walls" are indicated. Nevertheless, alerted by the Mountain Woman engraving, Figure 23, we are now encouraged to ask a fresh question: Were these two entry walls the equivalent of a pair of "horizontally laid *menhir* bodies" which originally led up to a dual entrance?

—It is possible that the horizontal layout surrounding the central vaginal sanctuary was intended to be something like an artistic compilation, adding the Mother's pelvic cross section in sideview? Were the entrance walls that funneled the dancers inward at two entrances—frontal and posterior, left and right—a sideview of the "maze," depicted from a butcher's perspective?

Fig. 25. Top view of Enclosure C, excavated to bottom level. Courtesy of DAI.

—We must not forget that full-time hunters were life-long butchers and students of anatomy. It would have been easy for them to conceptualize something like this about their Earth Mother. Every female mammalian they split exemplified this dual orifice structure. The combination of the three dimensions—of a vertical orientation for the center, with the pelvic lateral two-dimensional cross-section for the surrounding mazes—need not surprise in a "primitive" composition.

—But understanding this problem has become complicated, recently, by the fact that the illustration in the *National Geographic* essay, cited earlier, provides a more conventional style of adjusting concepts of entranceways, of doors in Göbekli Tepe maze architecture. I can empathize with that reasoning and admire the artistry, but I have preferred here to err conservatively on the side of the original German Archaeological Institute model.[33]

—On October 2, 2011, Professor Schmidt and I were looking at this still unexcavated portion between the ruined "Lions Gate" at the south end and the potential double entrance to Enclosure C. This means I had a chance to ask my question *in situ.* Because at that moment in time this stretch of some meters has not yet been completely excavated, both reconstructions—with a single or a double entranceway—continue to remain a possibility.

The One-Menhir and Two-Menhir Distinction

There is no question about the fact that orthodoxy at Göbekli Tepe did require two central *menhirs* per sanctuary. Inasmuch as the Lions fraternity at their top station erected two such pairs in their lodge, I suspect, this could have been an intra-Feline political concession of sorts. Not all large Felines were true brothers toward each other—some may have been tigers, leopards, or similar such relatives. We do not yet have enough data at our disposal to approach the entire puzzle. And there are other things to consider.

—Alongside the dominant orthodoxy at Göbekli Tepe, of setting up pairs of T-shaped *menhirs* at the center of each *temenos*, significant evidence has been found of a more scattered individualistic tradition that was exemplified by singular statues of the totem-pole variety.[34] Without sufficient data available to fully explore this matter I have, nevertheless, garnered a preliminary impression, to the effect that most iconoclastic reactions at Göbekli Tepe were inflicted on individualistic types of totem pole statues.

—To erect and to engage ceremonially two huge menhirs at the center of a sanctuary required a great amount of social cooperation.

---

[33]Compare in this regard the pictorial reconstruction in the Charles C. Mann essay, in *National Geographic*, June 2011, pp. 44f.

[34]This point will need to be revisited. Apparently more bird-ridden heads were found during the 2012 excavation campaigns, somewhere at the site.

By comparison, chiseling and setting up a totem pole to glorify the lineage of a creative individual could be achieved by a single sculptor with a little extra hired help. Most single standing totem pole monuments at Göbekli Tepe, at some point in time, appear to have been deprived of faces and/or places.

Fig. 26. Enclosure C— DAI reconstruction, at http://www.urgeschichte.org/DieBeweise/Gobekli Tepe/gobeklitepe.htm

—It seems as though the majority of miners at Abdomen Hill were able to spot potential bullies quite easily. They were not interested in supporting a personality cult of aristocratic individuals. Such individualism would have contradicted the societal function of setting up communal pairs of *menhirs*. It is possible that offended groups simply ganged up and eliminated the individualists that stuck out from the rest. A social system that can produce Lion aristocrats can also incite sculptor-rebels who are preoccupied with revolutionary or "prophetic" aspirations.

—One of the most creative geniuses on this holy mountain was the rather eccentric sculptor of the totemic Lions lineage (Figure 10). We no longer have the face of this man's Lion mask, because it was cracked off and presumably pulverized. But we know that the man identified with a Lion totem. Two feline ears

Fig. 27. Enclosure C— Author drawing based on a DAI reconstruction, at http://www.urgeschichte.org/DieBeweise/Gobekli Tepe/gobeklitepe.htm

of the totemic sponsor's mask are still in place at his statue. The Lion-man's face, as well as the presumed "feline head" of his female, but not the Shakti position of this female nor the fact that procreation and birth were being shown to happen contemporaneously, were deemed offensive by the iconoclasts. It was essentially the arrogant Lions identity, the aristocratic feline smirks on those faces, that seem to have evoked the anger of competing sculptor-priests and provoked their flint cleavers. Of course, the suggestions offered here, from a distance, will all need to be reconsidered when excavations at Göbekli Tepe are complete.

Animals for the Barnyard

The recent find of a "dual porthole" sculpture, on the Northwestern Hilltop, finally gives us the assurance that Göbekli Tepe flint miners were, after all, in tune with their time. According to independent scholarship, the domestication of emmer wheat was to have happened nearby at the time when the Göbekli Tepe cult subsided. This coincidence is an encouraging takeoff point for exploring the hunters' transition toward the domestication of plants and animals. Obviously, much more needs to be excavated before this and other aspects of the cult can emerge with clarity.

8. Animals for the Barnyard

The Bull: To this day I have seen only two or three images of bulls at Göbekli Tepe. Because the sculptors adjusted the sizes of their images to the rock surfaces they had available, some male bovines there are difficult to distinguish from rams. Moreover, as an ungulate, the bull does not qualify as an active totemic sponsor of hunters. He was respected and inducted into the "honorable order of masculine hunter totems," perhaps because he was a male and a master of herd animals who could kill—or because miners at Göbekli Tepe were becoming concerned about the regeneration of bovines in general, of cattle that belonged to bulls.

—Nowhere is totemic logic a clear-cut science. We also find cranes, a ram, some boars, a gazelle, and a donkey in the Göbekli Tepe totemic menagerie. Whenever it suited the Stone Age taxonomists, they could bring males of any species into their associations of huntsmen. Yet, with all their openness I still would not have wanted to be an only Crane initiate in a lodge of Foxes. There would have been no end to the teasing, I suspect. There is enough evidence, however, that Cranes and Foxes got along together nicely in the Göbekli Tepe cult—much better than either of these got along with Lions.

—Bulls maintained their ambiguity into times when, millennia later at Knossos, one was said to be hiding in a megalithic maze—to guard the enigmatic innards of Earth, it seems. He functioned as the supreme killer and bugaboo of initiates who were not supposed to know whether they could survive their initiation ordeals. Of course, the Cretan and Athenian myths that are still being told about mysteries at Knossos have diluted the secret society and initiation components, down to the weightiness of a simple royal romance. In the evolution of human culture, for every distortion toward one extreme there tends to be provided—by divine grace perhaps—an opposite that might be useful for restoring some semblance of balance and a renewal of hope.

–The Hellenic *taurobolium* (bull sacrifice), later, and the Spanish bullfights later still, have pushed the Knossos bull monster back into its hunters niche—as a prey-designate, suitable for heroic feats of killing. The size and high status of the bovine species has enhanced the *taurobolium* and the bovine's valorization beyond the point where the maze cult at Knossos left off. Eventually this newer trend justified the efforts of the domesticators to control and to butcher cattle —something which in the early context of Minotaur mysteries would scarcely have been an acceptable aristocratic theme. The Minotaur lost credibility when ordinary peasants figured out how to handle and tame those bulls. Hunter-aristocrats thereupon needed to undertake something more dramatic and "heroic" against the cattle species—something spectacular to bounce mysterium tremendum back on people. The bull sacrifices and the bullfights served that function.

–Males of the human species, from Paleolithic into Neolithic times, have been predators while the females kept their growing families balanced in the safer pursuits of foraging. Within the general category of predators, hominid males were initially inferior hunters by nature. But as hunters they desired to be descendants of more powerful predators. Of course, a living creature selects neither its own parents nor its gods. In the process of human living these gods were not made; they were all discovered. Active totems or gods, being greater-than-human, have all along had the power to adopt into their packs, prides, and totemic brotherhoods such human apprentices as were willing to join and to "ape" them.

–It was then left to *Homo sapiens,* divinely chosen, to come up with a credible story—or at least an interesting hypothesis—that would naturalize his divine totemic status in public awareness.

Domestication lies just over the horizon: To find a rational justification for the practice of animal domestication, the Göbekli Tepe men eventually needed to be chosen and be led by different totems—thus, to be led by gods who were not dragging humanoid devotees indefinitely into predator dilemmas and pangs of guilt. The sheer desire to ceremonially stimulate some types of propagation events has prepared their minds for cultural situations that were still evolving.

Gradually, it modified their six-million-year-old obsession with aggression, killing, and meat-eating.

—The men's initial wishes to see more prey animal offspring, and to speed up the hatching of flint eggs among limestone ovaries, combined to steer human thinking in the direction of cultural expansion. Before men could practice domestication, they needed to find broadly reasoned religion that would help rationalize human nourishment and appetites in line with the status levels they were willing to grant to animals and plants. The religions of humankind today are still fragmentary. They cannot possibly avoid splintering as long as human sciences and industries focus on random victories and opportunistic markets. Atonement cannot be won in any less scattered a mode than a culture's present sum of aggressive sinning requires. A dozen modes of cultural aggression require a dozen distinct styles of religious retreat.

—Entertaining the general notions of prehuman flux mythology regarding the unity of all life, propagation, death, and transformation, has softened the ancients for their new tasks of providing nurture to animals. But domestication needed to be developed under the tutelage of divine sponsors that had yet to be discovered. Thus, Professor Schmidt's insight, that the Neolithic Revolution was a religious occurrence, is developmentally sound.

—The miners' industry and cult at Göbekli Tepe, with their manifest concerns for symbols of life and atonement, have generated an impulse for cultural creativity that reached beyond basic hunger, violence, and food. The cult which populated its sanctuaries with limestone *menhirs* has nurtured a seed idea—the notion of the Earth's fecundity and growth, attended to by male efforts. For this reorientation to become effective among Göbekli Tepe hunters, the Earth-and-Mountain Woman needed to be rendered pregnant and her abdomen needed to grow, visibly, with support of the men's devotion. And this entire object-lesson needed to be staged by habitual killers under the pretext of life-enabling atonement. The Göbekli Tepe cult reveals the depth to which an inherited killer-culture required balancing, in order to to pursue domestication and nurture.

—People on the road to domestication eventually needed to abandon all their predatory hunter gods. They needed to find, and submit to, greater deities that create, that would bless and enable them by fresh sacrificial paths of legitimization to own plants and livestock. Those hunters who did not participate in this general reorientation and religious conversion, who refused fair styles of domestication, sacrifice, and trading, remained forever a nuisance to the domesticators. They eventually became the aristocratic purveyors of militarism and hyper-domestication.

—One of the earliest domesticates along the northern Fertile Crescent, until recently, seemed unaccounted for among the bas-reliefs of Göbekli Tepe. It was the goat.[35] Could this mean that the animal no longer roamed within the legitimate realm of the hunters? It seems too early in the excavation process to downgrade goats as some kind of "evil" species. Besides, "good" and "evil" appear to have been aligned quite differently among Stone Age hunters than among subsequent domesticators. If there ever existed an evil species—before Devil and almighty God could be credited as originators of good and bad conditions in the world—it was the human hunters themselves, as artificial predators and tricksters.

Predisposition: *The severe contrast between powers of Life and powers of Death (Good and Evil), in archaic hunter tradition, became clear to me in 1971 when Johnny Cooke and I noticed how a Diné woman was afraid of our recording activities. She turned pale. She understood that what we recorded were words from the Talking-god Rite, Wolf Rite, or Deer-hunting Rite, combined or interchangeably so named. According to her view, we men were trafficking in power-words from the realm of death. The counterpoint to her fear was the hunter-shaman's own worries that any trace of female secretions—of life power—could neutralize and destroy his hunting powers. His death-wielding powers were therefore protected and kept in check by his mystic transformation into a totemic Wolf-deity. Then, after hunting he needed to be retransformed—in the same transformational sweat-lodge setting—back into a safe human husband. He needed to function again in the realm of life, that is, in the realm where women lived and children played and grew.*

---

[35]The biblical concept of a "scapegoat," which supposedly refers to goats as being evil—whether Hittite or Israelite—appears to have resulted from a general misunderstanding of relatively late historical contexts. Below in Chapter Twenty I will introduce an alternate perspective on this question. I suspect that the same unease also applies to the goat stamp-seals from Tepe Giyan (illustrated in Schmidt, 2008, p. 215). I find it difficult to imagine that some owner of a goat herd would choose the imprint of an "evil goat demon" for his business seal. In each of these instances, postulating a predecessor religion in which goats had positive standing would answer our historical queries better.

The Holy Barnyard: As early as at Figure 4, in this volume, I began to acknowledge the presence of a duality principle at Göbekli Tepe. In this section I must return to the same subject matter with an important amendment, and from a broader perspective. In 2010 Professor Schmidt reported on recent excavations in fresh trenches, on Northwest Hill. An artifact (Figure 28), which he introduces, is several meters in size. It approaches a degree of excellence that corresponds favorably to the most ornately sculpted *menhirs* at Göbekli Tepe, on Level One at the Southeast center.[36] But before focusing on this object, a look back to Figure 23 might help provide perspective on the historical process. The anthropomorphic apparent graffiti engraving, in the Lions Lodge on the Southeast Hill, I have accepted as graphic commentary that explains Göbekli Tepe theology. While with the advent of the Neolithic Revolution human living conditions were changing, and while among successive generations religious responses were evolving, earlier faith positions tended to drift out of focus relative to changes in their culture. Future teachers within the cult therefore needed to be more explicit. They needed to explain the relevance of old answers in relation to new problems, and in fresh ways. Accordingly, this next edition of graphic "theological commentary" reveals a fresh pattern of thought that suggests that at Göbekli Tepe the Neolithic Revolution had begun.

—This particular slab of limestone features two parallel rectangular holes that lead down into earth. The archaeologists have catalogued such artifacts as *Türlochsteine* (porthole stones). The dual orifices immediately suggest that here we are looking at the reduced version of a floor plan for orthodox *temenos* enclosures, with dual pedestal-and-tub features—such as can be seen fully excavated in Enclosures C and D. But no T-shaped *menhirs* were associated with this new find on Northwest Hill.

—The rectangular shape of the "portholes" nevertheless suggest that matching *menhirs* must conceptually have determined the design, to associate them with rectangular *menhirs*. But *menhirs* themselves are absent at this reduced model of an otherwise dual-base sanctuary. Moreover, their general westward orientation bring this sanctuary

[36]Klaus Schmidt, "Göbekli Tepe—the Stone Age Sanctuaries. New results of ongoing excavations with special focus on sculptures and high reliefs." *Documenta Praehistorica XXXVII* (2010), pp. 239-256.

design under the general influence of the Lions fraternity. All the while, Professor Schmidt tells us that no traces of formerly inserted *menhirs* could be seen.

—Very well! This means that, for the artist who created this "double porthole" arrangement, the old procreation ceremonial that featured *menhirs* needed not continue for the time being. The sculptor no longer envisioned a procreation scene, nor did he bother anymore to indicate the Mother'ssubsequent pregnancy. Not much of a hill was needed right there. All these familiar notions were, of course, still implied assumptions. But in relation to his newer concerns, this particular sculptor-priest chose to show the Mother'sexposure after she had already given birth.

—So what has changed at this temple model? The time of gestation, from procreation to birth (or to the points of egg-laying and hatching) now is no longer illustrated in a single display as it was attempted on some totem poles or was implied with the bas-relief gaggles of crane offspring under the huge *menhirs* in Enclosure D (see Figures 12 and 17, above; and also Pillars 12, 27, and 43 in Klaus Schmidt, 2008). Hatchlings and newborns are crawling there over phalluses that dallied too long.

—In all likelihood, the sculptors in these *menhir*-related instances were not trying to invite laughs at the expense of the most sacred concerns of their cult; rather, they probably were trying to be prophetic and optimistic, showing happy results in advance. Offspring and more life were the aim of their cult of atonement. It was expected to be a reasonable result of the Mountain Woman's pregnancy and growth. We may interpolate that this Neolithic culture had no reasons, yet, to denigrate human sexuality. Human overpopulation had not yet become the festering curse that it did in later years.

—In the context of this newer sanctuary model, procreation, pregnancy, and even birth, have already happened. All these steps of producing offspring are acknowledged now as having occurred in linear sequence. The moment has arrived to manage the barnyard. The presence of permanently stationed phallic *menhirs* was no longer required at this updated sanctuary model. The births of animals, or the hatching of a serpent (fish?) were accomplished. The progeny appears to be lining up, almost as if to be suckled.

—The sculptor of this temple arrangement has answered our lingering key question with precision—regarding the transition of the

Göbekli Tepe cult from hunting and gathering to domestication. We now know that this transition had been happening in the area around the time when this sanctuary model was sculpted.

—In a single scene the sculptor-priest showed us… showed us what? No, not yet a manger scene with animals and a holy human family—but already something like a "holy barnyard."

Fig. 28. The Holy Barnyard. A recently found "porthole-stone" sculpture at Göbekli Tepe. Northwest Hilltop. A similar photo image was first published in Klaus Schmidt, 2010, p. 252. Courtesy of DAI.

Serpent or fish? The scene with the ambiguous serpent-fish has re-awakened a thought about the role of serpent imagery in general, at Göbekli Tepe. Earlier in this book I put to sleep this thought by way of merely acknowledging a male serpent's dual sexual endowments. But could it have been the case that at Göbekli Tepe the men's fascination with serpents got them started with their dualistic anatomical worldview?

—Most people know that serpent or lizard tongues, at some point along their length, divide into two tines; but it is less well known that male serpents, and some lizards, also have hemi-penes, which means, two phalluses. Envious zoologists, apparently, at some time recorded and down-graded these as "hemi" or "half" quantities. But have male serpents, endowed with two phalluses, encouraged men at Göbekli Tepe to anticipate pairs of orifices on the turtle-like Earth-Mountain-Mother? These men knew serpents inside out. They probably handled and "milked" them for venom, and butchered them for skins and meat. Or, did they begin counting two orifices merely at puberty, when human female anatomy became more interesting to them? With that many sculpted serpents meandering among Göbekli Tepe's base-reliefs, this research question does recommend itself for later, farther down along our road of inquiry. I have raised the question here to let it go to sleep again, unanswered.[37]

—The mammals to which the Earth Mother has given birth in this sanctuary arrangement appear to be bovine, goat, and the descendant of a predator. The latter may represent a specimen of the first domesticate that joined the human household—a dog. And if this is a dog, if the "reptilian" creature turns out to be a fish or a vermin-hunting snake, then this could be the first mini-sanctuary to function

---

[37]In 1976 I published *Olmec Religion...*, and I changed the overall perspective regarding ancient Middle American religion—to seeing a Serpent cult overall. I identified the Olmec "mosaic masks" at La Venta, which hitherto had been interpreted as jaguar faces, as representing Crotalus durissus durissus. I would become an easy target for ridicule if I were to exaggerate Snake symbolism at Göbekli Tepe even by a single millimeter. The absence of open serpentine mouths among Göbekli Tepe images, so far, does not render this line of inquiry very productive. I generously bequeath this challenge to other researchers, for now. Academic resistance was fierce in 1976. But after thirty-four years my work has recently been vindicated by René Dehnhardt, in *Die Religion der Olmeken von La Venta: eine religions-archäologische Analyse.* Doctoral dissertation, Philosophische Facultät der Rheinischen Friedrich Wilhelm Universität, Bonn, 2010.

for domesticator households. Perhaps it came into use while contemporaries were busy covering up the last of the Lions menhirs, of the new western excavation area.

—This sanctuary model, on the Northwest Hill at Göbekli Tepe, may have been functioning some ten thousand years ago—set up by a weapon-maker and limestone-sculptor priest. As an altarpiece of the Earth Mother it may also have been a holy place for hunters and gatherers whose sons and daughters were thinking about becoming herdsmen and farmers. It is possible that the priest of this small establishment remained a totem-sponsored huntsman—a flint-tool maker—for the rest of his life. But in his days, herdsmen and farmers needed flint cutting tools, too.

Acknowledging the Goat: I am delighted to see here at last, in the Göbekli Tepe repertoire, the first image of a goat. Its presence supports the hunch that I held all along—that during the era of hunting no animal was regarded as inherently evil. How could our ancestors have considered an animal to be evil, as long as human males submitted, mystically, to the most dangerous predators and revered them as totemic sponsors and masters?

—If there was any creature on earth that consciously and intentionally was most mischievous, tricky, or evil—one who understood much of what he was doing—then it was man. His habit of making tools, to kill and to cut, amounted to premeditating serial murders. Such behavior also suggests that goats, back then, could not very easily have been shunned as an evil species. How could they have become the first ungulates to be domesticated with such an evil reputation? We will know better how to answer this question when the bone count at Göbekli Tepe is complete.

—For now, the presence of even this single goat sculpture, at Göbekli Tepe, endorses what I had prewritten and then reassigned to Chapter Twenty. I expect to offer there an improved opinion about the domestication of goats, along with my reasons for discounting the Aza'zel/Scapegoat equation as a theological, and even as a modern social scientific misunderstanding. I am not writing playfully about this matter. My revised narrative on goats will begin seriously enough at Yom Kippur, the ancient Israelite Day of Atonement—below in Chapter Twenty.

—While domesticates were sculpted for Göbekli Tepe sanctuaries, there also was born a new type of human priest, serving a new type of deity for a changing human constituency. The priests on this holy hill have all officiated with a basic repertoire of totemic symbols. Originally they probably wore loin-cloths and masks, and then they added stoles. They also knew how to think about human and divine activities in terms of divine hands, arms, and genitals—symbolically visible as well as extending and blending into invisible symbolic dimensions—broadening out perhaps, to some theme like "She's got the whole world of living beings upon Her lap!" It was these priests who learned to assume responsibility for human creativity—not only for hatching flint splinters from flint nodules by violent splitting, but also for the replenishment and procreation of species that as a consequence of their successful flint weapons industry were becoming scarce. They became interested in species that were suitable to live nearer to the human homestead.

—The theological perspective of this type of priests, at Göbekli Tepe, quite likely remained totemic in orientation. While mentally they were still hunting and capturing, and physically they were "flattening" their hunter totems down to bas-reliefs, these sculptor-priests learned to appreciate their own human abilities, their tools and their paraphernalia, loincloths and stoles—all being pretentions that enhanced their sense of power and status. While an older generation of totemic gods was flattened to stone by artistic assertion, other greater deities were needed to replace them, to authorize fresh human ambitions. While the priests accommodated the Mountain-and-Earth-Mother as materially as they could, their very work habits as limestone quarry-men set them up for a fresh round of theologizing, and for much more. Their moment in evolutionary time stimulated them mentally, to prepare for encounters with "Mother Nature"—or simply with "Nature," as she would come to be known in the far distant future, in an age when this book could be written.

—From a somewhat later period, at a nearby cliff, a rock carving of what appears to be a cow (or calf) was found next to a natural effluent spout resembling a bovine vagina (Figure 29). The elliptic arc above the small animal figure may refer to the spout in the cliff on the right. It may signify a process of birthing. Hollows have been scraped from the limestone surface—some oval, and others round. These suggest that the same limestone-dust "medicine" that elsewhere, as in Figure 30, was used to treat male and female humankind was here scraped to also maintain the wellbeing of animals. Such an outpour of improvisation points to a unified theory of life, to workable presuppositions for the tasks of domestication.

—Did this Earth Mother "know" Heaven or Father Sky? Like we do our thinking today, so also the sculptor-priests at Göbekli Tepe needed to conceptualize by a method of seeing similarities and contrasts. It was not possible to explain all of Life and Death in terms of the rocky Mother Earth alone. Their industry of weapons manufacture, and their maintenance of a male cult for the procreation of life in general, could never be balanced with maternal sentiments alone. Thus, as contradictory as it might seem, and given their atonement focus on the Mother, Göbekli Tepe priests strayed unto a path of fresh religious discovery, eventually finding and recognizing the Sky Father. The basic question of conscience by which this divine Father haunted them, was probably: "By whose authority are you, hunters and miners, manhandling the Earth Mother?"

Fig. 29. Rock carving of a cow, near a natural outflow, resembling a bovine vagina. Photo by courtesy of DAI.

Echoes from Göbekli Tepe in Hesiod's Theogony: The Greek poet Hesiod, seven thousand years later, raised exactly that same issue. But he seems to have blamed all obstructions—every abstracted phallus that failed to get out of the way—not on limestone sculptors who plugged up their Mother with *menhirs*, but on the living Sky Father himself. In addition, Hesiod incriminated Cronos the Titan as wielder of a flint "sickle" (thus as a proto-farmer) for having castrated the Sky deity—as if to blame domesticators, and to punish the Sky Father for the presence of all these "severed" representational and obstructive limestone paraphernalia:

> Of all the children born of Earth and Heaven, the Titans were the most terrible, and they were hated by the Sky Father from the beginning. He hid them in secret places of the Earth as soon as each was born. He would not let them rise into daylight. The vast Earth groaned with pain. Thereupon she created gray flint and fashioned a sickle and told her plan to her Titan sons:
>
> My children, begotten by a terrible father! If you will obey me, we will punish the outrage of your father. He was the one who first thought of doing terrible things. Cronos, the cunning trickster, answered and volunteered to act on his Mother's wish —of wielding revenge on Heaven. Then Earth hid him in ambush. Into his hand she put the jagged sickle, and instructed him in her plot. Thereupon... Heaven came, bringing on night and longing to make love. He lay about Earth, spreading himself full upon her. Then the son from his ambush stretched forth his left hand and in his right took the great long sickle with jagged teeth, and swiftly lopped off his own father's members and cast them away to fall behind him.[38]

—Apparently only distorted rumblings of the Göbekli Tepe mythology reached the poet Hesiod seven millennia later. His story plot exonerated miners and flint-weapon makers and tried to turn Mother Earth and sickle-wielding farmers forever against their Sky Father. Indeed, Göbekli Tepe religion generated fresh questions and problems of which Göbekli Tepe miner-priests and sculptors of *menhirs* understood nothing yet. But domesticators eventually welcomed a more virile Sky Father—one that was more creative than the one that Hesiod was able to imagine.

—Implicitly, without fully understanding the symbolic potential of their own ceremonial paraphernalia, the cult members at Göbekli Tepe prepared for the eventual recognition of the Sky Father, and thereby got ready for their eventual reconciliation with him. From high upon his towering clouds, this deity continued to hurl his fiery lightning spears toward the earth, and to roll his thunder-boulders.

---

[38]Hesiod, "Theogony," in *Hesiod, the Homeric Hymns and Homerica,* trans. H. G. Evelyn-White (Cambridge, Mass., 1977), pp. 87-93. Text translation modified.

Having all along mastered symbolizing the procreative endowments of the Sky Father, in the form of inert limestone *menhirs,* the men at Göbekli Tepe could not avoid wondering about the living deity on high who owned the dynamics that were still out of reach. The antithesis to their inert *menhirs*, a living Sky Father, eventually dawned on them, and he acted more like a bull than a lion. Thereupon the men abandoned their juvenile habit of sculpting phalluses.

—Not only for the sake of the Great Mother's peace, but also for the dignity of Father Sky, the imitational limestone paraphernalia needed to be buried out of sight, eventually. This God on High could be expected to approach his Spouse again, in accordance with His and Her own nature. He would approach not as he was carved and mutilated by the flints of chiseler apprentices. After a time, those angular T-phalluses, in the eyes of this living God, must have seemed like littering. Of course, he noticed those limestone fakes that were dumped onto his spouse—seemingly to mock Him who, millennia later, still wanted to be proud about "begetting sons."

—Göbekli Tepe sculptor-priests prepared for a future when humans would want to be truer friends to the animals. By shaping images of animals with their hands and tools, from the substance of the Great Mother, the sculptors gradually came to regard their images like procreations, progeny, and personal property. They cared not quite as much anymore for the offspring of totemic predators—former gods who they diminished and flattened to stone by sculpting. They increasingly cared for prey animals whom they learnt to love and to protect. Up until that time they knew how to hunt, kill, and butcher. Now they experienced sculpting their images was not unlike an act of devout creativity—and as an experience of falling in love with offspring so created. One wonders how much of fresh human empathy went into those early artistic procreations.

—A short time after sculpting some of these, the artificers began adopting live replicas of those imaged animals, as step-children for domestication. After two millennia of bloodying their fingers on flint and limestone, as hunters and miners, the skin of any brute animal born into their corrals would feel softer to the touch than did those stones. However, vis-à-vis their former totemic sponsors, they needed to evolve an inverse defensive relationship. As the people adopted prey animals for domestication, they became obliged to expell predator totems who behaved hostile toward their domestics. Totemic deities were thereby re-evaluated as demons and thieves. Maternal love and compassion could not easily be lavished on tame animals and on wild predators at the same time—even if some diehard huntsmen still considered the latter to be divine.

Creation, sculpting, and ownership: The transitional Diné Master and Keeper of prey animals, the Black-god (Raven), had the power to herd and keep animals because at his homestead he also kept a full set of sculpted jewel-stone prototypes of those same animals.[39] Similarly, we may suspect that sculptor-priests at Göbekli Tepe, when they carved images of living beings in three-dimensional shapes, sensed that they were gaining creative control and parental entitlement regarding those creatures. Their empowerment increased, regardless of whether they sculpted grazing animals for increase and domestication, or whether they magically confined totemic predator deities to lithic inertia and imprisonment.

—Such reasoning about the power of imaging explains the preponderant absence of plain human figures in the Göbekli Tepe artistic repertoire. It also explains the hostility that was expressed against some of those individualistic anthropomorphized totem poles. Anyone who carved and set up his own personal image made himself vulnerable. The earliest images made by human hands were taken to be part and portion of whatever living beings they resembled.

—Individuals, captured so in shapes of statues, could be modified, controlled, owned, and destroyed. Such reasoning, then, could easily be transposed to claims of ownership for purposes of domestication, and for justified butchering. It also explains prohibitions that were imposed later in the history of religions, against the making of images of either human persons or divinities. "Thou shall not make any graven images of men or gods" actually was another way of saying "Thou shall not try to own them in the form of sculpted models."

---

[39]See Karl W. Luckert, *The Navajo Hunter Tradition*, 1975, pp. 125 ff.

9. Hiding the Mystery of Life

When all excavations at Göbekli Tepe have been completed, a final question will remain: Why, in the end, were the sanctuaries and their contents covered with miners' overhead and tailings? First, the cover-up implies that flint mining continued beyond the point at which menhir-focused cult activities ceased. It also suggests that some places needed to be filled to continue growth of the Earth Mother's abdomen. After conception, covering up may have seemed to be the proper thing to do. The basic concern of the cult—atonement for the killers' violence by assisting in the creation of life—was thereby attained.

When the Göbekli Tepe cult reached its high point, some families, or perhaps entire clans, needed to move away from the area to follow the prey animals northward through the mountains. Abandoned temple enclosures, tailor-made for groups that were devoted to specific sets of totems and associated with representative *menhirs*, would soon become an eyesore for those who wished to maintain the dominance of their own clan-line and totemic orientation. Those who moved away may have felt a need to cover up their intimate lodges before they left.

—Have the Lions who built at the top of the Southeast Hill outlasted all others? Have they reoriented the entire cult westward and thereby simply obliterated enclosures along the southern crotch? Such answers do not solve the remainder of the problem. If this was the case, then who buried the western enclosures in the end?

—Those who continued mining at Göbekli Tepe needed to insist on the relevance of what they did. The factionalism that developed between aristocratic and lower ranking hunters, that was defined by competition and totemic affiliations, downgraded every individualistic cult establishment to a temporary affair. Over the course of two millennia, managements at the holy mountain changed hands many times. To what degree could younger generations of men really became emotionally involved in the religiously sublimated sexuality of previous generations? Each generation was caught up in problems of their own ebbs and tides. Göbekli Tepe with its sanctuaries and *menhirs* was a place that focused on the creation of Life. Death in general was shunned if not deemed utterly defeated. This orientation could have remained intact as long as people felt disposed to assist the growth of their Mountain Mother's abdomen. Those who left the area hoped that fresh life from their Mother would continue to flow with them, and empower them, wherever they traveled.

—For everything on earth there seems to be a time and a season. At Göbekli Tepe there was a time to unwrap and then, for a similar good reason, there was a time when the Earth Mother needed to be covered again. So, what would have been easier than to empty the basket loads of tailings, of overhead debris, that all along had been added to grow the Mother's abdomen—to dump them into the holy depths that needed to be covered?

—This does not mean that megalithic hunter beliefs, as a religion and in their totality, were being buried. For most of the time that miners and weapon-makers came to Göbekli Tepe, to work on flint, remnant cults may have continued to nestle in along the hillside—at what archaeologists presently call "Level Two." At some point in their evolution, the sacred lodges ceased to function as cult centers while the hill itself continued to grow physically, as in its pregnant condition it was expected to. By the time all crevices at this hill were covered, some animals were already being born in barnyards in the surrounding area. A shift had occurred in cultural as well as religious valuations. The fill dirt, for a time, became more important than having limestone paraphernalia in full view. And why should that not be so? The general gestation period for new life was under way, and the Mother's abdomen was destined for expansion. To see her grow had, after all, been the hope implied in all the quarrying, sculpting, and celebrating over the course of two millennia.

—Complete destruction of older sanctuaries was unnecessary. It was easier to bury than to destroy them. The *menhirs* did not represent archaic gods that needed to be demolished to make room for competitors. Rather, they were sacred "organic" paraphernalia that simply had gotten too old to be used in the way they once were. Over the course of two thousand years the Great Mountain Mother had been impregnated repeatedly, cheered on by tremendous swells of ego, by men who devised and managed her symbolic insemination. Man the artificial predator has begun to reinvent himself now also as an artificial propagator. While the Mother's impregnation surely required climactic rituals, the growth of her abdomen was gradual. And gradually the miners' impressive limestone arts could be neglected.

—That the most likely evolution of the Göbekli Tepe sanctuaries was gradual, and that their entombment was gradual as well, is indicated by the numerous cup-shaped hollows that have been scraped into the tops of many of the menhirs. As the lodges were filled in, the "heads" of menhirs were permitted to protrude above the fill for a considerable duration. Even while the lodges no longer functioned, lime dust was scraped from hollows atop the menhir testicles, apparently to be used as a special potent paint or fertility medicine. And even though the sanctuaries were being filled in, the people's faith in the efficacy of the menhir substances and of the maternal support structure endured.

—Similar usage of powders, scraped from *menhirs*, has been documented in western Celtic areas clear into the twentieth century. There such powders were consumed, suspended in water, to enhance conception and fertility.[40] From the total profile of the *menhir* ideology, which emerges at Göbekli Tepe, it seems probable that scrapings from these more ancient *menhirs* were being collected for similar purposes. If my overall interpretation of the Göbekli Tepe archaeology is approximately on target, then this place will eventually be recognized as fountainhead for derivative Celtic practices and beliefs.

Leveling the Genders: While the cult of *menhirs* declined, the sanctuary lodges were intentionally filled in with miners' debris.

[40]For additional relevant sources see Mircea Eliade. *Patterns in Comparative Religion.* New York and Scarborough, 1958, pages 216-238.

And the crotch of the Earth Mother was being covered. As the Great Mother was allowed more privacy, there occurred a leveling process among the genders. This fact can be seen engraved in stone in an interesting manner. In the filled enclosures, gigantic *menhirs* were allowed to protrude above the surface of the debris for a span of time. People could continue to reach the crest surfaces of the testicle tops from which they scraped cup-shaped hollows, to obtain some dust that served as life-advancing medicine (Figure 30).

Fig. 30. *Menhirs* with hollows scraped into the top. Enclosure B.
Source: Klaus Schmidt, 2010, Photo by Irmgard Wagner, courtesy of DAI.

—But then, behold! From the limestone surface of the post-partition female sanctuary (Figure 28), similar hollows have been scraped along its rim. This points to a time at Göbekli Tepe when female life essences were respected as life-advancing substances next to those of the male *menhirs*. Because a single sculptor-priest set up his mini-sanctuary without male *menhirs*, the notion of female self-sufficiency could begin to dawn on human minds at this sanctuary. A female altar established concrete premises for mythic possibilities, of discerning the concept of a "virgin birth," perhaps at some time in the future.

—Limestone *menhirs*, anyhow, were substances extracted from the Mountain's limestone ovaries. Strolling across the quarry plateau I saw quite a number of cup-shaped hollows scraped from the raw limestone surfaces which, quite obviously, represented the Earth Mother's raw ovaries from which all those male *menhirs* could be cut. The systematically concentrated occurrence of cup-shaped hollows on squared menhir testicles, and on the Mother's altar (Figure 28), implies additional sanctity that the cult was able to attribute to uncut limestone ovaries.

—Of course, no religion in the evolution or history of humankind has succeeded in permanently balancing a society of "predators." But even with recurring failures, it is fair to ask how much worse our gender relations could have evolved without these quaint limestone improvisations twelve millennia ago.

Predispositions: *As more of those roundish temples at Göbekli Tepe are excavated down to knee levels, benches may appear along the enclosure walls which indicate approximately the size of groups that could be seated there. I was pleasantly amused, and afterward almost shocked, at how familiar some of these rooms appeared to me. I have seen and sat in chambers like these. I have visited Anasazi sites in the Greater Southwest, and the Hopi Indian villages that are still occupied by living humankind. Yes, even in Mexico (e.g. Malinalco) have I found such lodges from the time of the Aztecs. I have been a guest at Hopi village plazas to numerous traditional dance ceremonials. At Shungopovi I sat in a kiva and saw groups of masked katsinas, visiting from other kivas, entering by way of a ladder through an opening in the roof. I have seen them dance as close to me as a hand breadth from my knees. All these memories have produced an exciting historical realization, that, though they were separated from Göbekli Tepe by many millennia, and ended up at the opposite side of the planet, the Middle American, Anasazi, and Pueblo cultures all still lived at similar moments in evolutionary time. Their ceremonials were still all performed by men who, though sedentary at the time, were still stuck in the nostalgias of their vanishing religion as Stone Age hunter-gatherers.*

The menhir idea has travelled far into America, indeed—even in the opposite direction by way of Europe. I have found a menhir set up at a farm homestead, of a Welsh lineage in faraway South Dakota, where no other stones were in sight for miles around. When I inquired about its use, I was told that at this stone two generations of marriages had been sealed, according to a Methodist Christian rite.

—Such coincidences require rethinking of the processes of evolution and diffusion. Up to this point in my career, as a historian of religions, I have examined a variety of Native American traditions—

mostly the religions of men in the Greater Southwest and in Mexico. It was never terribly important for me to ask whether or how their habits might have spread across the width of Asia or into America. It was enough to learn and see human activities in some probable relationship to local geographical and cultural conditions. Such relationships could be observed and examined. But now, certainly, with the discovery of Göbekli Tepe, some turbulence has been introduced into eddies of this writer's mind. The Olmecs had approximately seven thousand years to receive impulses from Anatolia; the Anasazi and Pueblo Indians had eight. But what has happened precisely? When, where, and how? Such questions dare us enlarge our horizons. But then again, such dares also threaten this book with obesity.

—No, the religion of those men at Göbekli Tepe was not just a licentious "fertility cult" as that term is commonly applied and used pejoratively in Western studies about religions. Theirs was the burden of having inherited the hunter-gatherer style of culture, a strategy of violent survival that took millions of years to evolve—that has transformed us into violent *homines sapientes* and walking puzzles unto ourselves. Objectivity and perspective about the larger evolutionary process is almost completely absent in our contemporary self-awareness. And facing crises today—concerning life, death, and weaponry—our own socio-cosmological intelligence is still quite haphazard, and juvenile.

—Today, *Homo faber* (man the maker) still leaps ahead in his evolution, overtaking *Homo sapiens* (man the thinker). Man the maker can now meddle with the creation of life in many new ways that may not—and probably will not—prove to be wise in the longer run. Man the thinker does not yet understand the underlying subject matter that he/she is actually thinking about, nor does he understand how to identify positively the things for which thinking might actually be helpful—or might at least not be more destructive than passions are sometimes by themselves.

—When the light of reason dawned on our ancestors, they found themselves imitating "natural" predators.[41] These proved to be better

[41]Elsewhere in this discussion I am avoiding the terms "natural, supernatural, nature" because these people at Göbekli Tepe could not have held our concept of "nature." By "natural" I mean here "not imposed by humans."

hunters than the newcomers were. But being superior imitators—superior apes—our ancestors became devotees to successful mighty predators by way of accepting them as totemic models, divine tutors, and even as their honorary ancestors. Over the course of millions of years, living in this manner, our ancestors learnt how to be the most effective predators and nuisances on the planet.

—Phallic tools and symbols of life, which the men's societies at Göbekli Tepe have tried to dignify with their repentance-and-atonement cult, were nevertheless pre-defamed by their own pursuit of violence and their general use of weapons. As a result, certain remnants of their ancient symbolism that pertained to "life" have by now been excluded from decent discourse. All the while, the gory glories of the weapon-and-death industries are valued positively by modern propaganda, by the entertainment media and toy marketers, for considerable profit. Death-wielding has been promoted to a point where the natural tools of life are now sometimes blamed for death and decay. Of course, there is a rational linkage, of sorts. Life is indeed a prerequisite for death.

The Military Industrial Complex: Already in Chapter Two I have alluded to military-industrial complexes. Indeed, it appears that the earliest Near Eastern kingdoms and empires still sent workmen to flint hills in eastern Anatolia to mine flints for spear and arrow points.[42] These materials were used to equip the earliest armies that whipped Near Eastern civilizations into shape. It is possible that extravagant religious cults of weapon-makers, twelve thousand years ago at Göbekli Tepe, already sowed the seed for extravagant military adventures that were to be undertaken during subsequent millennia. Göbekli Tepe has not remained the last place on Earth where violence and religious extremes were being cultivated together—to justify and to incite each other. Moreover, religious solutions do not always succeed in their attempts of balancing, especially when acts of balancing are attempted by people who remain imitators, predators, warriors, and hunters at heart.

---

[42]If my memory serves me right, some years back, while reading translations of ancient royal Hittite texts, I came onto a royal degree that regulated the manufacture and acquisition of flint-weapon points, possibly up in the Göbekli Tepe flint hills region. I have no access to this citation right now, but it exists.

—Ten thousand years ago, men at Göbekli Tepe did not know what Uranium was. Nevertheless, while contemplating "progress" in the evolution of their weapons industry, I feel motivated to confess another predisposition which pertains to a more recent transition. Old fashioned atonement problems still resonate today.

Predisposition: *Toward the end of 1953 I travelled through Tennessee and took a photograph of the Oak Ridge plant in which the bombs for Hiroshima and Nagasaki were made—or at least this I was told. I learnt a little later that Oak Ridge at that time was home to the largest percentage of people with Ph.D. degrees, and also the highest percentage of Bible-reading people with such academic degrees—people who were inclined to take prophesies concerning Armageddon and their own roles in the Divine Drama seriously. The flint weapons industry at Göbekli Tepe, somehow, has reminded me of those rumors about the Oak Ridge situation sixty years ago. Weapon industries and fan clubs (e.g. National Bow associations), and organized religion for their justification, appear to have been dancing partners already 12,000 years ago.*

—**Lives, Knives, and Domestication:** Hunters came to the Göbekli Tepe area to mine flint, and they probably carried additional flint nodules up the hill from lower ledges. They would flake and knap these raw materials into tools and weapons. Hunters would come to this place to trade venison for weapons. The flint industry on this mountain was the cutting edge of the Stone Age hunter-gatherer culture, and that culture flourished, and then began to convulse and expire up there at the slope of their tailings hill. It was a sacred hill that hunters, miners, and weapon manufacturers compiled between 12,000 and perhaps 9,500 years ago. Hunter-gatherer culture expired there in stone temples—that is, in exclusive hunter lodges—where men staged pantomimes of atonement with the Earth Mother. An artificial predator, *Homo sapiens,* hoped to make amends for his general violence in hunting, mining, and weapons manufacture.

—When Göbekli Tepe miners found flint eggs under limestone slabs, amongst the strata which they systematically broke and crushed, they thought about flakes of flint, about sharp edges for cutting, scraping, and piercing. They improvised chisels, axes, spear-points, and arrowheads. And whenever these practical hunters saw a prey animal in the wild, their first thoughts were about spear, arrow, and knife.

Predisposition: *The cultural transition at Göbekli Tepe, which ordinary huntsmen could not possibly have foreseen, brings to mind for me the work of a good friend, Hansjakob Wiederhold, who introduced cattle into New Guinea. The natives there for whom he made these efforts were still hunters at heart. Men who considered becoming farmers were given some training, plus a cow to care for. The animal was to be paid for with returning her first calf to the ranch for redistribution. The cow and subsequent calves were then for the farmer to keep. The calf in payment would be raised and given to another farmer candidate. This was the plan. Years later I asked him about the greatest obstacle that he might have encountered in New Guinea. He made a memorable point: "These natives whom I taught animal husbandry have all along remained hunters at heart. When they saw a cow, their first thought was not calf, but knife."*

—People of the Göbekli Tepe flint-stone culture, who lived by killing, mining, and weapons manufacture, sought atonement by way of a softer limestone religion. Had we ended up in China some eight or seven millennia later, we could have met the sage Lao Tzu and he could have told us all we wanted to know about hardness vis-à-vis softness—about the balance of Heaven and Earth—about Yang and Yin. He could have done it abstractly without referring concretely to Flint Culture or to Limestone Religion. But he would have understood quite well what we are talking about.

—At some point in Chapter Nineteen we will touch down in China several centuries prior to the sage Lao Tzu. We will get to see quite a lot of Flint culture in the process of converting to Bronze metallurgy. In due time this culture of violence evoked protests on the part of Lao Tzu and other classics teachers—provoked complaints against imperial excesses in "hardness." A hunter/warrior culture, just arriving there, was trying to "civilize" the Chinese motherland. Much of that Yang abuse happened at the Shang capital city named "Yin"—a homonym with another meaning, of course.

PART TWO:
EVOLUTION, CULTURE, AND RELIGION

What is Culture? What is Religion?

Culture is the sum of human ego-assertions—is what
humankind think they are imposing on ordinary nature.
Religion is the response to apparent
greater-than-human configurations of reality—is
the awareness of what such configurations
are imposing on humankind.
The difference between "history of culture" and
"history of religion" is dalliance between the
two—is change of culture in light of religion,
and of religion in light of culture.
The difference between "history" and "evolution" is
the length of time of changes under consideration.
Had this book been written only for historians of
religions, Chapter Ten could have been offered as
introduction. But most readers with an interest
in Göbekli Tepe have evolutionary and
archaeological questions up front.
This chapter summarizes the author's theoretical
bridge over which he walked toward
Göbekli Tepe—to understand its religion.

10. What is Culture? What is Religion?

Toward an Evolutionary Theory of Religions

Since the days when some of my professors—not all—insisted that questions concerning "the origin and the evolution of religion" do not belong in the history of religions field *(Religionswissenschaft)*, almost half a century has gone hiding in soft lobes of human memory. "All questions about origins should be left to metaphysics," these men advised their students. They recommended steering clear of the "origin" questions, as well as of the "evolution" of anything religious. All previously attempted evolutionary approaches to the subject matter were judged as failures by these mentors. Their views were probably in agreement with the majority of historians of religions at that time, and perhaps at some schools today they still would be.

—With this bundle of cautions, so it seemed to me already back then, the boundaries of our academic discipline were being drawn unnecessarily tight. What harm could be done if the connotation of "historical change" were also to be considered under the larger rubrics of general "development" or "evolution?" And what would remain of the study of ordinary history if ordinary evolutionary processes of change were to be discounted? But then, different words mean different things to different people.[1] I read the literature of teachers who informed my professors, as well as the writings of those who concocted the theories of religious evolution that became problematic over time.

—It need not surprise anyone that early theories of cultural and religious evolution turned out to be unstable. Their authors were chasing abstract subject matter through fuzzy evolutionary sequences. The problem was this: If one started with qualitative definitions of

[1]Already back then, in the recesses of this writer's mind, it seemed as though the entire debate about "evolution" was a tempest in an English teapot. Whenever he switched to reasoning about these matters in German, the problem seemed to disappear. Yet, obstinately he stuck to working in English.

religious subject matter, such as with theisms defined essentially by the number of deities involved, or with concepts such as spirit, anima, mana, or the holy, it was not easy to link up with empirically anchored data. Attempting to project such concepts back to prehistoric eras—to early culture strata which themselves had been defined qualitatively as "savagery" or "barbarism"—resulted in additional vagaries. Such efforts have allowed us to pay only perfunctory attention to the physical data that paleontologists, archaeologists, anthropologists or zoologists were accumulating in the field. Such theoretical initiatives cast doubts on the "evolution of religion" models that had been proposed. Evolutionary approaches that were based on qualitative and abstract foci could not produce conclusions that were any sharper.

—My "experience-response spectrum," Figure 32, was designed to bring empirical data and general knowledge concerning religious behavior into closer proximity.[2] But my answer to the challenge of my teachers was not formulated until about five years later, during the fall of 1969. It was not widely published until 1991.

—A common misconception about "religion in evolution" has all along been that among successive stretches of time, as in a progression, each level has been supplanted by a next higher level of refinement. So for instance, the trailblazing anthropology of Lewis Henry Morgan (1818-1881) identified a hunter-gatherer stage and called it "savagery."[3] He progressed to domestication, agriculture, and metalworking and called them "barbarism." Finally he recognized the art of writing as being the hallmark of "civilization." Morgan's continuum of linear evolutionary progress provided Karl Marx and Friedrich Engels with their sequential structure and with sufficient gaps into which they could insert the "class struggles" of their own theory. Upon their general model of dialectics, of progress within a historical material process, these founders of Communism built a world model that required and deserved a Proletarian revolution.

—The pioneer of American cultural anthropology, Lewis Henry Morgan, was no fool; but his sketches about the functioning of ancient society never quite rose to the level of a workable field theory.

---

[2]See the Section below, "The Teeter-totter of Experiences and Responses,"with Figure 31.

[3]Lewis Henry Morgan. *Ancient Society*, or *Researches in the Lines of Human Progress from Savagery, through Barbarism to Civilization. 1877.*

I will not reject evolutionary hypotheses as failed attempts outright—especially not those of pioneers. Instead, I will again publish here my five successive levels of cultural adaptation, almost exactly as in 1991. All levels of human cultural adaptation, in their heydays, needed to be associated and balanced with matching religious responses—in context of thought as well as in physical behavior.[4]

ca. 300 years ago: ideologies of democratic revolts—

ca. 3,000 years ago: universal salvation protests—

ca. 5,000 years ago: hyper-domestication by warriors—

ca. 10,000 years ago—domestication by herders and planters—

ca. 6 million years ago—gathering, scavenging, hunting—

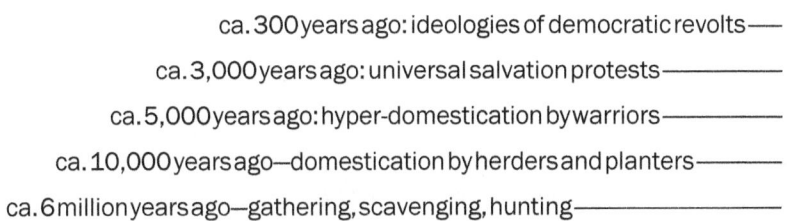

Fig. 31. The Accumulation of Five Levels of Culture

—It should be emphasized that the five levels of culture, and of adaptation, are "successive" only with regard to their beginnings in time. They do not displace anything. All five adaptive levels of cultural complexity and of concomitant religion that I am proposing, still exist today. I personally have been active at all five levels. None of them has been superseded. This means that Morgan's idea of a linear "progress" has no place in my teaching vocabulary. Relapses to simpler levels of adaptation may become necessary, or desirable, as more complex lifestyles run into their natural limitations.

—As a matter of fact, many exceptionally successful modern people, in the free time that they have earned as rewards for modern work and skills, are reverting periodically to earlier or simpler levels of human adaptation—such as hunting, fishing, gathering, gardening, handicrafts, and walking—and they call these returns into prehistory their personal "recreation." Both "rebirth" and "recreation" are concepts of the mythological and religious kind.

—As Morgan, Marx, Engels and many social scientists or historians have done, I am classifying types of human culture according to the material adaptations by which people sustain themselves. The link between culture and religion appears obvious. Types of culture

[4]My "five levels of adaptation," as evolutionary accumulations, were published in the "Introduction" to *Egyptian Light and Hebrew Fire*. Karl W. Luckert. Albany, State University of New York Press, 1991, pp. 21-27.

define a people's mode of aggression; they also set up those same people to experience corresponding modes of guilt and to respond, accordingly, with matching types of retreat behavior. Their types of guilt do modulate their religious experiences and affect their overall behavior. I will therefore attempt to link my "evolution and history of religions" model to existential, intellectual, as well as material human involvements.

The Teeter Totter of Experiences and Responses

Though I was largely aware of my personal presuppositions to learning, my approach to teaching about religions has been significantly affected by so-called scientific materialism. This confession will come as a surprise to some of my friends.[5] Indeed, teachers who wish to communicate with their students do, inevitably, end up using words that those students will understand most easily. I have also noticed how the applied sciences and technologies of the English Industrial Revolution have honed the English language to a point where it actually favors empiricism and scientific materialism. This is not to say that Marx and Engels influenced the English language, but rather, that both men prospered nicely within the verbal thickets of English empiricism. They struggled to crawl away from the entwining boughs —*dem Schlingen Gewächs*—of their native German tongue. Marx and Engels responded positively to English empirical categories. Marx wrote his most important works while he was surrounded by the noises of London. In stark contrast, his native German language never surrendered to experimental science its categories of *Geist* or *Geisteswissenschaften,* which have no precise equivalents in English.[6]

—After an interval of hesitation and astonishment, I felt obliged to acknowledge, regarding the formation of my personal theory of

---

[5]The references to Marx and scientific materialism, in this section, are an accommodation to the fact that Part Two and Three of this book were first written upon request from scholars in the People's Republic of China. On second thought, this coincidence may contribute fresh defining lines also to a Western dialogue.

[6]English is the perfect language for manufacturing scientific categories. Not even Sigmund Freud's psychoanalytic theory, in Das Ich und das Es (1923) sounded really scientific until "es" was mistranslated into English and objectified as "id." Thenceforth the "Es-Bezogenheit" could be studied scientifically as a specific, respectable something.

religion, indebtedness to the current English vocabulary of scientific empiricism and materialism. When in 1968 I gave my first college-level introductory lecture to the history of religions field, after some slowdowns in communication, I noticed that my students had been taught to think along the lines of raw English pluralism and Marxist materialism. So, with chalk in hand, at the blackboard, I adapted and transposed my explanations of religious experience to raw quantifiable and measureable categories. I did not notice at the time that I was also resolving a systematic problem for atheistic psychology as well as for Marxist materialism. Beyond this, the Teeter Totter scale can be used as a theoretical bridge between theism and atheism.

control experiment hypothesis analysis familiarity fascination awe fear/trembling surrender

I______I______I______I______I______I______I______I______I

range of cultural aggression ______I_______ range of religious retreat

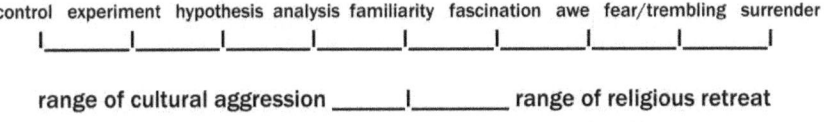

Fig. 32. The Teeter Totter of Experience and Responses

—Of course, qualitative words that define characteristics such as "holy" or "sacred," remain real and meaningful as well. There exist optional versions of linguistic "software." If communication requires, one can talk about qualities by using quantitative scales—thus talk about qualities which contain more of this or less of that trait. All one needs to do is to extend the experiential intensity scale (the Teeter Totter scale, Figure 32) from scientific experimentation toward the dimension of religion, and thereby bridge the culture side of the scale to the religion portion on the right. Together, both dimensions represent a continuum that is able to accommodate degrees of human experience. To distinguish religion from science, one does not really need to refer to "spirit" or "matter." All one needs to do is become aware that human awareness is limited.

—As long as we acknowledge the fact that all through life we are surrounded, we can encounter and experience (1) reality configurations that are less than we, (2) reality configurations that are greater than we and (3) reality configurations that are our potential equals. The latter category, at the middle of the scale, turns out to be quite narrow in scope. It comes into focus only at the fulcrum where aggression and retreat are balanced by egalitarian communication and harmonic coexistence.

—Religion is the human response to so-conceived and so-experienced greater-than-human situations or configurations of reality. The range of religious experiences extends (1) from the egalitarian midpoint of "familiarity" along the right side of the experiential intensity scale. (2) The mildest form of religious experience may so be designated as "fascination." (3) The midpoint of the religious portion, of the right half of the total experiential scale, may be indicated by "awe." For example, the kind of experience attributed to the Prophet Muhammad, upon seeing the angel: it is said that he froze in awe so that "he could move neither forward nor backward."[7] (4) The next intense religious experiential degree can then be marked as "fear and trembling." And (5) the ultimate religious degree of intensity amounts to full "surrender" of the self.

—At the midpoint of the scale, at the point of egalitarian "familiarity," the experiential Teeter Totter of any rational individual must balance. Potential equals communicate at this point and share. There they propagate and thrive. All species provide nurture and survive at this averaged center.

—The scale that is offered here is also suitable to illustrate the teachings of the Buddha—by subdividing the four segments along the right half of the scale into halves—thereby indicating the eight progressive steps along the Eightfold Path. A more common example would be the case of a human family. After a child is born, parents naturally assume de facto "divine authority" over the child, for a limited time. Beyond human examples our definition of religion is expandable to fit other species. One only needs to plot the average balanced behavior of another species at the midpoint of its own total scale. And thereby, for example, a dog becomes eligible to have revelations regarding its religious relationship of dependence vis-à-vis some greater-than-canine human master.

—A human person is too small to be "Nature." He or she cannot pretend to know where the "supernatural" dimension begins. Moreover, we face even greater difficulties when we try to distinguish the "natural" from anything else. Thus, our Teeter Totter scale does not

---

[7]Ibn Ishak (?-768 CE), as quoted in Thor Andrae, *Mohammed, the Man and His Faith.* New York, Harper Torchbooks, 1960, p. 44. "Awe" is also illustrated by St. Peter the disciple, as quoted in St. Matthew's "Transfiguration" account: "Lord, it is pleasant to be here; let us build three huts...." There was no need either to move higher or to return to the valley.

distinguish a supernatural dimension from reality. As one of Lévy-Brühl's "primitives," this author knows himself only as a human being that knows some of its limits.[8] He knows the line where the greater-than-human, the super-human, dimension begins for him.

—Every human mind thinks scientifically as well as religiously or theologically. Whenever we contemplate subject matter as greater-than-human realities we theologize. When we examine subject matter as less-than-human things, so as to consider them for analysis, experimentation, or control, we proceed scientifically. During some rare moments our thoughts may be balanced in "humanistic" fashion, among potential equals—at the midpoint of the scale. The experiential scale can be applied regardless of whether matter is greater than mind, or mind is considered more important than matter, and regardless of whether Hegel or Marx are accepted or rejected. To communicate rationally, we may orient ourselves along that intensity scale among facts that are measurable. Accordingly, Marx and Engels would predict that "religion" someday will wither away. But they forgot to consider the greater-than-human boundary that all humans are destined to bump up against. The greater-than-human dimension will never go away unless humans themselves become almighty—and then, obviously, it would be impossible to be religious anymore.

—Of course, people are great enough to target a word like "religion" and swear that they will never use it again, and afterward pretend that "religion" and the greater-than-human dimension have disappeared altogether. So, for Marx and Engels this seemed an easy prediction to make. In the evolution of languages, all words eventually wither away. But this withering process only changes words for superficial identification and communication. For every word-symbol that becomes politically inconvenient, several replacement words are invented. It is then only a matter of time before a favorite is selected by conventional usage. Indeed, a particularly scary word may become dominant during a period of civil commotion. Then, for a while, historians can build careers and become prominent by writing books about "revolution," about "war and peace," or about "terror."

---

[8]Cf. Lucien Lévy-Brühl. *How Natives Think* (1910). Lévy-Brühl distinguished two basic mindsets, "Primitive" and "Western." He describes the mental activity of primitives as "mystical participation." See also Footnote 19, page 170.

—Greater-than-human realities may be, or may not be, truly what we perceive them to be. In similar fashion, those arguing from the popular scientific side do not really know whether experimental scientific objects, the less-than-human units of reality, are really what they understand them to be. It only means that for the time being we think we can get away with manipulating them. I call attention to the fact that scientists today are as frightened as anyone else, because during the twentieth century their colleagues figured out how to split the Uranium atom into smaller units. Their fears are of an existential nature—which is, they are religious responses to inconspicuous, but nevertheless fear-inspiring and therefore "greater-than-human" subatomic fragments, "enriched" perhaps by ignorant administrative policies. In the course of human evolution, the gods have revealed themselves in various numbers and sizes. With a little bit of luck and effort, even a tiny virus can scare or defeat a mighty human hero—or an army. All the virus needs to do is enjoy multiplying among potential equals.

—While proceeding along the experiential dimension toward the right end on the scale, the need for precise definitions decreases. To share or not to share our experiences, or "how" to share them, is the central question for those who try to balance their lives near the midpoint of the scale—to share in the company of potential equals.

Religion as Process and Quest for Balance

Since my first day of teaching about the experiential scale I have envisioned it as the beam of a Teeter Totter. The metaphor served me well for all introductory lessons to the history of religions. Seeing this theoretical model as a children's playground fixture does suggest its expanded validity for all developmental stages in human life. Ascribing to the scale a pivot at the middle illustrates our need for balance. The principle of a pivoted Teeter Totter scale, and the need for balance, are never outgrown when children become adults. But as children prosper and succeed in the adult world, they are continually obliged to create fresh imbalances, for power and profit. Nevertheless, to the extent that humanity wishes to survive, it must dedicate its energies also to the quest for co-operational balance.

—The point to which all life on earth moves, with a great variety of religious and scientific responses, is ultimate surrender in death. In the course of every organism's life, death is prefigured by cycles of fatigue and rest, of falling asleep. We inhale and eat, but we must surrender our intake sooner or later. Ritualized paths recommend to their devotees "submission or surrender of the ego," to be achieved ritually already during lifetime—as something to be practiced and perfected. Nevertheless, all the religious paths of humankind, in one form or other, distinguish degrees of gradual surrender, of learning, or among shades of knowing. They carefully distinguish temporary and less intense surrenders—thus, changeable states of awareness that differ from the finality of surrendering one's ego unreservedly at the moment of death.

—The larger a society, the greater are the imbalances it creates—and the more organized must therefore be the religious efforts of harmonizing such imbalances. And then again, if religions fail to provide the goals which they set, certain perplexed pilgrims may despair and blame religion for their own cultural failures. Rational "retreats" from irrational battles may be identified as causes for having lost the war. In human struggles, those who interfere as peacemakers can easily get blamed for the embarrassing predicaments that combatants have gotten themselves into—which is, embarrassments that were exposed by the interference of a peacemaker.

—Alert reformers can try to resuscitate a weak religious tradition; they can also abandon a particular path as a hopeless venue. In this manner, some religions are being reformed with valorized theologies and with refocused concepts of salvation, while others are being trashed by reactionary atheists or by fanatic fresh theists. But then, inasmuch as no human mind has ever been able to reinvent itself from scratch, any fresh start must begin with paraphrasing older problems on hand of available solutions. In real life, new problems and solutions are the offspring of antecedents, of older problems and solutions. Older solutions must always first be understood in terms of the older problems which they resolved in bygone times.

—Persons who find themselves entangled in modern chaotic situations may evaluate inherited "Old Time religion" as being truer, simpler and purer. To the extent that older solutions are being preserved and ritually enacted, faithful followers of a Path may turn nostalgic. They may try to restore obsolete levels of early culture, in hope of making older religious solutions relevant. They reintroduce the old problems that initially made revelatory solutions necessary. But some older religious answers no longer can resolve all present human problems effectively. Still, older fragments of culture and religion will always be important to obtain rational historical perspectives.

—All problems and solutions, approached by human intellect at various levels of culture, tend to be made more complex over time. Those flint arrow heads, at Göbekli Tepe, possibly besmeared with serpentine venom, have meanwhile gotten enlarged to the magnitude of nuclear missiles and canisters of poison gas. New technologies and materials have gotten uploaded onto our personal experiential Teeter Totter planks. Religious retreats, of trying to escape back to earlier and to simpler days, may promise less ballast on our existential scales, but they cannot remedy all modern imbalances.

—Scientific experiments allow for only one category of human experience—just as eating a meal engages only one extremity of our total alimentary equipment—namely, the portion that is most suitable for aggressive behavior. Scientific experiments pertain to the left side of our scale, and they involve (1) the task of familiarizing oneself with facts, (2) analyzing these facts by reducing them conceptually to safe and manageable portions, (3) proposing a hypothesis that can reach beyond the known facts, (4) undertaking controlled experimentation that yields measurable similarities and differences, and finally (5) exploitation of newly obtained knowledge, for additional control, to determine starting points for future rounds of experimentation. Thus, from the center of our experiential scale, the scientific portion of the scale extends left from familiarity to analysis, hypothetical rearrangement, experimentation, and the entire realm of conquest and control.

—The entire pursuit of scientific experimentation is suited only for studying and for understanding reality configurations that are of less-than-human scope. This is so because the scope of experimental science is limited to understanding realities that are judged *a priori* to be inferior to man, and therefore controllable by experimentation. Any experimental confrontation with potential equals will naturally lead to interpersonal struggles on one hand, or to accommodation, compromise, and a possible measure of egalitarian interplay at the other. In either instance, the key objectives of science will be eclipsed. Then, any confrontation with greater-than-human realities may lead to fascination and poetic depth, to shudders, trembling and holy fear, and eventually to an ego's surrender.

—Metaphorically speaking, on the right side of the scale the scientifically inclined human manipulator becomes himself or herself an object of experimentation—an "object" at the disposal of greater-than-human reality—that is, if greater reality were indeed inclined to stoop to our style of scientific tinkering. Scientific control at one end of the scale is existentially negated at the other end where all activities fade in religious surrender. The starting point of scientific experimentation—as of religious experience—lies at the "familiarity" midpoint along the scale. It is the only point along the scale where the human mind is free to pursue neutral, unprejudiced observation.

—Also at this midpoint, labeled "familiarity," any would-be equals engage in egalitarian sharing in accordance with the Golden Rule—with the universal rule of ethics that governs egalitarian relations. If the Golden Rule were applied to dealings with scientific objects, one would be raising their status to a point of equality, and this would prohibit experimentation and transform science either into play or conquest. Of course, it is possible for an "aspect" or part of a human person temporarily to be considered a lesser subject matter, available for scientific research or medical treatment. But this step is ethically feasible only after that smaller portion of a person has been analytically and contractually differentiated from the remainder of the person that contains and retains ego awareness. The essential ego portion—the integrity of a person—neither can nor should be subjected to scientific experimentation.

—Egalitarian "experiments" at the midpoint of the scale may be no more than playfulness. By the same token, the relationship of potential partners, from that midpoint onward, can indeed be overwhelmed by stress if one partner utilizes the other scientifically as an experimental object, or simply as something less than equal. From the same midpoint of playfulness, moving to the right on the scale, it is also possible to idolize potential equals.

—In any case, the graduated steps of sensing religious intensities or weaknesses—are fascination, awe, fear and trembling, and surrender. Along the total length of the experiential scale, all the way from conquest to surrender, the language of scientific materialism is suited only to comment on the left half of the scale. Relations with greater-than-human realities require a different vocabulary and attitude. Scientific materialism cannot explain more than half the scope which disciples or comrades, as human fellows, are apt to experience from the day they are born until the day they die. A worldview that is fifty percent in tune, and fifty percent out of focus, will only be able to understand half the range of possible human experiences. Proponents of such an orientation have a chance of understanding other people perhaps slightly more than half of the time.

Types of "Religion" and "Religions"

In the universal/singular case, "religion" is a noun that refers to a pattern of behavior which tends to counter-balance culture-generated aggression. If religious retreats, i.e. attempts at balancing aggressions, appear faint or failing, or if battles are lost, then organized religion often gets blamed for conditions that it tried to prevent in the first place. Inasmuch as religion *reacts* to culture's ways, it earns blame for whatever its interferences help or fail to produce. Strictly speaking, there are no such things as religious victories. At best there are peaceful religious retreats, defeats, or avoided victories. In the history of religions some efforts at balancing human behavior have indeed been able to limit conflict and to postpone violence. Periods of calm have indeed been achieved. But insofar as calm must be sustained with mythological assurances of "justification," any kind of religious doctrine of justification may, in the end, be held liable if a religiously comforted culture mobilizes for rounds of revenge, thus perverting its religious justification into fresh liabilities.

—Any kind of creature that attacks anything or anyone, and that intermittently retreats, acts religiously. Living beings that are involved in a quest for food, and that capture, harvest, bite, swallow or absorb, also "retreat" for periods of rest—and thereby their religiosity is made manifest. If it is animals that do the retreating or balancing, we may categorize their behavior as "animal religion." However, to understand the point of this chapter, a reader need not go so far as to acknowledge the existence of animal religion. Let us consider here, simply, the religions of humankind. If large numbers of common folk manage to retreat to a behavioral equilibrium, we may call that "folk religion." If their levels of culture appear simple and primitive, we may recognize "primitive religion." Every religious solution, generally, is adjusted to the "primitiveness level" of its host culture. Every answer must respond, more or less, to the level of complexity of the questions that is being raised. On the other hand, every answer must establish its relevance to a culture's current degree of "complexity."

A religious innovation, in order to become rele-vant, must carry the proper amount of rational weight—not too little and not too much. Where rituals are being staged by shamans, we talk of "shamanism." If a single person finds his or her balance of retreat behavior in a personal style, we speak of "personal religion." Then, inasmuch as for millions of years, males and females have labored for separate goals at various intensities, it is also reasonable—though not always advisable—to distinguish between male and female types of religiosity.

—People that live in small tribal societies may have their religions classified as "tribal" or as "small-scale" religions. However we choose to name them, we are not really characterizing religiosity as such; rather, we associate religiousness with social or cultural features that are more easily nameable. Levels of cultural complexity, and sizes of populations, do indeed determine the type of imbalances that religious responses eventually are expected to solve. Among larger populations we find class strata, competition among nations, as well as entire clusters of civilization that have become visible in history. Accordingly, we may think about "national religions" or about major "world religions."

—Atheism does not necessarily render a person irreligious. The blessed Buddha taught an atheistic doctrine, concerning a path to enlightenment, and thereby he became the founder of one of the great world religions. Greater-than-human reality—because it exceeds the human ego all around—can actually be envisioned along both dimensions along the scale, and can be scored in both "positive" and "negative" numbers. Inexplicable "positive visions" (e.g. Heaven) and inexplicable "negative light" (e.g. Nirvana) can overwhelm a human mind with approximately equal intensity. Inexplicability by itself is sufficient to indicate whether or not we are approaching the greater-than-human dimension.

—Marx and Engels, in spite of what they said or wrote, submitted to the greater material Process of History. And as if to endorse the religious significance of these two men, somewhere in China one can find a temple built in honor of a more recent prince among atheists, Chairman Mao Tse Dong. Surely against his will, he has become recognized as a god. This fate, in China, has caught up even with a theist who recognized no God but Allah. Hu Dahai, a Muslim general who served the first Ming emperor, lies buried in Nanjing. He also sits enthroned as god in a boundary temple in Gansu, from which he benevolently faces in the direction of a population of Tibetans. I have visited both his tomb and his temple, thrice. Three decades after the Cultural Revolution, Tibetan "Buddhists" donated lumber to help rebuild this Han boundary temple.

—If a reader disagrees with the schema implied in the graduated experiential ontology of the Teeter Totter scale, I accept the fact that I am failing in my attempt at communication here. But there exists absolutely no doubt that someday will bring agreement, when the person endorses my scale at his point of final surrender in death. Of course, I will not then insist that he take time out and respond to the argument of this book—not at his most holy and private moment. If he happens to be a theist, let us say a practicing Muslim, he will have no trouble understanding the experiential scale. His prayer gestures anticipate his point of final surrender five times each day. If, on the other hand, he is committed to scientific materialism instead, his personal surrender can be cushioned by the fact that all along he has practiced thinking of himself as a material entity. This mental discipline, of seeing his ego diffused in matter, is a preparatory atheistic variety of religious surrender. Not much of his essence will need to change for him when he simply is being converted into a more authentic clump of it.

11. From Hunting to Domestication

The evolutionary transition from hunting to domestication has widely been named "Neolithic Revolution." Before considering religious responses for this transition, one must be aware of a variety of material and strategic implications. The dialogue of this chapter prepares for its continuation in Chapter Twelve, which will consider an alternate route of transition, from hunting directly into the exaggerated phase of "hyper-domestication."

The Fate of Roamers and Settlers

The hunter and miner religion at Göbekli Tepe (Abdomen Hill), as far as can be surmised at this point in its excavations, was for the most part a retrenchment for salvaging hunter-gatherer culture—more so than a confident step forward into an agricultural or biological revolution. But then, people who during ceremonial rounds enact rites of atonement are assuming a posture of religious retreat. They are repenting, and culturally they linger mostly at the defensive or submissive level. These huntsmen, as weapon makers, hesitated along the frontier of their Hunting and Flintstone culture. While wavering there they sought and found refuge in Limestone religion. But, having said this much about the boundary of progress along which men in sanctuaries at Abdomen Hill were having their second thoughts, one should also bear in mind that a predatory mind, that took millions of years to evolve, could be converted only very slowly. Alongside taking physical steps, mental reorientation needed to happen with many incremental intellectual discoveries. These needed to be planted in human minds, and be cultivated there, as many small axiomatic seed ideas.

—Excavations at the Southwest Hill of Göbekli Tepe, at the slopes of Level Two and on the Northwest Hill, have now brought to light fresh indications of change which point in the direction of domestication. One must assume that orthodox totemic hunter folk, who participated in the larger atonement and religious awakening trend, did so still mostly in order to balance their hunter existence. Eventually and probably, most of these people moved away from the area still as hunters, and many migrated northward through the mountains. They went on to populate Europe and Asia. Those who drifted east across Asia may have helped push Ice Age populations and advance migrations over the land bridge into the Americas, ahead of themselves, while following others. A group that drifted into Southeast Asia may have mingled with people who later carried megalithic habits into the Indonesian and Pacific realms.

—All this does not mean that people who participated at Göbekli Tepe's two millennia of growth and evening glow actually migrated to all those distant places themselves. But it is possible that traces of Neolithic cult places, of which modifications appeared subsequently in Celtic Europe and in the Americas, still await discovery across Asia. We can expect them to be found in association with limestone plateaus and flint mines.

—In any case, at some time between four and five thousand years ago, the megalithic vogue seems to have reached Middle America. There the roaming populations, whirling and eddying, proceeded to block the isthmus which was the natural geographical funnel for movements from North into South America. On that narrow strip of land, drifting and compacting populations could not survive by hunting and gathering. They needed to become sedentary planters, and so they were forced to coalesce defensively into political concentrations and systems of hyper-domestication. The most important American domesticated plants were maize in Mexico and potatoes in Peru. Both cultivars seem to have come into use there as early as ten to seven millennia ago.

—From Middle America the mound builders with their planter culture, propelled by population pressures, eddied back northward into the Greater Southwest and also further east into the Mississippi and Missouri basins. Generally in North America, Middle American influences of mound builders reverberated as far north as maize and potatoes were planted in pre-Columbian times.

—Ten thousand years ago, there also were populations that continued living along the Fertile Crescent and in Anatolia, and these people pioneered a variety of domestication enterprises. The general consensus among pre-historians still appears to be that goats, sheep, pigs, and cattle were first domesticated along the upper arc of the Fertile Crescent. For exploring the next larger picture in that area we are advised to keep an open eye on what is being excavated a little farther west of Göbekli Tepe, at Çatalhöyük. India and Africa are now also being mentioned as seperate places for the domestication of cattle. The practice of herding and animal husbandry may have spread from the Upper Fertile Crescent southward along the rivers of Mesopotamia. However, most of the early domesticator settlements there may have gotten buried under alluvial sands, over time.

—Domestication practices were brought from the Fertile Crescent into Europe by 7,000 years ago. The first Neolithic settlements in China began about that same time with the Yangshao culture, along the Yellow River. The Dawenko people in the Shandong region were roughly contemporary. The Longshan, 4,500 years ago, were beginning to populate the area where the Shang dynasty eventually took hold.[9]

—City-based "civilization," an indication of hyper-domestication, began in Egypt, Mesopotamia, and in the Indus valley almost concurrently, some centuries prior to 5,000 years ago. Organized hyper-domestication was under way in China at least by 3,600 years ago under the Shang Dynasty. Bronze metallurgy, wheeled carriages, as well as the art of writing, were added at Anyang three centuries later.

—If one does postulate the quest for a steady supply of food to be the primary factor in the human struggle, then, at the outset, the introduction of "domestication" must have seemed like a step backward from "the good old days" when hunting and gathering were sufficient. But for the most part it was not human planning; it was geography, the climate, and unforeseen quick increases in regional human populations that caused problems of the magnitude that in turn would cause migrations.

—As a matter of course, hunter bands, wherever they went were inclined to respond to their first food shortages by uniting

[9]For general introductory readings see Patricia Buckley Ebrey, compiler. Http://depts.washington.edu/chinaiv/index.htm.

into teams and hordes. They undertook larger hunting campaigns and invented methods to drive the animals into makeshift enclosures. Because meat shortages in those days were quite likely caused by a general decline among wild animal populations, under pressure from increases in human hunter populations, the technological improvement of weapons and the general intensification of hunting were, in the longer run, all self-defeating.

—Throughout the era of hunting, migrations of people have followed the availability of prey animals. Wherever wild animals moved about, there the hunters were obliged to follow. And the hunters' migrations were energized with fresh optimism when, in small steps, their weapons technology could be improved. This was the dimension in the evolutionary process for which Göbekli Tepe was able to shine for two thousand years.

—In the human quest for food, the domestication of plants and animals eventually were unavoidable measures all around the globe. Adjustments needed to be made wherever herds of wild animals were reduced or decimated, and where wild grains, vegetables, and fruits failed to fill shortages in the food supply. Domestic herds were assembled from among the most docile specimen and from the easiest species of prey animals that could be found. Goats and sheep topped the list of the earliest preferred species. Cattle were added when the supply of wild bovines was thinning out.

Predisposition: *The principle of slaughtering the "wild" and breeding the docile is common sense. As a young boy, this writer himself was the cause of such selective breeding. His father wanted docile cows that a seven-year-old boy could lead, on a rope in his right hand, with a stick in his left, while he himself was guiding the iron plow. The on-hand cow had to be gentle, and the one off-hand needed to have a steady gait and be a little taller to walk in the previous furrow. I had a favorite all-red (rust colored) cow for leading on-hand. Altogether we had five cows in the stall. By the time my all-red favorite was sold to the butcher, eight years after she had been bought as a heifer, three of her daughters had taken her place.*

—Gardens were planted with the most vigorous and most edible cultivars. These emergency measures became a style of survival that compelled groups of people into sedentary living. At some point in time, chasing rare animals was simply no longer practical. But men could not just become domesticators of animals or plants—not without first recovering their own archaic temperaments as less aggressive "gatherers." The Homo sapiens species, which during the era of large-animal hunting had split, culturally along its gender boundary, needed to find ways of living together again, to settle down and to invent their new livelihood together.

—The evolving interdependence between human groups and domesticated herd animals proved to be severe enough to affect human character profiles. As humans became sedentary, they established their own societies after the manner in which they already had entrenched and secured certain domestic herd animals. The herds they owned could at daytime be seen mingling amongst human guardians and owners. Together they all became easy targets for remnant hunters who insisted on pursuing animals in accordance with their old-fashioned ways. The most stalwart hunters continued roaming and scouting, and they were not accustomed to distinguishing between wild and owned animals.

—The clans that moved away from Göbekli Tepe, to continue hunting elsewhere, kept their options open longer for settling at other places at some time in the future. They aligned themselves with other adventurous hunters whose hopes and habits matched their own. Eventually these groups of mobile hunters coalesced to form bands and hordes of warriors. With combined strength, such people then extended and imposed their wills on territories that had been populated earlier—some of which had earlier grown too weak to keep moving. Human settlers were getting included in the target lists of those who persisted on hunting. Any trick that mobile hunters knew how to use against wild animals could be inflicted more effectively on domestic animals, and just as easily on human owners.

—Poorly armed herdsmen and farmers, equipped with tools not designed for combat, toiled among their possessions, scattered in small groups. As weak individuals they often were the only obstacles that stood in the way of gangs of robbers that happened to be craving meat the old-fashioned way. Large numbers of cultivators and nomadic herders were needed, therefore, to cooperate for mutual defense. This fear-induced necessity, even more than the sheer economic factor of an increase in food production, has been the dynamic that was responsible for the growth of human populations and settlements. If, as a male domesticator, you felt incapable of protecting your family, clan, and possessions; if you thought you were too weak, then you needed to raise more boys, more fighters, who eventually could help defend you and other settlers.

—When in the course of time some wandering bands of hunters coalesced to become warrior hordes, those who had settled earlier became vulnerable to ever increasing threats. Eventually it was necessary for sedentary folk to unite for their own security and defense, to withdraw and to corral themselves into walled villages and cities. But then, as people sought refuge behind adobe, wood, and stone, the stationary cities themselves became cherished targets. Organized warriors could conquer and control these cities and, in turn, they knew how to prevail against their own competitors in the name of defense and pre-emptive aggression. Having once fallen into the hands of warlords, villages and cities became fortresses from which victorious conquerors could launch their campaigns of aggression. Peaceful defensive settlements of domesticators were in this manner placed into the service of warlords.

Personal Changes wrought by Domestication

Agriculture, the domestication of plants and animals, implied an economy that entrapped and entangled its originators. Being sedentary enabled them to raise more children, and larger populations instantly made mobility and honest hunting more difficult. Sedentary people kept their nostalgia for hunting alive, of course, and surely some of them occasionally managed to return to the more exciting life of the chase. But by and large, sedentary farmers were stuck in their own progress. The more they prospered as domesticators, the fewer animals could be found in the wild.

—During the period of transition from hunting to domestication, some things that were essential to the self-esteem of hunters appear to have been lost to settlers. A systematic comparison of hunting with subsequent domestic nurture and butchering practices might expose what these ingredients of the hunters' self-esteem could have been. We will therefore compare "hunting" with its subsequent counterpart of "nurture and domestic butchering." We will focus on the general efforts that were required for each. To that end we will weigh these activities in terms of motivation, preparations, pursuit, confrontation, killing, butchering and transportation. We also will consider these efforts in relation to religious rationalizations that were maintained for achieving societal legitimization—required for existential poise and balance.

Motivation: The fact that archaic hunters were motivated by their need for food is obvious. This fact is vouched for by regularly and naturally recurring sensations of hunger. For above-average hunters, winning extra status could be an additional motivation; it could be earned by showing extraordinary valor and skill on the hunting range. By contrast, planters and herders acted with long-range anticipations of future needs. Because domestication labors do require long-range strategies and inventiveness, for storing foods, the momentary physical sensations of hunger are less decisive for initiating daily labors. Instead, strategies, work routines, and methodical sequences were brought into play to streamline the flow of activities. Momentary gratification was subordinated to planning, method, and work routines.

Preparation: Hunters needed to keep their tool kit simple and portable. Provisions also needed to be kept dry and light. Domesticators, in stark contrast, could accumulate larger quantities of equipment and provisions. They even could develop elaborate procedures for manufacture and could establish routines for regular maintenance. Defined somewhat whimsically, culture and civilization began with the accumulation of surplus goods, that is, wherever accumulated goods became too much to carry. Hoarders needed to become sedentary—as if waiting for robbers to lighten their loads before it would make sense for them to move on.

Pursuit: Hunters put most of their efforts into tracking, chasing, waiting in ambush and setting traps. By contrast, domesticators reduced hot pursuit to a minimum. They pre-arranged their quest for food as permanent trap-and-friendship strategies. They modified animal behavior through breeding, confinement, nurture, taming, and friendship. Their vigilance was instead directed against fellow predators—that is, exactly against those competitors whom their ancestral hunters once respected and imitated as totemic divine models. The excitement that hunters experienced while they engaged in hot pursuit was gradually replaced with methodical and ritualized activities—and eventually with grandiose sacrificial feasts to reduce boredom. Depending on the status of the human or divine guests that were invited, or on the amount of ceremonial status that could be earned, plain boring butchering events at group settlements could be magnified to immense feasts of slaughter and potlatches.

Confrontation and Killing: Hunters often enacted their killings as climaxes at the end of exhaustive pursuits. They experienced their "moments of truth" as moments of excitement and as transitions to well-earned rest. By contrast, domesticators prepared their confrontations methodically. Without the jubilant crutches or heroic enhancements, and in sharp contrast to the hunters' genuine joy of victory, domesticators could experience killing and butchering as disappointing acts of cowardice. Such emotions, obviously, lingered in stark contrast to the aforementioned opportunities for staging sacrificial feasts or potlatches.

Butchering and Transport: Hunters faced the arduous task of having to carry home their butchered meat. In cases where it was easier to move families to the killing site, considerable efforts had to be invested on camp reconstruction. In slaughters staged by domesticators, the animals and the celebrants were already in place. More energy could be devoted to formal meals and to intricate rituals that included communal feasting.

Normalization: Ritual procedures for the hunters' self-justification aim at alleviating the guilt of killing, and at justifying slaughters by communal eating. Hunting, pursued as divinely modeled ordained trickery was perpetrated against divinely provided and humanly targeted victims. By contrast, in domestic butchering the weight of ceremonial justification has shifted to claims of divinely guaranteed ownership of living animals, and of property in general. The guilt of killing and eating, among domesticators, became a problem of cult and culture-defined economics which, in turn, was based on divinely granted status and property rights.

Sacrifice and the Economy: Ownership of possessions could be demonstrated among domesticators by offering advance share sacrifices to the gods and contracting divine-human covenants for acquisition. For the legitimate acquisition of entire herds, in some early herder cultures, whole individual share-animals needed to be paid to an original divine owner. The price that had to be paid to the gods was often higher than what poorer people could afford. Thus, religiously justified status, demonstrated in the presence of some deity, might then justify and stabilize a lopsided social order. Full share payments legitimized owning the original breeding stock, not so much because a deity really needed food shares, but to stabilize ownership rights among humankind in a somewhat orderly manner. Theologically, the situation can be understood as the gods having played along in the rituals of humankind, by their grace, to enable human economies, trade, and exchange to begin.

—The modern academic disparagement over ancient sacrificial practices, therefore, is not so much an indication of superior civilized understanding, but rather an indication of ignorance regarding the practical reasons required for balancing a society of early domesticators and first-time owners. To arrive at a better understanding of the original problems, one need only imagine large populations in posthunting cultures, where every man is still a trained hunter and a butcher, but most are failed hunters with little else to do that would not be demeaning to male egos. One might also imagine people trying to run an economy that had no conventions according to which one could own animals or sell meat!

—The ceremonial elaborations that surrounded the killing of sacrificial victims, as they came to be practiced by domesticators, must first of all be understood as pragmatic social innovations—as the kind of things that belong into the philosophy basket of Immanuel Kant's *Critique of Practical Reason.* Socially, a sacrificial feast functioned as a substitute for the adventure and excitement that used to come naturally for men who were out hunting. Gathering and hunting are ways of living which, once upon a time, added up to a lifestyle probably more pleasant than subsequent domestication chores could be. On average, hunting seemed more dignified than shoveling manure or hoeing weeds. Hunting was more "aristocratic," first because it defined the lifestyle of hunters, who later became aristocrats. But it also was more edifying than constantly serving tamed animals—creatures that never even made an effort to control their bowels.

Domestication as Humiliation: Seen from a slightly different angle, after Homo sapiens has progressed for some millions of years in the art of premeditating murder technologically, his ego slowly got worn to where he began to see himself as a penitent victim—doomed perhaps, to perform domestication labors for atonement. Foolish animals, with their demanding needs, appeared to have become the masters of those men who succumbed to the need of serving them. Having once committed oneself to be a farmer, even to own as much as a single cow, for milking, required steady attention and labor—without hope for a day's vacation. Aristocrats, and even public officials in many places today, will still downgrade the status of a farmer who voluntarily, or by his status of birth, seems predestined to shovel manure, to remain forever unqualified for any higher calling.

–When large wild animals and huge loads of venison became a rarity for men on the open range, their families had to compensate by scrounging about in the vicinity of their camps for whatever they could find. Accidental spillage of gathered seeds, at the camp site, and discarded plant waste that sprouted, may have led to the invention of seeding and planting. And such elementary planting may have led to pioneering horticultural experiments—undertaken primarily by gatherer women. Such an evolution and sequence of events probably was the scenario at well-watered places.

–During the phase of cultural realignment known as "domestication," heroically exuberant artificial predators needed to relearn the lowly roles of docile gatherers, and then learn to be planters as if they were akin to squirrels. Within just a few generations, some of them needed to switch from predation to gathering. And on top of that they needed to learn how to tame animals that would have been so much easier to kill. This means they needed to replace their extermination impulses with maternal strategies that led to their own enslavement. Humankind may be the most adaptive species on the planet, but the speed of mental repentance and strategic conversion, from the heights of confident divine predation, back down to chores of the most primitive modes of gathering, was strenuous beyond anything else imaginable. Proud men needed to learn again the simple gathering skills in which any basket-carrying woman could outperform them.

–The combined economics conundrum, of navigating the transition from overhunting to domestication, sounds straight forward. But in reality it was more problematic than any modern mind can now imagine by hindsight. The masculine hominid hunter ego had evolved over six million years and was then challenged to radically reconstitute itself. It was trained and bred to endure dangers of every possible kind, during encounters with greater-than-human (divine) beasts as competitors. Hunters were able to sacrifice their own lives if necessary, to defend and to save their comrades and families. They were, however, unable to adjust in a timely manner to the environmental imbalances that they themselves were causing by weapons-engineering, overhunting, and overpopulation. The need to evolve rationally—to be Homo sapiens—to balance and to justify their actions, has been far more strenuous than any superficial pragmatism which can be ascribed to humanoids nowadays.

—If I were to think of only one fate that could have been worse for a proud Neolithic hunter than failing to bring home enough meat, it would be the fate of being born a male lion who, in lowered savannah grasses, found himself too visible and therefore easily surpassed by the hunting skills of the smaller lionesses. Is the male lion a "dependent" baby killer because savannah grasses now grow shorter? Do human males experience their occasional urges to go warring because long ago they learned how to knap better flints, because their women had more babies, and because there were less prey animals to hunt? Are human females really proud to have their men die as heroes in wars, embattled by machines? There seems to be no beautiful summation to this story.

—We must continue to dwell on the self-evident evolutionary travails of humankind. After some millions of years, humanoid artificial male predators, and maternal gatherers, needed to learn together how to become different kinds of marriage partners, different fathers who were less effectively roaming and all around less important human beings.[10] Today, ten thousand years later, the entire planet still suffers from the aftermaths of this male transitional crisis. This identity crisis, it turns out, has been the most enduring scar that the great Neolithic Revolution has left.

Sacrifices to Feed the Gods

Can anyone be sure that our earliest hunter ancestors actually gave food offerings to greater-than-hominid predator deities? Of course we can be sure. They did. And so did all their ape predecessors millions of years earlier. They could not have survived without occasionally surrendering to some superior and hungry competitor the carcass of a victim which they were unable to defend. After meat had been cut up into chunks, they would try to escape with portions. And if they failed to rescue portions, they counted themselves lucky

[10]Compare Kroeber, Clifton, Bernard L. Fontana. *Massacre at the Gila.* Tucson, 1986. Also Luckert, Karl W. "The Geographization of Death in Melanesia," in *Numen—International Review for the History of Religions 18.* Leiden, 1971.

to escape with their hearts still pounding. Under such circumstances, the probabilities were high that lives were lost. The gods could claim hominid victims on their own volition. To rethink such events as "sacrifices" was a face-saving ploy of humankind. The act of sacrificing one's self was therefore ordinarily not a voluntary option. Hominid hunters usually died when they ran out of saving strategies, tricks, luck—and of course, divine indifference or "amazing grace."

Predisposition: *These are the raw facts of predator life to which this writer will personally attest. Early, during the primitive years of his childhood, and growing up in a rural village, it became occasionally necessary for him to surrender his school lunch to a roaming dog—actually a pedigreed wolf, that was fed in a human dwelling but, apparently, was not subjected to any additional domestication disciplines. The budding intelligence of a weak boy has rediscovered—for the trillionth time on this planet—salvation short of existential surrender, by a method of sacrificial giving. Surrendering a school lunch was a humbling experience. It remained a secret about which the boy's parents were never informed. With the country on a war footing, tempers among villagers needed to be kept calm. Enlisting the help of a father usually made most situations worse. Children understood this fact of life.*

—Surely, our hominid ancestors were obliged to learn such tricks of survival early on in their careers as foragers and scavengers. They themselves robbed from those inferiors that succumbed to them. They also stole from mightier predators whose alertness they suspected to be less than what met the eye. Experimentally they were testing and challenging the superior status of all their divine competitors. This type of experimental competition is something for which ape aptitudes happen to be most suited. Indeed, we have proof that competition must have happened in that way, because some species of ancient predator deities have actually gone extinct, and others that survived have been dethroned. Even the royal lions and tigers are being forced, nowadays, to accept the indignity of semi-domesticated status in animal parks, under the protection and discipline of human wardens with rifles.

—In 1959 J. Häckel published a pace-setting summary concerning hunting rites. He mentioned deposits of skulls, bones, skins, bladders, and figurines in relation to a general belief in the reincarnation of hunted animals. He also referred, before he introduced the word "sacrifice," to the fact that animals were dispatched and sent home to their divine Master, presumably to deliver messages of goodwill.

Häckel introduced then, correctly it seems, sacrificial categories as he referred to certain deposits as "offerings"—as gifts that hunters presented to their divine superiors. Hunters have been observed to give "offerings of firsts" (*Primitalopfer*).[11]

—Before the meat of a victim was released to the hunters for eating, a small portion was put aside and burnt—frequently some vital organ. Häckel also mentioned the Samoyed practice of depositing reindeer skulls and long bones. He suggested that this custom may reflect a "similar" way of thinking. Häckel's glissando, from sacrificial "offerings of firsts" to bone deposits, and to "similar" presentations, is not altogether convincing.

—The archaic hunters' practice of giving offerings of first portions to superior hunter totems did indeed recognize divine sponsors of the hunt.[12] Presenting such share offerings must have had its beginnings far back at the animal level, rooted in scavenging and in social sharing.

—If we bemoan the fact that our human ancestors were losing too much of their prey to mightier predators, then by applying the Golden Rule, we may consider for a moment the next lower species of predators that fell under the sway of our antecedents. Surely, the first hunting wolves and dogs, canines who in our early evolutionary days still ranked above humankind by virtue of their better natural hunting skills—and who later functioned as divine justifiers in ceremonies—would have had more reasons to complain. As part of the measly human grace for coexistence, when humans became their lords, wolves accepted far more humiliation. They won the privilege of eating the worst leftovers of what they hunted, and of what they surrendered to their human masters.

—Hunting under the sponsorship of a divine tutelary was a theological solution, resorted to for resolving the problem of acquired guilt among increasingly self-conscious killers. To be a "toolmaking predator" was the profession by which our hunter ancestors apprenticed to become *homines sapientes.* Their deeds of weapon-making were difficult to justify ethically, and even more difficult to deny. A prefabricated bloodied tool, carried in a toolmaker's hand, testified

---

[11]See J. Häckel, "Herr der Tiere," *Die Religion in Geschichte und Gegenwart*, Vol. III, Tübingen, 1959, 511-513.

[12]Häckel shows no awareness of a need for the human hunters' justification.

against its bearer and in his own eyes his weapon convicted him of his crime. A hunter's crime was "premeditated murder."

—A variety of clever excuses, justifications, ruses, and sacrificial variations were used by primitive hunters to shift their guilt away. Among those methods, making share payments was religiously, perhaps, the most honest one. Futuristically speaking, these sacrificial improvisations have become foundational habits for actual human economies. Sacrifices established the values of livestock and properties. All the while, it was unavoidable that some presenters of sacrifices learned more quickly than others how to extract maximum advantages from the divinities with whom they dealt and covenanted.

—Share offerings of the type that I like to call "alpha-omega offerings" consist of lopped-off extremities taken from conquered animals. These could include snout, tail, horns, eyes, anus, or portions of the skin, frequently from opposite ends on whole animals—hence the "alpha-omega" designation. While a divine sponsor agreed to accept his animal in its essential outline, the human hunters walked off with the less essential "filler" portions of meat—and so they ate and grew strong as *homines sapientes*.[13]

—Share offerings can be presented to a tutelary sponsor that happens to be near, or they can be sent to one who may live far away. When dealing in the realm of gods, geographical distances are of little concern. And to the extent that a deity does indeed accept the penitent gestures offered by a human killer, the responsibility for the victim's death is assumed by the deity who accepts the offering. By logical extension, in ordinary hunting, the deity who accepts a share offering does, in effect, partake of the hunter's communal meal and of his guilt—which are both factual results of co-hunting. The divine-human bond of atonement extends to other guests at this meal who by eating become guilty of the victim's death. Their atonement at such a meal is certified by the participation of a divine sponsor, who by his presence assumes responsibility to redeem all guilt. All celebrants become atoned blood-brothers of the contract-hunter. The most effective bonding rites in the human repertoire are experiencing near-death together, as fellow victims or as fellow killers, jointly bleeding, accepting either guilt or clemency together.

---

[13]A short but useful account of pygmies in Zaire, including the successful hunt of an elephant, can be seen in an educational movie. Kevin Duffy, *Children of the Forest* (28 minutes). Pyramid Film & Video, 800-421-2304.

—In order to lighten the weight on his conscience a hunter could, if superficial gestures failed, surrender existentially to a greater-than-human totemic predator and explicitly become the divinity's share-hunter, to be owned by him.[14] It can easily be seen how this theological solution could have been ritualized and modified to reduce the size of share sacrifices. Payments in kind initially were offered as a religious solution for killer consciences. They were expanded, as in biblical tradition by herd-owner interests, to include first-born whole animal sacrifices. Giving share sacrifices in payment for herds has gradually evolved into our modern system of economics, according to which the first titles of ownership could be purchased in exchange for value-added sacrificial share payments. In order to own herds and harvests, our ancestors needed to purchase their first livestock and seeds from legitimate divine owners, from gods who created and therefore initially owned them. Those things could then be traded among humankind as commodities—they could be purchased in exchange for "sacrificial share equivalents."

Fig. 33. Stick figurine—replacement sacrifice for a fellow predator

—Beneath the range of bargain share sacrifices, still cheaper offerings were possible. A traditional Navajo *(Diné)* hunter has showed me how this can be done. He made a hand-sized stick figurine to replace and to pay for an injured or dead animal (Figure 33). Stick figurines were appropriate, for instance, when a man killed a divine predator, such as a mountain lion, in self-defense.[15]

---

[14]Luckert. *The Navajo Hunter Tradition*, 1975, pp. 17ff.

[15]Description in Luckert, *A Navajo Bringing-Home Ceremony*. 1978, pp. 193-195.

—This *Diné* hunter would never have dared to cut up such a deity as food—that is, someone who could function as a divine tutelary for the hunt. This meant that he also could not reasonably have considered cutting off some kind of preliminary alpha-omega segments. How could he offer these portions as if they were appetizer shares from a communal meal? Such an act could have been understood as a cannibalistic insult toward a divine "hunter colleague" or toward a potential totemic sponsor of the hunt. The hunter's debt, for an animal killed in self-defense, was forgiven when such a substitution figurine was accepted by divine grace.

—Share and substitution offerings can be enhanced with songs, with rhythms and dance steps of devotion and joy, with praises and speeches of appreciation. The basic notion of alleviating the guilt of killing—of killing for sustenance by submitting oneself to a totemic deity as "natural" share hunter—had far-reaching consequences later when hunters became domesticators. It set the pattern for human submission to slavery—for the ways in which inferior people were expected to submit to qualitatively superior hyper-domesticators.

—The accusation of being some kind of guilty killer or butcher could be leveled against any timid hunter or domesticator. Even in the aftermath of the hunter era, the chance of encountering a "shamanic" accuser—someone who knew himself to be ceremonially atoned—was always a possibility. Such an accuser would know how to obtain super-human forgiveness, for himself first. He also would know that you are keeping yourself foolishly in guilt. Then, if you accepted the forgiveness formula he offered, he became your de facto moral guardian—conjoined with you by the memory of your former guilt. This distinction between atoned hunters and guilty inferiors gave the world its qualitatively "better" aristocratic upper class.

—Driven by self-reflective intelligence and by a desire to make more effective weapons, the possibility of becoming ever guiltier increased; the need to find more suitable paths of atonement and of religious justification increased as well. Just as there were no limits to inventing more effective tricks of cultural aggression, so also were there no limits to potential paths of religious atonement.

—Killing and butchering an animal that showed pain, that showed anatomical similarities and red blood, and that exhibited a degree of intelligence during its last struggle for survival—all these responses a rational hunter was obliged to respect, because they also formed the building blocks for his own ego. A degree of learned fairness can be assumed in the case of any species of animals of which the young grow up playing and wrestling each other. From an amalgam of such snippets of learning, from the human ability to imitate, to experiment and to innovate, have also evolved the characteristics that define the souls of our species. Whatever amount of intelligence that is being mobilized for cultural aggression is, for the sake of balance, also required to be mobilized for religious retreats.

—In the service of culture and aggression, intellect is aimed outward. It reflects back inward in the shape of "*con*-science"—in a literal sense "against" or "*con*-trary" to the direction of experimental "science"—the latter of which, viewed broadly, represents the intellectualized mode of outward aggression. Hunting is trickery; good hunting is trickery well done. Greater-than-humanoid predators, who were both feared and admired by our ancestors, since times unremembered, have revealed themselves also as greater tricksters. To our ancestors they became models and totemic sponsors. Their existence justified human hunting. They accepted credit and blame.

—Just because some of those hunter gods in our repertoire of legends are now being degraded to the status of tricksters or buffoons—such as Coyote in America is sometimes demoted to the status of a bungler or a witch—does not mean that a higher status was not accorded them in earlier days of evolution.[16] It simply means that humankind now feels strong enough to laugh about some of their earliest gods. To tell a joke at the expense of a deity is a way of demoting him or her. It is less dangerous than a curse. A curse acknowledges that the object might still have power and may, therefore, need to be frightened away. Herein, in Diné discourse, lies the difference between a disrespectful laugh and a scornful curse—between Coyote the deity, the witch, and the bungler.

—Seen through the windows of domesticator culture, during the past ten millennia, ancient hunters and totemic gods could no

---

[16]During my fieldwork on *Coyoteway, a Navajo Holyway Healing Ceremonial,* University of Arizona and Museum of Northern Arizona presses (Tucson and Flagstaff, 1979), I discovered that in the context of this chantway, Coyote, the American prairie wolf, was still functioning as a positive totemic deity. However, in general Navajo folk belief the status of both Coyote and Wolf has suffered. The first of these is mocked as bungler and trickster, and both are frequently feared as witches. It would appear that "Renard the Fox" legends represent a similar degradation of totemic Fox mythology. Göbekli Tepe could have been the evolutionary breaking point for the Fox totem.

longer be trusted. Anyone could steal an animal and give an alpha-omega offering to a hunter deity. The archaic hunters' method of religious justification could no longer protect domesticators. Early tutelary sponsors of huntsmen were frequently rediscovered and redefined by domesticators as demons or devils.[17]

—Have a look at the appearance of the typical "Devil" in medieval European Christendom! He looks like a collage of odds and ends from the world of predators—fresh out of prehuman flux mythological conditions—including the artificial man-made three-pronged spear. Committed domesticators had no choice but to search for a greater-than-human Creator deity from whom they could legitimately acquire herd animals, plants, fields and other private property. The transition from hunting to domestication could not have happened without communal religious reform.

Resurrection versus Reincarnation

So-called "deposits of skulls and bones," as were left by ancient hunters, cannot be interpreted categorically as "offerings." And likewise, the process of "reincarnation" does not necessarily entail devotion to some Master of Animals, nor do reincarnation processes require sacrificial giving. For a hunter faced with the question of how much weight he should try to carry home, depositing the inedible remains of a carcass at the hunting site was a practical necessity. Sheer deposits of animal skeletons should, therefore, be distinguished from obvious sacrificial giving. Hopes of resurrection might have been cultivated and expressed in relation to both human and animal bones —but not necessarily.

—Bone deposits at *Diné* Indian hunting sites seem to indicate resurrection hopes, rather than what Häckel calls "reincarnation." I was told about such rites in 1971, as they were part of the *Diné* hunter tradition. The prime motive of Navajo hunters, in their farewell speeches to the bones, was alleviation of their guilt for having killed. The hunters were trying to minimize the gravity of their deed. With

---

[17]The denigration of ancient totemic deities, or dynastic crests, has also become necessary as a matter of course in recent secular political revolutions. Soldiers who fought against dynasties represented by totemic crests were, for the most part, unaware that they were still finishing off the remains of ancient totemic hunter religion. Ancient religion and politics never have been completely separated.

the essential soul left unhurt, in the form of bones, a hunter's victim thereby remained alive in futuristic terms—to be hunted again. The bones are expected to resurrect, and thereby the hunter's crime of killing is rendered null and void. There is no hint here of a faith in "reincarnation" in the sense that a spirit-soul is waiting somewhere to enter a new body. The bones *are* the soul, and new flesh and sinews will regenerate on them. The dead animal will rise and be seen running again. This is the classic distinction between reincarnation of souls and the resurrection of bodies. Resurrection was expected to happen with recycled bones.[18]

—A significant amount of confusion has crept into Western anthropological thinking in response to Sir Edward B. Tylor's theory of "animism." Predisposed by ancient Greek dualism, many Western readers have leapt all too quickly to explaining life and death in terms of bodies being occupied and abandoned by spirits. Instead of asking "what is it that leaves at the point of death?", one can neutralize this question and ask less prejudicially, "what has changed?" Wherever the hunters' prehuman flux mythology resonates in the background, there the concepts of "transformation" and "resurrection" usually are closer to the intended meaning than the Indo-European dualism that is implied in the concept of "embodiment" or "reincarnation."

—The subject matter of "resurrection" and "life after death" does deserve an afterthought. From general historical considerations it now appears that both "resurrection" and "life after death" could first have been conceptualized by hunters in relationship to their victims. Faith in life after death may have had more to do with alleviating the hunters' guiltiness of killing than with the hope of improving one's own destiny in the face of death. I came to this conclusion during field researches four decades ago. The discovery was a complete surprise, but it makes evolutionary sense. A Homo sapiens hunter who lives by causing death cannot complain too much if some greater power then also terminates his own life, in the end. Death seems to be the fair cost of temporary survival by eating.

---

[18]See Luckert. *The Navajo Hunter Tradition*, 1975, pp. 36, 206f. The ancient association of bones with the probability of resurrection is echoed in biblical traditions in the case of Ezekiel's vision of a "valley of dry bones" (Ezekiel 37) as well as in association with the crucifixion account of Jesus of Nazareth (John 19.32). The bones were not broken, according to the story, apparently in order to make subsequent resurrection appear more likely.

High Gods and Masters of Animals

In academic circles where primitive religions are being discussed, the anxiety over being classified as an "evolutionist" still feels somewhat stifling today. But Andrew Lang, in 1898, and Wilhelm Schmidt from 1912 to 1954, both courageously pursued the prospect of finding a more primitive stratum of belief in a single supreme deity among a variety of cultures worldwide. While answering these men, the problem concerning the evolution of religion could not be completely avoided. Perhaps to introduce some relativity into the enormous efforts for or against the theory of "primeval monotheism," or to shed some doubt on the universality of the High God concept, a host of scholars began to focus more closely on Master of Animals types in hunter religions. Could faith in a Master of Animals among hunter-gatherers, cited in support of a theory of primeval monotheism, be traced to any historical circumstances? Or, how important for understanding today's religions still were the roles of Animal Masters in the course of their evolution ?

—High God and Master of Animals types from all kinds of primitive culture strata were brought together for comparison, as if the spatial elevation attributed to "high up" deities, and the earliest traceable notions of such among the most primitive peoples, could together prove or disprove something about the greater-than-human dimension. How much of romantic Golden Age mythology has interfered with or stimulated this academic search? Other scholars tried to get to the root of primitive religion psychologically. They postulated a special type of primitive mentality that, supposedly, made religious thinking easier or necessary.[19]

—It seems as though below the surface the "primeval monotheism" debate was not so much about religion as it was about the

---

[19]See Lucien Lévy-Brühl. *How Natives Think* (1910). Lévy-Brühl distinguished two basic mindsets: "primitive" and "Western." Primitives do not distinguish the supernatural from reality. He described their mental activity as "mystical participation." By Lévy-Brühl's categories, the author of this book would certainly be a primitive. His teeter-totter scale (Chapter 10) does not distinguish "nature" from "super-nature." Instead, he assumes the presence of analytic aggressive human minds, owned and operated by artificial predators. This author, a finite human being, knows that "greater-than-human" begins along the same boundary line where his own influence ends. But he does not know the outer limit of "nature," and hence he cannot know what "supernatural" means.

beginnings of metaphysical arithmetic and counting. Does a child, or do primitive people, learn to conceptualize "One" before they distinguish "One" from "Two" or from "Many?"

—What was overlooked in the discussion of primitive hunter religiosity, by Western research agendas, was the core subject of hunting as such. This writer happens to be convinced that the blood spilled while hunting and butchering was the foremost reason for primitive hunters having tried to behave religiously when they were hunting.

Predisposition: *Before I am suspected of using the term "primitive" in a derogatory sense, let me put my clarification in writing here. I do consider the farming culture in which I was raised to have been quite primitive. In my home culture we all talked to our farm animals. They were more easily persuaded to work that way—and talking to them also put us children at ease, knowing and assuming that the animals, whom we had to guide with sticks, were able to empathize with us and understood our filial dilemmas. The circumstances which, in the history of religions field, obstructed our ability to understand true situations, was the fact that students were either hoping for historical proof that would establish a theory of primeval monotheism, or else were trying to escape from all theisms while looking back over their shoulders, agonizing for their secular souls while seeing the religion of their fathers still in hot pursuit, trying to save them. But then, gods from any pre-monarchic era cannot be meaningfully classified by how high up they sat enthroned. I never met, or saw, or heard of a hunter deity sitting on a throne. They were all roaming or riding as I was—unless, of course, one of these gods happened to enjoy standing still as a tree or sitting still as a mountain. But even at that, a non-roaming hunter deity never sat enthroned as High God.*

—Someone can, nevertheless, draw an experience/response spectrum—as in Chapter Ten above—which accommodates those who do encounter realities that seem greater-than-human. For the historian of religions, gods are more than names or adjectives. Gods are what they have done and continue to do alongside humans. And in order to establish what gods are doing, their deeds must be distinguished from what human protégés think that they themselves are doing. Primitive religions cannot be elucidated with a compilation of synonyms or adjectives. They require names, and above all verbs.

—Try this same method of investigation on the streets of New York, and ask people about the Christian Trinity. Nay, you may even go to any church of your choosing and ask for an explanation about the triune God of Christendom. The chances are slim that, at your first try, you will stumble onto a world-wise theologian who can make historical sense out of this doctrine for you. People with integrated theological and historical knowledge must be searched for and approached with an open mind and open questions.

—Meanwhile, I have sought my own ethnological delineations between monotheism and polytheism. I never really trusted questions regarding the number of gods and therefore, as a rule, I did not ask them. In 1971 and in the years that followed I resisted asking such questions of Claus Chee Sonny—who was my teacher of the Diné Deer Huntingway. I knew that the man was intelligent and that he would have been capable of concocting a "Great Spirit" theology on the spot—had I only mentioned as much as "Great Spirit." On his own, Claus Chee Sonny never mentioned such a deity.

—However, at a moment of initiation into the general mysteries of the Talking-god it became obvious that this "Grandfather of the gods" could have revealed universal monotheistic status at a moment's notice. But there never was a need for doing this. Doing so would have precipitated all sorts of incredulities among academicians as well as among the *Diné* people themselves. In Western terms such a universal deity would be difficult to explain in relation to the masked impersonations that appear in some of the *yeii* ceremonies. Thus, where the gods retain their lowest possible profiles, vis-à-vis humankind, there human devotees, too, will be more easily to understand, to approach, and to endure.

—Working with a *Diné* traditional hunter-shaman, and traveling on multiple occasions with him through his hunting range, I not only concluded that his religious vocabulary did not include a "Great Spirit"—and not even a "spirit" or "soul"—but also that his hunting range never was a "Happy Hunting Ground." The activity of hunting invariably loaded him with guilt and with the risks of divine reprisals. For every procedural mistake that he made while hunting and butchering, he needed to have a ritualized reconciliation procedure on hand to restore his relationship with divine animal-persons to a state of normalcy and balance. He considered such ceremonial first-aid—such atonements—to be more important than any physical skills needed to track, to kill, or to butcher.[20]

---

[20]I do not know for sure—and I would consider it a waste of time to research this question—but if pushed, I would look for a "Happy Hunting Grounds" eschatology not among Native American traditional hunters, but in James F. Cooper's 1826 work of fiction, The Last of the Mohicans. And incidentally, in actual history there has also not yet been a "last Mohican."

—The Navajo Coyoteway ceremonial that I recorded in 1974 was, as are all *Diné* "holyway" ceremonials, oriented toward reconciling humankind with the Holy People—that is, with the gods. During the performance and recording of this healing ceremonial I avoided asking any questions regarding its polytheism. After the ceremonial had been finished and recorded, Johnny Cooke and I returned to the shamanic practitioner for multiple rounds of supplementary questions, mostly to hear again the words and segments that we might have misunderstood. Only at the end of our very last session, when we were sure we had everything that we needed, did I risk asking a question concerning religious arithmetic. Very cautiously I probed:

—"During this nine-night ceremonial we have spoken prayers and brought offerings to sixteen Coyote-gods, and to the Talking-god and to the Calling-god. Is it possible that these many gods are only one god?" Without pondering, the Coyoteway Master answered with "Could be." The unspoken portion of his answer was obvious. In that case, one god has received all the prayers, songs and offerings at different places. It does not change anything regarding the content of the Coyoteway ceremonial.

Predisposition: *It is with no small degree of embarrassment that I remember my second day at Luke Cook's Diné homestead. I helped him and two of his sons fetch their young heifers to have marker clamps snapped onto their ears. As a farmer's son from Germany, with some exposure to farm-work in Kansas, I was handling those animals with more determination than my Navajo friends were trying to accomplish this task. I laid the animals on the ground, on their sides. While trying not to look too weak toward those cattle, it took me a while to notice that these heifers registered a few degrees closer to being full "persons" to my Navajo friends.*

The Problem of Sin and Guilt

Among the research questions that anthropologists typically ask about primitive hunter religion, problems related to the spilling of blood, resultant guiltiness, and the reconciliation with gods and fellow animal people have been conspicuously omitted. The scholars all seem to have been busy trying to find ideal primitive hunter societies who, somehow either were, or still are, in harmony with Nature—that is, trying to find situations where guilt feelings are still absent.

—It goes without saying that questions pertaining to sin, guilt, forgiveness, or justification cannot be asked directly—and the reason is, that guilt in all cultures is habitually denied and that reasons for such denial, or even reasons that justify general aggressiveness, arise long before the question of guilt can be admitted into full consciousness. A present awareness of sin or guilt will only be shared spontaneously, embedded in a trustworthy larger context, among people who can trust and feel secure.

—No! The American Natives were not living in a Western-style Romantic utopia of Nature under a "pure-spirit" deity. And yes, these hunters knew that they were killing "fellow animal people" whom they recognized as "persons." And many of these animal people were deemed divine and had totemic relatives in human clans and tribes, in men's associations with many initiates. The latter are being educated and are immersed into the presence of surrounding divine beings, still today during their world-renowned "vision quests." Tribal men's associations cultivate these traditions.

—Modern skilled academicians have been taught how to rationalize their own culture's mores with regard to killing—in terms of jurisprudence, politics, biochemistry, and sports. Our Western cult of hunting and fishing, as sport, supports the habit of seeing wild fauna as "game animals."[21] It refers to commercial hunting and fishing with domesticator vocabulary, as "harvesting." All these modern notions have nurtured our misconceptions about "primitive" hunters. In addition, the Hellenic distinction between human bodies and spiritual souls, and the expedient postulate, about animals being living bodies devoid of genuine souls, has remained a factor in our industrial treatment and exploitation of animal species.

—Indeed, one may wonder whether our life-sciences and our food-chemistry—whether our ways of defining food compounds—might not have been inspired essentially by the felt need to justify our culture's aggression against exploited forms of life. Sometimes I wonder what a "pro-life" science would really look like. Ethical issues of self-justification, and appeals to greater-than-human realities or norms, are always religious concerns. By the same token, modern secular minds are accustomed—for the sake of appearing scientific and rational—to hide their older religious justifications (and their newer secular "rationalizations") from public view.

---

[21]Father Berard Haile, the most successful Navajo ethno-linguist, utilized the English word "game animals." But for traditional Navajo hunters, their hunting never was a game. I struggled all the way from writing "game animals" to "prey animals" and "preyed-upon animals."

—My first laboratory session in a biology course at university had nothing to do with "life." We were asked to dissect a dead animal. Meanwhile, many names of ancient "gods," and even "icons," have been pirated by computer engineers. The Greek term *bios,* life, has been re-assigned to control programs for computer operations—thus, relegated to the rear ends of machines. To cover the tracks, our computer-steered English Thesaurus for *Word*, no longer recognizes the meaning of "life" in the "bios" root. By not acknowledging the word that gave us "biology," devotees to computer science help diminish biological issues, life and its sanctity, issues of guilt and ethics, and they help fascilitate our sliding down the slope of mechanized materialism.

—All the while, I confess that an awareness of guilt, as it pertains to the Navajo hunter tradition, has not come into view for me "scientifically." It came by personal communication, as a fieldwork surprise. The question about a people's "justification for killing" will never appear on the radar screen of a scientific hypothesis.

Human and Canine Domestication

If you are born a humanoid, clumsier than a chimp when it comes to climbing trees, and if you have half the chimp's tooth sizes lined up along shortened jawbones, what can you do? The answer is, you work with what you have—which includes a stiffer back, suitable for walking more proudly upright than a chimp needs to, an opposable thumb that you keep away from the chimp's stronger hand, and which instead you train to do precision work on inert sticks, bones, and stones. Above all, you use the gray matter between your ears.

—If you are born a primate with an acquired appetite for meat, and you are outhunted by a wolf—and are able to run only half the speed of that canine, what must you do? You must invent weapons and "false teeth" that you can toss at target animals from a distance, to wound them, and then invite a wolf to be your friend, and let him or her help finish the tracking and killing. Of course, you must utilize the gray matter between your ears consistently. You must compose an impressive ritual of flattery for the canine, which enables you to take possession of captured carcasses. After all, with your knives you are better at butchering than a wolf will ever be. And if you act your role magnanimously, as a wise master over life and death, then the wolf will be your religious devotee, your hunting slave, your dog, for as long as he or she and you might live.

—And then, when you are seventy-eight years old, you will have outlived the dogs of your younger years. A Black Labrador Retriever will correctly analyze your weakness. Her name is Skeena. She knows that you cannot run anymore and that you cannot throw anything very far—and still, this black dog loves to embarrass you by bringing you her sticks to throw. It is then that you must use what you have left between your ears to defend the honor of your species. You must summon your grandson Travis and pass Skeena's stick on to him. She has already trained the boy well, to throw her sticks great distances—spectacular dares for retrieval. The grandson gets his exercise and Skeena earns her self-esteem—as the Labrador Retriever—a status that far surpasses the level of old humanoid stick throwers. And I? I have won another while of peace without having to die for it.

Predisposition: *Some years back, in Missouri, I owned a plot of land on which I planted experimental pecan trees. Every time when I walked to fetch my tractor, the neighbor's two dogs threatened me. One was a Husky and the other a Coyote-mongrel. The latter always bared his huge canines, but held back behind the Husky, cowardly. I did not derive much pleasure from these daily threats of getting bitten. Therefore, one day I picked up four egg-sized stone pebbles and carried them—one in my right hand and three in the left. When the dogs attacked, I opened my hands to show those stones to the Husky who had come within two hand-widths of my legs. Both dogs retreated immediately without an extra bark. In the afternoon on that same day the Husky snuck up on me as I was hoeing weeds around a tree. I felt him touch my left leg and I quickly raised my hoe in self-defense. But the Husky had not come to attack. He wanted to submit. With my right hand I reached for his neck and pushed his head to the ground. I held him down some ten seconds and said "OK." He responded with a painful whimper and crept away. From that day on neither of these two dogs attacked me again. And even though I knew they were in the vicinity, I never saw them again. The Husky had accepted me as his distant master—as a deus otiosus of sorts (a homo otiosus, more precisely, if he had studied at the place where I taught). Apparently, the Coyote-mongrel concurred.*

—The action of pushing down a dog by its neck, in play, comes almost naturally to bi-pedal humanoids. By contrast, in an intra-species match among puppies, this act of wrestling a sibling to the ground by its neck, to establish rank, would have required significant more strength and talent—a delicate balance of power and friendship. In an inter-species playful contest with a puppy, however, even the arm of a fumbling human child, pushing from above, has the divine advantage.

—It is likely that the domestication of *Canis lupus* began long before fifteen thousand years ago in Asia and in Africa, at hunting sites where, in natural "chow circles," some packs of wolf-dogs invented manners of behavior that rendered them acceptable to human hunters. These encounters between two species may have begun when human hunters, while butchering with knives, cut off second-rate portions of meat and tossed them to packs of wolf-dogs that mastered the art of surrounding humans peacefully. In turn, the humans loved to watch the dogs scramble among themselves for the pieces that they tossed. The hunters may initially have fed them only to keep them from coming too close. They "sacrificed" playfully to inferiors who, had they been better organized as a pack, could have become greater-than-humanoid. At that stage it was probably the advantage of having a spoken language that enabled our species to communicate strategy and to fake greater-than-canine status.

—During successive hunts, the dogs learned ways to please their human benefactors by helping them locate and track the prey. They might even have found ways to distract dangerous larger predators that could have harmed their otherwise resourceful two-legged overlords. The dogs discovered the value of rational "religious" servitude. So it is possible that Canis lupus enslaved itself into the service of Homo sapiens by its own playful and religious sophistication. In strategic alliances with human hunters, these animals improved their chances of having better lives—better than they could have achieved by insisting on competitive and hostile encounters.

—The first softening of relationships could have taken place in a variety of ways. Whereas approaches by adult animals are thinkable, it may have been the case that the first domestic dog was a puppy that was adopted and weaned as a pet. Then again, wolves do habitually encircle the herds of grazing animals. With human hunters also present, trying to imitate their strategy of encircling and "herding" ungulates, it may have dawned on some of those wolves that it could be advantageous to allow humankind to participate in their roundups. And so the wolves used two-legged ones as their "hunting men," just as humans thought they were using the four-legged ones as "hunting dogs." The wolves may have realized that their unilateral victories could all too easily have been annulled by human hunters who had the ability to bite them fatally from considerable distances.

—Most probably, they learned this basic lesson the hard way. With rational cunning, canines opted to help humankind upfront and beg for rewards after the hunt. In the case that they should fail to be sufficiently rewarded for their daytime services, they could venture out and go hunting for themselves at night when humans rested. The primary benefit of this strategy was that they no longer needed to compete, or fear being hit by poisoned arrows.

12. Hunting to Hyper-Domestication Direct

Three questions dominate the background for this chapter: (1) What happened to hunters who wandered away from Göbekli Tepe to hunt elsewhere? (2) Who were the warriors that filled the ranks of armies five thousand years later when city states and empires were forming in Mesopotamia, Egypt, and India? (3) What drove the construction of cities in regions populated by domesticators? Each of these questions helps answer the others, but all answers remain hypothetical.

Göbekli Tepe Dispersions

Neolithic *homines sapientes*, the industrialized heirs of predatory Primate dreams, twelve thousand years ago at Göbekli Tepe, began fulfilling the ambitions of their ancestors to establish themselves as the best-skilled flint weapon makers and nuisances on Planet Earth. Wild prey animals could not keep up with their numbers, and not in the hunting drives they staged. When the miner's sense of guilt and enthusiasm for their religion of atonement reached its peak, possibly around eleven thousand years ago, there apparently followed a period during which many hunter clans gradually started drifting away from the area.

—Hunters and gatherers, on average, have left light footprints in archaeology; on that account the Göbekli Tepe *menhir* weights appear all the more remarkable. At the end of the Ice Age the climate along the Fertile Crescent was getting warmer. And, while glaciers along mountain ranges in the north were melting, all living beings beneath the slopes were prospering. Each species and variety was bent on filling the land with its own kind. The industrialized and partly sedentary human hunters also thrived and populated the land. Their own growth in numbers generated the dynamic that drove them apart.

—For brief cold spells perhaps, at irregular intervals, the glacial runoff slowed to a trickle. As a result, living conditions fluctuated and deteriorated not only for hunters but also for sedentary domesticators. Not enough settlements in the area have been excavated for us to know for sure exactly what happened. But we can assume that two millennia of climate transition, and periodic glacier thaws, could not have occurred in peaceful regularity and tranquility. Once a sizeable population of settled domesticators was hit with an erratic drought, with two seasons of crop failures in a row, food shortages would send them adrift. Our historical climatology studies are not sufficiently refined to date such brief disasters.

—One can assume that over the span of one or two thousand years of human increase, while glaciers melted, animals were overhunted. When the mountain passes opened up, prey animals and their hunters began to slip away. And with the hunter clans went their representative industrial craftsmen who used to work as miners and weapon-makers at Göbekli Tepe. As they travelled toward Europe and into Asia, these men would have kept their eyes open for limestone escarpments and flint nodules.

—As they moved into new regions, in small troops and waves, they found prey animals and edible plants to sustain themselves. It also seems reasonable to assume that, along their paths into Europe and Asia, they chanced upon groups of people who had scattered there previously, and also some who later ended up in the Americas. They met hunters whose ancestors had generations of Ice Age experience and survival skills to boast—hunters of mega-fauna who knew where to find wild oxen and where in the cold lands still to find mammoth. These continents were not empty places. *Homines sapientes* entered Europe and Asia, the Indonesian archipelagoes, and probably scattered all the way to Australia by following others who went there perhaps thirty thousand years earlier.

—One can assume that wherever hunters from the Göbekli Tepe region moved, they carried with them a growing body of knowledge about alternate lifestyles. They knew the fates of kindred who quit hunting and stopped traveling—they knew the challenges that those who continued wandering tried to avoid. And they understood the hazards of travelling in an environment where human populations were on the increase; they knew some things about inter-clan hostilities. In some areas, where the abundance of wildlife seemed too good to be true, it probably was that. Wild animals were more numerous in areas where tribes of human hunters fought each other for territory. If they ever decided to become sedentary, they sensed the dangers and understood many of their options.

—There were specific emergency steps of downscaling—of hoarding seeds and nuts, and of drying fruits, beets, tubers, or fishes. Such steps needed to be taken when the lifestyle of mixed hunting and gathering deteriorated beyond endurance. Practically every group went through rounds of downscaling before they surrendered to the meager alternatives of settling permanently. When the fauna was thinning out it became necessary to look for places with lush vegetation, with streams inhabited by clams and fishes. As key family members got older, and were reduced to gathering labors, such sedentary opportunities needed to be pursued, even if only temporarily. Larger river valleys would support larger populations who had similar expectations and needs. Larger numbers of people could band together and make better arrangements for security. Marriages and totemic clan alliances were contracted. Old bonds loosened when people moved away. New bonds were established as people mingled and joined.

—For every major group that travelled away from an ancient center, small numbers of nostalgia-laden loners drifted back on pilgrimages from afar, seeking the legendary homelands of parents and grandparents. On average, they probably found those ancestral lands less attractive than their nostalgic elders had remembered them. Lost clans could be found and reconfirmed at far-away places, generations later, while totem stories were being shared, repaired and amended.

—If you were a leading elder, responsible for divining the path ahead—which often meant guessing—you probably needed to tell "a story which you heard your grandfather tell, long ago." This could be a convenient and a polite ruse by which to nudge your group to move in a direction of your liking. If the geography of your story turned out to be mistaken, and if the people ended up suffering, you could not really be blamed for the fact that your grandfather had been wrongly informed so very long ago. Life in those early days was already a quest for knowledge—a competition of storytellers. In a sense, for Homo sapiens it still is that today.

—Reasoning backward in time, *Inuit* (Eskimo) clansmen seem to have reached Alaskan shores still a few millennia after Göbekli Tepe. Their relatives today are still found at both sides of the Bering

Strait. Before them, perhaps during or shortly after the Göbekli Tepe boom years, arrived Haida and Athabascan speakers in the American Northwest.[22] Some of those who hunted large sea animals at the American side might have returned to visit relatives back at the Asian side. They probably helped feed a network of rumors between Asian and North American populations. Many an orphaned totem pole along America's Northwest Coast (if there were any wooden totem poles that long ago) could so have gotten re-associated with long-lost relatives—or with new relatives who miraculously appeared out of nowhere and who spoke some recognizable words or who learnt new words quickly—who could make themselves understood as relatives from faraway places.

—Lone adventurers, when they fear for their lives, can learn a foreign language with remarkable speed—especially in storyteller traditions like the Athabascan, where the primary subject matter to be communicated is frequently huge chunks of silence. Comfortable silence will reveal two people's compatibility faster than any words. Having the proper demeanor—such as pointing with your lips rather than with fingers—could be more important than mastering the content of a story that was under contemplation. Wanderers appearing out of nowhere, who just happened to be roaming about—just "coyote-ing around"—are no rare sights even to this day. Some *Diné* whom I have known had a habit of disappearing and roaming for days without telling anyone in the family. Such habits, in fact, have honed the alertness of the remaining family members and made them good at guessing—and thereby also made them compassionate toward people who occasionally guessed wrong.

—It was possible to guess and to decipher the story of a totem pole, as we ourselves have tried to demonstrate in Chapter 5, above. One simply "remembered" what this other one, far away, signified and used to look like. Hosts generally were curious and willing to negotiate the differences.

---

[22]Of Athabascan-related languages in Asia, along the Yenisei River, only fifty-five fluent Ket speakers can still be found in the far north. All are now more than fifty-five years old. See Edward J. Vadja, "The Dene–Yeniseian Connection," in Anthropological Papers of the University of Alaska, June 2010. The Haida, who may have been the first totem-pole carvers along the Northwest Coast, have not yet been linked linguistically.

—To communicate enthusiasm for a carver's family could be easy, especially if the host was proud of his work and when the new-arrival was a likeable fellow, who enjoyed remembering stories of long ago, and who did not mind being rediscovered as the Raven, as the Killer-whale, or the Wolf whom he resembled—or if the host was desperately looking for a trustworthy kin, a replacement son, or a good son-in-law.

The Road to Hyper-domestication

Hyper-domestication means that something extra has been added to domestication—some kind of over-plus. To simplify this discussion we begin summarizing again at the level of gathering and hunting.

—Hunters and gatherers interfered in the existence of minerals by destroying, reshaping and modifying them. In the existence of plants and animals they interfered to terminate lives. Then those who became domesticators also assumed ownership and control over the nurture of cultivars and livestock. They interfered in entire life cycles —in breeding, birth, and nurture. Planters staked out gardens and fields for cultivation, while herders piled up boughs in the form of round corrals for camps of concentration. Thus cultivars could be systematically harvested and animals could be herded, kept, and held for slaughter.

—The "prehuman flux" genre of mythology of earlier hunters tended to accept all living beings as "persons." Notwithstanding this high valuation, domesticators eventually needed to find ways of reducing them conceptually to the status of impersonal consumables. While animals were being domesticated they became eligible for any kind of nurture and empathy that a human family was able to provide. But all the same, before any tame animal could be butchered it needed to be mentally reclassified, in present and in future tense, as some kind of owned property and food substance. "Flesh" needed to be mythically transformed into meat. During this process of religious reclassification, human balance and justification were being defined.

—Beyond the efforts of pure domestication, some hunters and part-time owners reasoned how to surpass the basic limitations of just owning animals and things. They became grand-domesticators, that is, "hyper-domesticators." They claimed ownership and permanent control over fellow humankind. At the onset of the Neolithic Revolution there were no traditional constraints, yet, that would obligate converts from hunter status to limit themselves to the pure domestication of plants and animals. It was ethically easy to surpass levels of domestication of minerals, plants, and animals—to cross a barely noticable boundary in order to meddle in the lives of other humans—regarding matters of propagation, birth, or nurture. Parents in all epochs have been doing so temporarily with their offspring, anyhow. It was not too hard to impose bondage on humans who surrendered good-naturedly in play. It was not impossible to inflict death on men who at initiations were already trained to "expect death."

—Hyper-domesticators inflicted on humankind many of the same tricks that hunters and herders had invented for the management of animals. But hyper-domesticators also would magnify their controls to horrible extremes. They would poke and whip, chase and yoke, scalp, castrate, slaughter and roast. And by inflicting extraordinary constraints, they would not only ignore natural bonds amongst their own species, but even disregard boundaries that used to exist between humans and their greater-than-human totemic superiors. After learning how to manipulate and "domesticate" hunter totems, they proceeded to rustle rank-and-file human protégés that used to answer to those deities. Collectively we classify all these exaggerations as hyper-domestication.

—Based on their traditional reasoning, persistent and arrogant hunters did not need to be bothered by conscience about their hyper-domestication style of daring. Most issues could be resolved within the comforts of ancient religious tradition. Hyper-domesticators could take comfort in the fact that it was neither they nor their sacred tradition that has worsened. They could view themselves as the true kind of orthodox heroic hunters of the kind that the very best among their ancestors had always been. By contrast, those many poor and extra drop-out hunters for whom there were no longer enough wild animals to hunt—who had sunk to the level of being livestock nannies—these were the ones that really have changed. They have abandoned the old-time culture and religion of successful ancestral hunters. It was these incompetents who have dropped away from their totemic calling and destiny. Multitudes of failed hunters sank to the level of being burrowing moles and cultivators. After the manner in which destitute grazing animals scratched the earth with their hooves, human planters scratched with hoes and sticks. Proud orthodox hunters knew why they would rather be heroes and aristocrats.

—In hindsight, it appears that the earliest domesticators, everywhere, adapted and took to peaceful planting and herding too soon for their own good. It is easy to see how cliques of hunters, or clans that remained armed and mobile longest in the interest of hunting and conquest, ended up claiming the lion's share of lands, usually in the form of larger hunting ranges. They ended up controlling most of the land and more than early domesticators ever could use or would have thought to claim for themselves. Aristocratic marauding hunterfolk would insist on capturing and robbing the earliest settlements. As booty they would take the fruits of sweat and labor that settlers had invested—and they took the settlers too.

—Still in the aftermath of recent antimonarchic revolutions, what continues to distinguish remnant aristocracies and royalties from common sedentary folk is the fact that, like their ancestors, they claim extensive hunting rights on huge tracks of land. Such lands would be deemed necessary and proper for aristocratic hunting. Their strategic wavering over time, between conquest and assuming responsibility for the defense of chosen groups of weak domesticators, was the manner in which they used both ends of their spears, while grabbing the middle. They secured rights to every stretch of land that subordinates would hunt upon, including spaces held by the settlers whom they conquered.

—Of course, with the "game animals" that lived in forests came the trees that grew there, naturally, to shield and to cover the wild fauna. By special elongated "planter logic," aristocratic hunters would assert ultimate ownership of the animals, land and trees combined. The only things they left to domesticators to own—when they spoke among themselves, joking aloud, was the peoples pride in their labor. This concession was profitable. Warriors, aristocrats, and royals persisted in hunting the orthodox way. They would become quite annoyed when presumptuous commoners followed their own nostalgia to also hunt a wild animal now and then. Back in the Stone Age, before there were commoners and elites, all human ancestors claimed the right to do so. Once upon a time all our fathers were hunters and all our mothers gatherers, and none owned any land.

—This hunters' "paradise" was quickly lost when the first Homo sapiens pair adopted, tamed, and claimed a prey animal and when they planted seeds in a patch of ground which they then claimed to be their property. Tamed and adopted animals needed to be protected against hunters who disregarded adoption rights. Planted gardens needed to be shielded against gatherers who honored neither property rights nor boundaries. When hyper-domesticators added their spin to the turmoil, the human species itself fell under the domestication spell of elitists. Aristocratic hunters counted vulnerable humankind among their legitimate possessions.

The Great Roundup: From hunting roundups to domestication and hyper-domestication roundups there is direct continuity. The hunters' strategy of rounding up prey animals is older than humankind. Humanoid hunters learnt this skill by way of imitating and interacting with wolves and by observing some of the larger felines. Those predators had been rounding up prey long before our human ancestors became interested in capturing meat fresh off the hoof. Imitation was the skill that enabled our ape-ancestors to become Homo sapiens—to mimic what lions, wolves, and tigers already knew how to do well. Skills of hunting by ambush were older still. Our ancestors learned those skills while observing reptiles.

–Keeping hoofed herd animals corralled was an activity that humans experimented with as soon as those animals were becoming somewhat scarce. The first intuition toward building a corral probably dawned on hunter minds when they were still hunting on the open range. It may be assumed that, quite early on, groups piled up brush circles in which to spend their nights in safety. After that, group hunting could be pursued by taking advantage of topographical features, such as canyons, rivers, and cliffs. Natural pits could be augmented with brush barriers, with V-shaped funnel routes into which animals could be driven while scaring them with torches of fire. Nets and other entanglements were probably added later. The method of domesticators, stacking sticks and boughs to build circular corrals, was probably first anticipated when they learned how to encircle animals at the open range. With their corrals, domesticators invented the idea of a "concentration camp" for taming and containment. In the era of hyper-domestication, the domesticator's corrals were converted into walled cities, fortresses, prisons, and selectively more solid concentration camps for keeping humankind confined.

—Sheep dogs, nowadays, perform their ancient roundup chores in the service of human shepherds. They perform the same labors which ancestors of their present human overlords, superior in the art of aping, have learned by observing the tactics of the wolf-ancestors of these very sheep dogs. Human owners appreciate the intelligence of their sheep dogs, of course, thinking as they do that servile wolf off-spring at some point were taught rational strategy by humans.[23]

—In the same style by which women of hunter-gatherers invented basket-weaving, to enhance their grasp for gathering, so the male hunters became herdsmen when they rounded up tameable animals into corrals—to be kept there as if in larger baskets.

—The act of organizing huntsmen, and of contriving their coherence as "hordes" of warriors, is to some extent an outgrowth of plain hunting and gathering. The traditional cohesion of hunter bands, of hereditary and voluntary totemic hunter associations, came under stress early on—at least in the days of Göbekli Tepe. Elementary notions regarding the roundup of people, enhanced persuasion, coercion and pain, were anticipated quite early during hunters' initiation rites. Subsequent domestication and hyper-domestication tricks, such as castration and torture, were direct elaborations on the butchering skills of hunters. What was done to wounded prey could also be inflicted on human slaves, experimentally—on all those whom hyper-domesticators claimed as their own.

—Later hordes of warriors, as they began to round up humankind, behaved like wolves encircling their prey—or like sheep dogs encircling tamed sheep. Warriors were intellectually quite capable of ranking anything they rounded up—including human herdsmen—at the level of prey animals in the wild. Under conditions of war, domesticators could simply be perceived as lingering there like lead animals, waiting to be hunted and rounded up as part of the throng.

—When totemic hunter associations were transformed into warrior hordes, shamanic leaders of hunting associations became commanders of men. When these commanders waged war, they appreciated their warriors as if they were still fellow comrades with

---

[23]Circular control became an archetype in Navajo Indian thinking. For example, it is considered rude for visitors to drive around someone's hogan, even where a path exists. While it might be easier to drive around than to back off, the archaic and aggressive meaning of "encircling" still lingers.

whom nostalgically they used to hunt animals on the open range. But over time, while planning wars, those same commanders fell into thinking about their men as their own horde of predators, theirs for combat and destined for slaughter. The supreme status of the ancient totems, their supremacy over human hunters, was thereby preempted and usurped by the first aspiring shamanic commander who went beyond pure hunting expeditions and became a warlord.

—We can contemplate parallels by scrutinizing a modern military situation from the inside. Soldiers invariably notice a qualitative difference between exercising on training grounds near barracks and camping in the field. In the open field a commander depends on his men as comrades, for his own wellbeing. Near the barracks he has a hyper-command structure to back him up—that is, a structure that enables him to treat soldiers as subjects, or even as objects toward whom he can express hyper-authority and scorn, quite freely.

—Civilization, or as we call it here, "hyper-domestication," at its beginning implied taking control of humankind. Civilized conditions, as far as their origins can now be traced, have arrived on this planet neither by peaceful design nor with organizational plans drawn by wise economists, not even by the advice of the best skilled domesticators. Civilized groups in antiquity were far more likely to have been rounded up by gangs of warriors—that is, by hordes still led by the obsessions of obsolescent archaic hunters, whose subjects were habitually redefined as prey animals. And of course, the commanders of warrior hordes borrowed a few basic tricks from the very herdsmen whom they raided. They viewed their "roundups" of human domestics in the manner of rounding up animals—from a hunter's point of view such humans were animals of prey.

—Measured along the value scale of hyper-domestication, the most ideal domesticates from among terrestrial animals turned out to be the human species itself, those very same creatures that reinvented themselves as domesticators and owners of plants and animals. Once subdued by warriors, their ability to communicate by way of language proved to be a rather dubious asset. For people taken to be sedentary captives, elementary language turned out to be an additional fetter for their enslavement. Humans could be subjugated with threats and be enticed with lies, flattery, and poetry to come into enclosures. On that account they were easier to be reasoned with, to be enslaved and turned into domestics, than a herd of wild goats.

—In contrast to goats and cattle, humanoids were in the habit of building their own corrals and barns. As soon as their creative energies and sweat were kneaded together with clay, and their hands left signature imprints in the mud that daubed their wattle walls, they were mystically bonded with their dwellings. They planted themselves emotionally to stay rooted in place. If hyper-domesticators were not overly reckless, their domestic humanoids would remain in place even without placing guards (herders) of the warrior variety. But, of course, not all hyper-domesticators in history were intelligent enough to recognize this possibility. Those without rational sensibility coerced their people to build fortresses, and prisons, instead.

—What sort of people were these hyper-domesticators, and who are they today? From the records of history we know them as warlords, monarchs, emperors, and dictators—all still driven by a hunter mentality with deeply felt inclinations to kill. Their genes survive in all of us—a little fiercer in some. They are people of aristocratic demeanor and of the highly praised "leadership ability." Many of them have remained passionate hunters by temperament and poise. Under more democratic circumstances, some of these people still continue to manage governments, parliaments, and industrial corporations. And some continue to "hunt" by newer technological means and strategies. With cybernetic technology they are now able to entangle their victims in *net*-works and circuitry. Flightless bi-pedal creatures no longer need to be captured in nets of hemp. Cybernetic "virtual nets" also serve this function. These nets will, of course, eventually entangle the net-makers themselves.

—Short-sighted greed will drive most hyper-domesticators to overreach themselves. Their greed regenerates ancient quarrels and revolutions with promises of fake freedom. How can freedom ever be won by a species of compulsive tinkerers—i.e. compulsive net weavers who, having achieved material prowess, continue to weave greater entanglements in badly understood empty space?

Militarism: As a category in actual life, militarism highlights the most violent skills of which human ingenuity is capable. In an organized manner it cultivates skills of murderous tricks and strategies that were imagined long ago at the hunter level of evolution. Those skills were boosted dramatically by inventions of flint weapons during the

Neolithic period. Hunting is strategic trickery that human males developed and mastered first vis-à-vis the animals. It called for, and inspired, basic improvements in weapon technology.

—But unbeknownst to the Neolithic weapon makers, their hunter technology is equally well suited for establishing hyper-domestication systems that a little later would enslave the very children of those master flint-knappers. Neolithic hunters had several million years training to become professional killers of animals, of prey ranging from mammoth and hippo, down to wild bovine, buffalo, moose, and deer, including dagger-to-claw combat with bears, lions, and tigers. Following the Göbekli Tepe industrial bubble, some hunters from that region roamed five to six millennia as bands of hungry wanderers. They evolved into hordes of robbers and warriors. At last they assembled and trained armies of warriors that whipped our planet's first imperial "civilizations" into shape.

—A little over five millennia ago, a point of critical mass was reached when sedentary domesticators, in fear of roaming hordes of warriors, no longer could avoid entering into defensive alliances with those whom they feared most. Their treaties usually were made in desperation. With a worldwide increase in domesticator populations, warrior groups that haunted and preyed on them prospered in proportion. Domesticators who lived in settlements proceeded to build and to organize mutual defenses in alliance with some of those who otherwise would conquer them. In other words, to save life and limb, domesticators needed to negotiate surrenders wisely. Together with their new overlords, they stood up against hordes that still roamed in the hills looking for more vulnerable settlements to raid.

—The lowest common denominator in hyper-domestication was residual hunting at the level of sports. The highest amount of force was exerted in fierce competition among hordes of warriors. The continuity of killer vocabulary remains intact and fluid among modern languages of sports and warfare. Our perpetual international wars and armed conflicts are not recent accidents. They are amalgamations of aspiring egos, still caught up in the mentality of decrepit Stone Age huntsmen who evolved into pillaging bandits and who scouted to devise the most lucrative schemes of "protecting" docile settlers in exchange for servitude and booty.

—Throughout the millennia after Göbekli Tepe, the ability to hunt fauna with bow-propelled flint arrows boomeranged on humankind. At some point, our ancestors needed to fear the very weapons that they invented to advance their quest for food. Defensively, they herded themselves into corrals which, originally, they had made of mud, wood, and stone for the control of animals. These were self-made fortresses which, when overwhelmed as defenses, defaulted to their original function as corrals and prisons. Once the first cities were surrounded with walls to keep hostile people out, the self-defeating process of voluntary self-incarceration proved to be unstoppable. There always were more people to be kept out by those who tried to save themselves and their properties within.

—With great interest, and a measure of anxiety, we anticipate the full excavation of all the Lions lodges at Göbekli Tepe. A very early act in the drama of human hyper-domestication has probably been memorialized there. And the overall drama they played there, in all likelihood, was a prototype of modern tragedy. Ten thousand years ago, only those gods that were many sizes greater could have appreciated these aristocratic behaviors as comedy. The social configurations that hyper-domestication produced are now obvious. Totemic deities served as pillars for aristocratic pride, power, and status. Persistent hunters despised those who quit the ways of hunting early on. The more they despised, the easier it was for their warrior descendants to rob and to subjugate those "loser settlers" later.

Ownership and Slavery: Ancient overlords never acknowledged with much precision the distinctions between farmers, herdsmen, and beasts of burden. A hyper-domesticator arrogantly assumed that he was entitled, or even called upon by deity, to own and to manage all naturally and artificially constituted herds and hordes.

—Entire nations have so been enslaved. And this includes groups of warriors that organized under ancestral totems, as well as some totem-inspired warrior-herders who themselves have moved beyond enslaving animals and included among their subjects weaker indebted herdsmen and farmers. Ownership and slavery, over time, have come to be defined in terms of whichever people could be subjected or be branded "inferior." An intelligent predator that has vanquished his own totemic gods with impunity, had no lingering ontological, theological, or ethical scruples—about also subduing human underlings that once upon a time were devotees of those totemic sponsors—later deprived of their mandates.

—Religious counter-movements against the styles of warrior empires have occasionally protested under the aegis of martyrdom and victimization. Some of their saviors posed as sacrificial lambs, as martyrs, beggars, humble hermits, prophets or humanistic reformers. Any concept in human language can become a symbolic candidate for opposition and contrast, and some of these contrasts may indeed have succeeded, for a while, in shaming the hyper-domesticators. But still, there has appeared nothing new under the sun. Already back in hunting days there were hunters, disguised in totemic deerskin for camouflage. In organized hyper-domestication systems there would be "wolves dressed in sheepskin," "foxes that managed chicken coups," or sheep who tried to pose as mighty liberator-wolves. According to a somewhat milder version, "apparent sheep" might later flaunt their piety as being "atoned," and thereupon as having become mandated hyper-domesticators—"by the Grace of God."

Human Sacrifice: In early hyper-domestication cultures a custom has spread that was a direct derivative from the hunters' share sacrifices. Sacrificial shares needed to be paid, especially for large possessions, to greater-than-human powers—such as to some aristocrat's ancestors or special totemic gods. In Part Three of this book we will feature several examples of such "conspicuous consumption" among seemingly hungry gods and totemic ancestors. At our present level of understanding a coherent woldwide evolutionary outline on human sacrifice is not yet possible, but some examples can be identified to serve as benchmarks along the general path of human evolution. A more detailed outline for this subject matter must wait for a time when more data will have been gathered—a time when interested historians are able to focus on the theme of hyper-domestication earlier in life than this writer was able to do.

—Archaic hunters have evolved strict rules of atonement for basic killing and butchering; for various reasons (for divine assistance in killing as well as for justification) they accepted the supervision of totemic deities. Then, during the eras of domestication and hyper-domestication, an increase in ceremonial "sacrificing" has elevated ordinary butchering to the vanity status of high-priests and representatives of supreme gods. High-priests functioned as exalted butchers (i.e. as pious orthodox hunters) in the "kitchen-sanctuaries" of later domesticator high-gods. Hyper-domestication cults were complex accumulations of many simple tricks and moments of atonement that ordinary hunters and butchers have managed to intuit and to compile in the course of their evolution.

—Eventually, full-fledged hyper-domesticators enlarged their festivities with adding human sacrificial victims, to frighten and to own increasingly more human groups. Nothing culturally new has been introduced into the legitimization process for justifying human sacrifice—other than an improved tool kit and the valorization of ordinary killing and butchering. Elaborate killing feasts, potlatches, and excessive victory celebrations—all these are derivatives of simpler archaic hunters' acts of killing, butchering, and ensuing celebrations. Pompous celebrations after successful communal hunts, flattery of heroic organizers and their aggrandizement, could all be hyped by way of adding human victims. Spectacles of terror are the grandest tools of hyper-domestication. They are suited to impress and to manipulate human populations. With sacrifices the hyper-domesticators celebrated the evolution of their species as artificial killers and butchers. At the fulcrum of these festivities stood the archetypal supreme Homo sapiens, as totemic hunter and sacerdotal butcher.

—Hyper-domesticators assume, in principle, that it is proper for them to own humankind after the manner in which domesticators claim to own animals. As proof of their ownership of humankind they offer nothing but the hunter's archaic point that they "can" kill any prey they choose. Their logic is still stuck on paying some share offering to an ancient predator deity—"in kind." Wars in some regions, such as in pre-Columbian Middle America and in Shang China, have been waged to capture prisoners for sacrifice. In modern warfare such struggles have become more secular and more extravagant. All those killed at either side of World War battle lines could be counted as victims and sanctimoniously be laid to rest into the hands of some almighty totemic sponsor—some eagle-, bear-, lion- or dragon-faced Fatherland or Motherland—for eternal legitimization of conquest, peace, and the victim's well-earned rest.

—In spite of such sanctimonious hype and hysterics, people are executed and sacrificed mostly for the sake of emphasis—to maintain an environment that, supposedly, is pacified and thereby balanced successfully, by terror and blood. The difference between "sacrifice" and "execution" lies, essentially, in the nomenclature by which hyper-domestication mandates define the victims either as rightful "possessions" or as subjects handed to administrators by greater and purer predator authority, in trust.

The Growth of Populations: On the total scope of our planet's size and evolution, seven billion grazing animals and foragers would not seem to be a dangerously large number. But seven billion primates, experimentally inclined omnivores, whose ancestors over the course of six million years have learned to "ape" exemplary wolf, lion, and eagle totems—that is, carnivores—and whose deadly technological skills have grown to outwit every creature on earth with only a few species of bacilli and viruses remaining undefeated. Well! Such creatures can create problems even unto themselves. If they were any species other than ourselves, we would long have recognized the predicament with apprehension and fear. In the eyes of a hypothetical other intelligent species we surely would have been identified as a plague to ourselves—a perilous and suicidal infestation of the planet.

—An increase in human numbers has been the ultimate blessing and reward that the gods of all eras have bestowed on humankind—among gatherers and hunters, domesticators, and hyper-domesticators. The generosity of that blessing appears to have increased over time. Unprecedented growth of the human population, in the Göbekli Tepe area, was likely stimulated by the booming flint industry during its final two millennia of fulltime gathering and hunting. It produced an imbalance of numbers between human hunters and the fauna. Improvements in flint weapon technology definitely helped increase the yields of communal hunting drives.

—But the technologically exaggerated blessings of human numbers were actually extorted from the gods at weapon-point. The gods were either unable or unwilling to replace all the prey animals that were being killed by flint-tipped arrows and spears. Larger human numbers provided an apparent sense of security. Over-hunting increased the food supply at least temporarily, as it also increased human numbers. When then, with hyper-domestication emphases the hunting drives were being enlarged to the size of military campaigns, human victims took the place of prey animals.

—More human babies were born and raised. Half of all offspring were males and potential hunters. And by so generating its own population bubble, the flint-based industry at Göbekli Tepe drove hunter culture in the direction of over-population and sporadic prey shortages. Dissatisfied hunters hoped for a more settled and better life. But with a shortage of prey animals their crises were accelerated and reasons for more people to go wandering were multiplied. Food substitutions needed to be increased by way of gathering, planting, and herding, and be made regular.

—Even though humankind was periodically threatened with starvation, the option of intentionally limiting the number of human births would have entered into few people's minds. Traveling was the ultimate solution to all problems that would arise in archaic hunter and gatherer societies, and before hunters tried to become sedentary, the hardships of travel themselves limited the number of children whom one could carry along. All the while at Göbekli Tepe's transitional cult, the entire thrust of a new life-oriented consciousness, and religiosity, was intended to encourage more procreation, more hatching and birthing. All sacred enclosures and menhirs, and most bas-reliefs at Göbekli Tepe, illustrate this message.

—Millennia later, in hyper-domesticated environments, population growth still remained a crucial factor. One never knew when the army of another warlord might arrive, break down one's defenses, kill lots of people, loot the resources and lead the able-bodied people away as captives, to turn them into slaves or sacrificial victims. Still, even while human lives were being wasted and hyper-domestication systems collided, human populations fluctuated and, on average, their numbers increased. The driving force for their increase in numbers was fear.

—Every conquered society and every warlord and occupier hoped and called for larger numbers of men. All threatened people prayed for the same. Men were needed for defense as well as for preemptive strikes and general schemes of conquest. This means that at any step of military activity, in any conflict, both sides of combatants hoped for short term victories on the basis of having superior numbers, provided as blessings from a God superior to other gods.

They mistook the larger intrinsic absurdity, of victorious competition among hyper-domestication systems and numbers, as constituting divine blessings. Much blind faith was needed to believe in the ways of human progress. There were no alternatives. Armies hurtling people into walled cities to keep them out of harm's way presented themselves as the best solution in emergencies. If a family felt weak and insecure, if a king estimated that he was short a thousand men, there was no better long-range plan than to encourage an increase in numbers. In addition, one might also pray that the ruling dynasty would forever be able to protect its people. In some modern lands, the encouragement for mothers to raise more sons is not subtle at all.

—Within the larger evolutionary process, the necessity of military defense entailed an increase in general controls. What started as simple domestication of plants and animals was amplified to a "hyper" stage, to establish greater controls with an increasing number of yokes and chains, put on animals first, and then also on people. For greater efficiency, human beings were assessed as property and resources. They were owned even while they themselves were still trying to own plants, animals, wives, children, servants, and even slaves—all in the name of inborn dignities and entitlement. To own and to be owned became an implied necessity, driven by the fear of losing security and life itself.

—Let us for a moment reflect a little more intimately: where is there a teacher today in democratic lands, and in open competition, who at one time or other has not been given the friendly advice to sell himself or herself a little more enthusiastically. Wherever the commercial valuation of people is being applied in earnest, in competition, there opens up the road that leads from pride of acquisition straight to self-enslavement. At that point the next round of hyper-domestication has already begun.

—Religion, consisting of submissive responses toward greater-than-human reality, can sometimes be counted on to dampen hasty changes. With the words "be fruitful and multiply," the supreme deity of Judaism, Christianity, and Islam has been blessing its people—as has Shang-Di and the supreme ancestors of China been blessing their offspring. These they blessed with population numbers that grew by hundreds of millions, reaching billions. So, how can a deity that once upon a time has blessed humanity with numbers amend its eternal promises? For an "eternal" deity to be permitted to update ancient promises seems unthinkable. An updated revelation, however, might specify a little more precisely the point at which an exploited blessing translates into a curse. Not only blessing-loaded religions lack such precision, modern promise-loaded political ideologies also do. And then, can selfish human rationality really be trusted with an updated divine revelation? Or can it be trusted to distribute secular political benefits any better?

Monotheism: Much has been made of "Hymns to Aton" whereby the Pharaoh Akhenaton addressed his Sun deity, Aton, as the Only One. Based on a few of his chiseled lines, this eccentric ruler has been credited with having been the world's first monotheist. Indeed, if the wisdom of the entire world were limited to this one man's own royal inscriptions, he would have been that first. But if we let the Sun-deity Aton shine a little brighter onto Akhenaton's inscriptions we discover that his hymns attest to a monotheistic relationship only between the jaded pharaoh himself and his personalized Sole God Aton, who loved only Akhenaton the pharaoh—and his spouse as an add-on. This was the religion of one person who aspired to absolute rule and to supreme divine honors, something that, lucky for Egypt, eluded him during his career as a Horus-Falcon on the throne of Egypt.[24]

—If a comparison were to be attempted, then Akhenaton's religion shows very little in common with the reactionary monotheism for which Abraham and Moses, along with priests and prophets of Yahweh/Elohim, under the administration of King David, have been credited. Their religion—though it was sponsored by a royal dynasty as well—was not promulgated for the advantage of a sole ruler, but at least for a confederation of tribes. Some prophetic checks and balances were present in the latter type of monotheism.

—Akhenaton's theocratic dream stood in a direct line with the ambitions of earlier Egyptian pharaohs. About the hyper-domestication habits of First Dynasty pharaohs more will emerge below, in

[24]The theological dimension of hyper-domestication (over-domestication) has been dealt with extensively in Luckert, *Egyptian Light and Hebrew Fire: Theological and Philosophical Roots of Christendom...*, SUNY Press, 1991.

Chapter Seventeen. The direction and pace of evolution for Western civilization and monotheistic religion were set in ancient Egypt. A comparison with ancient China, in Chapter Nineteen, will assist by having these two civilizations illuminate each other.

—It turns out that monotheism as such never quite was the cure-all for imbalances that beset human cultures, economies, or organized religions. The mathematical possibilities in everyday living are too numerous to be reduced to a single monad. Beyond the consoling vision of living under a sole divine authority, monotheism continually tempts human arithmetic with the next larger number—a dualism. By trying to bundle "salvation" all into one, monotheists easily end up in the hands of an apparent "Opposite." The world can then conveniently be explained as a warring dualism.

—Within a postulated dualism of "Good and Evil" (God and Devil), the evil portion usually turns out to be scientifically more demonstrable than the "Good" side—the latter of which sits enthroned, imagined as a unified and inexplicable someone, self-contained. Logically it cannot be otherwise. Analytic human minds are easily duped by their own smoke and mirrors. Scientific experimentation requires prior analysis, which means "breakdown into a multiplicity of aspects or parts." Accordingly, scientism is far more efficient and generous toward the fragments that it produces, by analysis and for experimental control. Analysis, breakdown, control, conquest and destruction will therefore always be easier to achieve along the road of science than will be synthesis, growth, or organic wholeness. And we cannot forget that *homines sapientes* are imitational creatures that evolved while honing their skills of rational analysis, as artificial killers and butchers.

—As far as one can track imperial monotheisms historically, such politicized religions may indeed have taken root a little over five millennia ago, to support the consolidation of imperial powers in Egypt and Mesopotamia, and possibly elsewhere. Also, for a span of time domesticators of cattle rediscovered images of themselves within the circles of their own reasoning. They saw themselves as livestock, similarly so owned. Living under the whip of hyper-domesticators, some ancients were taught that they themselves were livestock, owned by the gods and managed by royals on behalf of the gods. Of course, those who wished to liberate themselves from the fetters of hyper-domestication needed, for that reason, to first learn transcend the myths and ideologies that defined them as livestock and property to begin with.[25]

—Whatever ideology is used by hyper-domesticators to justify a people's enslavement, a rational critique of that same worldview, good or bad, is also required in the victims' struggle for liberation, as a starting point for "un-installment." The ancient version must be upended and modified, to forge a stream of counter-weights that are suitable for rebalancing. Rebels who start reasoning entirely from scratch, who ignore the former gods that used to underwrite the worldview that lost utility, or who prefer to rationalize on the basis of a modern atheistic ontology, are in danger of ending up with still older predatory primitivisms—such as, for example, some predatory heroic and totemistic nationalisms. Moreover, on the sheer basis of modern axioms which ascribe "impersonal matter," "energy," or "blind force" to the nature of the universe, it is difficult to argue in support of human rights, dignity, or the legitimacy of any life at all. The history of religions, therefore, remains an important intellectual tool of reorientation in the ongoing human quest for dignity and life.

—In Chapter Seventeen we will see how the first pharaohs of Egypt—the god-kings of the First Dynasty—ran their courts. As deified hunters, mutated hunter/herders, they operated them like barnyards stocked with humankind. Ministers and servants were sacrificed to patch the ruptures that got torn in the dynastic fabric when immortal pharaohs accidentally died and were temporarily transformed into Osiris, the god of death. At a god-king's funeral, human victims were added to the royal burial for shock effect, to strengthen the dynasty by way of terrorizing all would-be rebels. Even pet lions, as progeny of archaic totems, were obliged to accompany the divine-human Osiris during his moments of transition—while he was becoming his own successor. Peeping through the curtains, and reading a little between the lines, I suspect that the sacrificial deaths of those victims had little to do with the pharaoh's

---

[25]The idea is blatantly stated in the Mesopotamian Enuma Elish. It is reflected more gently in the hymnody of the Hebrew Psalms (e.g. Psalm 23). In the latter texts people are sheep, chosen by a divine Good Shepherd to graze on his watered green pastures. In a modern setting, where the deity no longer insists on having anything butchered and roasted for him, such poetry has become suitable to be read even at funeral ceremonies, for comfort.

wellbeing in a hereafter. It appears to have had everything to do with empowering the imperial dynasty, that is, with enabling god-kings to rule Egypt more effectively. These generational funerary sacrifices added weight and an air of calm—of peace imposed by terror and fear—imposed by the single deity of Egypt who rotated his Falcon manifestation in order to continue the dynastic royal spectacle from one generation to the next.

PART THREE:
EXAMPLES OF CHANGE AND TRANSITION

Hunting Coconuts and Butchering Yams

Dema mythology, as recorded by Adolf Jensen, has become a mainstay in the history of religions for explaining paleo-planter religion. The publication of extracts of these materials, in English, so far has led to a neglect of what otherwise could also be understood as a degenerate phase of the Wemale "hunter tradition."

This means that the dynamic of the Neolithic transition from hunting to domestication has been neglected and obscured. Our present discourse is based on a revised assortment of Wemale legends and myths, along with Eskimo and Navajo texts for comparison.

13. Hunting Coconuts and Butchering Yams

Adolf E. Jensen's monumental report regarding Hainuwele mythology and *dema* theology was co-published with Herman Niggemeyer under the title *Hainuwele: Volkserzählungen von der Molukken-Insel Ceram*—in the first volume of "Ergebnisse der Frobenius Expedition," Frankfurt am Main, 1939.[1] The first English translation of the Hainuwele myth was made available in Joseph Campbell's *The Masks of God*, in 1959.

—The evolutionary phase of paleo-planter culture and *dema* theology was brought to my attention in the classroom of Professor Mircea Eliade, at Chicago, during the early 1960s. He explained how to understand the mythical origin and functions of various edible cultivars in paleo-planter fashion, and he recognized the role of secret men's societies and their peculiar understanding of life and death. Above all else, he explained *dema* theology as the key concept by which one could begin to understand the religious world of Wemale paleo-planters. The contrast between heaven-oriented mythology of rice-planters, and of earth-oriented *dema*-theology among Wemale planters of tubers seemed fascinating, indeed.[2] Mircea Eliade raised relevant questions toward understanding the orientation of men at secret society centers, where human sacrifice as well as head-hunting were being practiced. The extreme behavior of Wemale men's associations was rationalized as a tragic consequence of the paleo-planters'

---

[1]Jensen, Adolf E., *Das religiöse Weltbild einer frühen Kultur.* Leipzig, 1939. Jensen, Adolf E. and Heinrich Niggemeyer. *Hainuwele: Volkserzählungen von der Molukken Insel Ceram.* Copyright 1939 by Klostermann Verlag, Frankfurt—Portions are translated here and used with permission. *Die Drei Ströme: Züge aus dem geistigen und religiösen Leben der Wemale.* Leipzig, 1948. *Mythos und Kult bei den Naturvölkern.* Wiesbaden, 1951. English Translation: *Myth and Cult among Primitive Peoples.* Chicago, 1963.

[2]For the model of a rice-planter religion see Hans Schärer, *Ngaju Religion.* The Hague: Martinus Nijhoff. 1963.

mystic identification with the realm of vegetation—in short, as the tragic consequence of a philosophical plant mysticism. Much of Professor Eliade's empathic reasoning on this theme was based on works by Volhard and Jensen.[3]

—The "Hainuwele" materials have been translated from German into English as a rule in abridged form. They were streamlined to best accommodate the general paleo-planters import given to the texts by Jensen himself. However, certain sentences in the original record, which could have cast an oblique light on Wemale hunting as well, were neglected and omitted by this approach. It must be understood, of course, that within the presupposed context of "the planters' *dema* theology," some of the neglected portions appeared non-essential to the translators and editors—and understandably so.

—It is on account of the crucial importance of these omissions that I have undertaken a fresh examination of the text, in German and in English, by way of including some of those omitted sentences—albeit, still abridging and all the while trying not to preempt the entire German text in the second language. Neither this nor any future studies of Wemale religion will ever exhaust the original implications without systematically returning to Jensen's unabridged German texts and contexts. It is my aim here to add my humble opinions to a series of commentaries that have already been published and that one might expect to be added in the future. For personal digestion I translated some sentences beyond what so far has been made available in English, and for the sake of economy I omitted others which, in turn, I judged to be less important to make my personal points. My aim has been to translate just enough to enable English readers to rethink Wemale mythology as pertaining not only to Hainuwele the divine maiden, but perhaps even more importantly as pertaining to Ameta, her father who was a hunter. While reconsidering these materials, I have become convinced that the mythological personage, Ameta, is not only significant for understanding Ceramese Neolithic planter religion, but is downright essential for understanding their mythology in relation to worldwide processes of Stone Age hunter religion in transition—in addition to head-hunting, human sacrifice, and cannibalism.

---

[3]Mircea Eliade, *Patterns in Comparative Religions*, Cleveland, 1963 (1958). *Myth and Reality. 1963. From Primitives to Zen.* New York and Evanston, 1967. See also E. Volhard, *Kannibalismus.* Stuttgart, 1939.

—Rather than enabling this mythology only to reveal paleo-planter religion, it needs to be mined for evolutionary glimpses of the Stone Age hunter tradition expressed by nostalgic Wemale huntsmen. Notwithstanding the Romantic uplift that a Neolithic sacrificial Hainuwele Girl might have provided for the international folklore market, the actual horticultural dimension of the Wemale women appears to have been only obliquely illuminated by the men's sacrificial Maro ritual. Our presupposition is that, before Hainuwele mythology was initially shared with Jensen for recording, it had been processed by the minds of obsolescent hunters who had been involved in headhunting and in human sacrifice. These men were trying to frighten the women into believing that the secret men's societies did indeed control the essence of the women's tuber horticulture. Being aware of these intentions, we recommend that the Hainuwele myth should, henceforth, be approached more appropriately as the combined myth of "Ameta and Hainuwele."

—Some twenty years after my first exposure to Wemale religion, at Chicago, and after some fifteen years of periodic fieldwork in American Indian hunter traditions, I revisited the Jensen materials concerning the Maluku Island of Ceram. It happened at the request of the editors of *East and West* at IsMEO, Florence and Rome, during the late 1980s.[4] It was then that I noticed a dimension that I had nearly overlooked the first time around—namely, the severe tension between the genders in decadent hunter societies, which tended to increase during crises and in times of transition. My own fieldwork among American Indians in the Greater Southwest has sensitized me to this issue.

—In the Maluku Islands, the dynamic tension between headhunters and their women appears to have been far more complex than a mere obligatory philosophical or mystic identification with the latter's garden produce. By hindsight, most of this philosophical plant mysticism which Volhard, Jensen, and Eliade identified as having been central to *dema* theology—the thought that it furnished the key to understanding head-hunting, cannibalism, and human sacrifice in the context of tuber horticulture—should now be reconsidered. It

---

[4]See Luckert: "Hainuwele and Headhunting Reconsidered," in *East and West,* vol. 40, nos. 1-4, pages 261-279, IsMEO, Florence and Rome, 1990. Portions of this publication were made available at www.historyofreligions.com, in 2000.

needs to be considered under the rubric of "Crises and self-justification among obsolescent Neolithic hunters."

—Certainly, Professor Eliade was aware of the Wemale gender conflict, at least at the level of their storytelling. It is merely the Professor's philosophical rationalization on behalf of the Wemale men, to the effect that they were mystically immersed and rationally balanced planters—and perhaps his underestimation of their demoralized condition as obsolescent hunters—to which I address my reservations here. It is for the purpose of explaining my revised understanding of the Adolf E. Jensen legacy, concerning Wemale religion, that I offer my German re-examinations in English, for consideration by readers in both languages, of course.

—In this writer's revised opinion, the "Hainuwele" story is a men's narrative of the hunter-butcher burlesque type, primarily. It represents planter mythology and *dema* theology only in the twisted perspective of desperate obsolescent hunters. We do not have here a myth that the women, the actual owners of Wemale horticulture, would have been pleased to repeat or to explain. We do not know how low the women valued any stories that their men were telling at their *baileo* center. Chances are quite high that the men's stories never were intended to be even heard by female ears, and that they were not expected to be appreciated by females. For us in the English-speaking world, this discernment must eventually lead to a reconsideration of the "*dema* theology complex" in its entirety, as prelude to a better general understanding of the so-called "Neolithic Revolution"—the transition of hunters and gatherers to horticulture, world-wide.

The Myth of the dema Ameta and Hainuwele

In the days when the nine ancestral families of humankind emigrated from Nunusaku they lived at several places in West-Ceram.... Among the people of that time lived a man named Ameta, who was unmarried and had no children. One day Ameta went out hunting with his dog. After a while the dog found a [wild] pig in the forest which he chased toward a pond. The pig ran into the water, while the dog remained standing at the shore. Soon the pig was unable to swim anymore, and it drowned. When Ameta arrived at the place, he pulled the dead pig ashore. At its tusk he found a coconut. In those days, no coconut palms existed yet on earth.

—In a dream, Ameta was instructed to plant the coconut and he did so.... In three days, the palm tree had grown to a considerable height. After three more days, it bloomed. He climbed up the tree to cut the flowers in order to make a drink from them. Doing so, he cut his finger, and blood dripped on a palm blossom. He went home to wrap his wound. When he returned after three days, he saw that his blood on the palm leaf had become mixed with juice of the flower, and he saw that a human being was taking shape there. The face of a person was already formed. When he returned after another three days, the body of the person was there, and after another three days, his drops of blood had become a small girl. Commanded in another dream, Ameta brought the girl to his home.... He called her Hainuwele (limb of the coconut tree).

Fig. 34. Wild Boar with Coconut. Adapted to "Ameta and Hainuwele" by the author. Based on Richard Bartz, Munich, habitat photo. Http://creativecommons.org/licenses/by-sa/2.5/deed.en.

—The girl grew up quickly. And already in three days she was mature enough for marriage. But she was not like ordinary people. When she yielded to necessity, her excrement consisted of valuable objects, such as China-ware and gongs. Her father Ameta became therefore very rich.

—In those days, a great Maro Dance was held at Tamene Siwa, which lasted nine nights. The original nine human families all participated. They danced in the pattern of a nine-fold spiral. When the people dance the Maro at night, the women sit in the middle. They do not participate in the dancing, but they do hand out Sirih and Pinang for chewing to the men who dance. During this great dance, the girl Hainuwele stood in the middle and gave Sirih and Pinang to those who danced.... On the evening of the second night... she handed out corals instead. All the people thought the corals to be very beautiful.... During the next, the third night... she distributed beautiful China plates, one to each of those who were present. During the fourth night she gave away still larger China plates. During the fifth night she distributed large bush knives, and during the sixth night she gave nicely worked Sirih containers made of copper. During the seventh night she gave earrings of gold, and during the eighth night beautiful gongs. In this manner the value of objects that Hainuwele distributed was increased night after night. And these happenings seemed increasingly more mysterious to the men. They met and consulted with one another. They were very jealous (i.e. envious) of the fact that Hainuwele was able to distribute such wealth. And they decided to kill her.

—During the ninth night of the great Maro Dance, Hainuwele was stood up again in the middle of the place, to distribute Sirih. The men, however, had dug a deep hole at the place.... Inside the slowly moving spiral dance formation, they edged the girl Hainuwele toward the grave and pushed her in. The loud Maro song, chanted in harmony with three voices, drowned out her cries. Earth was thrown and heaped on her, and with their movements the dancers trampled solid the dirt on the grave. When morning dawned, the Maro Dance was over. The people returned to their homes.

—When the Maro Dance was finished, and after Hainuwele failed to return home, Ameta knew that she had been killed.... He went to the dancing place and dug up her corpse and cut it up into many pieces. The individual portions of the body he buried over the entire area surrounding the dancing place. Only the two arms, which he had not cut up, he did not bury; but he brought these to Mulua Satene—to that woman who, in the beginning when people were created, was transformed from an unripe banana. It was she who in those days ruled over the people. The buried pieces of Hainuwele's corpse, however, were transformed into things which hitherto had not existed on earth—that is, into tubers which humans have used as their staple food ever since. The stomach of Hainuwele became a large pot, which has been preserved to this day and is in possession of the village chief of Honitetu.... At this point in the story are described the nine body portions of Hainuwele and the nine fruits into which these portions were transformed.

—Ameta cursed the people, and Mulua Satene was angry with them, because they had killed. She built a large gate at a place in Tamene Siwa. It consisted of a nine-fold spiral, fashioned after the Maro Dance formation. Mulua Satene herself stood on the trunk of a large tree at one side of the gate, and she held the severed arms of Hainuwele in both of her hands. She assembled the people at the opposite side of the large gate and spoke to them: "I will no longer live here, because you have killed. I will leave you this day. Now you all must come to me through this gate. Whoever comes through the gate remains human, and whoever does not pass through, with them it will be different." The people all attempted to pass through the spiral gate, but not all succeeded. Whoever failed to come to Mulua Satene through that gate became an animal or a ghost. In this manner originated pigs, deer, birds, fish, and many ghosts who live on earth. They had been people, but they could not pass through the gate behind which stood Mulua Satene....

—Satene said, "I will leave you this day, and you will see me on earth no more. Only after you have died will you see me again...." Then Mulua Satene disappeared from the earth, and she has been living since then as nitu (ghost) at Salahua, which is the mountain of the dead, in southern West-Ceram. Whoever wishes to reach her place must die first.[5]

Hainuwele Mythology in Historiography

The plot of the central events in Hainuwele's murder received careful scholarly attention several decades ago and has at some point been judged historically, as a "situational incongruity." Hainuwele's curious mode of production, the excretion of valuable articles, has provided a hint for literary dating. Such trade goods, which on Ceram functioned as money, could not have antedated the spice trade of the sixteenth and seventeenth centuries when these

---

[5]Translated and abridged from Jensen and Niggemeyer (1939: 59-64).

things first appeared in the Maluku Islands. They may even belong to a much later time—to a "cargo situation" that was brought about by the intensification of Dutch colonialism, between 1902 and 1910.[6]

–The apparently recent date of an "archaic" myth need not be cause for alarm for those who have assumed its greater antiquity. Three or four centuries would, anyhow, be a full enough running time for a story plot in oral tradition. Living oral traditions, of archaic provenance, of the kind which some among us have been recording, were constantly being recycled by each successive generation of storytellers—and were updated as a matter of course. Those miraculously lengthy running-times of oral Near Eastern legends—which some scholars have postulated to double the time frame of biblical prehistory—and which supposedly have remained true to form over a millennium of oral sharing—do themselves belong in the realm of legendary subject matter. In the case of anonymous recorder scribes of antiquity, we may safely suspect that their powers of imagination have been consistently underestimated. After half a millennium of so-called "oral tradition," the distinction between an orally documented historical event, and the bare historical evidence that the thought of such an event scored in the mind of a storyteller—matters very little anymore, unless the "event" is also substantiated by archaeology, and is detectable.

–Traditional narrators told their stories for the sake of contemporary relevance and not to conform to recorded antiquity. They had no recorded antiquity to conform to. Thus, if Chinese porcelain ware was present on the island of Ceram, and if on top of that fact some such ware was used in native ritual, then, surely, mentioning it in revered traditions was required of every teacher-narrator worth his keep.

–For the time being, however, the concrete historical context of colonial circumstances under which Hainuwele became known as producer of "all sorts of valuable articles, such as Chinese dishes and gongs," is a most welcome benchmark for the history of Wemale religion. It helps us adjust the almost certainly overstated dynamic of philosophical food mysticism among archaic domesticators. It is amazing how much historical realism a few imported dishes and gongs can contribute to our perspective. Nobody can deny that these

---

[6]See Jonathan Z. Smith, "A Pearl of Great Price and a Cargo of Yams: a Study in Situational Incongruity," in *History of Religions,* 1976.

goods had to be imported and had to become known before Jensen's version of the story could have been told.

—However, the greater part of the question still remains: What is the more archaic core of this "Hainuwele" myth? The central human sacrifice of the dema girl Hainuwele and the propagation of edible plants of her body portions, together appear more basic to the myth than the presence of Chinese "currency" that supposedly was distributed as gifts during a ritual. I therefore suggest that the archaic core included some version of Hainuwele's creative activity and her mode of production. While her actions may seem absurd to modern urban dwellers, Hainuwele's excretions cannot be simply discounted as "filthy lucre" or as an ironic primitive version of "dirty money."

—The creative excretion motive has been recorded elsewhere in the world, much earlier, and independent of Western colonialism, in ninth century Japan. In the Nihongi we read that the goddess of food, Uke-mochi no Kami, was killed by Tsuki-yo-mi, a heavenly messenger deity, who felt insulted on account of the dirty food that the goddess offered him. Then, from the dead body of Uke-mochi no Kami, domestic animals and foods for the future continued to come forth.[7] Where her hair was parted, on the head of this goddess, originated cow and horse; on her brow originated cob-millet; on her eyebrows originated silkworm cocoons; in her eyes originated another variety of millet; in her body originated rice; in her vagina originated barley, large beans, and Adzuki beans.

—Likewise in the Ceramese version, excrement and dirt (*Kot und Schmutz*) do not exist in opposition to life-supporting food plants. In primitive awareness, excrements are here no more and no less than edible foods expressed [pun intended], contemplated, and then renamed in future tense. Moreover, the dirty female method of creation "between excrement and urine" is sufficiently highlighted at other places in Ceramese lore, wherever females function as cooks and presenters of food. For instance, in mythical primordial times, female excretions were cooked to become edible sago [Metroxylon]. And an ever-so-dirty grandmother was transformed into a sago tree.[8]

---

[7]Florenz, Karl. *Die Historischen Quellen der Shinto-Religion.* Göttingen und Leipzig, 1919, pp. 144f; translated by the author. Anyone who ever harvested barley with bare hands knows that the origin episode, in the Nihongi, was narrated by rowdy men and was understood to be burlesque to the extreme.

[8]See Jensen and Niggemeyer, 1939: 69f.

—The problem of purity and impurity, to the extent that it burdened primitive hunters, cannot be dealt with here in its entirety. Let it suffice to observe that feminine secretions, since the ape level some seven million years ago, have been evaluated as life fluids that flowed in stark contrast to the masculine drive for hunting, killing, and death-wielding. Still very recently, a trace of such life-generating fluid would have spoiled any traditional Navajo hunter's chances of killing a deer. The feminine opposition to masculine aggression, even the confiscation of stone weapons held by males, has been observed in contemporary chimpanzee behavior.[9]

—Then there is the evolutionary happenstance, on the island of Ceram, that human female resisters to violence, the men's partners in pleasure, at some point in time succeeded in growing more nourishment for their paleo-planter households than their men could hunt. The evidence of this crisis of transition to domestication lies scattered worldwide—to the effect that, as the result of a change in livelihood, male hunters have lost much of their self-esteem. Such basic evolutionary considerations go a long way toward explaining the Wemale men's corpus of chauvinistic and scatological Hainuwele mythology.

—A measure of common-sense equality is achieved when some Ceramese stories, again after the pattern of scatology, tell how a male's act of urination could have produced pregnancy (Hainuwele, pp. 269, 356). In addition, one can learn how Wemale men associated pollution with the presence of urine and excrement, and also with insult and with the power to kill and to expel (Hainuwele, 172f, 177, 224, 327, 329f). But none of these chauvinistic negatives are sufficient to overcome the positive and creative significance of feminine excretions. That significance is supremely anchored in the universal feminine function of giving birth—and everyone who is alive has to acknowledge his and her derivative nature.

—We must return specifically to Hainuwele's creativity. She first created by way of excrements, that is, without sacrificing her own body. Thus, during her first round of gift-giving her body served as a resource and container, as naturally as such a creative function can be assigned to a womb. Only later, after her body had been cut into

---

[9]See Chapter One, above; also Frans De Waal. *Chimpanzee Politics: Power and Sex among Apes.* New York, 1982.

pieces by male hunters, and after her remains decayed to a smelly substance of excremental quality, would edible bodies of tubers and other plants begin to bud from the planted portions. In this context, the reader is encouraged to contemplate the entire fertilization – planting – burial – growing – digging – cutting – cooking – eating – nourishment – excretion cycle of a tuber, first with and then also without its detour through human digestive tracts. As soon as one contemplates realistically this entanglement of the planters' symbiotic relationship with humus, dung, and dirt, then everything concerning paleo-planter existence becomes clearer.

—Meanwhile, it goes without saying that historians of religions, who venture beyond the domain of sanitized written history into dirty fields and primitive customs, must also dare to investigate beyond a historian's own theoretical *"Sitz im Leben."* Even the word *"Sitz"* (seat) is out of order in this context. Primitive tuber planters dig in dirt to dispose of excrement, as well as to harvest sustenance.

—"Ethnology" can be defined as the top layer of archaeology, the layer that still smells. And expressions from urban commerce, such as "dirty money," are too negative and hopelessly out of context in the garden patches of Hainuwele's people. On the other hand, the gold-shitting asses or cattle in Eurasian fairy tales belong only partly in the realm of literary fantasies. Their concrete incarnations graze, still, on pastures of the real world. Unto valuable fields and soil, and unto the grass that in turn nourishes them, animals bestow their divinely endowed blessings.

—Adolf Jensen has repeatedly expressed despair about his inability to explain the central meaning of Hainuwele mythology—that is, its existential connection with headhunting as well as the implied necessity of ritual killing. He must have sensed that pure philosophical plant mysticism did not provide enough of a rational connection. Our own interpretation of the central theme in Hainuwele mythology, therefore, does not only concern Hainuwele's more recent creation of foreign trade goods, but more so her elementary participation in the universally "dirty" creativity practiced by womankind. The basic role, that females universally have served as birth-givers, gardeners, cooks and presenters of food was, of course, continually modified in contention with the attitudes of their men. One must remember that the Wemale men were nostalgic huntsmen who would rather eat meat that they hunted than accept vegetables or fruit from the hands of their more successful women.

—A competing Ceramese foil to the Hainuwele excretion theme is on record and is most revealing. There is a tale that attributes the ability to create by excretion also to a heavenly hunter. A heavenly hunter went out hunting together with an earthly one. He excreted a *kussu* and urinated into existence a streak that became a snake. The earthly hunter subsequently killed this snake (*Hainuwele,* 77). Of course, everyone knows that earthly hunters who tell such a story are already in the habit of killing snakes and *kussu*. Is this dualistic hunter story therefore older than the Hainuwele theme of the planters' ritual killings? Or is it simply a late hunters' tale concerned with such justification as still could be derived for "dirty creativity" from a heavenly hunter's domain? Hunting as an occupation is mentioned here as the common denominator between the celestial and the earthly realms. Is this story told, then, to demonstrate that excreted or born creatures belong to hunters, to be killed by them?

—The moment has come to move a little ways beyond Hainuwele's scatological creativity, to another point in the myth which is central to the Maro sacrifice itself. In the narrative rendered above, Hainuwele's primary ceremonial function during the Maro festival has been identified several times. Her role was to distribute to the dancing men the customary *Sirih* and *Pinang* for chewing (i.e. medicine to heal and to revive). As the ceremonial approaches its climax, on the ninth night, no latter-day embellishments involving distributions of treasure items are mentioned anymore by the narrator.

—Such earlier distributions in the story, apparently, served only to upstage the people's traditional expectations of the girl being of ordinary service to the men. As it turned out, the men became angry when she surpassed their expectations and revealed herself as a divinity of extravagant wealth. Thus, knowing that the final night of the ceremony featured only Sirih and Pinang, and considering the recent age of Chinese porcelain in Ceram, we can assume that the presence of luxury goods during the earlier nights of the ceremony were simply a storyteller's free elaborations. Thus, inasmuch as in the ceremonial context of the final night, Sirih and Pinang (i.e. medicines to heal and to resuscitate) have again been assigned centrality, the suspicion which has been raised concerning the recent age of Chinese porcelain in Ceram, reveals therefore an entertainer's value-added elaboration, from the second through the eighth nights. This elaboration serves then to elucidate the resentment that the dancers developed when they found Hainuwele to be an archetype of creative womanhood—thus, not only a goddess food, but also a general goddess of wealth.

—Hainuwele's killers were jealous about her ability to procure and distribute wealth—or so goes the lame excuse. Judged in the light of an elongated evolutionary perspective, however, this rationalization of the Maro sacrifice, as a result of envy, may stem from the colonial decade when the older struggle for maintaining sheer authority had already gone out of focus. Certainly, it was not only men-to-goddess envy that motivated archaic Wemale men to kill her? The Hainuwele myth was structured to depreciate the girl's person-hood and womanhood. Hainuwele was a goddess, created by an unmarried male without the involvement of a woman. It took a Maro sacrifice, and the telling of her myth, to establish her place in horticulture and to place her powers completely under the authority of the men.

—An answer is floating closer to the surface now. Wemale men sought ceremonial control over Hainuwele's domain of food plants, over the village with its dancing place and the general realm of feminine horticulture itself. They envied the "real" economic status of their women, as contrasted with the unrealistic hunter nostalgia that, after the decline of hunting, became a doomed residual inheritance.

—They sought ways to become real men again, which meant reinstating themselves as their families' chief defenders and providers. These men turned into violent nuisances because, during village skirmishes, their violent behavior established them at least as the apparent defenders of their kin. They filled their deficit as providers with ritual authority and with the terror of head-hunting and cannibalism. Pathetically maladjusted for their evolutionary role in horticultural adaptation, these obsolescent huntsmen failed the balance test. Of course, they failed primarily by our standards, because our standards are based on hindsight.

The Hainuwele Myth and its Hunter Legacy

Before the Hainuwele tale can be approached again as a central myth of paleo-planters, it must be aligned in the evolutionary context of the men's failing hunter culture and religiosity. The story bears the full imprint of the men's authorship. Indeed, the onus of doubt regarding the antiquity of this tale fosters a welcome sense of unease.

What, in academia, will happen now to Adolf E. Jensen's innovative and famous category of "*dema* divinities"?

—It is amazing how uncritically the Hainuwele story has been accepted as the most central and typical myth of paleo-cultivators. As such, it can henceforth be held only with the proviso of seeing it in a larger evolutionary context. Scholars have fallen for the Romantic chauvinism of cannibals and headhunters in broad daylight—in spite of the fact that the "hunter context" of the story's plot, and of the Maro cult, was not in the least disguised. But then, sacrificial theories in general, whether religiously smooth or politically jagged, are seldom completely straightforward or honest.

—The transformation of people into animals or ghosts, toward the end of the Hainuwele narrative, is a typical "prehuman flux" theme in hunter mythology.[10] But as far as the sacrificial theme of Hainuwele is concerned, the tale would have been better titled "Ameta and Hainuwele." The principal *dema* deity in this Wemale story is Ameta. As a hunter he is neither killed nor mutilated.

—Ameta comes onto the scene as one who has gone out to hunt a boar, and in this effort he obtained the first coconut seed. The man was put in charge of planting that seed—the seed that he had hunted. The seed was his because, traditionally, a hunter owns whatever he captures or retrieves while hunting. In order to avoid the silliness of having a hunter chase a coconut, the narrative aligns the seed with a wild boar as its carrier.

—The events that follow the hunt not only clarify the fact that coconut trees belonged to Ameta the hunter, but also that the food goddess, with all her wealth-producing powers, and all cultivars that were formed from her substance later, were Ameta's legitimate offspring and possession as well. Hainuwele may have been the specific substance from which cultivars grew, but Ameta was her creator and owner, and even her essence. He is the man who, with his own "blood," has fertilized the coconut blossom on the tree that he owned. Blood happens to be an ever-present byproduct not only of menstruation and birth, but also of every type of hunting. He procreated and raised the Coconut-Limb-Girl without the participation of a woman. The divine girl was his property alone.

---

[10]For "prehuman flux mythology" see Luckert, *The Navajo Hunter Tradition*, 1975. See also Chapters 14 and 15, below.

—Then it was the men—obsolescent hunters—who with their spiral dance pushed the *Dema* Girl into a grave of their making. It was not individual hunters that killed her; rather, it was the whole spiral-snake of hunters that did it. And after that, it was her owner and progenitor, Ameta, who dug her out and cut up her body, planting her dormant portions as tuber seed. After all of this, it was a Wemale hunter—a *dema* deity perhaps by virtue of having bled and fertilized his own coconut blossom—who owned the cultivars and the horticulture that came to sustain the people. And so, in a process of claiming all agriculture, ceremonially with the support of mythology, the men claimed the right to control the females. Regardless of what the women might have claimed traditionally as their domain, the credit for their own inventions and advances in horticulture was usurped by the less successful and obsolescent male hunters.

Sedna, Mistress of Sea Animals—an Inuit Dema Deity

Alongside Jensen's *Hainuwele* materials, historians of religions have also been pondering Rasmussen's version of the Eskimo *Sedna* myth as featuring a similar *dema* divinity. The mythic father of *Sedna* cut off his daughter's fingers when she was clinging to the edge of his canoe. In this manner, she was drowned by her own father, who was a hunter of sea animals. Her severed fingers were transformed into a variety of sea animals, and the mutilated *Sedna,* herself, became their ruling mistress. Henceforth all Inuit huntsmen—regularly guilty of killing sea animals, of continuing to cut off their divine sister's fingers—were obliged to follow her wishes. A shaman was periodically required to comb her tussled hair—to calm the waves of the sea.[11]

—Reflecting on this myth of sea-animal hunters, one cannot help but marvel. These hunters managed to weigh their guilt of hunting against the hardships they themselves suffered on difficult seas. By way of narrating the origin and destiny of the sea animals, which they hunted, they managed to assimilate—by the grace of *Sedna*—as artificial predators with their guilt-engendering occupation in a more or less balanced and functioning world order.

---

[11]See Rasmussen Knud. *Intellectual Culture of the Iglulik Eskimos.* (Report of the Fifth Thule Expedition 1921-1924. Vol. VII, Nr. 1.) Copenhagen, 1929. See also Franz Boas. *The Central Eskimo.* Washington D.C., 1888.

—The evolutionary, cultural and societal implications of this Inuit story have yet to be sufficiently explored or understood in context. My reference here to *Sedna* mythology is therefore limited to two points—first, to the fact that historians of religions have referred to her as a *dema* deity comparable to *Hainuwele*, and second, to the fact that this myth belongs squarely into a world of hunters of sea animals—of Iglulik Inuit hunters of sea animals.

—I wish it were possible to relive Rasmussen's original recording sessions of this narrative. Were his male Iglulik narrators joking here about the clumsy flippers of sea animals—in contrast to having nimble-fingered human hands with opposable thumbs? Or was this Iglulik story told seriously to explain greater-than-hunter sacrificial ontology in its totality? Was it told as a burlesque joke on their victims or were these men serious about resolving hunters' guilt? I do not know. I am, however, a little more familiar with Navajo Indian storytelling. And yes, the Navajo story about Bear Maiden, to be summarized next, can safely be classified as an example of hunter-and-butchers' burlesque.

Bear Maiden, a Navajo (Diné) Hunter Dema

One cannot stop arbitrarily after mentioning only Hainuwele and Sedna mythology. There also is a Navajo Indian myth that approximates the plot of Hainuwele's dismemberment—and it most certainly is a story of hunters. The only element in the Navajo story that can possibly be attributed to planter influence is the habit of classifying animal species in accordance with four-directional colors. But this feature is a peripheral element—a clear accommodation to Hopi Indian cosmography which, in turn, happens to be a frontier emanation of Middle American cosmology. But at its core the Navajo "Bear Maiden" story represents hunter burlesque at its purest:

—In mythical times a maiden, wife of the primordial Coyote, succeeded in killing all her brothers, except the youngest. In an attempt to kill him too, she transformed herself into a ferocious bear. But with the help of other divine helpers and animals, the youngest brother managed to kill her instead. He proceeded to resurrect his dead brothers. Then he butchered the carcass of his Bear sister.[12] As

[12]See Father Berard Haile. O.F.M. (Karl W. Luckert, editor). *Upward Moving and Emergence Way*, 1981, pp. 207-216. See also *Navajo Coyote Tales*, 1984, pp. 82-84.

the Wemale hunter Ameta had done to Hainuwele, his Navajo counterpart cut the Bear Maiden into pieces. Nevertheless, true to hunter limitations, no words are wasted on any planting of her remains. It would have been pointless, because Navajo women have become owners of sheep, not gardeners. *Diné* men faced no competition from gardeners and vegetable growers. So, the butcher of Bear Maiden simply left the pieces to themselves. Somehow her vagina became broad-leafed yucca. One of her breasts became the pinion tree, which resulted in nut-bearing pinion cones that still today resemble the nipple on that original breast. Her second breast became Porcupine. One arm became Black Bear, and the other arm became Blue Bear. One leg became Yellow Bear and the other became White Bear. Her intestines changed into slender snakes, and her colon became the head of Horned Rattle Snake. Her small intestines became Long Snake and her spine became Stubby Bear. Altogether, this constitutes a Navajo *Diné* hunter's burlesque story about creative butchering.

The dema Divinities of Hunters and Butchers

At the very least the possibility has now been established that some genre of *dema* mythology was current among primitive hunters. And then, upon closer reflection, it also appears quite obvious that the killing and butchering of sacrificial bodies matches well the skills of men who are experienced hunters. The basic theme of this mythology—creative butchering—fits less well into a planter culture unless, of course, the planters are still hunters and butchers at heart and are compensating for having to adjust to the less exciting ways of domestication. Obviously, domestic animals are kept to be killed and butchered eventually. But domestic animal-related activities are neither the subject matter of Hainuwele mythology, nor are they among the objectives that the Maro rite was meant to achieve. Like the Sedna myth of the Eskimo and the Bear Maiden myth of the Navajo Indians, the Wemale myth seems to express the interests of men who are clinging to the dreams of remnant hunters and butchers.

—Now that we have started to reconsider how hunters and planters got caught up in an evolutionary dialectic, a new set of questions emerges: Can it still be said that, at its core, the Hainuwele myth on the island of Ceram was a primitive planters' way of explaining horticulture? Can such a conclusion still be maintained on the small point that portions of Hainuwele were said to have been planted? What kind of a feminine rational planter mind, by any stretch of the imagination, would have told such a narrative? The livelihood of females rested on a clear knowledge about what was seed and capable of sprouting. Inasmuch as Hainuwele is said to have been killed and cut up by male hunters and butchers, should one not rather look for original motives in the occupational dream-and-sports world of these men? And finally, can "*dema*" still be maintained primarily as a unique theological category for paleo-planter religion as some people have proposed?

Tuber Butchering and Coconut Hunting

Increasingly, it appears as though the cutting up and planting of Hainuwele's body—as a prototype for planting tubers—represents a maladjustment on the part of male hunters for whom the boundary of the realm of hunting and butchering had become problematic. Butchering an animal would have been a noble task for them. But having to "butcher" a tuber—yams or taro—in order to survive seemed like an ipso facto silly spoof that apparently women had been inflicting on their men. It was paid back as an insult on feminine dignity.

—The men's horticultural origin myth, as it has been told to justify Maro sacrifices, reduced the general status of women to the level of tuber seed. The sacrificial procedure, performed by obsolescent hunters, reduced the Hainuwele victim in proportion to how the men's own functionality as butchers had been reduced by culture change, to the level of burlesque. To the extent that the parallel between tuber meat and the flesh of a sacrificial girl could be imagined, the "Ameta and Hainuwele" myth, together with the Maro festival, placed all edible plants into the ceremonial domain and under the jurisdiction of the men.

—The first Western colonial encounters with Ceram happened already back in the 16th Century, and they lasted into the Twentieth. Western Ceramese peoples were hunter-gatherers and slash-and-burn planters of tubers. The men engaged frequently in small-scale warfare and headhunting.[13] The most recent headhunting incident may have happened as late as 1992 (or as recently as a few weeks ago). During

[13]G. Knaap, "The Saniri Tiga Air (Seram); an account of its discovery...1675, and 1950." *Bijdragen tot de Taal-, Land- en Volkenkunde 149* (1993), no: 2, Leiden, 250-273.

the 1930s, Adolf Jensen still noted two secret men's associations in West Ceram. These are the older Wapaulame society of the Wemale and the more recent underground Kakihan which, by the 1930s, had proliferated from the Alune across all of West Ceram. None of these were still espousing the mythology or older ceremonial information that Jensen collected concerning the Maro cult, Wemale headhunting, or cannibalism. Therefore, we are still dependent on ethnological literary samples to postulate the older Wemale planters' worldview, powered by *dema* deities, headhunters, and cannibals. Here is how Wemale men, as storytellers, explained the beginnings of headhunting:

—Initially the men built a meeting house *(baileo)* to celebrate feasts there. To decorate the baileo, they hung up a variety of fruits, such as coconuts, bananas, and pineapples. But they did not consider these to be beautiful. They also hung up dogs, deer, and pigs, but they did not like the looks of those either. Then they thought that a human head would decorate the baileo rather nicely; though, it was difficult to obtain such a head.

—Then the Latulisa (war chief and leader of the baileo) decided to get the head of his sister Silai. He told the people: "Go, and cut down my banana tree!" They did not understand what he meant, and when they returned they said: "We have found no banana tree!" Then the Latulisa himself went to his sister who, at the time, was weaving a skirt worn by Alune women *(a kanune)*, and he cut off her head.[14] He hung up the head in the baileo, which now was deemed nicely decorated. From that time on people practiced headhunting. And when they went to war, they said to one another: "Get this coconut!" Or: "Climb that kanari tree!" One who has never taken a head will not understand this. But the others know what is meant.[15]

—Transposed into a concrete evolutionary perspective, this story gives more than just an explanation of headhunting. It reveals why it

---

[14]Wemale women were not supposed to weave; they wore beaten tree bark instead. In contrast to Wemale planters, Alune people are 'makahala' which means 'rice eaters' The Wemale people were planters of tubers and they were organized according to matrilineal principles. Wemale females isolated themselves during menstruation in special huts outside their villages. Marriages between Wemale and Alune were not supposed to happen. See G. Knaap, "The Saniri Tiga Air (Seram)," 252.

[15] Portions translated from Jensen and Niggemeyer 1939; 115f.

is necessary to have men's associations and lodges in the first place. Their lodge had to be a very special place. Fruits and plants from the gardens of womenfolk were the least acceptable symbols to decorate this haven of bruised hunter egos. Trophies from carcasses of hunted animals might once have sufficed to establish the status of huntsmen. But hunters who used to be able to bag real animals, in the forest, could not impress each other with such animals anymore while suffering boredom in lodges. Hunters had become less and less successful in finding animals. Their ability to procure animal flesh was diminished and the men's dependency on the women's garden produce had increased. The men felt pressure to find new ways to save themselves. In the aforementioned legend, not even a superior leader of men could hunt enough animals to earn respect. The men needed to find other ways to maintain their relevance and dignity. They stuck to the skills they learned as hunters. They chose to use the terror they knew how to inflict on animals, and they unleashed it upon humankind as well.

—The chief in this historical legend forcefully reasserted his authority over his family—also his ownership—by cutting off the head of his sister. This show of force has to be understood against the man's older style of raw hunter existence. Traditionally, what a hunter could butcher, he had already brought under his control. An archaic hunter first made and owned his weapon, and then he took possession of his victims.

—At least by the time this story could be shared with outsiders, a broader justification for the murder of the chief's sister—beyond a raw hunter impulse—needed to be mentioned to justify such violence against a member of his family. In the hour before Silai was beheaded she was in the process of escaping the brother's household and his authority. She was weaving an Alune skirt, almost certainly in preparation for a forbidden marriage to an Alune man. Therefore, this brief interpolation about what the woman was doing appears to have been added to the story to provide extra justification for the chief's violence—indeed, she wove a *kanune*.

—Upon closer examination, much in the Hainuwele corpus of the Jensen collection, even the Maro cult, appears to be custom designed for justifying exactly the course of action that this chief took, as well as the actions of his followers. While females raised plant foods by some dirty method approximating excretion and decay, members of the secret men's society assumed aristocratic responsibility not only for the wider world of animals out there, but also found ways to become more relevant and to guarantee propriety around the home camp. The home is a place where a planter family survives. But in order to sustain vulnerable hunter egos at such a place, to assuage hunter nostalgia and to maintain their obsolete perspective on male superiority, for a way of life that had already been lost when the last of the great predators fell, traditional Wemale men needed to kill a Hainuwele Girl now and then. They progressed from being nostalgic hunters directly to become hyper-domesticators—owners and killers of humankind.

—Back in the days when defunct and defensively resourceful hunters composed Hainuwele mythology, real men went headhunting amongst their neighbors. They danced Maro spirals and killed Hainuwele girls. They butchered and planted female flesh as a parody of the women who planted pieces of tubers. And knowing themselves guilty, they told a cosmogony of justification, claiming that such sacrifices were necessary for cosmic balance. Moreover, considering the women's important role in the entire planter ecology, it should not come as a surprise when the hangovers that followed headhunting were blamed on women and accredited to them as their botched innovations:

—In the days when human beings still lived at Mainala, the practice of going to war was still unknown. The people then played a game of contest, still without weapons. That game was *Souwe*. People fought with their hands, and whoever touched the head of an opponent had won the game. The one who was defeated was considered dead and was out of the game. This they played together, frequently, and they also went to a neighboring village to play that same game with the people there....

—Once when they played there, a raptor bird flew toward them, with a mouse in its beak. He tore out the hair from the head of the mouse and let the dead mouse fall to the ground. Then the people said: so we also must do it in our game; he who defeats another pulls out his hair. But because the pulling out was not possible, they cut off the hair with knives and machetes. This new game by which the people of Mainala imitated the raptor bird was called Topiulu. The people of Mainala always won in this game when they met with the neighboring village....

—One day thirty-one women from the neighboring village came to Mainala to play Topiulu, because in those days the women competed as much as the men. On their way, they saw that same raptor with a dead mouse. They saw how this bird bit off the head of the mouse and dropped its body. The women were angry about the fact that the people of Mainala were always winning and therefore said: "The raptor has shown us. From now on, we will do it in that manner too, and cut off the head." When they came to Mainala, all the people were still in their gardens. They only found an old man, and they cut off his head. They took his head home with them. On their way home they rested by Mount Batu Kokoba and there placed the head on a rock. Only one of the women, who still had a three-month old baby, went straight home and told her people that they had cut off the head of an old man at Mainala. Meanwhile, the men of Mainala returned home and found the body of the man without head. They tracked the women and caught up with them at Batu Kokoba. When they saw the head of the old man on the rock, they attacked and beheaded all thirty of them. From that time on, war was waged with weapons, and there was headhunting. Losing the heads of thirty women for having taken the head of one old man was a misfortune for the village. It was therefore agreed that women should never fight again.[16]

—As a story of this kind, told by men to rationalize their practice of headhunting, this tale tells it all. In all hunter religions, some predator animals served as totemic models for imitation. Thus, imitating a successful raptor appealed to the hunters' common sense. Nevertheless, only men who were bona fide predators were entitled to the kind of justification that could be had by way of imitating predator totems. In this instance, the men also chose to remember their "ideal" lost hunters' paradise as a time when they used to merely cut off the hair of their defeated victims. As they now saw it, the real problem began when ignorant women wanted to be hunters and killers, and wanted to behave like men.

—Or, did they really mean "when women began nagging the men about not bringing home enough meat"? Transposed onto their current evolutionary context, this sentiment implied that the real trouble began when women usurped the roles of men and thereby became the chief procurers of food. The men therefore needed to be

[16]Portions translated and summarized from Jensen and Niggemeyer 1939: 113f.

cautious that women would not also usurp their substitutional prop, the privilege of proving their greatness in war. We already have seen another story, earlier, which is more upfront about the culprit who started headhunting. There, a chief of men, who cut off the head of his sister, was given full credit for having been the first headhunter. By contrast, our present story shifts the blame for headhunting to the women, and the story explains more specifically the twisted logic of the hunters' justification. As the men saw it, their killing and headhunting needed to be pursued because of pressures by the women —as surely they also remembered having formerly pressured wild animals.

—We read between the lines that headhunting frequently was done in preparation for marriage, to impress and to assure brides—similar to the way men once needed to establish their worth as hunters of animals, butchers, and providers. They proved their worth in the same manner as males in other animal species still do—by engaging in battles. Fist fights in certain human frontier societies still today serve that same purpose. The practice of head-hunting and its necessity, in the head-hunters' final analysis, therefore always appeared to have been the women's fault.

—Even though not every Maro dance required an actual Hainuwele victim from the village, Jensen still learned that Maro dances traditionally followed in the aftermath of headhunting expeditions. Thus, headhunting raids at "enemy" villages preceded human sacrifices at home. Men hunted heads among people in other villages, perhaps to get even with those who had caused them earlier losses, but also to redeem lost hunter status with substitutionary warrior honors. Back home Hainuwele victims were killed—more sparingly perhaps—but were sacrificed nonetheless for emphasis and for balance. A species divided into female foragers and male artificial predators was, in accordance with its own nature and culture, a species in conflict with itself. In times of transition from hunting to domestication, tranquility between the genders and peace among neighboring villages were fated to be more of an exception, rather than a rule.

To students in the history of religions, the Ainu Bear Sacrifice has become a favorite ethnological benchmark that helps throw some light on the religious behavior of archaic bear hunters. Inasmuch as this book focuses essentially on the transition from hunter to domesticator religion, the inclusion of this benchmark sample will help us highlight pivotal moments of the Ainu ceremonial. Contact points for comparison with the Navajo Hunter Tradition may be found in the next chapter, especially regarding the subject matter of "prehuman flux" mythology.

14. Bear Hunters on Hokkaido

From among anthropological themes pertaining to native Ainu culture, on the island of Hokkaido, the Bear Sacrifice has become most notorious. But today, very little about this ritual seems to be verifiable anymore on Hokkaido itself. All accounts of Ainu bear hunting, nowadays, are stories that refer to times past. The island today does feature extensive agriculture of wheat, soybeans, potatoes, corn, as well as pastures for cattle.

—Nevertheless, for students of the history of religions, the Ainu Bear Festival has become a favorite. Killing a bear with bow and arrows, after all, was something that archaic hunters did.

—But then, if this popular festival named *iomante,* at the island of Hokkaido, were to illustrate what archaic Ainu bear hunter religion actually was like, its lesson would surely be misleading. A former Ainu bear hunt in the forest, the *omante,* at which an adult bear was killed, was one thing for the Ainu bear hunters. The latter-day *iomante,* at which a domestic bear cub was sent back to its divine owner in the forest, was another.

—The *iomante* is reviewed in this book to help us see what hunter religion, already romanticized, looked like at some point during its history of transition. Indeed, from the nostalgic memories of early Ainu domesticators, from their transitional adaptations while learning to live in a village, still something extra can be learned. The *iomante* ritual appears most meaningful if we try to understand it as the spectacular product of a certain moment in human evolution—a climactic and cathartic moment, perhaps—at the conclusion of Stone Age hunting. It signifies a people's entry into the cultural phase of adaptation to domestication. Bear hunting at Hokkaido was reduced to a sedentary feast of nostalgic slaughter.

—Similar emphatic and transitional activities could have happen-ed at Göbekli Tepe between twelve and ten thousand years ago. As far as we can tell, that ancient cult still has sought its religious solutions in esoteric isolation from families and their settlements. Comparable dramatic responses to crises of cultural transition have been erupting since those early days quite regularly, all around the globe, featuring the likes of headhunting, cannibalism, and slaughter sacrifices. It was by a variegated process of adaptation that the descendants of hominid hunter-gatherers—with some six million years of evolutionary depth—are still now trying to get used to the effects of their recent Neolithic convulsions. Ten millennia ago, the Neolithic Revolution precipitated in human culture a conversion shock that, still today, reverberates with ever deepening aftershocks. Societal maladjustments, revolutions, and wars, appear to be emanating, still, from this largest transition brought on by human culture. Those ancient traumas have thrown upon humankind as many suicidal tragedies as they have victories.

—Customary interpretations of the *iomante* all recognize that a sacrificial bear is being sent home to its Master, a deity that lives far away, in or beyond the mountains where some bears in animal form are still known to live. The Ainu Master of Animals appears to have been some type of divine elder or chief of the bear species. The sacrificial *iomante* bear is dispatched to this distant Master with a traditional message, to the effect that more bears should be sent, so that Ainu men could hunt and butcher more of them. In addition, the young messenger bear himself is invited back, to return to the Ainu people and be welcomed there again as a guest.

—But in spite of this apparently normal bear hunter request, of having more bears sent, the message of latter-day Ainu bear-butchers, during *iomante* celebrations, no longer fully communicated the traditional bear hunter sentiments. It rather reflected the festive mood and wishes of domesticators. The victim was a two- or three-year old captive and "domestic" bear. On that account the prayer that was sent communicated something else.

—A feast was staged in honor of a sacrificial animal. Men ganged up on the celebrated victim. Boys shot blunt arrows at it with small bows. These projectiles were neither large nor sharp enough to kill the animal; they were only sufficient to torture and to incite rage. The bear was doomed to die a slow and painful death. At the climax, when a larger arrow was mercifully dispatched into the victim's heart, all the men rushed in and everyone hoped to have his hand involved in the animal's death.

—If one were to interpret this rite on the basis of its most recent celebrations, when mostly teenage boys did the mock shooting, one could, perhaps, explain the proceedings as a method for boys' initiation. With only a single bear available, many boys could so achieve adult bear hunter status, all at once. While at one point in time the purpose of initiation may have become the ritual's primary purpose, it nevertheless seems as though that strategy could not have been the festival's original intent. In the nineteenth century, when John Bachelor lived among the Ainu and reported their ways in some detail, it appears that there still could have been enough bears in the forest for most boys to prove themselves as mature men by actual hunting. In addition, John Batchelor provided sufficient circumstantial information to help identify the dynamic of the event in his days.[17]

—To begin with, the sacrificial victim was always a domestic caged bear, namely, one that was captured as a small cub some two or three years earlier by hunters who had killed and butchered its mother. From the hunters' general behavior, it can be assumed that, back then, they were not so hungry as to kill the young ones. Moreover, they were sensitive and humane enough to take them home to their wives and children as living "teddy bear" pets. Until the cub learned how to lap its own food, it was suckled at the breasts of human foster mothers. The young bear was so not only adopted as a pet-child, but was welcomed into the human family as a notorious and honored divine guest. It grew up under human foster parents and in the company of human step-siblings.

—In the Ainu cultural context, the welcoming of this bear cub as a divine being reflects a typical mythic orientation of the "prehuman flux" variety. It stands in full harmony with prehuman flux mythologies such as that of the Navajo Indian hunter tradition, to be summarized in the next chapter.

—According to an interesting Ainu source, "gods sometimes come to this world of men to play, where the god, a bear, comes in the disguise of a black fur, sharp claws, and big form; the wolf, a god named Horokeu-Kamui, comes in a white robe; the fox, a god named Chiron-Nubu-Kamui, comes in a yellowish-brown disguise; others in disguise of birds, of insects, or fishes.... The hunting deity is always a beautiful young goddess in the kingdom of the gods, but she comes

---

[17]John Batchelor, *The Ainu and Their Folk-Lore* (London, 1901), pp. 483-95.

into this world in the disguise of a small bird, such as a Japan-Jay.... Nusaburo-Kamui, who is the god of land and agriculture, appears in the form of a snake.... The small long worms, such as earth worms that live in the mountain rivers, are the deities of water."[18]

Fig. 35. Ainu *iomante*. Japanese hand-scroll painting.
Courtesy, Trustees of the British Museum

—Perhaps one ought to interject, at this point, that such early adoption of infant animals may have been the secret of taming some of the species with which human domesticators have been successful. As it turned out, human experiments with taming most wild predators permanently, such as bears, were doomed to fail.

—When a young domestic bear grew big enough to hurt someone, it had to be caged and fed with proper caution. But even then, the initial emotional bond with its human family could not be eclipsed entirely. When the day of sacrifice arrived, its human foster mother proceeded to explain the inevitable fate of the animal, in various ways: The bear has grown too big to be fed. He actually belongs to other parents, or to a Master in the mountains. It ought to return there and tell about the good care it received from its human foster family. Then the animal is encouraged that some day in the future it ought to return to the Ainu people, and participate again in

[18]Kyosuke Kindaichi, transl. Minori Yoshida. *Southwestern Journal of Anthropology,* Vol. 5, No. 4, 1949.

its festival of honor. These last thoughts, obviously, were mentioned to diminish the guiltiness of the killers and to lighten the weight of their activity as butchers. These words also were intended to comfort and to assure human family members who mourned the loss of their pet child or sibling—or mourned the passing of days when it was still cuddly and young. Their separation would only be temporary.

—In any case, it seems safe to say that, in all likelihood, the Ainu bear sacrifice does not represent what one commentator has suggested for bear festivals in general, it being "a perfect hunt"—unless by "perfect hunt" one means figuratively a domesticators' butchering feast.[19] Or, unless one means the heroic burlesque of a bear hunt, staged to leave an impression on women and children whose knowledge about bear hunting would otherwise have been even more limited than it was. To merely stage a perfect bear hunt, the great ceremonial and comical amplification of killing the animal would not have been required. An array of many small bows and arrows would not have been needed; the bear would not have needed to be roped at all four legs to be conveniently spread-eagled whenever it displayed its will to run. In other words, the animal would not have needed to suffer a torturous slow death. A victim's suffering and dying are precisely what, in the context of widespread apologetic orthodox hunter religiosity, has made every successful hunting expedition an imperfect hunt. As a matter of fact, the Ainu bear festival amplifies this imperfection.

—By artificially evoking an animal's rage and fury, the Ainu huntsmen-farmers jointly displayed their would-be heroism for everyone in the village to admire. During actual hunting in the forest, very few hunters would have been needed to bring down a bear. But here these villagers, in unison, grabbed their only chance to demonstrate their basic worth as potential bear hunters—as the kind of boys who, in earlier heroic days of real bear hunting, would have grown up into real men. The bear butchering feast was staged by all the men of the village, for their joint revalorization as heroic providers of meat–a role for which, once upon a time, they would have earned real status. They staged this festive display at a time when their opportunities to hunt bears in the forest were dwindling. What they failed to provide in the form of actual meat, they now compensated for with violence and circus. This is exactly the type of violent compensation that one

---

[19]Compare Jonathan Z. Smith, in *History of Religions*, 1980, p. 126.

can find elsewhere among cultures transitioning into early stages of domestication—and then one encounters it again, in the form of violent warfare, among people who might be attempting a meaningful transition into hyper-domestication, thus into what sometimes is called "civilization."

—Nevertheless, "prehuman flux mythology" assumed the unity of all types of people in the world. External appearances were considered transitory and more easily depreciated than real essences could be altered. So what was there in the Ainu prehuman flux "ontology" (i.e. their theory of being) that permitted a celebratory show of torture? Kyosuke Kindaichi obtained his information about Ainu gods from a teenage Ainu girl.[20] This is a significant datum for consideration. To her, when she was little, the *iomante* sacrifice had been explained in the following manner: A bear cub deity has come into the Ainu domain to play. It came and grew up, playing together with human children.

—Accordingly, the final circus round of torture showed the god still at play.[21] It is reasonable to assume that during the period that preceded its sending-off festival, the bear would indeed have behaved quite rambunctious and violent among its human step-siblings, had it not been caged. Shortly before this bear was restrained, its human playmates complained that it had been harrying them. Now those same human friends taught it one last lesson on how to behave in human society. It was all in a manner of good-natured siblings' "bear play" and rivalry, of course.

—But, did Ainu men really believe that they could communicate to their greatest among hunter deities, the Master of Bears, the fact that they loved the bear-child that they fostered, and then keep the big god completely in the dark about the fact that they were torturing it to death? Indeed, the days of bear hunting were coming to a close for the Ainu people. As obsolescent huntsmen, as neophyte domesticators, they struggled to preserve some sort of continuity that would help balance their new way of living and help them preserve, somehow, the remembered tradition of bear hunting, which had built their identity and provided self-esteem through years past.

---

[20] Kyosuke Kindaichi, transl. Minori Yoshida. *Southwestern Journal of Anthropology*, Vol. 5, No. 4, 1949.

[21] To modern outsiders this attitude may seem unfair. But is our modern sport of killing deer really a "sport," with fairness implied for all participants?

15. THE NAVAJO HUNTER TRADITION

This chapter is a take-off on the author's 1975 book by the same title. A brief assortment of themes is offered, because they are the type of insights that have helped disentomb some of the Göbekli Tepe secrets: prehuman flux mythology, the burden and legitimization of hunting, mythic geographization of the landscape, the release of prey animals for hunting, and justification for the ownership of herd animals. The 1975 volume was the author's first entry into Diné Stone Age religion. Several more contacts followed.

Hunter Mythology

In 1971 I began doing weekend field research on the Navajo Indian *(Diné)* Reservation in Arizona and New Mexico. The academic definitions of "religion," together with social structures and suspicious evolutionary sequences that we struggled with in school, were altogether impractical for explaining to *Diné* (Navajo) traditionalists what I wished to learn from them. After reading the available anthropological literature on Navajo ceremonialism, it became obvious what was missing. I needed evidence of traditional *Diné* huntingways—hunting songs, rituals, prayers, and mythology. With the help of Johnny C. Cooke I found the last retainer of an entire ritualized huntingway. I did not need to ask any questions about the "origin" or "evolution" of this huntingway. The mythology began answering such questions from within.

—Of course, the human caretaker of this Stone Age hunter tradition, Claus Chee Sonny, did not know anything about absolute origins either. No human story will ever explain absolute first causes, because whichever First Cause can be named, it will immediately beg the question about "antecedents" of any cause so mentioned. But then, any storyteller worth his voice knows that a story must move forward and that he need not waste time on infinite regressions demanded by someone else's formal logic.

—In Claus Chee Sonny's Stone Age hunting myth, all hunter gods were, in some fashion, still members of the "animal" or "divine-animal-people" category. Only one hunter deity, the Talking-god, seemed to be an exception in that he was an advance and humanlike "talking" personage. However, this apparent exception did not disturb the larger picture that was coming into focus. In the context of this myth, which refers to prehuman times, the prototype of present-day humans, along with other predators and gods, were all present as variant appearances of "people" who lived in a state of mythic prehuman flux. "Prehuman flux" refers to mythology pertaining to man's primeval kinship with all creatures of the living world, and to the essential continuity among them all. In prehuman times, all living beings existed in a state of flux—their external forms and appearances were as easily changeable as clothes.[22]

—"Prehuman flux mythology" stands in stark contrast to what Sir Edward Burnett Tylor and others have told us about "animism." In the traditional Navajo sense of "prehuman flux" it cannot be said that all things contain spirits or souls—rather, it should be said that, according to this archaic mythology, all "people" used to be able to transform themselves by way of changing their outward appearances, much like changing clothes. The emphasis is on people, on persons and their appearances, not on invisible spirits or souls that are supposed to empower people like dynamos from within. The "origin of hunting" myth, extracted and summarized next, is an example of just how "people" in the condition of prehuman flux have changed their disguises and then sometimes reappeared again in the shape they held originally:

---

[22]Luckert, *The Navajo Hunter Tradition*, 1975, p. 133. A nice example of "prehuman flux" mythology is also found in the Ainu tradition: "where the god, a bear, comes in the disguise of black fur, sharp claws, and big form; the wolf… comes in a white robe…." Minori Yoshida, Kyosuke Kindaichi transl., see Chapt. 14, above.

An Excerpt from Claus Chee Sonny's hunting myth: The first (human) hunter had four arrows. The first deer at which this hunter aimed was an adult Buck, and the large buck transformed himself into a mountain mahogany bush. The leaves of this bush resemble deer antlers. The second deer at which the hunter aimed was an adult Doe, who promptly transformed herself into a cliff-rose bush. The bark that flakes off the stem of this bush was used for the maternal function of bedding down babies. The third deer at which the hunter aimed was a Two-pointer, who instantly transformed himself into a dead tree. The Navajo name for a Two-Pointer is a homonym to Dead Tree. The fourth deer at which the hunter aimed was the Fawn, who transformed itself into a lichen-spotted rock. The Navajo name for Fawn is a homonym to Lichen-spotted Rock. These four deer people, having appeared under conditions of divine transformational "prehuman flux," revealed the necessary hunting rules in exchange for not being killed. Thus, the ethics of hunting, the proper rules and safe procedures, were established according to the targeted divine victims' own specifications.[23] In this manner, hunting was permitted under the Deer People's own stated conditions. Following their rules would eliminate the need of feeling guilty or of reaping their anger.

Prehuman Flux is not Emergence

Discovering the "prehuman flux" mythic theme as the starting base for *Diné* hunter mythology was totally unexpected. Pre-oriented, like everyone else in the American Southwest, Johnny Cooke and I expected that any Navajo "origin of hunting" myth would be set in some type of an emergence context—with a story that told how the first hunters, and/or their prey animals, emerged from several layers of underworld existence into the surface world. We expected *Diné* hunters to have been born, perhaps, from the Earth Mother through some kind of a vagina-like crevice, or by climbing upward inside a hollow reed. This is what Hopi Indian clans nearby—though not all—have been telling their children, and also have told some outsiders. Hopi Indians even point to the exact spot of that emergence in the canyon of the Little Colorado River, alongside the stream.

—The Emergence myth does figure substantially among *Diné* healing chantways. The Navajo singers of the "Upwardmoving and

[23]Karl W. Luckert. *The Navajo Hunter Tradition*, 1975, pp. 29-31.

Emergence Way" tell an extravagant version of the emergence myth to help them classify and remember the repertoire of Navajo ceremonials from an Emergence Way perspective. These shamanic practitioners saw all other *Diné* chantways as having branched away from their own Emergence Way ceremonial reed. A diagram several meters long, drawn from the perspective of this chantway tradition, was found among Father Berard's papers in the archives of the University of Arizona. I published and explained this document in my "Editor's Introduction" to Berard Haile's *Upward Moving and Emergence Way*.[24] The Emergence Way rationale adopts the cultural context of the surrounding Pueblo Indian cosmography, and it conceptualizes the basic creative healing processes as "re-emergence from underworlds."

—Blessingway singers have constructed a similar mnemonic synthesis to account for their own epistemological orientation. And then, inasmuch as Blessingway songs appear to be positioned, in our time, to outlive the older Navajo chantway versions, the general myth of emergence is being accepted by most commentators for the sake of its popularity and simplicity. It is being treated, by some people, as the "approved standard" *Diné* version. But the historical dynamics of *Diné* chantway evolution were far more complex.[25]

—Two-and-a-half years after recording the Deer Huntingway, I also recorded, in 1979, the nine-night Coyoteway ceremonial. The Emergence myth for that ceremonial is severely abridged, and limited to a narrative concerning the discovery of Coyote People in the underworld. There is only sufficient narrative to enable the first Coyoteway shaman to go and learn his Coyoteway chants in the underworld. Thus, the Coyoteway tradition respects the human origin by "emergence" and uses it to narrate the first shaman's empowerment in the underworld. Nevertheless, the most recent initiate, Luke Cook, introduced typical emergence mythology more fully into his personal understanding of Coyoteway—including the typical "First Man and First Woman" family. An outline of his larger

---

24See Berard Haile. *Upward Moving and Emergence Way*, 1981, pp. vii—xv.

25For a summary description of the process of ceremonial evolution, in the case of the Coyoteway ceremonial, see the Introduction in Karl W. Luckert, *Coyoteway, a Navajo Holyway Healing Ceremonial,* 1979, chapters 1 and 2. For historical research, all "Blessingway" ingredients in Diné chantways should be examined at their own merit, in the historical context of their specific host ceremonials. Some of the Blessingway ideas, in our days, are explained as well-intentioned linguistic simplifications, sometimes even as defensive "fundamentalist" reductionisms.

ontology, compared with that of Claus Chee Sonny, can be found in connection with the Navajo Deerway Ajilee tradition.[26]

—As a former student of Claus Chee Sonny, alongside Johnny Cooke, however, I feel obliged to attest to his words. When he was finished telling his Deerway origin myth in terms of "prehuman flux" type transformations, I asked him why his hunting story does not refer to the story of Emergence or to gods at the Four Directions—all of which are recognized in many schoolbooks. His answer was quick and clear: "The Emergence story and gods of the Four Directions do not belong with the *Diné* Deer Huntingway; they belong with Blessingway."

This Master of Animals is not yet a natural Owner

While recording and examining the Navajo Hunter tradition, I noticed that there was no obvious legitimate Master of Animals. There was the awareness of former buffalo bulls that used to, and mule deer stags that still do, function as masters of their herds. This general logic belongs to a standard system of traditional Navajo proportional thinking. For example, Claus Chee Sonny, as a healing practitioner, recognized a tall medicinal plant as the chief who ruled over similar smaller plants that grew in the vicinity.[27]

—Instead of a full-fledged Master of Animals, Claus Chee Sonny's hunting myth tells about multiple predator contestants for that mastering role. In the beginning, human hunters were among them. There was also an assertive raptor type, the Black-god (Raven), who for a while had the others out-maneuvered. In mythical times, when hunting was begun by people, the Black-god was one of those first divine hunters. In the beginning, all "people" that roamed were potential hunters. According to Claus Chee Sonny, the prey animals were being abused, and therefore the Black-god rounded them up "for their protection." They became rarer on the hunting range.

—It all means that this new keeper of animals, the Black-god, ceased being a hunter and became a warden to protect the prey animals. He kept the animals corralled, and now and then he fetched and butchered one for himself and his family. The herder mentality of Claus Chee Sonny appears here fully developed, one full step

[26]Karl W. Luckert. *A Navajo Bringing-Home Ceremony…*, 1978, pp. 17-20.

[27] Luckert, *The Navajo Hunter Tradition.* 1975, pp. 54-57.

beyond the point of the traditional pure hunter who earlier in life he still wanted to be.

—The logic of this hunter myth nevertheless is clear and coherent. Aside from their oral tradition, Navajo hunters in the field have seen how the Blackgod (Raven) warned his animals when human hunters were approaching. So, already in mythical times, the conservative Black-god must have been endowed with a herder's motivation. He was suspected by fellow hunters of having something to do with the disappearance of the animals. In time, it became obvious that this god had corralled all of the animals into his underground moun-tain hogan (hut). But this discovery happened early on, at a time when human beings had not yet taken their present shapes.

—Even at our late date, in 1971, Claus Chee Sonny still had not admitted to himself that overhunting was possible, or could by itself have caused the shortage of prey animals. For a hunter's mind, religiously set at ease, there would always be enough animals to hunt. The problem for him was that hunters had been hunting with the wrong manners and attitudes, and by the wrong rules. For punishment, the Black-god withdrew the animals and hid them—hid them for himself and for the animals' own protection.

—But then the Blackgod was tricked by an advance representative of human hunters. Still caught up in the primeval condition of prehuman flux, the new competitor to the Black-god, who was going to release the animals for fellow hunters, has variously been identified as Puppy in disguise, Wolf, the Talking-god, and as the first human hunter. Under prehuman flux conditions he could easily have appeared as any of these, at any moment he liked. Therefore, his huntingway is known variously as Deer Way, Wolf Way, and Talking-god Way.

—Claus Chee Sonny's hunter story reveals hunter mythology at a point of reorientation, in transition toward some kind of herder religion. The Navajo reality in the 1970s was that herds of sheep were kept at most homesteads. Most often the sheep were owned by women, though not always. Some cattle were also introduced which then belonged to the men, though not always. Nevertheless, out on the hunting range Claus Chee Sonny, as a hunter in transition, still had to maneuver his conscience around the presence of "natural" Ravens (Black-god), and also around the Mule Deer stag types. Both were quite visible in their habit of protecting herds of deer. They herded them protectively as though they really owned them.

—Claus Chee Sonny's myth has led me to search for traces of it back across the Bering Strait along which ancestors of American Indians have travelled millennia earlier. Remnants of the "Release of Animals" mythic theme, out of some hole in the earth, can be found in the mythology of ancient Aryan herdsmen. The theme was recorded in the Rig Veda, among the credentials of a warrior deity named Indra. This deity was given credit for liberating cattle for his Aryan people. The cattle had been sequestered inside Vala Mountain. Perhaps the god Indra (or a similar deity known by a different name) enabled his people to become herders before he led his Aryan herdsmen into struggles with other people from the Indus Civilization, not quite four millennia ago. This much the Vedic mythology seems to suggest. The god's demolition of the Vala Mountain became his model for also demolishing Vasyu cities.[28] Some type of justification of violence is clearly intended by this mythos.

Hunter Deities in Transition

Not all hunter gods have evolved into sponsors of herders, and Indra's evolution into a warrior deity, as displayed in the *Rig Veda,* is not replicated by all herder gods. Not all of them have lapsed into hunters' violence or mutated directly into gods of war and hyper-domestication, though the opportunity was present for all at one time or another. In general, the step up from an animal-bodied Master of a herd to an anthropomorphic Master who owns all animals is of a considerable magnitude. It is the step that archaic hunters took when they began thinking about anthropomorphic Masters, Owners, or Mistresses of Animals. In all probability, this step also was taken by participants in the Göbekli Tepe cult twelve to ten thousand years ago, when Mother Earth and Father Sky were re-envisioned in forms of gender-specific essentials. This change has piqued the minds of scholars regarding another deity—namely, the High God who was master, creator, and owner of animals, and who, by logical extension, could also be expected to be creator and owner of humankind. This additional conversion, to gods who own humankind, takes us another step in the evolution of human culture—into the era of hyper-domestication.

---

[28]Karl Friedrich Geldner. *Der Rig Veda* 1, 62, 4. 5; 1, 121, 4; 1, 130, 3; 3, 32. 16; 6, 18, 5; etc. Harvard University Press, Cambridge Mass. 1951-1957.

Totemic Sponsors: In the traditions of archaic hunters there generally are two types of divine contestants for the ownership of animals, just as there are two types of adaptation levels for humans who live on animal meat. The *Diné* (Navajo) Master of Animals, the Black-god, was already a de facto "herder deity" who, for a while, appeared to have been keeping the dwindling stock of wild animals away from die-hard hunters. But then, there also was the still older *Diné* hunter authority, one whom we might identify as a traditional predatory Sponsor of the Hunt. While the Master of Animals type was already active as a herder, this older "totemic sponsor" deity was someone who protected the enterprise of hunting itself. He needs to be acknowledged at this point in the discussion. Both types of deities were destined to impact the theologies of later cults of domesticators as well as those of hyper-domesticators when these emerged.

—In the course of field research I have come to suspect that, among fulltime hunters, share offerings of the hunt used to be given mostly to tutelary sponsor-type gods who themselves were still active hunters. A human hunter's impersonation of his totemic model could be intensified to a point where the human protégé surrendered his entire humanoid identity, to participate mystically in the activities of the superior deity. Thereupon the totemic sponsor and his human protégé, together, were a mystically comprised dual persona. They hunted together, united in the form of a singular possessed, owned, and atoned divine-human being—as some kind of a "god-man."

—To begin with, a religious encounter with one's greater-than-human sponsor of the hunt does not require that the hunter immediately convert from an experimental scientific mode into a religiously immersed "faith and trust" mode. It needs only be said that, by encountering great totemic sponsors, primitive hunters asserted their egos more cautiously. They approached totems with proper ceremonial respect. And all the while, the hunters hoped that they had chosen and learned the sponsors' atonement rituals sufficiently well. In any polytheistic pantheon, as in any human society, certain individuals rise while others lose status. And, generally, a human ego that shows good manners towards an ascending deity may also manage to gain some public respect and uplift for his efforts.

—The Navajo shamanic practitioner, Claus Chee Sonny, has credited the chief of all *Diné* deities, Grandfather of the Gods (the Talking-god), as author of his entire hunting ceremonial. He has also acknowledged the presence of the Calling-god, Mountain Lion, and

Wolf (the latter type accounts also for Coyote and Fox). In addition, he recognized such avian Holy People (gods) as Raven, Hawk, and Robin. Whether all of these deities could maintain their status today as better-than-human skilled hunters was not an issue for Claus Chee Sonny anymore. As a shamanic healing practitioner who served hunters, he needed several divine sponsors that would assume responsibility for hunter transgressions, and who would help him along in bearing various human burdens of conscience. With a little extra persuasion, these deities could be moved to withhold some of their punishments and illnesses.[29] Material sacrifices to any deity, at any evolutionary level and with the proper attitude, could be reduced to inexpensive stick figurine substitutions. They could even be reduced to bare words of flattery or nicely chanted songs.

—Should it happen that a shaman begins to doubt the effectiveness of any of his sponsoring deities—or that he sees a need of dealing with some herder type of Master of Animals as well, there is really no need of abandoning any older sponsor prematurely. "Conversion" and reliance on a different deity could easily be postponed. Men who interact with a number of gods, politely, usually are able to keep their options open longer.

—Claus Chee Sonny, before he dared to go on the hunting path, underwent a psychological and mystical transformation in a Sweat-lodge ceremony. He became a Wolf-being, and even the very Talking-god himself. He identified with Wolf, and therefore he bent his knees while walking (somewhat lowered like an Australopithecus). As Talking-god he also was the "Puppy in Disguise" who at the beginning of human hunting liberated the prey animals from the

---

[29]Wyman, Leland C. and Clyde Kluckhohn. "Navajo Classification of their Song Ceremonials." Memoirs of the Anthropological Association, vol. 50, 1938. Navajo shamans used to know of thirty-two different totemic animals that could be offended. These divine animal-persons had at their disposal thirty-two different illnesses. A trespass against one of these divine "custodians of illness" invited his specific brand of revenge in the form of a disease. This essay by Wyman and Kluckhohn explains the etiology of illnesses. Of course, what a god inflicted, he also could take away. The divine custodians of a specific illness were also in possession of the specific remedy—that is, of a combined proprietary illness-and-healing bundle. Different shamanic practitioners specialized in different types of these "bundles." Shamans who became famous in their profession were in danger of being branded as witches. A healer suspected of inflicting one of the illnesses he controls, or who withheld service, was perpetually in such danger. In reality, all Navajo "Holyway" healing ceremonials were rites of reconciliation and atonement.

Black-god's underground corral. In this case the combined Puppy Talking-god person was also the first human hunter—known later as the man Claus Chee Sonny, who in the sweatlodge was transformed into that Wolf-man and into a legitimated hunter.[30]

—It is by way of his mystic union with the Talking-god as a Wolf-puppy—with his totemic sponsor of the hunt in prehuman flux—that the human protégé could unload responsibility for the deaths of roaming Deer People whom he hunted. After the hunt, the protégé returned to the sweat-lodge to undergo a reverse ceremonial transformation, to become again a benign and safe human husband and father. He was cleansed of his death-wielding predatory powers.

—Theologically speaking, this means that all hunter salvation was based on a rational awareness of the original sin of eating, and on a fear of non-atoned killer liabilities. His hunting never became a question of an evil deity tempting him to kill, nor of a god who "made him do it." He was always absorbed in the persona of the sponsoring deity, who acted on his own volition through the joint hunter persona which he owned. In his totemic ally possessed state, the Deer Huntingway story of Claus Chee Sonny became the hunter's personal religious confession and profession. It could be talked about very factually, as a simple story of how hunting happens. During his sweat-lodge ritual the Talking-god took on human form so that the human hunter could participate in his divinity—sufficiently divine to hunt in an atoned state, together, as the deity. Hunting by the grace of a divine sponsor is the ultimate in ancient hunter atonement.

Prayers and songs on the hunting path: Prayers and songs, with minutely prescribed actions, served as checks and balances for Claus Chee Sonny's hunter religion. In his state of intimacy with the Talking-god, he spoke prayer words like "you will give me." They

---

[30]Still after 1975 I encountered a Western-educated person on the Navajo Rervation who accused Claus Chee Sonny of being a Wolf-man or Skin-walker Witch. Apparently that person had gotten wind of a half-truth about the sweat-lodge hunting ritual, to the effect that participants used to "turn into Wolf and then go hunting." Obviously, this person no longer understood the Navajo hunter tradition, nor much of the pre-Western *Diné* hunter mysticism. I sensed danger, because this person's demeanor seemed hostile, and there appeared to be more such people roaming at the place where he was. I am providing this information for the historical record, now, because both persons, the Western educated person and Claus Chee Sonny are now deceased.

implied familiarity toward the divine giver. With these and other words, he requested a deer from the Talking-god:

> "Talking-god, my Grandfather!
> A Son of Early Morning, a Turquoise Prairie-dog,
> A Turquoise Horse (a Deer Buck) you will give me today.
> With the black bow in my hand, you will give me.
> With feathered arrows in my hand, you will give me.
> With the arrow that will not miss the heart in my hand,
> You will give me.
> Before the Sun sets, you will give me.
> Before I am tired and worn out, you will give me.
> My Grandfather, the Talking-god, you will give me today."
> (pp. 52f)

—Then the hunter Claus Chee Sonny, out hunting while impersonating the Talking-god, stands ready to kill and sings:

> "Ah'eh na-ya-ya, I am standing nearby, na-ya-ya (repeat).
> I am the Talking-god, I am standing nearby, na-ya-ya.
> I am standing atop of Black Mountain, I am standing nearby,
> na-ya-ya.
> A Son of the Male Wind (a deer) stands nearby, na-ya-ya.
> I have a black bow in my hand, as I am standing nearby,
> na-ya-ya.
> I have a feathered arrow in my hand, as I am standing nearby,
> na-ya-ya...." (p. 24)

—Claus Chee Sonny has managed quite nicely to avoid mentioning the actual killing. In stark contrast, the song of Billie Blackhorse dwells on it. But by way of transferring the event into holy space it is he himself, atoned and fused with the deity who he addresses as "Young Man Talking-god"!

> "Na-yah na-ya-yah-ah-ah.
> At a holy place it happened (repeat),
> At a holy place it happened, a-ya.
> Young Man, the Talking-god!
> This happened at the holy place, a-yah (repeat).
> This happened to the Big Buck,
> This happened at the holy place, a-yah....

There is the cutting of the throat. Na-eh-ya-yah.
Now Talking-god, Young Man!
There is the cutting of the throat, na-eh-yah (repeat).
Now there is the Big Buck.
There is the cutting of the throat....
This happened at the holy place, a-yah...." (p. 65f)

—Meanwhile back with Claus Chee Sonny—while he continues to impersonate the Talking-god, and while he smokes his pipe, he prepares to carry home the meat:

"Ah'eh na-ya-ya.
I walk away with it (three times), na-ya-ya.
I walk away with it (three times), na-ya-ya.
I am the Talking-god.
I walk away with it (repeat), na-ya-ya.
On the top of Black Mountain, I carry it away,
I carry it away, na-ya-ya....
With white smoke at my finger tips....
Around my eyes white smoke....
White smoke mingling with my voice....
I carry it away, I carry it away, na-ya-ya....
I carry it away, na-ya-ya." (pp. 47f)[31]

—When Johnny Cooke and I met Claus Chee Sonny in 1971 he told us that he was seventy-two years old. And even though the man hunted deer throughout his long life, as an atoned hunter he was never really responsible for killing as much as a single one. It was always the Talking-god and him, together, who did it.

[31]Excerpts from Karl W. Luckert, *The Navajo Hunter Tradition,* Tucson, 1975, pp. 24-26.

16. CATTLE CULTURE FOR EUROPE

Some 7,700 years ago, a people from the Near East migrated toward Europe, leading among them small herds of bovine, sheep, goats, and pigs. They settled in the Hungarian Plain and from there spread west and north beyond the Rhine River. In archaeology, these people are known by their banded pottery designs (Linear Band Keramik). During their slow trek westward, conflicts and cannibalism were on the rise. Maximizing domestication measures, it seems, has generated its own excesses and has advanced to schemes of hyper-domestication.

A Near Eastern Variety of Cattle for Europe: Some people who descended from Göbekli Tepe hunters and miners learned to tame goats and sheep, and their herding style was culturally influenced by them. They also succeeded at domesticating cattle. Around that same time, other breeds of cattle may have been brought under human control in northern India and in sub-Saharan Africa. But from the upper arch of the Fertile Crescent, domesticators spread downstream into the Euphrates and Tigris flood plains.

—Two thousand years after the cult lodges at Göbekli Tepe went silent, hunters that earlier began dispersing across Europe were discovering the need to retreat from, and having to put up resistance against the next wave of migrants from the Near East. Some 7,700 years ago, a Mesopotamian people of the Banded-Pottery-Maker culture (LBK or *Linear Band Keramik*) intruded into Europe and brought cattle, sheep, goats, and pigs to the Hungarian Plain. In less than a millennium, their settlements spread westward along the Danube across Europe and northwest beyond the Rhine River. Eventually, out west, both hunters and domesticators were halted by the waters of the Atlantic Ocean; all were obliged to become more or less sedentary. People that remained true to the roaming lifestyle of hunting and gathering have remained largely invisible to archaeology. But eventually the descendants of sedentary domesticators stood up megaliths along the western fringes of Europe. Those monuments served the gamut from celebrating the mysteries of procreation, birth, and life, to stabilizing the domains of death.

—The new settlers from the Near East, in Europe, used their advanced Neolithic toolkits to cut clearings into the forests where they chose to build. With flint axes, they cut timber to build fences and palisade fortifications. They learned how to erect walls for their houses by the wattle-and-daub method, and they fitted beams to support their roofs.

—In areas surrounding their settlements, the first cattle farmers of Europe continued to hunt wild animals, including bear and auerochs. Back home in their houses, everyone drank as much cows' milk as they were able to digest. An analysis of bones has revealed that, back in the Near East, the ancestors of these immigrant cattle-farmers were not yet able to digest lactose. By contrast, most of the later LBK people who settled in present-day regions of Austria, Hungary, and Moravia had acquired this capacity.[32] Their insistence on drinking milk, accompanied presumably by a high infant mortality rate, brought on this adaptation quite speedily. Lactose digesters distinguished themselves as survivors already at the age of infants. Around 7,000 years ago, these farmers were grazing their cattle all across Central Europe and westward beyond the Rhine.

—In archaeology there appears, among numerous LBK sites that have been found, the unmistakable pattern of an increase in violence. By contrast, less violence still seems to have been associated with their first homesteads in Hungary.[33] By the time these settlers reached the central and western portions of their European expansion, that is, present-day Austria and Germany, their lives seem to have become significantly more violent and precarious.

---

[32]Dairy farmers living in Central Europe around 7,500 years ago may have been the first human beings to drink cow's milk comfortably. See Lynne Peeples, "Did Lactose Tolerance First Evolve in Central, Rather than in Northern Europe?" *Scientific American*, August 28, 2009.

[33]Wild, E. M. et al. "Neolithic massacres: Local skirmishes or general warfare in Europe?" *International Radiocarbon Conf. 18,* Wellington, NZ, 2004, pp. 377-385.

—We are inclined to interpret this increase in ferocity as a gradual build-up of resistance along their western and northern frontiers. But whence would this build-up have come? I suspect that earlier hunters that were scattered thinly over Europe, still surviving on adequate populations of wild animals, having no settlements to defend, slowly retreated ahead of the intrepid wave of cattle farmers. When then by this movement the hunter populations became more compacted, the fauna would have become sparse more quickly. Concurrent still with the farmers' intrusions, a spattering of hunter clans probably preceded the farmers on their trek westward, wandering at a slightly faster pace. The herds of cattle, sheep, goats, and pigs of the domesticators could not be moved as quickly as hunters were able to get out of their path. When in western regions the beleaguered hunters were forced to yield increasingly more territory, their defensive skirmishes against the intrepid settlers needed to be intensified.

—The general situation of the LBK advance at the time may have been analogous to the "Wild West" frontier, that a couple centuries ago was being played out in North America. Battles were probably fought between intrusive LBK clans and native groups of hunters while, concurrently, some clans from either side might have achieved some modest degrees of accommodation and integration. And so it appears that, for a time, western hunters shot flint arrows into the bodies of intrusive settlers—the arrows that archaeologists found embedded. Obstinate settlers swung stone axes against the heads of those slightly earlier and more "native" hunters.

—Who won this conflict in the end? Inasmuch as earlier waves of hunters came probably from the Near East as well, genetic differences between the conflicting sides will remain difficult to detect. Near Eastern peoples were present at both fronts of this slowly westward shifting wave of conflicts.

—A significant number of LBK settlements have yielded evidence of violence and murder. Thirty-four victimized bodies have been found at Talheim, Germany. Inasmuch as adult females were missing in those burials, while child-corpses were present, the preponderant evidence seems to suggest that this massacre was motivated for the capture of women. The Aparn-Schletz site in Austria yielded sixty-seven bodies; Herxheim in Germany has been estimated at more than three hundred bodies. The latter place may have been a five-hectare ceremonial site for cannibalistic sacrifices, three to five victims at a time.[34] Additional Stone Age sites in the German realm with evidence of possible cannibalism are Fronhofen, Zauschwitz, and Honetal.

—In France, at Fontbregoua, a pattern of archaeological evidence suggests that some of this early cannibalism could already have been practiced among indigenous hunters. Some of these hunters tossed human bones on their refuse heaps, mixed with the bones of other prey with similar butchering marks. Thus overall, we do not really know who did what to whom during the late Neolithic period in Europe. Was it the hunters themselves, or mostly early cattle farmers who lapsed into decadent hunter nostalgia and harbored dreams of hyper-domestication? Or were both sides in-volved equally? The presence of cannibalism means that a clear ontological demarcation between humankind and the prey animals had not yet been achieved at that time and place. At least such a demarcation had not yet been balanced religiously and rationally among those Neolithic forebears.

—There are hundreds of archaeological sites that beg for a more detailed examination of the settlement and the disappearance of LBK culture. At this point, we dare to speculate only in very general terms about the process by which domestication and cattle-raising began in Europe. Some 7,000 years ago, the LBK culture area ceased producing its telltale linear banded ceramics. Did native hunters win this struggle? Did potters simply get tired of making the same products? Did cattle farming continue and increase? *Linear Band Keramik* potsherds, by themselves, do not explain the total lifestyle of a people. A ceramics style does not embody the essence of a culture. LBK shards serve as archaeological time- and group-indicators only for general approximation. Evidence about the treatment of human bones, to the extent that these can be identified, could teach us a little more. Who were the people that continued living in Europe and started making plain ceramics? Which of those were lactose digesters? What did they do differently for survival? In time we expect to learn more.

---

[34]Archaeological evidence for cannibalism exists practically everywhere in Neolithic Europe, around and prior to 7,000 years ago. Reports and commentary have been published widely on the Internet. A place to begin would be an English essay by Edward Pegler, "LBK massacres—who killed whom?" See also his bibliography, at http://armchairprehistory.com/2011/01/16/lbk-massacres.

—Cultural analogies provided by more recent headhunter and cannibal cultures around the globe, such as we noticed in the Maluku Islands, introduced here in Chapter Thirteen, beg to be compared in greater detail. In Middle America, multiple obsolescent hunter cultures coalesced in a struggle for headhunter and cannibal hegemony. They gave shape to a ceremonial monstrosity that outwardly, seen from a safe distance, resembled a majestic "civilization."[35] The four millennia older LBK culture in ancient Europe seems to fit the general pattern of transitional Neolithic disorientation of humankind that worldwide was trying to transit from hunting and gathering to something that resembles domestication.

Epilogue: Before we allow ourselves the self-righteous luxury of being shocked by the behavior of our primitive European antecedents—or by primitives elsewhere—we might contemplate the continuation of the human path of violence into our modern era. The violence during our most recent two centuries, amplified by modernity, has been far more massive than any ancient peoples could have accomplished. Colonialism, imperialism, slavery, world wars, revolutions, and genocides continue around this planet, each to outdo another in brutality. The excesses of hyper-domestication have not been halted, nor have democratic and socialistic revolutions improved much on the basic inhumanity wrought against humankind itself. As we fight tyrants by imitating them, and then surpassing them in their manners, we typically generate more of the same. I am writing these words in the year 2012, while much of the Near East is ablaze —as if all these people wanted to help me modulate my sentences.

—Glib clichés, which pretend to derive human values and the advancement of human dignity from scientific discoveries, are for the most part propagandistic exaggerations. While ancient prehuman flux mythology has demonstrated its goodwill by trying to assure reverence toward all fellow "animals," it was nevertheless unable to prevent cannibalism, so our corresponding modern "theory of evolution," has not yet helped us infer a fundamental ontology that might help us value human life appreciably above the levels we

---

[35]See Karl W. Luckert. *Olmec Religion, a Key to Middle America and Beyond.* Civilization of the American Indian Series, Volume 137. Norman: Oklahoma University Press, 1976.

ascribe to our pets. In fact, scientific principles by themselves, without the importation of ancient religious values, cannot even buttress our self-esteem sufficiently higher than the animals that we slaughter for food. On our battlefields we degrade humankind far beneath the value of livestock. The more of scientific chemistry and mathematics we impute on DNA, and string alongside the human genome, the more obviously pretentious and accidental our human status does emerge. Today our values, and human dignity, still need to be maintained with support from diverse scraps of ancient mythology. Modern wars roll around the planet and are rationalized scientifically—slightly beneath the standards of justification that we insist on for exterminating insects.

—The widespread antagonism in America, between so-called "Creationism" and "Evolutionism," really has very little to do with the scientific study of evolutionary causes or sequences. It is being fuelled rather by concerns for the implied status and destiny of humankind. The issue is not whether the first man, Adam, was a mutated ape. Creationists do not mind deriving him from a lump of ordinary clay. The concern is therefore, rather, how arrogantly our modern scientific hypothesizers—if they were to grasp majority powers to educate and to govern—might treat people who earlier have conceded that they are children of apes rather than dignified children of God. Most parents believe, if only for a while, that their own children are angels of sorts. This writer lived the first ten years of his life under a political system that applied "value-neutral science" disastrously to political policy. This is why he now thinks that one should try to recognize the inhumane killer-excuses that slumber at the foundations of modern scientism for what they are—before we use them to enwrap the ontology of our combined human destiny.

17. Hunter-Rulers in the Near East

Hungry Neolithic hunters depleted the fauna. As hordes of warriors their descendants raided settlers who, less well-armed, retreated behind defensive walls. The Egyptian empire was unified by Menes, a passionate hunter who initiated Egyptian "civilization." The Narmer Palette depicts him doing what he knew how to do best. His three victims probably were hyper-domesticators with similar ambitions, but they were less successful than Menes. Human burial-sacrifices at royal tombs of the First Dynasty show the extent to which the totemistic Falcon-kings of Egypt advanced their agenda of hyper-domestication.

In the so-called Near Eastern "cradle of civilization," some five to two thousand years ago, when cities were being built and texts were being written, stories were composed about how all those good things supposedly came to be what they are. We are given hints about some mighty heroes, sons of gods, who lived in prehistoric times. These belonged to the human species and they took for their wives the daughters of humankind *(Genesis 6:4)*. We are given a few names of heroic hunters who transformed themselves into men of war, into kings and builders of cities. Kings then gathered an entourage from among progressive scribes who themselves were anxious to compete with earlier more old-fashioned skilled elites, such as stone masons and limestone sculptors of the ancient Göbekli Tepe ancestry, and other kinds of public actors.

—While orators recited epics and told legends to educate and to entertain, scribes recorded similar subject matter to practice writing. On fragments of their writ we find the names of ancient kings and hunters like Gilgamesh and Enkidu, Nimrod, Sargon, Esau, Menes, and the likes. The actual historical content in these story fragments is meager. Some may identify earliest mighty men while others may only prove that there was a time when a scribe knew that before men built cities there were hunters and wild men—and also that mighty men and hunters sometimes became the conquerors and controllers of cities.

—Such legends occasionally reveal the courage of scribes to think afresh about history, but by themselves these literary productions make poor history. Fortunately, in some situations archaeology has brought to light material vestiges for fresh interpretations and challenges. In our days, when bones and mummies of god-kings can be gathered into museums and displayed, certainly, some polished layers of ancient glories are being scoured.

—While in accordance with nostalgic dreams, some of the earliest cities supposedly were built by hunters, suspicions may be justified to the end that first settlements were more often destroyed by hunters than built. Defunct bands of hunters did not easily convert into peaceable domesticators. It was more likely for them to become robbers and warriors. Some early cities probably were destroyed, held in submission, and then rebuilt by the command of conquerors who, quite likely, were interested in having fortified walls for their own protection. They converted domesticators into crowds of denizens, to enslave them and to exploit. Warlords found protective walls useful for spending their nights, and within these walls they employed writers who knew how to write housekeeping ledgers and supportive propaganda in the form of legends and myths. Thus legends, about early conquerors who boast about having built cities, are lacking in precision. Most likely they were aristocratic propaganda.

—Orthodox and roaming hunters, when hungry, turned into robbers, warriors, conquerors, and then became creative as planners of various hyper-domestication schemes. They made policy and virtue out of rounding up not only animals, but people too. Thereby, they enhanced the ambitions of their distant ancestors who used to make "artificial teeth and claws" of flint. While early hunters quite likely were not the actual hands-on builders of ancient civilizations, perhaps they nevertheless might be recognized as history's "sheep dogs"—those that drove human gatherers, planters, and herders of animals into tighter corrals for security, control, and availability as resources.

—After the first rounds of city conquests and rebuilding had played themselves out, when competition among marauding armies became fierce, the wiser among warlords decided to become sedentary protectors of the cities they conquered. If they robbed and destroyed the places completely each year, and then retreated to their hills, there would be nothing to return to and to rob after a skipped harvest. It was more profitable to colonize a settlement like a living beehive, to confiscate a share of its produce regularly, in a somewhat disciplined manner, and in return provide its laboring inhabitants with protection, who thereby would become slaves. If a conqueror did not watch his booty, another hungrier horde would lurk in the hills, waiting to replace him.

—Such was the warriors' way of practicing hyper-domestication. In those arrangements sedentary people were made into domestics and slaves—owned after the manner as livestock was claimed by domesticators. Systematic fleecing of a city's denizens became established as an honorable profession. Such was the beginning of individual city kingdoms, and annexing additional city kingdoms was the beginning of empires. In common history books such hyper-domestication schemes are now termed "civilization." Indeed, by way of administering the better policies of a wise ruler, with the help of decent officials, hyper-domestication systems sometimes began to look almost normal—until misfortune befell the royal dynasty, or until a foolish princeling was enthroned and deified.

—Occasionally a stark contrast is needed for us to notice the commonplace and the obvious. Several years ago it was an eye-opener, when at last I got around to looking at the earliest known organized stratum of Chinese "civilization." Among the earliest scratches of Chinese writing, engraved on oxen shoulder blades and tortoise shells—collectively known as Oracle Bones—one can still discern the testimonials of marauding hordes of ex-hunters, arriving as warriors to claim domesticator settlements as properties along the Yellow River. The Shang aristocracy itself was such a horde, fully engaged in puffing themselves up as hyper-domesticators. They invented the art of writing for extra ornamentation and leverage. Divination was supervised and manipulated to justify the royal decrees. Some three thousand years and a few centuries ago, a bureaucracy of about two hundred scribes and diviners was managed by an ambitious Shang ruler who had veto power over everything that was written—over everything that the gods and ancestors would communicate through the practice of cracking Oracle bones with hot metal rods.

—As a great surprise, the first historical strata of Chinese civilization closely resembled those that I had been exploring decades earlier among Middle America's political and ceremonial domains. Primitive hunters, there, were perfectly capable of building something that looked like a jade, serpentine, flint, obsidian, basalt, and limestone-laid civilization.[36] The highest "spiritual" level to which some of those ex-hunter warrior-priests and butchers were able to sublimate their skills was to cleave rock boulders instead of just smashing skulls or cutting open rib cages to sacrifice hearts to a celestial Serpent.

—Hunters were our first deified rulers. The Mesopotamian Gilgamesh, a hyper-domestication prince, quested and sought a level of divine status that had been attributed to totem-devotees of old. His story provides insights into how the first aristocrats wanted to be seen by those whom their stories were intended to impress. Whereas Prince Gilgamesh achieved for himself something like a low-level divine status, his more archaic huntsman partner, Enkidu, acted the role of a bygone hunter buffoon, for comparison. Prince Gilgamesh's quest was aimed at deifying ancient Mesopotamian nobility—that is, aimed at embellishing hyper-domesticators with fake piety.

—By contrast, the earliest Egyptian pharaohs, as devotees of the genuine Falcon totem, a natural raptor, were less humble and more forthright about their divine status. Egyptian rulers aspired to high divine status early on and for those ambitions they are still being admired today. But let us look at their careers historically, in the context and dialectic of their evolution as hunter, robber, and warrior upgrades. Rather than merely enacting the role of a lofty Falcon totem named Hor, or Horus in Latin, the ruling god-kings of Egypt, throughout most of their history, can also still be tracked as earth-bound passionate huntsmen who upgraded themselves enough to pose as justified killers of men. They arranged and governed what came to be called "Egyptian Civilization" straight from the depth of their hunter egos and passions.

Menes (Aha), ca. 3100-3038 BC: Menes was the founder of the Egyptian empire, the beginning of what came to be known as Western Civilization. He set Egypt's direction. He combined two

---

[36]See Karl W. Luckert. *Olmec Religion, a Key to Middle America and Beyond.* Number 137 in the "Civilization of the American Indian Series." Norman: U. of Oklahoma Press, 1976.

kingdoms that became known as Upper and Lower Egypt. The names by which he has been identified in history are Menes, Narmer, and finally Hor Aha. The last of these names was ascribed to the occupant of the first royal tomb of the First Dynasty. Under the name of Menes, this first pharaoh earned the reputation as an all-around heroic hunter. Among pharaohs who still thought of themselves as ex-hunters, the most meaningful manifestation of their authority to govern was their ability to kill. Of all the skills that archaic hunters were most proud, killing ranked as their *summum bonum.*

Fig.36. The Narmer Palette. Courtesy: Trusties of the British Museum.

—There is a story about Menes being attacked by his own hunting dogs. He rescued himself by riding across Lake Moeris on the back of a crocodile. This reversal of fortune and achievement, by daringly mounting a most dangerous reptile, demonstrates transcendence over ordinary hunting skills and strategies. In the awareness of his people, this king was the huntsman of a new superior order—a tamer of crocodiles who, definitely, also knew how to make people toe his line.

—The hyper-domestication element in this story becomes transparent by the claim that the tale was first told by a priest whose god was Sobek, the divine Master of Crocodiles.[37] By way of these incidental circumstances, Menes was implicitly given credit for founding the city of Shedyet (Crocodilopolis). A priest of the primary sanctuary at Crocodilopolis had a vested interest in insinuating that their temple and their city were as old as Menes, the founder-pharaoh of Egypt.

---

[37]Diodorus Siculus, in *Bibliotheca Historica.* See Joseph, Frank. *The Destruction of Atlantis….* Rochester, Vermont: Bear and Company, 2004, p. 99. Citation in *Wickipedia.*

While tillers of the soil domesticated cattle, the aristocratic priests of Sobek kept crocodiles at their temple.

—Apparently not all of Menes' extraordinary hunting feats were remembered as fantastic legends. A realistic sounding story about the death of Menes also has survived. Having been a hunter all his life, and after having reigned over Egypt for sixty-two years, he was out hunting by the River still at an advanced age. There, he was killed by a hippopotamus.[38] Grave goods in the tomb of Aha, the First Dynasty's first Osiris, included over four hundred sculpted bull heads with natural sets of wild bull horns. Also buried with Aha were dogs, young lions, male servants, women, and dwarfs. It is conceivable that the pharaoh himself accumulated his four hundred sets of wild bull horns over the course of his life-time, as trophies.

Theology from Heliopolis. According to the earliest written theological hints, in the Pyramid Texts, any ancient Egyptian pharaoh became the god Osiris when he died. By way of continuing his divine mystery drama according to the Heliopolitan version, this Osiris then "arose" in the person of his successor, as a totemic Horus Falcon—so as to appear at the proper time, completely transfigured for his coronation—to sit on the throne of Egypt in his full human shape and glory. In this manner, every ancient pharaoh was his own predecessor as a ruling Falcon and a transformed Osiris mummy when he died. Eventually he became also his own successor again, as the next Horus manifestation. Thus, with each generation of rulers, this ancient deity transformed itself into a new Horus for re-enthronement—into the Falcon totem who had endured in human memory as a supreme raptor deity since hunting days.

—Still quite in harmony with transformational prehuman flux hunter mythology, a dying pharaoh went to his tomb transformed into the god Osiris.[39] He rose to rule over Egypt, retransformed into

---

[38]Galvin, John. "Abydos: Life and Death at the Dawn of Egyptian Civilization." *National Geographic.* Washington D.C. Apr. 2005, 106-121.

[39]As this entire range of subject matter has been dealt with extensively in Karl W. Luckert, *Egyptian Light and Hebrew Fire: Theological and Philosophical Roots of Christendom in Evolutionary Perspective*, State University of New York Press, 1991, this reference is provided here to supplement our present theme. Because the earlier book has been out of print for some years, the reader is referred to five essays in the bibliography at www.historyofreligions.com which, but for some improvements in the Introduction, correspond to the book.

Horus the Falcon totem—as a single deity, comprising each pharaoh in the lineage: past, present and future. At some point between his funeral as Osiris and his reappearance as Horus occurred his transformation, by resurrection.

—The Egyptian mystery of death was not confined by the shapes of visible material royal bodies, whereby each body would house a divine spirit. Rather, those divine kings together formed one personal and divine essence, each with dual emanations of life—comprised of the flashy *ka* as well as the lingering *ba*.[40] Thus during his reign, a ruling pharaoh was always engaged in the routine of showing himself as someone who continues to be divine, almighty to kill, and everlasting. It was the inherent logic of totemism, of transformation and resurrection based on prehuman flux ontology, that furnished the dynamic of ancient Egyptian hyper-domestication.

—The hunter-derived totemic mysticism of ancient Egypt supported imperial sons of God who ruled as divine Horus Falcons. It has held Egyptian hyper-domestication together for about three thousand years. Apparently this same Egyptian political ideology was embraced, at least in part, by King Solomon at Jerusalem, then by Darius the First of Persia, by Alexander the Great of Macedonia, and Caesar Augustus of Rome. These rulers all used the title "Son of God" or had it ascribed to them.

—The theocratic imperialistic tradition eventually provoked opposition on the part of commoners. People of the Roman Empire began to prefer a crucified victim—rather than one of those deified proponents of violent hyper-domestication. Though their Son of God was a commoner, they nevertheless insisted that he was born of, and resurrected by, God the Father. The Gospel of Jesus of Nazareth proclaimed the "Empire of God" as a religious alternative. The "divinely begotten" status of Roman emperors was implicitly undercut in the Nicene Creed which clever Christian theologians (e.g. Athanasius) got approved under Constantine's own supervision. Jesus Christ was thereby recognized as "the only begotten Son of God." The divine title for Roman emperors was officially abolished under Flavius Theodosius Augustus, Roman Emperor from 379 to 395. He ceded the title "Son of God" to Jesus Christ—the Anointed.

---

[40]A brief introductory distinction between *"ka"* and *"ba"* might be as follows: "ka" was the bright spirit soul that returned after death to Atum, the Godhead; "ba" was the shadow soul that lingered with the body, around the mummy Osiris.

—If some of my suspicions about Göbekli Tepe were moving in the right direction, then the first monuments expressing hyper-domestication ambitions might need to be sought there, at the Lions Lodge and beyond. First Dynasty human sacrifices. The Egyptian early style of hyper-domestication is documented archaeologically, by human sacrifices that are associated with all the imperial tombs of the First Dynasty. According to the archaeological record, the royal tombs of the First Dynasty (ca. 3000–2800 BC) have yielded a total of 860 so-called "subsidiary burials."[41]

Aha	Tomb B10, 15, 19	33 subsidiary burials
Djer	Tomb O	318 subsidiary burials
Djet	Tomb Z	174 subsidiary burials
Merytnit	Tomb Y	41 subsidiary burials
Den	Tomb T	136 subsidiary burials
Anedjib	Tomb X	64 subsidiary burials
Semerkhet	Tomb U	68 subsidiary burials
Qa'a	Tomb Q	26 subsidiary burials

—In light of the fact that these graves have been looted and disturbed, one cannot be sure that all subsidiary burials were actual sacrifices, as we also cannot be sure that some of them were not. However, it seems that a large portion of these tombs, if not all, may have held retainers who were given no other choice but to die at those divine-royal funerals. The heirs and successors of deceased pharaohs, or their handlers, probably thought that Egypt would be a better place, or at least easier to govern, if some of these people were promoted into the underworld.

—Even though these numbers sound a little better than those of the Middle American sacrificial cults, where totals ran into many thousands, or better than Shang and Chin Chinese numbers where totals may turn out to be tens of thousands—the notion that human beings were regarded and wasted as inferior property, and captured by early Egyptian hyper-domesticators as if they were cattle or trophies, was present clearly enough. If you took a divine scion from totemic hunter stock, grafted it onto the throne of Egypt and let it be born of (or hatched by) Isis, then the deity that grew from that nest would remain a Horus, a raptor, a killer.

---

[41]Caroline Seawright, *Human Sacrifice in Ancient Egypt.* http://touregypt.net/feature stories/humansac.htm.

—Some historians have been inclined to interpret the number of subsidiary burials and sacrifices to reflect the greatness of the kings for whom they were sacrificed. Indeed, there had to be a corresponding degree of stability, of fatalism sustained by fear, if significant numbers of the former king's retinue could be sacrificed for him. But in this writer's opinion, these numbers reflect an offset sequence. Djer apparently sacrificed 33 retainers for his secure take-over from Aha. Djet thought he needed to eliminate 318 to secure his position, and his widow Merytnit and her military backers together colluded that they needed to rid themselves of 174. The system, then, seemed to have held itself afloat with a transitional queen-widow on the throne. When her son Den was old enough to rule, the system had by and large been cleansed, and the trustees were already committed to support him. He and his closest retainers felt they needed to get rid of only 41 questionable characters. Den himself probably had little say in these matters. But on the whole, I suspect that the weaker the political position of an adult heir, the greater a compensational impact was required, and a greater sacrifice, so that the next leader might win status for himself as well as empowerment for his allied "executioners" who were then to rule as ministers. The first king of the Second Dynasty, Hotepsekhemwy, sacrificed a token 26 victims to his predecessor at Abydos, to assure his inheritance of the First Dynasty's mandate. Then he left Abydos and moved downstream to Sakkara. For all we know, his successors there abolished burial sacrifices and substituted carved figurines of servants to be entombed.

—Most commentators on First Dynasty human sacrifices tend to accept the original cult story at face value—to explain proper afterworld arrangements for the deceased king. But to this writer's mind, such apologetics for human burial sacrifices are not very convincing. The additional rationalization, that in First Dynasty days a distinction was made between slaves and devoted free servants—suggesting that servants might have been willing victims at royal funerals—also seems doubtful. While dying kings may have given a few hints of advice, the primary decisions of who should die and who should live were made, effectively, by slated successors—by royal heirs and their conspiring collaborators.

—The system was implicitly structured to create its own victims. If you were a servant and wanted to be kept alive by the next Horus, you might ingratiate yourself to the prince as best as you could. But everyone would notice what you were doing. If in the last moment the inner circle of priests and regents enthroned a successor whom you did not expect, you have bet on the wrong Horus. You likely would have been sent on a second tour of duty with the old king. You would be under suspicion because you demonstrated uneven loyalties. From a royal successor's point of view, the safest solution was always to promote ambivalent servants to serve the Osiris in the underworld.

—But certainly, it is a reprieve to see that Egyptian pharaohs, at their dawn of hyper-domestication, were not the worst exploiters of humankind whom our planet so far has seen. Nevertheless, deified masters expected their servants, and even some of their high-level ministers, to accompany them into their afterworld. If this is what the pharaohs expected of those who helped them build up their inheritances, then what could one expect of their behavior toward common people whom they never needed to face? Their system implied that the sovereign owned his subject people as property. The rule of hunter-born totemic emperors facilitated the expansion of domestication culture into hyper-domestication, resolutely.

—Perhaps it was the moderating influence of smaller nomadic herder clans, surrounding ancient Egypt, which contributed some bargaining power that helped subsidiary burials to be discontinued after the First Dynasty. Perhaps it was an influence similar to that exerted by Hyksos invaders a millennium later.[42] It may be assumed that in surrounding realms, freedom-loving herders roamed and tried to resist when hyper-domesticators garnered too many privileges for themselves. Lesser royal upstarts, and to some extent the pharaohs themselves, appear to have added some herder ethos to their hunter instincts. Pharaohs were depicted carrying symbolic whip insignia, as drivers of animal carts and supervisors of slaves did. Already during the First Dynasty some were shown carrying the symbolic crooks that shepherds utilized to hook animals by their hind legs, to manage them in the herd. Obviously, domesticator symbols by themselves could not humanize the system. The destiny of herd animals still

---

[42]The *Hyksos* had their capital at Avaris, in the northeastern part of the Delta. Their occupation lasted from about 1783 to 1550 B.C. through the "Second Intermediate." Dynasty Fifteen (1663 - 1555 B.C.) consisted of foreign "Shepherd Kings" or "Princes of the Desert."

was to get slaughtered, just as surely as wild animals were killed and butchered by hunters.

—It was probably the cultural exchanges between Egyptian hyper-domesticators and marginal Near Eastern herder traditions that, to varying degrees, made a "good shepherd" ethos eventually possible. This ethos has been imprinted on Judaism, Christianity, and Islam. The "good shepherd" idea presented itself as an antithesis to bad shepherds, or to hunters who were known to lurk in the dark. But all this meager "herder humanism," together, failed to save many domestics of Egyptian and subsequent civilizations from slavery and serfdom.

—The fate of being owned has also overtaken those who were captured as prisoners of war, as victims in conflicts that they did not cause, and also groups that were being enslaved by divinely mandated emperors. Hunter totems, those that were flattened down to limestone bas-reliefs at Göbekli Tepe, were still up and about, everywhere, roaming freely at the beginning of sedentary civilizations. Egypt, the birthplace of Western hyper-domestication, was first ruled by totemic "Horus" falcons. This is why eagles in Western lands still dominate today as emblems on the insignias, flags, and monetary notes of Western nations. Here in the United States, we honor our Egyptian roots with our bald-headed native American eagle, with a gigantic obelisk in our capital city, and with the image of a pyramid printed on our dollar bills which, for the sake of authenticity, still sports the very eye of Horus.

Gaia, El Elyon reject Human Sacrifice.

Human sacrifice has been and still is the ultimate act of hyper-domestication. Acts of divinely sanctioned homicide are performed in warfare as well as to upstage sacrifices of owned livestock. Historically, animal sacrifice was a means to pay the highest gods in hunter fashion, with meat; in domesticator fashion, bodies were sacrificed for ownership of livestock. By 3,700 years ago, human sacrifices were not uncommon worldwide. The Earth Goddess at Anemospilia, at Minos, apparently stopped such an event that was staged in her honor. Then the myth of Abraham, that may first have been recorded some three thousand years ago, tells of a herdsman who might have lived some seven centuries before the story was written. The narrative exposes the idea of human sacrifice as foolishness. It features a soon-to-be patriarch who was willing to sacrifice the only son he had left. The story explains how the cult of Yahweh-El Elyon, sponsored by King David at the city of Jebus-Salem, came to prescribe substitutionary sacrifices of livestock, by herders.

18. Gaia, El Elyon reject Human Sacrifice

Torched by Gaia, the Earth Mother

"Gaia" in ancient Greek means Mother Earth—she was *"Maka"* in Minoan Linear B script and *"Cybele"* in Phrygian.[43] In Part One of this book we identified her archaeologically. We saw her Abdomen as Göbekli Tepe, the pregnant Mountain Woman. Then, about three thousand years ago, the name *"El Elyon"* (God on High) was combined with the ascription *"Yahweh"* (the deity of ancient Israel) when, at a tent sanctuary at Jebus, the Davidic monarchy combined the Hebrew Levitic cult with the Canaanite cult of Melchizedek. It was the time when Jebus City was remade into Salem, which later became known as Jerusalem.

—The most amazing evidence of a ritual human sacrifice, for Gaia, was found in 1979 by archaeologists excavating the Minoan civilization on the island of Crete. It was found in a triple-chambered temple ruin that had collapsed as the result of an earthquake, some 3,700 years ago. The upper structure of the temple was burned to ashes. Then, on mainland to the east, conditions from that time period approximately match cultic activities attributed to the legendary Hebrew patriarch Abraham.

—This particular earthquake, at Crete, collapsed a rural temple structure at *Anemospilia*, seven kilometers south of the great palace of Knossos, on the hillside terrace of a northward facing slope. Three parallel chambers were connected along their northern front entrances by an entrance corridor that ran along the combined width of the three chambers. The middle chamber contained the remains of the divine statue, namely, two anthropomorphic feet of burned terracotta that survived the destructive fire. Rows of vessels sat arranged before the statue. In the east chamber, rows of more pots and vessels had been placed. The total number of pottery vessels found at the site was in excess of four hundred.

---

[43]For Linear B see <http://www.palaeolexicon.com>.

—In the temple's west chamber the excavators discovered the remains of a human sacrifice in progress. The victim, an eighteen year-old male, was lying on his side in a fetal position as though he had been bound. This probably was standard procedure, because even if the victim was drugged, his life instincts could have awakened for a last moment of struggle. Suddenly the proceedings of the sacrificial rite were interrupted by an earthquake. When the wooden cover-structure of the building collapsed, the torches that were being used to illuminate the interior ignited a conflagration. The greater divine dimension of the terracotta-footed image, next door, apparently was aroused by this ritual. The Earth Mother Gaia herself quavered, stirred awake, and thereby she stopped the officiating priests in their tracks. These personages were pinned to the floor to be broiled and roasted there—to be preserved as evidence for historians in the distant future.

—From the body of the victim, laid on his side on a raised platform, only half of the blood had been drained by the time the flames started burning him. The fire charred the bones of the upper portions white and left the bones in the lower portion, where blood was still present, smoldering in a darker hue. The holy sixteen-inch blade of a bronze knife was found still lying by the victim's body.[44] At both sides, it showed the nicely stylized image of a boar's head, engraved with elegant lines. The priest and his female helper had fallen to the floor near the victim. Altogether three priestly insiders in this holy ritual were caught and pinned to their places by this event.[45]

—The authors Yannis Sakellarakis and Efi Sapouna-Sakellarakis, with additional historical perspective contributed by Joseph Alsop, were keenly aware of the stir that their publication would evoke. They anticipated that their discovery would upset many people; that it would affect the feelings of all those who hitherto had sought their identity among the glorious intellectual achievements of the ancient Greek civilization. As far as we can tell from a distance, the archaeologists provided their readers with an adequate summary of the material facts. But then what! A human sacrifice has been offered at the very root of the great Minoan-Greek civilization? Most Western

44This was already the Bronze Age. But bronze has not reformed Stone Age mentality.

45*National Geographic Magazine*, February 1981, pp. 204-222. For the sake of precision we will cite source page numbers from this essay in our text.

peoples were prepared to think of this ancient civilization as being as grandiose as the architectural styles and philosophies that emerged from it—and among those innovations the execution of Socrates has long been written off as a freakish mishap. One could expect that all readers were unprepared to judge their civilization critically as hyper-domestication. The discovery was disturbing news, indeed. And to that effect, the authors hesitated, and then at last confessed:

—"Never before, for one thing, had there been strong proof that Crete's prehistoric Minoans practiced human sacrifice, although it had long been suspected." But, before the archaeologists "dared to utter the dread words 'human sacrifice' aloud"—and before they risked publication—"they spent agonizing hours pondering the evidence." (p. 210)

—Indeed, anyone familiar with Minoan mythology knows something about the Minotaur in its maze. Most readers may know about its habit of devouring lost human entrants. They may also know some comparative materials about the survival of maze rituals elsewhere in the world.[46] They could have suspected blood-dripping sacred daggers somewhere near the birthplace of this veiled Minotaur initiation tale.

—When the authors finally published their evidence it came in the shape of a beautifully rationalized White Paper. Surely, the ancestors of this great civilization should be excused because, "under unusual stress, the ancients grew desperate and offered human lives to angry gods. Plutarch tells us, for example, that Themistocles sacrificed three men to assure victory at the Battle of Salamis…, a seer ordered a human slaughtered to rid Athens of a plague in the seventh century BC." On the basis of these records the authors reasoned toward their conclusion: "If a crucial battle and a devastating epidemic produced abnormal stress, we can be quite sure that earthquakes would do the same." (p. 218)

—With the situation thus brought into focus, we can grasp the sentiment of the archaeologists' summation: "We are more than reasonably certain of the salient facts: Thirty-seven centuries ago, in a time when earthquakes were rocking the island of Crete, a Minoan

---

[46]Regarding the meaning of labyrinths see John Layard. "Maze Dances and the Ritual of the Labyrinth in Malekula." *Folklore XLVII,* 1936. Also, A. Bernard Deacon, *Malekula, a Vanishing People in the New Hebrides*, 1934; and "Geometrical Drawings from Malekula and other Islands of the New Hebrides," *JRAI*, 1934.

priest sought to avert the final catastrophe with a rare, desperate act: to the deity of this hillside temple, he offered up the ultimate sacrifice—a human life. But the victim died in vain." (p. 205)

—Obviously, this archaeological summary, with its "desperate deterrence" theory, is built on a serious historiographical and archaeological error. As far as the historiographical mistake is concerned, the archaeologists failed to honor the proper sequence of cause and effect. This human sacrifice had been planned, begun, and was half completed before the earthquake struck. With the logic of these authors one could as well claim that Jesus of Nazareth was crucified to avert earthquakes—a quake is said to have struck while he died.

—A much better explanation for this Minoan human sacrifice is contained in the archaeological evidence itself. The data explain quite nicely what was on the minds of the supplicants while they prepared their sacrificial ritual. While the authors conscientiously presented additional archaeological data, they apparently were at a loss about how to relate these data logically to the seismic event.

—"In the corridor we uncovered rows of vessels that had contained offerings such as fruits, grains, peas, and possibly milk, honey, and wines. In some of the jugs, many of them miraculously unbroken, we found charred fruit seeds." [47] (p. 213)

—Additional rows of vessels were placed before the statue of the deity that stood against the back wall of the central chamber. The clay vessels and the deity's own terra-cotta feet, in that room, survived the fire. The exact composition of the foods in any of the vessels would be of great interest.

—The total architectural layout of the foundation walls and the functional arrangement of the temple have survived the earthquake and conflagration of some 3,700 years ago rather well. They read today like an open book on sacrificial symbolism. In fact, they probably can be read more easily by us today than by contemporary farmers who, some 3,700 years ago, fearfully saw the fire and eyed those mysterious ruins from the outside and never dared to go near or to mention them again.

---

[47]Reading the authors' words while looking at their photographs, we suspect that the "corridor" that contained the rows of many vessels may not have been the earlier identified entrance "corridor" that connected the three parallel chambers, but it appears to have been the easternmost of the three parallel chambers. There is no reason to dispute this minor ambiguity. It makes no real difference where in the temple most of these extra vessels were.

—On the fateful day on which an earthquake wrought disaster, the ceremonies in that temple were not an immediate emergency measure. They were regular and long-planned harvest affairs. The more than four hundred full vessels, placed there for the deity, are proof of extensive public participation. The contents of these vessels were brought as offerings by people representing families, and the priests did not buy them. Historically reasoned, it cannot be said that the earthquake-event had anything to do with these peoples' preparations—not until the tragic deed was done and the young man had already been bled half empty. Not until one priestly helper was already underway, having either served the deity in the central chamber a first drink of fresh blood or was about to do so.

—The divine statue in that central room stood back against the southern wall. This central room was the most sacred chamber in the temple compound. It was the holiest of holies. A priestly helper might just have exited from that chamber, before he/she could turn west again toward the room of sacrifice to fetch another pitcher of blood. The collapsing roof trapped all three officiating priests inside the building. All movements were stopped, and the temple became a freeze-frame of the tragic evolution of religiously legitimated human violence—for the chronicles of civilization.

—The overall architecture of the temple facilitated quite conveniently the bringing together of agricultural produce and human blood—for the deity stationed at the center, to eat and to drink. Agricultural products came from the god's own storage room—the east chamber. Human blood was brought fresh from the tab in the god's "kitchen," the west chamber. It was the place where the altar platform stood, where the victim had been bound and was found. All these matters were logically arranged for such special days on which the deity in the middle would be served her banquet. The overall evidence, therefore, suggests a regular seasonal agricultural hyper-domestication rite. While this sacrifice, certainly, was the last human sacrifice at this temple, in all probability it was not the first.

—Nevertheless, it would be possible to argue that human sacrifices may not have been on the deity's regular menu in this tri-part temple. The vase in which the human blood was carried to the statue—which got shattered in the corridor—bore the dominant image of a bull. This could mean that bull's blood was the most common sacrificial drink at this temple. But the fact is undeniable that, on that fateful day 3,700 years ago, a young man was the victim before fire consumed the structure and roasted his sanctimonious killers. Certainly, on that day their "bull" had human bones.

—Clearer evidence toward the regularity of ceremonial functions and blood sacrifices can scarcely be expressed through the medium of architecture. Domesticator sacrifices of this sort, to which human victims were added to upstage the presentation of mere agricultural produce and livestock, are stock examples in the logic of hyper-domestication. Fruits, grains, peas, honey, and wine were in those vessels. The presentation of slaughter products, supplemented with agricultural and horticultural produce, were logical combinations for divine banquets under those circumstances. The human blood was drained to put the fear of God into the bones of all those living peasants who devoutly brought their vessels filled with gifts of produce. Some of the produce was probably meant for eventual consumption by the priests. We should not forget that the evolutionary prototype of all food sacrifices for the gods was the meals that hunters would afford themselves after a successful kill. They ate portions together with their totemic sponsors.

—I suspect that in the context of Minoan stratified society, where farmers and herdsmen were able to fell and butcher bulls as well as any aristocrat could, the ordinary bull sacrifices would no longer have seemed sufficiently uplifting. The hunter-derived egos of aristocrats, and those of their shamanic priests who graduated as hyper-domesticators without having first learned simple domestication, felt threatened under these circumstances. Where ordinary domesticators could own cattle and slaughter mighty bulls, the priestly servants of royalty and aristocracy could no longer elicit the *oohs* and *aahs* that they craved by performing their sacerdotal slaughters. This, in all likelihood, was the reason why royal diviners went to the next intensity level, to crank up the *mysterium tremendum* effect with human sacrifice.

—The blood of oxen was probably more precious than the blood of lesser animals, and the blood of humankind was more precious than that of oxen. And, of course, the blood of nobles would have been more precious than the blood of ordinary folk. While ordinary human blood might normally have sufficed to teach extra-ordinary lessons, even the sacrifice of an aristocrat may have been risked now and then. Any chief could get into a situation where a sibling or minister would threaten his status and position. By and large, I suspect that the human victims in this society were mostly common domesticators—just as common as were the contributors of those four-hundred-and-more jars.

What might have happened next at Anemospilia?

The victim died and three priests went silent under the flames. The people were dumbfounded and stole themselves home in fear. They mentioned this event only in subdued voices and whispers. The area was probably avoided entirely until the event was forgotten. No one touched the temple ruin, not for 3,700 years. The archaeologists came, and as pious descendants, they defended the rationality of their distant ancestors. In spite of this one incident of seemingly irrational behavior, these Minoan ancestors obviously must have been people who could reason.

—If we spin this story a little farther we ask: "What could this event have meant to those who devoutly believed that they were sacrificing to buy divine grace?" Indeed, the victim did not merely "die in vain" as the excavators concluded. At the moment the blood was offered at her statue, the Earth deity seems to have been downright angry when she refused or devoured—depending on one's perspective—all sacrifices presented to her on that day. Is this how the gods ordinarily ate and drank? Was it an unworthy victim? Were the priests guilty of improper procedure?

—Had the priests survived they probably would have thought of a way to insinuate that the villagers have not brought the full amount of offerings. But as it turned out, for the people this was their last sacrifice at this place. The deity refused all that the priests offered to her on that day. All three officiating priests were trapped. Their royal superiors, seven kilometers north in the palace at Knossos, probably needed to lie low for a while with this group of peasants to their south. It is even possible that their palace at Knossos was taken down as well by this same earthquake. Nevertheless, with every additional ordinary earthquake, the memory of this particular one faded. The aristocrats and priests may have lost authority for a while. But in time, we can assume, another type of sacrificial ceremonial replaced the one that was abandoned. Neither the rulers nor their subjects could coexist in an ontological vacuum. At that moment, reformers had their chance to change their path of religious evolution—if they had relevant issues simmering at the time. The details of the reformed ritual probably would not have mattered greatly, not as long as the new practice would have mollified fear and cheered the people onward in their daily quest for survival.

—We do not know of a prophetic protest reaction in the Minoan kingdom. Before 1979 we did not even know anything about this sacrifice that terminated a local cult. But now we know that this practice was stopped by a greater-than-human power. The grandest pious Stone Age habit, of killing someone for a deity, was halted and locally abandoned. The Earth Mother from whom the seismic tremors came has stopped the proceedings herself.

—The Earth that quaked was the same that the people tortured while working their fields. Just imagine yourself being the Earth Mother, getting regular "haircuts" with hoes of flint. The aristocrats and their priests probably managed to use the disaster to mollify the people into a slightly different style of subservience. As penitent gatherers, as retainers of hunter mentality, most of them knew instinctively that they needed to repent from something and become better people. All primitive hunters knew something about the original sin of killing and eating. But what was the original sin of a human being that converted to domestication? Was it killing and eating a forbidden garden-fruit—as a storyteller in the book of *Genesis* has narrated? We know that it had something to do with ownership, with authority, with eating, and with all the fruits that were being offered in those four-hundred-plus containers.

Sacrifice downscaled by Yahweh/God on High

Three thousand and seven hundred years ago we might have sailed from the island of Crete to the nearest continental shore and then wandered east and south. Within the same lifetime we could have stumbled into our next episode. We have just left a hillside temple in ashes, back at Anemospilia. A human sacrifice was offered by a community of believers who practiced blind faith. The Earth Mother destroyed her own temple, and she rejected all the offerings that people brought. She killed her priests. Concurrently and throughout much of the world, similar slaughters of humans by humankind were going on. As we look at various cultures and religions, however, let us not jump to disdain-driven judgments. Let us bear in mind that any sentence of interpretation that we utilize to illuminate archaeological data is hypothetical narration. It adds up to being commentary on legends about stones, bones, sheep skins and brittle papyri.

—For the response of the Earth Mother at Anemospilia, we have archaeological data, whereas with the actions of Yahweh/El Elyon we must make do with ancient words. To the extent that those words were rooted in history, in something that happened some 3,700 years ago, the Hebrew story only holds what, two-and-a-half thousand years ago, scribes in ancient Israel were able to make of fragments and hearsay.

—What if God asked a man to sacrifice his only son? What if a prospective patriarch were to obey such a command and thereby eliminate his offspring? What if this patriarch had been in line to be our own ancestor? What would have become of us and of all the holy truths we study? These are the existential puzzlers that the story about Abraham and Isaac entertains.

—Any story about human sacrifice, narrated or explained by killers and butchers, or by the beneficiaries of haloed martyrs, will end up being warped in one fashion or other. After Abraham banished his firstborn son to the desert, along with his mother, God on High told him to sacrifice the only son he had left. The same God, it was said, promised he would increase Abraham's progeny to the size of multitudes and nations—to numbers as uncountable as stars in the sky or as grains of sand along the seashore. The requirement for this blessing was that Abraham would sacrifice his remaining son as a burn-offering to the Lord. The would-be patriarch proceeded to demonstrate his blind faith. In a gesture of ultimate piety—and apparently also of greed for the rewards promised—the man gambled his self-same progeny. However, before any of this blind piety could be enacted, the deity changed the rules for Father Abraham's religion.

—Contrary to the low-lying Earth-Mother at Anemospilia, Abraham's God-on-High noticed what his devotee was about to do before blood spurted forth from a wounded artery. A moment before Abraham could apply his holy dagger, God stopped him.[48]

—The storyteller saved himself a lot of trouble by not trying to rationalize the motivations of God. Was this God cruel? Was he

---

[48]Abraham, if he lived, could have lived in Palestine during the early Bronze Age. But we have no proof that Abraham owned a bronze dagger of the royal quality that has been found at Anemospilia. There is no reason why a herdsman who is said to have lived at Harran, near Göbekli Tepe, could not have carried with him a favorite holy flint knife, as a memento from that northern holy homeland.

hungry? Was God trying to measure the amount of reason that could survive an old man's blind faith? If this man really hoped to become an ancestor of multitudes and nations, at what point would virtuous blind faith have begun? At what point would his intelligence as a herdsman and progenitor have failed? Was this shepherd's mind sharp enough to enable him to even help in raising a grandson?

—As far as we can surmise now, from historical clues, the story of Abraham's attempted human sacrifice could have been written as early as three thousand years ago. It could have been edited over the course of five more centuries, mostly by scribes in the employ of the Davidic dynasty. And stories written for a royal dynasty always have had political objectives. King David ruled circa 1003–971 BC. The king and this patriarchal story-character, Abraham of long ago, had interests in common. An ancient would-be patriarch needed offspring, followers, territory, a troop of fighting men, as well as a covenant with God Almighty. David needed these same things.

—King David knew at the outset about who in Abraham's story would need to be the descendants. He labored to unify a group of tribes and small city states—preferably under some divine mandate bestowed on patriarchs they all had in common. Could all of David's solicited tribes be persuaded to belong under the genealogy of a single patriarch? This was the challenge that the would-be monarch accepted for himself. To accomplish his goal he needed people, territory, and a divine mandate—all wrapped into a single patriarchal narrative. Any legend which assumes the involvement of a living deity will, effectively, be elevated to the status of a guiding myth. We define "myth" as a narrative that relates human existence to the greater-than-human dimension. Legends differ from myths in that they do not, or do no longer, explain an active engagement with the greater-than-human dimension.

—King David needed more than just an army and a story. Numbers of people, territory, and a divine covenant also did not yet add up to a functioning kingdom. To secure his monarchy, the king needed people who would be loyal to him and who would accept his divine mandate, preferably in total obedience and blind faith. This was the royal wish-list, and these points also were the subject matter to which the king managed to obligate his writers. The Abraham epic was a foundational story that was recorded piecemeal, for a religious cult that was organized by a king, to help consolidate his rule.

—Unifying a conglomeration of diverse tribes does not happen merely on the basis of a religious story. The political realities need to match. Like every ancient upstart king since the beginnings of hyper-domestication, David was scouting to find groups of vulnerable people to whom he could offer military protection. In exchange for security, these groups were expected to integrate their regional claims into the new kingdom. The divinely anointed kingdom-builder skillfully labored to create trustworthy friendships, secure political as well as religious alliances.

—For his seat of government King David took over Jebus, a Canaanite City. It cost him some advance secret diplomacy, a well-staged take-over, the re-employment of former city elders, and the combination of the Levitic cult of *Yahweh* with the Canaanite city cult of *El Elyon* (God on High). Organizationally his plan required bringing together Hebrew and Canaanite priests. Theologically it meant that "Yahweh" and "El Elyon" were aliases used to refer to the same almighty deity.

—The Abraham myth in *Genesis* (or the presumed "history of faith" starting approximately seven centuries earlier) tell of a friendly encounter between Abraham and the priest-king at Jebus City. The latter's name was Melchizedek. The Canaanite high-priest who was installed by David, for the unified cult seven centuries later, was named Zadok. He evidently was known to the king's scribes as a scion of the ancient royal and priestly family of Melchizedek.

—David's kingdom was being stitched together and legitimated by the patriarchal myth about Abraham. A divine covenant was required and the scribes drafted a number of suitable "covenants" between God Almighty and his chosen patriarch, as well as additional covenants with subsequent kings. These covenants multiplied and were rearranged over time. The most ambitious of these versions bequeathed to Abraham's offspring a territory that stretches from the Wadi of Egypt (Wadi El-Arish or the Nile Delta) to the River that flows past Ur (Euphrates). The problem with this claim—unbeknownst to all involved back then—was that the world's busiest thruway for drifters, from Africa to Europe and Asia, ran precisely through that patch of real estate.

—As a chosen patriarch, Abraham was promised offspring as numerous as stars in the heavens and as plentiful as grains of sand along the seashore. His descendants would conquer and possess the city gates of their enemies and, eventually, they would comprise an empire—a multitude of nations. The cost of these special favors for the divinely chosen herdsman was obedience and blind faith, including obedience on the part of all his offspring peoples. The possibility that those descendant nations might turn into each other's enemies was not yet anticipated by those early writers.

—Actually there were three patriarchs—Abraham, Isaac, and Jacob (aka Yishrael). They were combined by David's writers to comprise a single original patriarchal family. This joint family of ancient patriarchs, extending from father to son and grandson, were Abraham at Hebron, Isaac at Gezer, and Jacob at Bethel. The story of this combined family of triple patriarchs tied together a kingdom by representing the south, the west, and north of the land in a generational sequence. The patriarch at Bethel lent his name to the united kingdom as Yishrael—"Partisan Fighters of God."

—Telling a significant story requires a weighty subject matter. The weightiest of subject matters by the time King David came along, three millennia ago, were the universalistic political schemes of hyper-domestication—including the burdens of slavery, the dominion of robber barons, and slaughters by warriors and priests. Apparently, David and his entourage tried to avoid some of the worst schemes of "hyper-domestication." The existence of the Abraham story itself suggests that King David plotted for the abolition of ritual human sacrifice. His goal may not have been as pure as first hindsight suggests, however. David was a shrewd warlord and schemer. He was not against having people killed in devious ways. Reading among some of the ambiguities inserted by his own chroniclers, his first motivation may have been to wrest execution authority from the two high priests whom he appointed. Apparently, he hoped to hold such powers in his own safer hands, as supreme commander of the military. Nevertheless, by teaching blind obedience he paved the road to dictatorship for his successor son, Solomon.

—Whatever else David's original political motivations might have been, the story about the first patriarch Abraham was initially told to lure the chosen and declared "children of Abraham" into the new king's political confederation, in obedience toward both God and himself. The same end-goal also was on the minds of the Levite writers of the "Exodus" epic, who tried to define the new Kingdom of Yishrael by contrasting it with the God-damned civilization of Egypt. All the same, the monarchy was blessed for a while with a semblance of coherence. By installing high priests from both the

Yahweh and the El Elyon tradition, the powers of the two high priests were halved. This strategy held theocrats in check who otherwise might have tried to function as executioners and supreme judges. The Abrahamic herder and founder myth kept hyper-domestication in check and limited the kingdom's sacrificial cult to an earlier level of religion—sacrificing no humankind.

—On Mount Moriah the God-on-High did not spell out his new religious statues in clear words of law, instead he taught an object lesson. Abraham's blind faith earned him a reprimand. God let the would-be patriarch discover a ram caught up in a thicket. Abraham quickly recognized the ram as a preferable sacrificial substitute for his son. The patriarch, an experienced butcher who already had a holy knife ready in his hand, knew what he needed to do. The miraculous introduction of an unexpected sacrificial ram, into the story, thus underscores the divine reform.

—David's moderate hyper-domestication efforts managed to shoo back his people to the more primitive practice of sacrificing herd animals—thus, to shoo them back into an ordinary domestication cult. The development of the patriarchal myth, which slanted theology toward styles of blind obedience, could have happened after Solomon, with imperialistic ambitions, was enthroned as an Egyptian-style "Son of God." Solomon died having earned the reputation of a tyrant. His kingdom broke up, irreversibly.

—In the larger evolutionary context assumed for this book, one can recognize in this ancient Abrahamic covenant myth an issue that was much older than David's writers could have known. Those who before Abraham's time, in the tracks of the god-king Narmer (Menes, Aha), sacrificed humankind were still hunters who derived their hyper-domestication temperaments from divine predator totems. In contrast, the writers of the Abraham story were, in effect, putting their quills and ink on the fulcrum between scavenger and hyper-domestication religion.

—Hunters on their direct path to hyper-domestication have been terrorizing and sacrificing humankind. And even though the patriarch Abraham, according to this *Genesis* story, heard the God on High promise hyper-domestication rewards, the scribes of the Davidic dynasty were already working to define a more universal and moderate monotheism for the future. The step that they took has necessarily set back the clock to the culture level of domestication and herding. Amidst hyper-domestication experiments that have surrounded and tempted them on all sides, these scribes emphatically reformed, and took back their hyper-domestication cult to the more limited rites that required only domestication sacrifices of animals and plants. In practical terms, theologically, they thereby reduced the appetite of their God Almighty in harmony with the ordinary pursuits of common domesticators. Even though these men helped build a monarchy, they worked to defeat hyper-domestication culture as much as seemed possible at the time.

—Abraham has so become a distant legendary founder of three streams of world religion—the Jewish and Samaritan traditions, Christianity, and Islam—plus a number of ethnic and confessional rivulets. Abraham is recognized as father of Ishmael and Isaac, as a grandfather of Jacob *(Yishrael)*, and as an ancestor of religious founders like Moses, David, Solomon, Ezra, John the Baptizer, Jesus of Nazareth, Paul of Tarsus, and of Mohammad of Mecca and his descendants. Among the ancestors of religious founders who have become historically significant, Abraham has no equals. Followers of the aforementioned monotheistic traditions regard Abraham, if not as their tribal ancestor, then as the religious antecedent in whose tradition subsequent founders and prophetic reformers have apprenticed and were commissioned. Abraham stood at the turning point between simple herder culture and hyper-domestication. He was stopped by almighty God, the Herdsman of All, from finishing his hyper-domestication sacrifice.

19. Hunters and Ancestors in China

Excavations at Anyang and Xian have opened new vistas for prehistoric understanding. How did China's earliest warrior clans and dynasties emerge from their prehistory? Some of the texts on Oracle Bones give hints of what was on the minds of those elites. The earliest royal hordes were diehard roaming hunters who turned into marauders, warriors, and aristocrats. They established their own brand of hyper-domestication. Thanks to what we now know about Göbekli Tepe, it was hunters, weapon-makers, and potential warriors that subsequently roamed across Asia—hunting mammoths perhaps, but also robbing domestic animals and enslaving domesticators. Oracle Bone texts depict hunter-warrior clans still in a process of arriving.

Ancient hyper-domesticators in Western lands, whose domains adjoined the Mediterranean Sea and the Persian Gulf, have at times managed to rule humankind by claiming leadership status as "begotten" heirs of the sole creative power. If challenged on that point, their fallback position was that they were "first representatives" of the mightiest totem-modeled deity. It may be assumed that over time elements of paternalistic herder logic and ethics have trickled into some of these theocratic schemes.

—By some small contrast, in China, the rulers of the first imperial dynasties emphasized a still purer—or wilder—aspect of totemic hunter religion, namely, the centrality of a predatory ancestral lineage.

Such a lineage essentially was the message that every totem pole during the Neolithic was trying to crow. It seemed logical to assume that the grandest totemic ancestor would also have engendered the grandest offspring.[49] To the extent that within a hunter culture everyone was already accustomed to be proud of his totemic predator lineage, no one could really afford to doubt the significance of anyone's ancestor—especially not of someone who, as emperor, acted as though he was the supreme huntsman of the world. Wherever the descendant of a huntsman lacked in heroism, he could take up boasting about the greatness of an ancestor who, still at his funeral, was presiding over the grandest, most memorable killing spree.

China's Deer-Hunter rides a Dragon

Pertaining to the beginnings of Chinese civilization, as to the origin of civilizations elsewhere, the archaeological sources yield their data in small trickles. And also in China those first trickles may be sought in Stone Age strata. About the time when one finds sedentary Neolithic hunters in China, one also finds the first traces of human burial sacrifices. Indications are present already in a prominent Yangshao burial of about 6,000 years ago. In 1953, archaeologists found the remains of Stone Age ancestors who established themselves as sedentary hunters, farmers, and fishermen. They worked as fishermen along the Yellow River, and they planted millet on fields nearby. Our reference is to the "Shell Dragon and Tiger Tomb," at the Xishuipo site of Puyang, in the present province of Henan.[50]

---

[49]On the basis of what we have learned since starting our narrative at Göbekli Tepe, the differences between ancient Western and ancient Chinese civilizations are now diminishing. This has become apparent as we reconsidered the First Egyptian Dynasty, and it will become increasingly apparent as we proceed in China.

[50]For much of the data and references in this section I am indebted to Du Xiaoyu, a doctoral graduate in history at the University of Nanjing. Her interpretation assistance shall also be acknowledged for my visit at Anyang, concerning later portions of this Chapter. See also, "The Cultural Relics Management Committee, Brief Report of Trial Digging of Xishuipo Site in Puyang,"濮阳西水坡遗址试掘 简报, Cultural Relics of Central China, 1988(1). "Cultural Relics Management Committee, Brief Report of Trial Digging of Xishuipo Site in Puyang" in Huaxia Archaeology, 1988(1). "Cultural Relics Management Committee, Brief Report of Trial Digging of Xishuipo Site in Puyang," in Cultural Relics, 1988(3). "Archaeological Team of Xishuipo Site in Puyang, Excavation Report of Xishuipo Site in Puyang of Henan," in 1988, 年河南濮阳西水坡遗址发掘简报, in Archaeology, 1989 (12).

—The most prominent male occupant (M45) in an elaborate three-chamber burial place was flanked by man-sized shell displays of a tiger at his left, and the oldest dragon image so far found in China at his right. Thus, one of two dragon mosaics laid out with mussel shells, on the floor, was company to the man's skeleton in the main chamber (Figure 37). The other design was laid out two rooms farther to the south and appears to portray the ghost of the deceased, mounted on the back of his dragon (Figure 38).

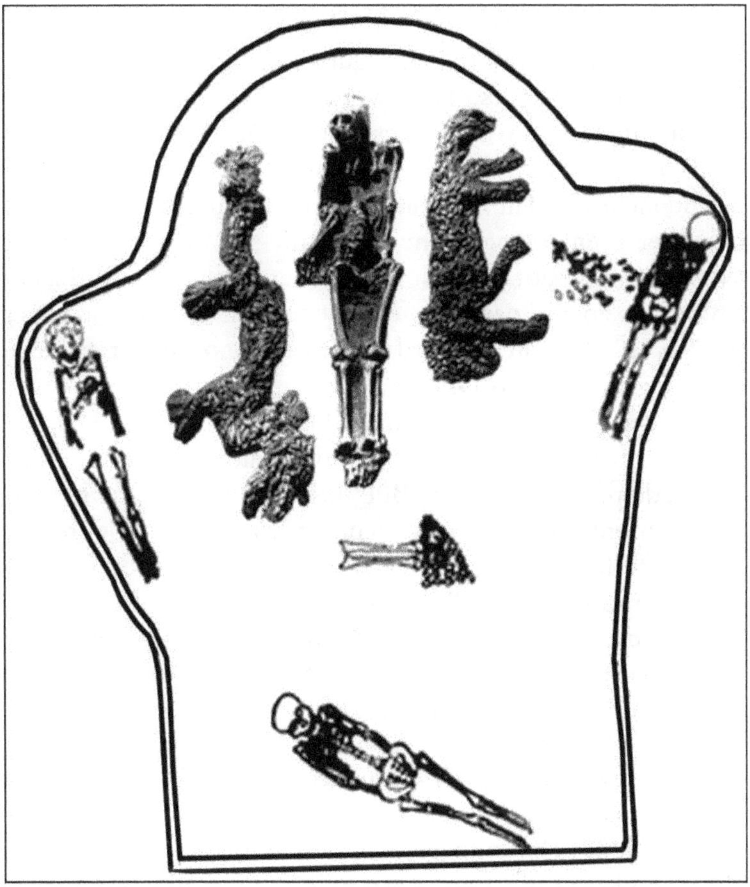

Fig. 37. Chamber One of Burial M45 of Yangshao grave at Xishuipo, Puyang. Source: Pictures 6, Page 5, Plate One, in *Cultural Relics of Central China*, 1988 (1). Courtesy of Du Xiaoyu. Redrawn and composition by the author.

Fig. 38. Dragon Rider. Burial 45, Chamber Three of a Yangshao grave at Xishuipo, Puyang. *Archaeology*, 1989, 12, p. 1069, 4. Courtesy of Du Xiaoyu; Excerpted by author.

—I refer to "his dragon" because I reckon that the deceased was a shaman of leadership stature who, during his lifetime, commanded at least two totemic helpers. They were a Dragon and a Tiger. There may be included with the Tiger also a Deer. But those images, depicted in Room Two of this man's underworld (not shown here), appear inconclusive. The "exquisite stone ax" that is mentioned there is no longer seen between the deer and the tiger. And from the limited data, it was not possible to rule out the likelihood that Room Two refers to an ordinary hunting scene with the deer as a regular victim. Nevertheless, in his third chamber, the occupant seems to be shown riding away on his Dragon.

—The deceased may have earned his reputation as a Dragon Rider on account of having done so already while alive, during shamanic séances perhaps, in the dark. But this cannot be known with any certainty. Among the designs woven into later Han burial robes, and in Chinese folklore, some fierce horses have been metaphorically transmuted into dragons.[51] Warriors as far west as Europe, mounted on horseback, loved to think of themselves as dragon riders *(dragoneers)*, well into the Twentieth Century. But Yangshao people, in their days, had no horses yet to ride on.

Three Subsidiary Burials. We must contemplate the significance of three additional "deposits" associated with this Stone Age burial (Figure 37. M45). The corpses of three young persons in their teen years were added in niches and according to measured distances, like a team of surrounding servants. Together, these extra skeletons from six thousand years ago hint at the start of a long trail of ominous

---

[51]See for example the *Han Tomb 1 in Ma-wang-dui of Changsha,* 马王堆一号汉墓, *Picture 38, Cultural Relics Publishing House, 1973. (Image not shown here.)*

subsidiary burials—of prototypes for human sacrifices, as found associated with subsequent Chinese royal and aristocratic tombs.

—As Western readers, who are used to finding their oldest written sources among the ancient texts of Egypt, and who have read rumors about the hunting exploits of King Menes, we may wish to rethink the Egyptian tale in light of Yangshao archaeology. When Menes' own hunting dogs turned on him, he escaped riding across a lake on the back of a crocodile. Inasmuch as Chinese dragons were also clouds, the Chinese "Menes," about a thousand years earlier, probably dreamt of riding his Dragon airborne among the clouds.

—This early Yangshao Dragon Rider had a successor who sacrificed to him three human servants. Injuries were evident on the neck bones of at least one of the three. Of course, these victims were sent along by the dead man's successor who, we may assume, was not without an ulterior motive—such as demonstrating and establishing his own authority at this Xishuipo place.

—Obviously, my reading of these data must be considered hypothetical. Even before I had a chance to consult all the documents, my position was disputed by some early commentators on grounds that a "classless" Neolithic society, and a tomb of 6,000 years ago, could not possibly contain sacrificial human skeletons. But then, present-day heirs of ancestral cultures generally try to deny the atrocities of their ancestors. Judging by responses of present-day Europeans, our suggestions of cannibalism for the LBK culture in Europe, and reporting a human sacrifice at Minoa, are no exception. Honoring and defending one's ancestors is a praiseworthy posture of filial piety in any culture. On the other hand, ideological dogmas regarding "classless societies," that obligated Chinese archaeologists in 1953, are now rarely mentioned anymore. Specifics regarding the evolutionary theory of Marx and Engels, and the "class struggle," have retained cogency for only a century or so. It now seems as though hyper-domestication abuses began early, among hunters of the Stone Age, when first aspirants to heroic status raised their heads and proudly stood up individualistic totem-pole monuments.

—From this point forward in Chinese history-telling, one need not ask anymore when Chinese emperors got their idea of impersonating dragons or large felines, and why some of these emperors, as dragons, also accepted the responsibility and credit for administering good climate for farming. The Chinese genius of imperial government ruled as the people's chief agricultural Rain-Dragon and benefactor.

Those imperially inclined totemic hyper-domesticators have deciphered the secrets of managing docile domesticators already among those Neolithic Yangshao people, there, along the Yellow River, six thousand years ago.

—After contemplating human sacrifices which were executed by the Shang later, and after revisiting the venerable tradition of Confucius and of his educational Reform, I will reconsider a modern comparative moment of the Xishuipo scene. I will revisit the ceremonial events that I filmed in the year 2002 with the help of Zhang Zuotang (see Figure 41, below). We will then have an occasion to remember the three Yangshao victims who had their throats cut during a funeral at Xishuipo, six thousand years earlier.

Dogs, Horses, and Chariots of the Shang

The Shang pantheon, according to David N. Keightley's reconstruction and stratification, includes (1) Shang-Di the High God; (2) Nature Powers such as River, Mountain, and Sun; and (3) Former Lords. These three levels of power together comprise the "Higher Powers" category of the pantheon. Then, follow (4) some famous Pre-dynastic Ancestors who were being bundled into the Shang mandate; (5) Dynastic Ancestors, and finally (6) Dynastic Ancestresses. Generally speaking, the cult emphasis was placed on the ancestors at levels 4 through 6. From among the Higher Powers (1 to 3), Di appears to have been least involved in the physical dimension of the Shang ancestral cult of sacrifices.[52]

—The most conspicuous stratum of dynastic hyper-domestication in China was discovered at the site of the last capital of the "Shang" (aka "Yin") dynasty (ca. 1300-1050 BC). Near present-day Anyang, a dynastic totemic ideology was being rationalized that justified the killing of thousands of human victims. While Professor Keightley follows the reasonable convention of distancing Shang-Di as some kind of *deus otiosus* from the worst of the physical cult, I am in addition inclined to see this supreme being, "Shang-Di," as a remote "totemic ancestor" who, historically, was never quite definable. The

---

[52]See David N. Keightley. "The Making of the Ancestors: Late Shang Religion and its Legacy," in *Religion and Chinese Society,* vol. 1, John Lagerwey, editor. Chinese University Press, Shatin, N.T., Hong Kong (2004), 2006; pp. 5ff. Keightley has acquiesced to talking about a Shang Pantheon for "analytical purposes." Literally speaking, ancestors alone would not add up to a "pantheon."

archaeology of sacrificial evidence at Anyang tends to overwhelm all attempts at linguistic systematization. Sacrifices appear to have been at least as systemic a component in Shang imperialism as has been the concept of "Shang-Di." And Shang-Di appears to have been the earliest and highest totem-possessed ancestor of the Shang lineage. He became the apex and fountainhead for all subsequent dynastic ancestors. The Shang dynasty probably began at Shang-Di's totemic moment in mythical time.

—The general religion of ancient China has variously been classified as ancestor religion, family-ism, or as something entirely non-religious. Students of comparative religions have therefore always differentiated between ancestors and gods as they have taken pains to distinguish Chinese from Western religions. But the question of whether the Egyptian Osiris-Horus theology is essentially different from Shang-Di's pantheon remains debatable, at least in terms of political and functional consequences.

—The thrust of Keightley's essay recognizes that the Shang ancestors were "made" for subjugating masses of people about whom we still know very little. In our evolutionary and politically sensitive vocabulary, this could be stated as "a Shang pantheon, contrived for goals of hyper-domestication." In an academic symposium on religion, the Shang "pantheon" of divine ancestors would then, logically, belong under the heading of "religion"—as much as does the Heliopolitan theology of ancient Egypt. Among cultural and political considerations, both would also score as "legitimization efforts and propaganda" in support of Shang or Egyptian hyper-domestication. Neolithic totems used to function as gods who were both predators and ancestors.

—The most ancient core of the Shang mandate has been spun straight from the most primitive wool of artificial predator law—from the raw behavior of archaic hunters: "You own what you can kill." Kings, emperors, and usurpers throughout human history have claimed power over their domains by various methods of hunting and sacrificing humankind—by paying "in kind" for what they pretended to own. But no sooner had anyone attained such authority, than he needed to begin his struggles to maintain power, for his dear life's sake. He needed to justify his mandate against usurpers, continually, with fresh demonstrations of his ability to kill. The point of his demonstrations was not merely that he *could*, but also that he *would* kill—in order to own.

—In this manner, the violence of hyper-domestication was doomed to whirl in vicious circles, always in danger of spiraling beyond circular limits. Even highly principled sovereigns and idealistic revolutionaries have inadvertently stepped into the terror trap. As the means to a desired end, they tried to utilize terror defensively, and temporarily. Their hope was to reach a point along their road after which they would be secure enough to do mostly good. However, the equally primitive law of "enforcing balance by engaging in revenge," never left enough freedom for switching over to "good" after having done "bad for the sake of defeating evil" so very well.

—Early Chinese civilization, like others in the world, began with Neolithic technology and later was accelerated by the inclusion of fire and metallurgy. Flint weapon points were duplicated and reshaped in metal, and stately heatable bronze vessels proved their practicality as cooking pots in cannibalistic victory celebrations. Alongside the art of bronze casting, there was another component that added power and stratification to the diverse inheritance of Shang hunter culture. At Anyang this addition was the domestication of horses, a skill that eventually was combined with wagon technology.

—Aside from warriors and herders, the Shang aristocrats also controlled planter folk. According to hints in the Oracle Bone records, these were people who were expected to sow, tend fields, and reap millet. But very little is known about Shang commoners. As far as the Shang elites and the management of their domain were concerned, what counted most was their royal skill of preserving and expanding their ancient lifestyle of hunting. Indeed, in ancient China most hunters have persisted in force, haunting and subduing local domesticators. Foreign herdsmen, possibly Xiongnu or Samoyeds in the north and west, together with their animals, were all memorialized on the Oracle Bone records as captives. Some people may have been taken and kept as "prisoners of war" for a while. But how could prisoners be distinguished from ordinary peoples when war campaigns were not distinguishable from marauding and indiscriminate pillaging?[53] It appears as though early Asian domesticators, herders

[53]Herbert Plutschow identified in addition natives of the sheep-raising Ch'iang tribe among those victims. "Archaic Chinese Sacrificial Practices in the Light of Generative Anthropology," *Anthropoetics I*, no. 2, p. 5, December 1995, University of Los Angeles, CA

as well as planters, were never able to escape being controlled by totem-dogged archaic hunters who reorganized and reinvented themselves as warriors and aristocracy.

—From the first written records of the Shang, the Oracle Bones, we learn about large troops of men engaged in hunting expeditions. The king worried a lot about his horse-drawn wagons. Under off-road conditions, these Bronze Age cavalry contrivances apparently were prone to accidents. They may have been better suited for supervising a hunt from the sidelines, to carry the king as commander a few feet higher than his hordes, or to haul equipment, rather than to drive into the middle of a hunt or into the melee of a military battle. The Shang king fretted about how to avoid hunting accidents. His preferences, of using "dog soldiers" for the hunt, were not attained without good reasoning—all those professionally staged oracle consultations notwithstanding.

—Shang kings of the early Bronze Age used two kinds of officers in their retinue. First, there were men who ran with dogs. The infantry attacked jointly with dogs. They attacked like dogs. All these officers and their animals were simply referred to as "dogs." And then there were officers who manned and drove the royal horse-carriages, and they were named "horses" after the animals that they tamed and used.

—This linguistic peculiarity of calling soldiers "dogs" and "horses" not only betrays the beginning stages of a written language that masters the art of abbreviation, but it also exposes the ideological profile of Shang hyper-domestication. In the eyes of the Shang elites, ordinary soldiers really were dogs and horses. Ordinary human beings were ranked significantly beneath the elites, as other animals were. And judging from the extent of human slaughter at Anyang, human beings were indeed treated there like domestic livestock—and worse.

—Dogs were domesticated some fifteen thousand years ago and earlier; or rather, they might have domesticated themselves when by their own volition they became camp-followers of human hunters. The first presence of domestic dogs, or wolves, among human hunter folk did not yet produce a culture of domestication. Domestic dogs merely improved the effectiveness of an alliance of predators. When later this combined pack of human and canine hunters came to be reorganized under human chiefs and kings, they were assigned to serve the same basic function—to hunt like dogs. And all of them together were utilized by totemic ally mandated kings who assumed that they personally owned all of them as their "domesticates." The top echelons of the human species had, in fact, elevated their humanoid ethos to the aristocratic approximation of divine Wolf Culture.

—If at this crucial moment in human evolution there really was a competition between human and canine culture, then the canines won the contest by virtue of their obedience modeling. Dogs became the exemplary models of their human masters. What a dog would do for a human master, all humans were henceforth expected to do equally well for those totemic ally deified human masters. And to this very day, in colloquial Chinese, the infantry soldiers and police officers are referred to as dogs—or, even a little farther down to earth, as dog-legs.

—But what has hyped the royal power of the Shang even more, what elevated the rank of the first ancestor Shang-Di over High Powers, ancestors, and kings, and what established horses, was the additional rattle of horse-drawn wagons. It is therefore necessary to take a quick look at horse domestication in Asia.

—The earliest fence-post enclosures, with significant amounts of horse manure to vouch for occupancy, in Kazakhstan, have been dated around 5000 BC. Like cattle, sheep, and goats elsewhere, the horses at Krasni Yar, Kazakhstan, were kept for meat and milk.[54] The earliest evidence of horses being ridden, that is, of horse teeth having been worn down by bits, was found in Kazakhstan as well, dating 3,500 to 3,000 BC. Only a few of these horses were ridden, perhaps to hunt or to round up wild horses. The earliest horses that drew carts or chariots were used in Mesopotamia by about 2,000 BC. The carts showed up in China some eight centuries later, during the Shang Dynasty, as dual-hitched two-wheeled contraptions. Horses have been found sacrificed, together with chariots and charioteers, alongside thousands of captives and dog-officers (Figures 39, 40). Yin (ca. 1200 to 1045 BC), near Anyang, was the last capitol of the Shang Dynasty.

—With the arrival of horses and wagons, the methods of hunting and warfare began to change toward greater complexity. But

---

[54]Marsha A. Levine, "Domestication, Breed Diversification and Early History of the Horse," McDonald Institute for Archaeological Research, Cambridge, UK: Http://research.vet.upenn.edu/HavermeyerEsquireBehaviorLabHomePage/Reference.

the link between hunting, military training, and warfare was still strong during Warrior States centuries (475—221 BC) and onward. Heroic warriors would face wild animals such as bulls and tigers with bare hands and a short sword. Strategically there was not much difference between military campaigns and hunting drives. Hunting roundups were undertaken to net animals for slaughter and sacrifice to the ancestors. Warfare was used to capture human groups for labor and sacrifice—as well as herdsmen and their herds for slaughter and sacrifice—all in honor of the same ancestors. Hunting, as virtual "war" against animals, was excellent training for warfare against humankind. Even foreign conquerors of China, such as Kublai Khan (13th Century), fell in line with ancient traditions. He conquered people as he conquered animals. Marco Polo, who loved to hunt wild sheep all over Asia, found the Khan's hunting parties difficult to distinguish from military campaigns. Tens of thousands of people participated in those hunting drives.[55]

—All warfare of the Shang was pursued analogously to hominid evolutionary beginnings. Humanoid artificial predators were grouped against prey animals and were marshaled in rivalry against their natural predators. Shang dog-officers and horse-officers served under the command of a divine-human king who was the descendant of divine ancestors of a self-made totemic dynasty or "species"—a military force of fighters. They were led against buffalo, deer, and wild pig—also against the tigers that were circling and herding them long before humankind imitated their strategy. Presumably, chariots would be used by kings to scout the whereabouts of herds, and to haul nets and other gear. Dog officers would be stationed to hold the nets that then would slow down and entangle the driven animals, to be tied up or killed as the situation permitted, or as the king demanded.

—The Shang king, in order to determine his official strategy for a hunt, or a strategy for any other campaign activity, had propositions for ancestral assistance inscribed on shoulder bones of cattle or on tortoise shells—collectively referred to by excavators as "oracle bones." These items were cracked with the application of a red-hot metal rod to divine the amount of help that the king could expect from his ancestors. The king maintained a staff of approximately

[55]See Mark Edward Lewis, *Sanctioned Violence in Early China* (SUNY Press, 1990), pp. 145-146.

two hundred learned men who kept records of his official divinations, official decisions, and corrected results. He remained in charge of the process in that only he did the final decoding and interpreting. Verifications were then inscribed on the same bones, after the fact, to certify the king's accuracy—perhaps to flatter the king and impress his ancestors. Aside from his thoroughly controlled bureaucratic attendants, and the king's ancestors, no other humans were trained enough, or were authorized, to read these records anyway. Thus, by way of a formalized bureaucracy, and with the help of China's first literate engravers and diviner assistants, the Shang king ruled from a position beneath his own ancestors.

—While the king managed to legitimate his decisions and to justify his commands, the full obedience of the masses was expected to happen beneath that manmade cloud of literacy—of literacy wrapped up in elitist ancestor-dedicated magic.

—But then, while the king's method, of governing by written oracles, demonstrated great strength and inventive shrewdness, it also introduced a new standard of implicit precision and vulnerability. Why was it necessary for the king to explain everything to his ancestors? Did he not have control over the entire system to begin with? Was it a matter of demonstrating to his ancestors that he could deceive and manage underlings better than they were able to do without the art of writing? In an earlier chapter I have postulated that the first word spoken by a humanoid artificer-predator probably was a denial and a lie. It appears as though the evolutionary process at the cradle of civilization has produced a duplication of this first spoken advance. The first written words beyond household ledgers were probably also false and fancied.

—The commands of hyper-domesticators needed to be recorded with precision to impress their underlings. Moreover, without issuing commands absolutely, the kings could not even have impressed their own ancestors effectively—nor could they have intimidated literate officials who gradually must have become cognizant of inconsistencies. So it came about that surreptitious "divination" could not rule ancient China forever. While literati, on the basis of their duties and labor, were unable to challenge the royal manufacture of oracles, subsequent generations of scribes enabled themselves, nevertheless, to master the linguistic skills which, apparently, could turn hyper-domestication lies into official truths. A written language could be studied objectively for what it was. From among earlier rounds of administrative notations and interpretations it could help detect inconsistencies. Thus, without the Shang king's earlier bureaucratic cover-up, the hundred philosophical schools later on—including the Confucians, the Daoists, and the Legalists—would not have had any handles to grasp, no tools with which to detect lies and discrepancies, or to find faults for which to insist on improvements.

—The people who were preyed upon included warriors as well as herdsmen with their cattle, sheep, and horses. All domesticators could be declared enemies or legitimate prey, and their possessions could be confiscated. And surely, some of the king's own engraver apprentices, who on account of youthful innocence might have asked embarrassing linguistics questions, could easily have been rendered victims. Of course, the existence of any warrior kingdom could, by the Shang method of literate divination, be justified in the name of practicing defense. Any aggressive troop of warriors could be mobilized as easily. Love of survival required defense, and pre-emptive strikes were the surest way of keeping one's defenses intact. Greater amounts of violence were required, and in most instances sufficed, to suppress lesser amounts of violence.

—Four Oracle Bone inscriptions provide an outline for the outcome of what was deemed to have been a good hunt: "Today, the *yi-day*, if the king hunts, the whole day he will have no disasters, he will not encounter great rains" [145]. "On *guimao* (day 40) (we) really did burn the brush (while hunting) and caught [wild buffalo] eleven; pigs, fifteen; tigers…; young deer, twenty [146A]. It should be the Dog-officers whom the king joins with, (then) there will be no disasters" [146B]. "If the king joins with the Dog-officers he will catch (game)." Human prisoners were memorialized on Shang Oracle Bones as a king's payments to his ancestors in exchange for their endorsements and assistance. The divination process was the same whether the king paid his dues with cattle or with men. It was the king who proposed his sacrifices, and the ancestors could accept or reject by determining the chance cracking lines on the oracle bones. But the king did the final interpreting, and we know what the hungry ancestors received in the next instance: "If he offers Qiang (prisoners), ten men, the king will receive assistance." [144][56]

---

[56]David N. Keightley. *The Ancestral Landscape…*, 2000, p. 3, 106, 108f.

—What has been found near Anyang, at the birthplace of Chinese imperial civilization, can be taken as an especially amplified example of early hyper-domestication. Progressive hunters, aristocratically familiar with all types of domestication schemes, overshot the goals of ordinary domestication. From controlling plants and animals they progressed to subjugating human beings. To legitimize their aggressive style, they manipulated their communications with the superior ancestors and gods. The distinction between ordinary human fighters and the dogs or horses that the Shang royalty led into battle was erased when, as the Oracle Bones attest, the ruler proceeded to divine the fate of any of these subjects. The king was chief scribe, diviner, interpreter—updater and recorder of his Oracle-Bone-based legitimization bureaucracy.

—Under this system, neither the gods nor the ancestors nor the Supreme Ancestor (Shang-Di) himself were able to convey anything that the Shang ruler would not permit. Meanwhile at Anyang, skeletons of human "dogs" were found and excavated along with those of four-legged dogs, horses, two-wheeled chariots, and two-legged charioteers. There was even an elephant. The numbers of archaeologically documented sacrificial victims from the Wu Ding period ran into thousands.

—Here is an example of the king's pledge to Father Yi, inscribed on an Oracle Bone by a royal diviner: "In making exorcism of Father Yi, (we) will cleave three cows, and pledge thirty dismembered (human) victims and thirty penned sheep" (I. Bin—*Heiji* 886; Y891.2). Drowning animals in the River was also a strategy that the Shang kings used for sacrifice: "(We) make burnt offering to Tu, of three young penned sheep, split open one bovine, (and ritually) drown ten bovines."[57]

—Modern scholarly rationalizations generally begin by assuring us of the religious disposition of ancient Chinese people—assuring of the intimate relationship they supposedly maintained with their ancestors. Thus, whether certain commentators sympathize with ancestors that became victims during ancient Shang slaughters, or whether they apologize for sagacious royals who staged those spectacles, or whether, motivated by politeness certain foreign scholars refrain from asking anything to avoid offending anyone, we cannot expect sober historical assessments from any of these.

---

[57]David N. Keightley. *The Ancestral Landscape…*, 2000, pp. 9, 32, 64.

Fig. 39. Anyang, China: A Shang Dynasty excavation pit in a field of human sacrifices. Author photo, courtesy of Anyang Museum.

—The fact remains that for sensitive modern minds, with evolutionary hindsight, human sacrifice offered as proof of piety to ancestors, or to inflict strategic terror on subjugates, is reprehensible in any shape or form. But then, modern societies of the West, the Middle and Far East, have all killed in excess of a thousand times more human beings during the Twentieth Century alone. They have sacrificed more human victims than even the bloodiest rulers in ancient Middle America, in ancient China, or in between might have managed in pursuit of their archaic modes of vanity—or for the elusive stability of their priestly or royal dynasties.

Fig. 40. Chariot and charioteer sacrifices. Author photo by courtesy of Anyang Museum.

—Regardless of what kind of religious apologies one might offer for aristocratic sacrifices, our historical observations should include recognition of the fact that these alleged devout rulers could hardly have cherished the same religious faiths as did their victims—or vice versa. There never was a single unified Chinese ancestor religion, unless it was the portion that can better be studied, self-contained, as imperial propaganda. The common people could not escape the sway of this ideology.

—Honors were intended exclusively for the supreme ancestors of the royalty; that is, for what David Keightley has identified as the "made" royal assembly of ancestors, beneath Shang-Di.[58] Ancestors for whom you were killed were not yours. When, as a Shang warrior, you suddenly found yourself surrounded by a team of armed dog-officers, and had your hands tied behind your back, the only religion that you had left for yourself was the one that ended with a pious surrender to their Shang-Di, and to your Ming (Fate). The dog-officials who "honored" you as a noble victim were not your relatives and might also be honored likewise the next time a royal died—or had a toothache.

—At any royal funeral, a new ancestral candidate—the deceased monarch—was inducted into the already deified ranks of Shang ancestors. While the deceased king was thereby promoted to the rank of his divine predecessors, his successor staged a most grandiose and noteworthy spectacle for his entry into life hereafter, as well as for the successor's increase of power over the living population. The entire slaughter of animals and people, apparently, was staged to increase the status of the combined generations of royal predators, dead and alive. This ancestor religion promised stability for the dynasty. On common people, it bequeathed slavery and a constant reminder of their finitude.

—The deceased royals for whom thousands of human lives were wasted were not even actively participating in these pious pretenses at their funerals anymore. Their days for killing humankind were over when they died. It was a successor's turn to clean the deck of power to his own advantage—to get rid of people of the old official structure, and to pick his own generation of warriors. His own human "fighting dogs" were men whose souls he managed to load with fresh culpability—to create a new generation of killers who, for their own protection, needed to be loyal to each other as blood-brothers,

---

[58]David N. Keightley: "The Making of the Ancestors: Late Shang Religion and its Legacy," pp. 3-63 in John Lagerwey [ed.] Religion in Chinese Society. It goes without saying that beyond scant scholarship in English, there is a massive amount of scholarship in China itself.

and also be loyal to him, simply because everyone else in the world would have despised them individually. They needed to cling together through inducement of fear, to enforce their joint honor.

—The inducement of fear is what aristocratic sacrificial piety came down to in the end. A predecessor's funeral was the opportune moment when the government could be purged with the pretense of official piety. The regime could not be cleansed this easily again throughout the remaining lifetime of the next ruler, unless—yes, of course, unless with his rites of purification and self-legitimization, a successor overreached himself. He could then face insurgencies and be forced to join his family of sublime hungry ancestors, under Shang-Di, more quickly than he could consolidate a loyal following. The dynasty could fall and the king's body (or head) could be cooked in a stately bronze pot, cast especially for the next usurper and winner of the divine mandate.

Confucius: Teacher of Decorum in the Dragon's Lair

In preceding sections of this chapter, we have provided glimpses of how Stone Age hunters in China contributed to the earliest stages of hyper-domestication. We noticed that the mere substitution of malleable bronze for flint did not change the essence of Stone Age hunter culture or religion. Metallurgy simply sharpened the killers' weapons and rendered them more effective. Moreover, those famous Shang bronze containers apparently served as vessels for a swankier level of cannibalism. Hyper-hunters became hyper-domesticators and hyper-aristocrats.

—The same stride forward also introduced the art of writing to enhance the control of property and people. Thousands of human victims were sacrificed at Anyang, as if the rulers were learning their basic arithmetic by scoring corpses.[59] An archaeologist cannot help but be less impressed by the filial piety of these Shang kings than by the tyranny that they inflicted on the living.

---

[59]More than 1200 sacrificial pits were unearthed in 1934-1935 at Anyang, the capital of Shang. In 1976, archaeologists discovered 191 pits containing more than 1200 victims. See Herbert Plutschow, "Xunzi and the Ancient Chinese Philosophical Debate about Human Nature." *Anthropoetics 8*, no. 1 (Spring/Summer 2002), East Asian Languages and Cultures, University of California at Los Angeles, CA. For a sample pit see Figure 38, above.

—Some seven centuries later, it was left to the Sage Confucius, and other reformers, to labor for whatever human dignity and religious balancing that could be salvaged for humankind in China. Their options were limited. Confucius could not come down from a mountain as Moses supposedly did, with a new divinely inscribed tablet and announce a set of new commandments of God. Shang-Di, in evolution, was still closer to a totemic sponsor, a "super hunter," than he was to a creator or father of all living species. He had no prophets among the people and he would not issue public laws. That function was pre-empted by the Shang king and his esoteric divination bureaucracy. Archaeological evidence shows that the first two historical dynasties of ancient China, the Shang (ca. 1570-1045 BC) and Western Zhou (1045-771 BC), practiced human sacrifice. Then, in the subsequent "Spring and Autumn" and "Warring States" periods, human sacrifice was discontinued as a state ritual. However, actual killings of this sort were abolished "officially" only in the year 384 BC, when live burial victims were replaced with clay and wooden figurines.[60]

—For a summary, we refer again to the diligent work of Herbert Plutschow: None of the other prominent Spring and Autumn and Warring States period philosophers took issue with human sacrifice —not Confucius (Kong Fuzi, 551-479), Mozi, (ca. 480-390), Mencius (Meng Zi, ca. 382-300), Zhuangzi (ca. 365-280), and Han Feizi (died 233). While they were idealizing the first dynasties and their wise rulers, it seems enigmatic that none of these philosophers even so much as mentions human sacrifice, not even as a negative, no-longer-desirable state-supporting ritual. They write as if such sacrifice never existed. They ignore the fact that the wise Yao, Shun, Yu, King Tang of Shang, Wen and Wu of Zhou, whom they all idealized as the fathers of good statehood, actually practiced human sacrifice.[61]

—Some differences of scholarly opinion do exist about the extent of the alleged Confucian "silence." Professor Xu Changqing

[60]Herbert Plutschow. "Archaic Chinese Sacrificial Practices in the Light of Generative Anthropology," *Anthropoetics I*, no. 2, p. 5 (December 1995), University of Los Angeles, CA.

[61]Herbert Plutschow, in *Anthropoetics 8*, no. 1 (Spring/Summer 2002). Yao and Shun were legendary wise kings of antiquity. King Tang was the dynastic founder of Shang. King Wen (reigned 1099-1050 BC) and King Wu of Zhou (reigned 1049/45-1043 BC) were dynastic founders of Zhou.

headed the team of the Archaeological Institute of Jiangxi that excavated a 2,500 year old aristocratic tomb, discovered in January 2007. The tomb contained the remains of forty-seven human victims, and all the while Xu Changqing explained that Confucius "spent a lifetime criticizing blood sacrifice."[62] Indeed, I agree with Professor Xu that this sentiment was implicit in the teachings of Confucius. Nevertheless, like Plutschow, I also have not found direct indications that Confucius spoke against the practice openly. I must continue to consider the historical circumstances that could have produced the Sage's ambivalence.

—When considering Shang-Di's presiding role over the Shang government, dynastic sacrifices and atrocities, Confucius and other reform-minded historians must have been dumbfounded. As students of history, they probably knew a few things about these atrocities—also about the fact that, in private aristocratic circles, the practice continued into their own days. Criticizing these practices openly probably would have brought nothing for the teachers except death sentences that would have helped authenticate the practice itself. These hyper-domestication practices endured because they amplified fear among potential victims, and they increased status and privileges for the ruling elites. Had the teachers spoken straight, their words in debate would very likely have legitimated such sacrifices as administrative necessities. Therefore, it seems, Confucius modified religion by way of ignoring the ancient supreme totemic Ancestor of Shang (Shang-Di). As much as he possibly could, he oriented himself toward a broader dimension and less intimate Heaven (Tien).[63]

—The trouble with having special people become special friends of almighty personal deities—or with descendants of almighty ancestors and lords—is that such people may grow too big to coexist in the world of ordinary mortal humankind. "Tien" was the name by which Confucius referred to the supreme deity. It meant something like "Heaven-and-Sky" combined. It implied a deity that was more spacious than Shang-Di, but nevertheless attentive to human affairs. Under

---

62Kevin Holden Platt, reporting on January 29, 2008 for the *National Geographic News* (October 28, 2010).

63Founders of religions, in general, have focused on reshaping ontology and theology, and have limited themselves to changing the presuppositions of various social styles. See for instance the silence among founders of Christianity, Buddhism, and Islam regarding the hyper-domestication practice of slavery. While one trims the toenails of a system, trimming fingernails must be postponed.

the circumstances, and within the Confucian perspective and balance, the almighty name *"Tien"* needed to be established as a highest standard and norm and at the same time be kept out of the reach of emperors. By contrast, *Shang-Di* was much too closely linked with all the dynastic Shang ancestors who were known to insist on a cult of human sacrifice.

—Of course, the overall structure of Confucianism has presented a number of problems for those who depended on it over the past two-thousand-plus years. There is no room in this book for such a discussion, but I recommend a lecture by Wm. Theodore De Bary.[64] Some Confucian ambiguities remain intransigent for modern minds; but be that as it may, for the purpose of resolving those difficulties, the historical situation and the intentions of reformer Sages must first be understood.

—Confucius taught ritual *(li)*, which amounts to improvements on behavioral style and decorum. Reforms were expected to result from pressures generated by improved societal behavior and decorum. For example, it was left to Mencius to expound on an almost demo-cratized enthronement practice for emperors, based on an episode where the ruler Yao selected Shun as his successor instead of his own son. According to Mencius, Shun presided well at rituals. All the musicians and people liked him—and "Heaven sees according as my people see; Heaven hears according as my people hear." (*Mencius 18*, 7-8; the James Legge translation).

—Thus, as a next broader step in the Confucian view of things, it was the scholar's hope to avert human rulers from overriding the true intentions of Heaven. And so these scholars sought to lessen the dangers of theocratic hyper-domestication. Confucius and other classical scholars did not have many solid exemplary historical precedents to model and to recommend—perhaps none.

—Against the general danger of supporting imperial tyranny, while still wanting to maintain a semblance of humaneness and order, Confucius needed to recommend rituals for both societal dimensions, upward and downward along the social status scale. Upwardly he needed to check the power of the emperor and the elites, and downward he needed to empower ordinary people—to help ritualize

[64]Wm. Theodore de Bary, "The Trouble with Confucianism." *Tanner Lectures on Human Values.* Delivered at the University of California at Berkely, May 4 and 5, 1988. Http:/ /www.tannerlectures.utah.edu/lectures/documents/debary89. pdf.

Fig. 41. The third-year anniversary of the funeral of Zhang Jucai, in the summer of 2002, at Fanmagou, Ningxia. Four Yin-Yang shamans officiated (lower left). The deceased was an ordinary farmer who, on that day, became a full ancestor and acquired the afterworld status of ancient lower gentry. Burial sacrifices for him were paper-mâché replicas that included a mansion, two servants—male and female, two pavilions, a male horse-attendant and the stallion he cared for. All these were burned at the gravesite. The invitation to this event was by courtesy of Zhang Zuotang, nephew of Zhang Jucai. Zuotang can be seen, slightly bent forward to tend the fire, at the lower right. The man with the hat, standing behind him, is Zuotang's father—brother of the deceased. Photos are extracted from author videos.

their lives and render them competitive with the elites. In the upward dimension, Confucius posited ideal models of the past, embodied in the form of imitable Sage Kings. Downwardly, he encouraged a web of simple rituals to expand the funerary cult of the common people. The ancestor cult of the elites had been used all along to dominate the comings and goings of the masses. However, the more the common people learned to respect and celebrate the ancestors of their own families, the more the status of royal ancestors was diluted in comparison.

—To boost the self-confidence of the living without involving their ancestors would have been revolutionary. However, to teach common people to bow to their own ancestors could be rationalized as being noble imitation of the piety that elites demonstrated for their own ancestors. So the common people were taught a way to raise their status by pious ritualism—humbly imitating the elites.

—How ancestor veneration among the common people in China has competed with and has mimicked the sacrificial ancestor cult of imperial elites can still be seen today by the paper-mâché substitute offerings shown in Figure 41, above. When in 2002 the means for a ceremony became available, Zhang Jucai, an ordinary peasant in an ordinary Ningxia village, was promoted to full status as a family ancestor, three years after his burial. The funerary gifts still mimic, and thereby compete with, those sacrificed by ancient elites. There was a mansion, a male and a female servant, two pavilions—representing Gold Mountain and Silver Mountain—and a male attendant with the horse he cared for. All were sacrificed along with bundles of home-printed afterworld money and libations of sorghum wine.

—The three sacrificial human representations appear to correspond, still, to the Stone Age burial at Xishuipo of six thousand years earlier (Figure 37). It is indeed amazing that here, even at this late date in modern Chinese history, no taboo in folk religion, or in theoretical principle, has been established against the basic notion of representational funerary human sacrifice.

—Confucius taught his upward-bound students how gentlemen and educators *(chüntzu)* might live and teach suitable ritual *("li")* for people at both upper and lower social levels. But how could a dance-and-decorum instructor hope, or dare, to reform the cult of glorious divine predators—of emperors, totemic tigers, lions, and dragons? Certainly not by trying to teach them the behavior and ethics of sacrificial sheep, head-on! But with some luck, reforms could be encouraged by a method of positing improved models of royalty that could be imitated. And by that method of "show and tell," Confucius said some things about the best kings who ever ruled. The need for presenting models of "wise kings" was more urgent than communicating what today we consider to be "factual history." In actual ancient Chinese history, we surmise, one could find far too many kings who prided themselves as being topmost killers. Confucius, as a teacher of reform, needed to eclipse the gory-glory ethos of the predatory totemic elites. He needed to indoctrinate them with wiser and softer models, worthy of emulation. In that regard, the Great Teacher's commentary on the aforementioned legendary wise ruler Shun (23rd-22nd century BC) is quite revealing:

> "Among those that ruled by inactivity *(wu-wei)*, surely Shun may be counted. For what action did he take? He merely placed himself gravely and reverently with his face due south; that was all."[65]

—Just imagine for a moment! Confucius, the country's notorious educator of public servants, of would-be advisors of kings and emperors, giving this advice! And then imagine being an emperor, expecting practical political "how-to-do" ploys of how to whip the people into line. It must have been maddening. Confucius did not give any hints of practical procedure that could have helped improve the logic of an ordinary imperial decree.

—Of course, advice was not solicited from Confucius for its practicality to educate humankind, but to give advantages to rulers. Therefore, instead, the *chüntzu* was given stories to tell about wise kings who ruled long ago (wiser and older than the one who was to be advised and wiser than anyone might ever have heard or read about). Such a ruler lived long ago. He disciplined himself with a method of *wu-wei*—with meditational inactivity.

—The implied rebuke for rulers was clear and twofold. Firstly, Confucius was redefining and softening the imperial ideals of ruthless ancestral kings into models for contemplation and emulation. And secondly, he was saying that zero governing would be better than the present style of violent active governing. Or at any rate, that *wu-wei* would do less damage to the people and to the land. Of course, a dance-and-decorum instructor could not dispense such wisdom

---

[65] Arthur Waley, trans. *The Analects of Confucius,* Book XV, 4. Vintage Books, 1938.

straight as his personal judgment. Instead, he hoped that his fictitious sagacious kings of long ago would inspire, and would to some extent be imitated. A little less arbitrary assertiveness, and a little more inactive contemplation, certainly, would have helped improve all human lives in ancient China—and would have helped soften imperial hyper-domestication.

20. Aza'zel's Goats near Göbekli Tepe

Almost all rituals in primitive hunter religion, and many in domesticator religion, were attempts at atonement, normalization, and justification. For hunters, the regrettable deeds were wounding, killing, and eating; for domesticators the new dimension added was wrongful possession of property. Acts of butchering were implied in either lifestyle. Some herders paid for herds with whole share animals; first-born animals would redeem siblings born of the same mother. Sacrificial animals at Yom Kippur were killed for what domesticators owed God. Sponsored by a king, an atonement ceremonial paid homage to both God and King. Back in days of hunting, Aza'zel was a Master of Goats, interested in keeping wild goat herds alive.

Yahweh's Cattle for Atonement

There once existed an ancient sheepskin, covered with old Hebrew letters. Two-and-a-half thousand years ago it was compiled, and copies of it have survived because the parchment scroll has become part of a larger holy book collection. The text is known as *Leviticus,* or as the third book of the *Torah.* The revised scroll was written by confident offspring of Judaic priests, apparently during their Babylonian Exile (597&586—539 BC), and these writers hoped that their book might serve as a textbook for later use. Someday, they might return to Jerusalem and have their temple rebuilt. And in that case, they would need a good manual for performing the ancient temple rituals, including the sacrosanct rites of accurately killing and butchering specified animals.

—These Judaic professionals have composed, rewritten, and edited what they remembered of stories and activities pertaining to the first tent-tabernacle cult of Israel's semi-mythical desert wanderings—of stories which once upon a time were posited as prototypes for the cult that King David (ca. 1003–971 BC) established for his tent-sanctuary in Jerusalem. His son, King Solomon (ca. 971–931 BC), upgraded the nomadic tent tabernacle to a temple of stone. So the textbook of worship and rituals, which those priestly aspirants compiled and edited during their Babylonian Exile, contained recollections of historical records and probably also some wishful improvements for the future. Any of these elements contribute to our understanding of the living tradition which continued to evolve in the minds of retainers.

—An unexpected passage in *Leviticus* provides us with a clue about religion at the time of the beginnings of the domestication process in the Fertile Crescent. Some of it recommends hypothesizing about domestication attempts regarding goats, sheep, as well as cattle. The text we choose for this discussion is Leviticus 16—the same portion that is still read by practitioners of the Jewish rite at Yom Kippur, their Day of Atonement. A few sentences in this text provide a glimpse into prehistoric Near Eastern domesticator religion —including inferences that possibly reach back as far as their inception in the Göbekli Tepe vicinity.

—It must be told up front that, in this instance, we are dealing with a puzzle-spot in the text that perhaps not even the Babylonian editors of *Leviticus* fully understood. But to their credit it must be said that, even while it conflicted with the major tenet of monotheistic *Yahweh* religion, they did not purge the problematic "goat episode" from their story. What saved this episode from being discarded was probably its unique fit in the ritual sequence of the traditional Yom Kippur (Day of Atonement) celebrations at Jerusalem's first temple. These rites were contemplated later, during their Babylonian Exile, when access to the temple was no longer possible. The disenfranchised priests continued to cling to what little they remembered about the annual sacrifices of goats—perhaps precisely because the cultural circumstances surrounding those peculiar rites had otherwise become unclear.

—During Israel's semi-mythical desert wanderings the first high-priest of the Yahweh cult was Aaron. Priestly recollections, later in Babylon, pondered the "original" divine instructions that might have been given by God to Aaron, the brother of Moses, concerning the proper performance of the traditional rites:

Fig. 42. The Scapegoat, painting by William Holman Hunt (1827-1910). Courtesy of Wikimedia Commons.

Excerpts from Leviticus 16—(RSV translation)

(3-4) Thus shall Aaron come into the holy place: with a young bull for a sin offering and a ram for a burnt offering. He shall put on the holy linen coat....

(5) And he shall take up from the congregation of the people of Israel two male goats for a sin offering and one ram for a burnt offering.

(6) And Aaron shall offer the bull as a sin offering for himself, and shall make atonement for himself and for his house. (7) Then he shall take the two goats, and set them before the Lord at the door of the tent of meeting; (8) and Aaron shall cast lots upon the two goats, one lot for the Lord and the other lot for Aza'zel. (9) And Aaron shall present the goat on which the lot fell for the Lord, and offer it as a sin offering; but the goat on which the lot fell for Aza'zel shall be presented alive before the Lord to make atonement over it, that it may be sent away into the wilderness to Aza'zel....

(15) Then he shall kill the goat of the sin offering which is for the people, and bring its blood within the veil, and do with its blood as he did with the blood of the bull, sprinkling it upon the mercy seat and before the mercy seat; (16) thus he shall make atonement for the holy place until he comes out and has made atonement for himself and for his house and for the assembly of Israel....

(20) And when he has made an end of atoning ... he shall present the live goat; (21) And Aaron shall lay both of his hands upon the head of the live goat, and confess over him the iniquities of the people of Israel, and all their transgressions, all their sins; and he shall put them upon the head of the goat, and send him away into the wilderness by the hand of a man who is in readiness. (22) The goat shall bear all the iniquities upon him to a solitary land; and he shall let the goat go in the wilderness.

(26) And he who lets the goat go to Aza'zel shall wash his clothes and bathe his body in water; and afterward he may come into the camp.

The Missing Scapegoat

People who have inherited *Leviticus* among their holy books have asked their teachers how this extra deity, Aza'zel, fits into the monotheistic sacrificial drama of Yom Kippur. The line-up of explanations over the millennia has become quite impressive, even though most of them amount to no more than ingenious concealments of ignorance. In addition, a mistranslation of "Aza'zel" into English has enriched our language with the category of a "scapegoat"—referring to someone who is being falsely accused and burdened by others. This misnomer, if reflected back to the First Temple rituals, would portray the officiating high-priest there as someone who professionally bore false witness against a goat.

—Nevertheless, the term "scapegoat" is now a bona fide English mistranslation which some social scientists meanwhile have adopted at face value and converted, rather a-historically, into a category for scientific discourse. This humorous twist, the scientific respect for the "scapegoat" mistranslation, frees me today from having to deal with it apprehensively. I am therewith liberated to tell my hypothetical story about the original Aza'zel, Lord of Goats, as about a divine personage that can be fitted into an approximate evolutionary context. It is well-nigh impossible for my evolutionary hypothesis to be more wrong than the sciences that have defined "scapegoat" to fit a mistranslation. As a byproduct, my story will also be fairer toward Aaron, the first high-priest of the Yahweh tradition, as well as toward all the priests and scribes who served at the First Temple, in Jerusalem.

Cattle, Sheep, Goats, and Priests. The priestly rite of sacrificing a male goat to Yahweh, and of giving an identical goat to Aza'zel, acknowledges two deities. This seems to imply a conflict for the avowed monotheism that was being affirmed regarding the God referred to as "Yahweh." It even suggests that, once a year, at the Jerusalem temple, something like a "dual cult" was acknowledged. The primary divine recipient of a bull, of a ram, and of a goat was of course Yahweh/El Elyon, whose combined Levite/Canaanite cult was centered at the Jerusalem sanctuary. The other recipient was a deity named "Aza'zel," who roamed in the wilderness. This means that Aaron, known as brother of Moses and the first high-priest of Yahweh, is on record as having not only modeled a golden calf-idol, but also as having acknowledged a separate Lord of Goats that may have looked like a goat—one that lived in the desert and, like Yahweh, was entitled to receive an annual goat offering.[66]

—There was an obvious difference between these divinities. Yahweh was the God of domesticators and butchers who, appropriately, insisted on having his goat killed and roasted as he had all his other animals. Aza'zel was known for having his goat delivered alive. This difference begs for an explanation.

—People who study the history of religions comparatively do have a fairly good idea who this Aza'zel could have been. He probably was a Master of Animals type of deity of earlier hunters, in the wild. Away from the progressive Near East, this type of deity has survived into later times and has scored in some of our ethnology books as a master of wild herds. In the Near East, traces of his cult seem to have survived seven millennia along the ancient margins of domesticator culture—long enough to be still reckoned with in the temple books of the Davidic dynasty.

---

[66]There is no need, at this point, to enter into a broader discussion of latent polytheism during the period of the First Temple. The Yahweh-Ashera evidence from Sinai is widely known by now. Our aim here is not to illuminate the limits of Judaic monotheism, but the antiquity of Aza'zel religion.

—Aza'zel apparently owned the wild goat herds while there still were any. With the advance of domestication practices, he saw many hunter-devotees leave his domain. One by one, human hunters killed off the god's remaining wild animals. And, as they themselves became fulltime human masters of goats and cattle, one by one they stopped acting reverently toward this ancient Master of Goats. However, it seems as though at least one, or perhaps several, priestly goat-herders must have been sending an annual share-goat to this deity, still three thousand years ago. Historically speaking, the custom must have been alive then, enough that the monarchs David and Solomon, or some of their successors, could still have accommodated a ritual gesture for Aza'zel alongside the royal Judaic cult of Yahweh/El Elyon. The Aza'zel passage in Leviticus could not have been invented very easily by rigorous monotheistic priests of Yahweh, whereas, from the point of view of the monarchy, the sacrifice of a goat to Aza'zel could have allowed a measure of administrative generosity if not also a measure of theological levity. It could have been a political accommodation to some poorer goat herder groups or clans.[67]

—Goats were deemed inferior to sheep and cattle; they were appraised as poor people's livestock. But all the while, goats were kept near homesteads to train young shepherds and to secure a steady supply of milk. Goats could feed on inferior pasture where cattle and sheep would fail to thrive. Moreover, a politically anonymous peasant culture of poor goat herders could have been lingering along the desert for some thousands of years.

—We suspect that, in earlier Neolithic days in the greater Near East, several divine animal Masters were recognized as supervisors and owners of certain species of wildlife. There almost certainly was a Lord of Sheep, a Lord of Bovines, and perhaps also some lords of camels and donkeys. But then, approximately ten thousand years ago, some of the wild animals of these lords began to be claimed by human captors and tamers. At the historical focal point for *Leviticus* 16, when 7,000 years after the beginning of domestication the royal Yahweh cult was organized, all the original divine lords of sheep

---

[67]It is quite possible that our picture of the Davidic/Solomonic dynasty here is unduly enlarged. Much of what has been ascribed in the texts to their First Temple cult may indeed be exaggeration. But then, the case of an archaic goat-liberation episode would still appear as an extraneous datum. There existed no good reasons that some exiled priestly scribes in Babylonia should have wanted to invent such an episode from scratch.

and cattle had surrendered their animals into human ownership. This means that sheep and cattle no longer grazed in the wild. The central cult of Yahweh/El Elyon had by that time absorbed all earlier species-specific sacrificial rites and demanded allegiance of all owners of sheep and cattle. But for some lingering socio-political reason, an extra allocation was made for sacrificing goats—probably because it was still customary to offer some goats alive.

—On the Day of Atonement the royal priests sacrificed to Yahweh first a bull, then a ram, and finally a goat. Animal sacrifices that earlier might have been given to a variety of divine animal Masters, as share payments for herds they owned, have by these devout proceedings gotten drawn into the larger cult of Yahweh, of the God who was revered as Creator of all species. People were thereby knitted into the monarch's organizational schemes, public sacrifices, census and taxation policies, market economy, and currency valuations—in short, into his entire net of hyper-domestication leverages. A domesticator who became obligated to sacrifice animals to a royally sponsored deity was also obliged to obey this human overlord who provided security under a mandate obtained from that same deity.

—With goats having been domesticated in the Göbekli Tepe area some seven thousand years before King Solomon built his temple, the memory of Aza'zel as a species-specific Master of Goats must have endured the entire span of time in order to still be included in Leviticus. While other Masters of Animals were being absorbed into the theology, the domain of some single universal Creator and Owner of all life on earth, Aza'zel apparently has retained his independence. The cult of a singular Aza'zel archaism could have been tolerated by a king only as long as it was politically harmless—and while it seemed theologically negligible to his priests.

—A single goat per year, given to Aza'zel, posed almost no competition to the central cult of Yahweh/El Elyon, a sole deity who ruled over everything. The priests of Yahweh were literati who, as such, competed successfully with image cults that were prevalent in Egypt and the entire Near East. These priests despised graven images and forbade man-made likenesses. Their God Yahweh was a speaker of words and a patron of scribes.

—Goat herders, who at Yom Kippur donated two male goats, one for Yahweh and the other for Aza'zel, were negligible poor illiterates in the eyes of the priests of Yahweh. Apparently the king preferred to maintain such marginal people as his outer ring of loyalty and safety. Back at his tent-sanctuary, Yahweh had priority claims on all roasted sacrificial animals of any species, including goats. He was given his choice of a male goat first, roasted; and then he even got to utilize Aza'zel's goat for his own ends. From this accommodation emerges now an answer.

—It looks as though the priests of Yahweh used the goat of Aza'zel as a convenient "trash hauler" for purposes of their own cult —quite useful for symbolic clean-up at a Festival of Atonement. Such condescending reasoning may have accounted for the fact that the presence of Aza'zel posed no threat to the Yahweh-centered monotheism. Yahweh's royal functionaries simply used the folk-religion of Aza'zel as a means for hauling and dumping Israel's sins. The poor goat-herders may never have completely understood the implied insult.[68] But fortunately, times have changed. Nowadays, archaeologists and paleontologists are quite happy to study trash in whichever strata or shape it can be found. Cultural trash-heaps contain great "has been" data.

A hypothetical Domestication Scenario

So far in this chapter I have introduced a literary source from the hyper-domestication era, one that suggests historical continuity for constructing an earlier Stone Age hypothesis. My aim is to shed a little extra light on the evolution of herder culture and religion in the ancient Near East. And to this end I will here compose a hypothetical narrative about how, under the best of circumstances during the closing phase of Göbekli Tepe, the domestication of goats could have occurred.

—All the while, I feel quite confident that Aza'zel's cult did not evolve as smoothly as my story will have it. But I think we ought to find some hypothetical trailhead that opens a path beyond the wide-spread Childean archaeological theory that explains Neolithic events essentially as an economics-driven "revolution."[69] It is quite unlikely

[68]Even if the priests of Yahweh arranged their atonement ritual to mock the Aza'zel religion, some kind of live goat offering had to be known, at the time, to be available for mocking. If it had not existed, the priests would have been in danger of mocking their own butchering sacrifices, in contrast to live offerings.

[69]Cf. Childe, V. Gordon. *Man Makes Himself.* A Mentor Book, New American Library, New York, 1951 (1936).

that ancient *homines sapientes* decided one day that domestication would be a more rational strategy of survival than was either hunting or gathering. Existential reforms of this magnitude could not possibly have resulted just from reasoning about economics. The human dependence on material necessities was whatever it has become over million-year stretches of encrusted evolution.

—In form of a hypothetical narrative I will therefore speculate how a Lord of Goats, Aza'zel, could have ended up being recognized along the periphery of King David's or Solomon's official cult of Yahweh—while these kings were engaged mostly with some advanced issues of hyper-domestication. We will try to visualize a larger context in which the prehistory of Aza'zel might be postulated in relation to both, to *Leviticus 16* as well as to data now coming to light at Göbekli Tepe.

—As far as we can tell, the first goats were domesticated in the upper Euphrates valley, in Anatolia or in northern Iraq, some 10,000 years ago—about the time when the Göbekli Tepe cult seemed ready to weaken. The domestication of sheep happened around that same time—probably in a similar manner and in that same region. Bovines were domesticated in that area perhaps a few centuries later. Some variety was still being hunted in the wild, a millennium or two later, at Çatalhöyük.

—It seems reasonable to assume that clans of progressive hunters did not experiment at the outset with the domestication of goats and sheep simultaneously. But once success was evident in dealing with one species, interest about experimenting with another could not be held back for very long. Over a relatively short time, one can assume, the successful domestication strategies spread to the lower Euphrates valley, right into the homeland where the Israelite saga of herding, of herder culture and herder religion, continued the evolutionary thread some seven millennia later. The herder sagas of King David's moderate hyper-domestication experiment were romanticized to help procure mythological support for his politics and statesmanship. Thus a narrative, featuring life-like situations more ancient than those of Abraham, appears well enough suited to sketch an early domestication hypothesis. With pertinent presuppositions put in place, our story about goat hunters and Aza'zel's goats can now be told:

The Goat Story: Somewhere along the upper reaches of the Euphrates River, a huntsman went out to hunt. He was following the trail of a small herd of wild goats. He killed and butchered a buck and gave a small share offering to Aza'zel, the Lord of Goats. The deity accepted the offering, and so the remaining carcass became legitimate property of the hunter. He carried it home and his clan ate meat.

—In spite of his successful chase, the hunter was disquieted. It seemed as though during recent years, even though pastures seemed lush and green from regular glacial run-off and rain, the wild goat herds had gotten smaller and fewer. Something tragic was happening and something radical needed to be risked. Politely asking the Lord of Goats to provide more animals did not seem to have brought any positive results lately. So, the next time the man went hunting he killed a doe—something that decent hunters tried to avoid doing. He paid his token share to the deity, butchered the animal and packed the meat into the animal's own skin. The doe's twin kids, only a few days old, he carried home alive. Several mature women lived at this camp. They were members of his extended family, and two of them were mothers who nursed babies. They suckled the goat kids until they could be weaned, far enough to slurp gruel from a pot—fooled of course by a false nipple which was a human finger.

—Then, several years later at this hunter's camp, one could see a small herd of tame goats grazing nearby, surrounded by their playful but tame offspring. The little herd at that point was still thought to belong to the human foster mothers who nursed the original orphan kids, substituting for the doe that the hunter had killed and turned into meat. The ladies never had any dealings with Aza'zel, the divine Lord of Goats, but they became accomplices in usurping the deity's authority. In those days it was the mothers and their older children who took turns watching over young tamed animals. They watched them constantly, just as they were accustomed to guard the family's human children. Thus, human mothers and their children came to be the first human masters of these domestic goats—and thereby their first actual domesticators. Had we visited this hunter's campsite still another few years later, we would have found an even larger herd of lively tame goats, grazing a little farther away from the camp, and guarded by an older boy. The young man held a long staff that featured the stub of a fork-branch modified into a hook.

—Meanwhile, on the open range, the residual wild goat herds were dwindling and disappearing. Hunters barely survived on hunting alone. Less foresighted traditional hunters at neighboring camps were starving and planning to move away—and meanwhile some were plotting to poach from their neighbor's tame herd. Of course, the owners of the tame herd suspected this danger well in advance. For that reason, the young man with the long staff had become a permanent fixture alongside his herd of goats.

—But with what justification could newfangled goat herders claim private herds and squat forever on the same stretch of hunting range? Why should hoarders be eating well while numbers of honest orthodox hunters were starving all around them? The visible stick of a goat-herder was no longer sufficient to shoo all of them away.

—As a matter of fact, the boy had been instructed by his father not to use his stick against a hunter who might come to rob one of the goats. The father would not want to lose a human son for saving a tame goat. In addition, the father remembered well the days when he, too, was still a full-time goat hunter. He understood that with an alpha- omega offering to Aza'zel, any goat hunter could easily justify robbing one of his tame animals. Aza'zel, the hunter deity, was not known to support human ownership of his living goats. All these animals belonged to the god until an alpha-omega share of their carcasses was paid. This appears to have been the religious bedrock for as long as any Neolithic huntsman could remember.

—Very well! The ancient law that governs mishaps was in effect ten millennia ago, as it still is: Whatever can go wrong will go wrong, eventually. A hunter from a neighboring camp walked up to the tame herd, killed a goat and gave his share offering to Aza'zel. The boy did not fight for his goat; though, predictable verbal grunts of complaint were exchanged between the Have and the Have-not. The boy's stick was ill suited, anyhow, to physically threaten a hunter who carried a spear—a shaft tipped with a flint point, manufactured at Göbekli Tepe, probably. The hunter draped the goat over his left shoulder and carried it away to butcher elsewhere. In his right hand he carried the spear. Both men felt bad about this encounter, about each other, and about themselves.

—In the evening a long conversation was held between the goat-herder father and his sons. The older man, meanwhile, had become father of several grown-up goat herders. Fortunately, he also was a wise man. He knew that his small clan was no match for all the hungry orthodox goat hunters who were still roaming. He needed to come up with a wise plan—a scheme that would grant his clan full title to the goats that they tamed. And of course, the legitimization required some kind of unprecedented approval by Aza'zel, the Lord of Goats. The father gave himself a full week to think about a plan, and to weigh all the words that he needed to speak. One week later, he estimated that the robber's clan would have finished eating the goat. After this, they might be tempted to strike again. But the father was determined to forestall this misfortune. He decided henceforth to act the role of an intercessory priest vis-à-vis Aza'zel on behalf of himself and all his neighbors. Thus, in order to acknowledge this man's wisdom and courage, and for the clarity of our story, we will name this first priest of Aza'zel—"Aza."

Aza, Priest of Aza'zel: Our very act of designating "Aza" as a first lay-priest revises the religion of Aza'zel from a religion of hunter-butchers to one that could become functional for domesticators and butchers. Had it been possible to convert all the hunters in the Near East quickly into rational domesticators of livestock, under a master deity a little greater than Aza'zel, or under some Lord of Sheep and Cattle that later could have been re-envisioned as universal deity for domesticators of livestock—or possibly under a God-and-Goddess pair—then, perhaps, the transition from hunting to domestication in that vicinity could conceivably have happened peaceably. But, almost certainly, it did not. It took humanity twelve millennia to rid themselves of some of those totemic hunter deities. Moreover, some archaic predator totems are still haunting us today as deadly political demons, on every continent.

—Teetering along cultural boundaries between three evolutionary steps, toward mostly man-caused shortages of food, was brought on by: (1) an increase in human intelligence and skills, which led (2) to the manufacture of better and more weapons that facilitated more effective hunting campaigns, and (3) resulted in an increase in human numbers. Men could kill animals faster than animals could reproduce. On top of this, (4) with the mountain glaciers to the north melting, increasingly more animals were able to wander away from the area, through the mountains. This is why in spite of an improving climate, a growing population of hunters created shortages and was obliged to either leave the area or to adopt domestication strategies and the accumulation of dried foods.

—Aza's story is told here to illustrate how a change from hunting to universal domestication required painful mental conversions of humanoid hunters, who had been habituated over millions of years.

Hunting and gathering were the only subsistence strategies that had been universally inherited and understood. But domestication and cultivation required that all people enable themselves, mentally and quickly, with the skills to tame goats, sheep, cattle, and donkeys, and to become servants to animals they hitherto only cared to kill. To have all people convert from predators to peaceable domesticators, in unison and voluntarily, would have been unthinkable even with the most modern methods of communication and persuasion. To accomplish this evolutionary adjustment evenly, throughout the ancient Middle East, would have surpassed the miracles of both "creation" and "evolution" together.

—For animals to be owned by humankind, and for hunter deities in competition with men to accept reduced roles, the entire experiential teeter-totter scale (introduced in Chapter Ten), needed to be rearranged. Status levels needed to be readjusted vis-à-vis animals and plants, as well as toward what seemed greater-than-human. Whatever domestic species were destined to become economically important, such as sheep, cattle, or grains, they all needed to be incorporated into the larger theodicy that was being intuited by progressive priestly shamans of the time. Visionaries would need to see traditional divine masters of animals residing at increasingly more distant places, and by their retreat legitimize humans as masters of any animals that the latter were able to keep near. Greater divine masters of humankind needed to be discovered and acknowledged by ritual. Before a post-hunter cultural order could be legitimate, safe, and possible, new greater-than-human boundaries needed to be explored, visions needed to be seen, auditions heard, and covenants negotiated with mightier gods. Different rationales needed to be adopted for sacrifice, and different procedures be found for payment and atonement.

—As far as anyone can tell, up until this Neolithic crisis, while human populations were doubling and tripling, no human hunter-mind had yet been worrying about starvation on such a large scale. Emergency domestication cults, inspired by new types of gods, required time to demonstrate the reasonableness of the strategies they offered. Divine owners who could legitimize derivative human ownership needed to be discovered, contemplated, understood, and befriended. New hopes needed to be intuited and shared.

—A new domesticator culture required time to find its focus, to legitimize the needs and rights of potential herders and planters.

We know what eventually happened. Hunters and domesticators all over the globe overshot their points of balance and ended up justifying methods of hyper-domestication, of controlling humankind.

End of the Aza Story: Finishing the story somewhat positively: the priest Aza called his three sons and told them to pick a three-year-old buck from the herd, and to follow him. They led the animal toward the camp of their hungry neighbors. Alert as hunters generally are, the huntsmen at their camp saw the four men approach. They saw that the father was unarmed, and that only the three sons were carrying sticks with which they guided a goat. What in a goat hunters' world was such strange behavior supposed to signify!

—At the edge of the camp the goat herders waited politely until the hunters came forth to meet them. There was a slight delay before the hunters could decide among themselves not to carry weapons, but to meet the visitors as four men with only three bare spear shafts between them.

—Father Aza was pleased when he saw the staffs they had chosen, and then he spoke: "Let there be peace between us! I know you are uncertain about why we have come, but we are here to express goodwill. We also need to communicate that we regard the herd of goats which we have been taming and raising as being part of our family. Our own human mothers suckled the first set of kids as though they were our extended family. We were fortunate that the twin kids we adopted were male and female. We did not butcher them. We raised them as pets for the children first, and then allowed them to breed. The buck that we adopted was pastured three years, and then we led him back to the wild range. We turned him loose as our payment to Aza'zel. For five consecutive years we have taken back a three-year-old buck as our payment to Aza'zel for the twin kids that we took. In this manner, we paid shares to Aza'zel. The buck that you see us leading here will be our sixth offering. We are on our way to the hunting range to release him.

—"Of course, we know that within a very short time hunters will find this goat. This animal will not be difficult to hunt. It has been tamed to seek the company of men. In this manner, various hunters in the area have been killing Aza'zel's friendly bucks, one each year, for five years now. We know that one animal will not go very far in feeding every hungry hunter family in the region. Therefore, we will offer you a proposition. We will lend you, and to each head of neighboring clans who comes to us, a pregnant doe to begin breeding your own tame herd. In addition, if in the future while you are out hunting you still do find some kids running about in the wild, do not kill them for food, but take them home and let them join your herd. Then, after your herd has multiplied for four generations—and several does in your herd are pregnant—you may bring one back to us in repayment for the one we let you borrow.

—"As far as we are concerned, you need not present three-year-old bucks to Aza'zel each year as we do, at least not for animals that are descended from our herd—although, as long as there are hunters roaming out there, starving, I think it would be a good idea to do so, regardless. Doing so would teach these hunters that, with domestication strategy, the scarcity of goats can be turned into sufficiency. From our camp at any rate, as a holy tradition, we will present a live goat to Aza'zel each year. We will act as presenters for all of us, and make payments to Aza'zel for the herd that we have started. Regarding the fresh kids that you might be adding to your herd from the wild—share offerings for them will be a matter between you and Aza'zel."

—"Now, my sons, let us take this buck out among the hills and turn it loose!" And turning once more to his neighbors, Aza said: "If we happen to see any of you people following us to get to the liberated goat first, we will not take notice. Whatever you do to the goat after we turn it loose is something that happens between you and Aza'zel. We will quickly return to our camp and hold our peace. And we will wait there for your visit, so that we may lend you a pregnant doe to start breeding your own animals, with our good wishes, in appreciation of the blessings of Aza'zel."

—At this point our Neolithic goat story may be allowed to end. We do not know how the hunters responded to Aza's offer. As narrated here, perhaps the story assumes an overly optimistic outlook on the ways of Neolithic humankind. Several thousand more years of learning may have been needed until closer neighborly collaboration regarding matters of domestication could be achieved. Even the exemplary herder legends about the Patriarch Abraham, recorded centuries later by scribes in the employ of King David and his successors, are still filled with economic disputes regarding water rights, grazing lands, and ownership of livestock—including the ownership of human families—which led to livestock-rustling, hot pursuits, kidnappings, and the formation of fighting alliances.

—I cannot even begin to estimate how much human blood might have been spilled in the Near East during those early millennia of transition from hunting to herding, or how many people were killed in subsequent conflicts among herders and farmers—during times when the glaciers melted, dried up, and people migrated to the two River-bottom Lands where irrigation channels could be dug more conveniently. Assumedly, many centuries of religious learning and compromising, under covenants contracted with ever mightier gods, were needed before the social and religious vision of a man like Aza could become commonplace. And by then, violence among fortified cities grew to hyper-domestication excesses, including warfare and slavery. Hordes of people were fighting each other in the names of newer and mightier gods. To feel a little better about the outcome, modern people have named the ailment that resulted from this struggle "civilization." It is the designation that is being taught in most of our schools, nowadays, as something to be thought about with a touch of satisfaction and pride.

Bibliography

Allen, Thomas George, trans. *The Book of the Dead or Going Forth by Day*. Studies in Ancient Oriental Civilizations 37. Chicago: University of Chicago Press, 1974.

Andrae, Thor. *Mohammed, the Man and His Faith*. New York. Harper Torchbooks, 1960.

Bartz, Richard. Http://creativecommons.org/licenses/by-sa/2.5/deed.en. Munich, "boar" habitat photo.

Bonnet, Hans. *Reallexikon der Aegyptischen Religionsgeschichte*. Berlin: Walter de Gruyter, 1952.

Boas, Franz. *The Central Eskimo*. Bureau of American Ethnology, Smithsonian Institution, Washington D.C., 1888.

Breasted, J. H. *Development of Religion and Thought in Ancient Egypt*. New York: Charles Scribner's Sons, 1912.

Burkert, Walter. *Homo Necans; the Anthropology of Ancient Greek Sacrificial Ritual and Myth*. Peter Bing transl.. Berkely. University of California Press. 1983.

Childe, V. Gordon. *Man Makes Himself*. A Mentor Book, New American Library, New York, 1951 (1936).

Clark, R. T. Rundle. *Myth and Symbol in Ancient Egypt*. London: Thames and Hudson. 1959.

Deacon, A. B. *Malekula, a Vanishing People in the New Hebrides*, ed. Camilla H. Wedgewood. London. Routledge and Sons. 1934.

____. "Geometrical Drawings from Malekula and other Islands of the New Hebrides," ed. Camilla H. Wedgewood. *Journal of the Royal Anthropological Institute, LXIV*. London. 1934.

De Bary, Wm. Theodore, editor. *Sources of Chinese Tradition vol. 1*. New York. Columbia University Press. 1960.

De Waal, Frans. *Chimpanzee Politics; Power & Sex among Apes*. New York. Harper and Row. 1982.

Dehnhardt, Rene. *Die Religion der Olmeken von La Venta: eine religions-archaeologische Analyse.* Doctoral dissertation, Philosophische Facultaet der Rheinischen Friedr. Wilhelm Universitaet, Bonn, 2010.

Dhammika, Ven. S. *The Edicts of King Ashoka, an English Rendering.* Buddhist Publication Society, 1993. Dharma Net Edition, Berkely, 1994, http://www.cs.colostate.edu/~malaiya/ashoka.htlm.

Diodorus Siculus, *Bibliotheca Historica.*

Eliade, Mircea. *Patterns in Comparative Religions.* New York and Scarborough. Sheed and Ward. 1958.

____. *Shamanism: Archaic Techniques of Ecstasy.* New York. Bollingen Foundation, 1964.

____. The Forge and the Crucible. Chicago. University of Chicago Press. (1962) 1978.

____. *A History of Religious Ideas,* 3 volumes. Chicago: University of Chicago Press, 1985.

Eno, Robert. "Was there a High God Ti in Shang Religion," in *Early China 15*, 1990.

____. "Shang State Religion and the Pantheon of the Oracle Texts," in *Early Chinese Religion,* John Lagerwey and Marc Kalinowski eds. Leiden and Boston: Brill, 2009.

Erman, Adolf. *Die Religion der Aegypter: Ihr Werden und Vergehen in Vier Jahrtausenden.* Berlin und Leipzig: Walter de Gruyter, 1934.

Faulkner, R. O. *The Ancient Egyptian Pyramid Texts.* New York: Oxford University Press, 1969.

____. *The Ancient Egyptian Coffin Texts.* Warminster, England: Aris and Phillips, 1973.

Freud, Sigmund. *Das Ich und das Es* (1923). Studien Ausgabe, Bd. III. Psychologie des Unbewussten. Fischer Verlag. Frankfurt a.M. 1975.

Galvin, John. "Abydos: Life and Death at the Dawn of Egyptian Civilization." National Geographic. Washington D.C., April 2005: 106-121.

Garstang, John. *Burial Customs of Ancient Egypt.* Great Britain: Kegan Paul Limited, 2002.

Geertz, Armin W. and Michael Lomatuway'ma. *Children of Cottonwood; Piety and Ceremonialism in Hopi Indian Puppetry.* ATR series vol. 12. Karl W. Luckert, general editor. University of Nebraska Press, 1987.

Geldner, Karl Friedrich. *Der Rig-Veda. Erster Teil.* Cambridge, Mass. Harvard U Press. 1951.

Goldin, Paul R. *Ancient Chinese Civilization: Bibliography of Materials in Western Languages.* April 8, 2009.

Goodall, Jane van Lawick. *In the Shadow of Man.* London and Glasgow. Collins Clear-Type Press. 1973.

Guthrie, W.K.C. *The Greeks and Their Gods.* Boston: Beacon Press, 1955.

Haile, Father Berard, O.F.M. *Women versus Men—a Conflict of Navajo Emergence—the Curly To Aheedliinii Version.* American Tribal Religions, Volume Six. edited by Karl W. Luckert. University of Nebraska Press, 1981.

Hali, Awelkhan; Li Zengxiang and Karl W. Luckert. *Kazakh Traditions of China.* Lanham: University Press of America, 1998.

Hantl, Otto. *Der Urglaube Alteuropas, Die Edda als Schlüssel zur Steinzeit,* Tübingen. Grabert-Verlag, 1983.

Hesiod. "Theogony," in *Hesiod, the Homeric Hymns and Homerica,* trans. H. G. Evelyn White. Cambridge, Mass: Harvard U. Press, 1977.

Hodder, Ian *The Domestication of Europe.* Oxford: Blackwell, 1990.

____. *The Leopard's Tale: Revealing the Mysteries of Çatalhöyük. London:* Thames and Hudson. 2006.

____. editor. *Religion in the Emergence of Civilization: Çatalhöyük as a Case Study.* Cambridge University Press, 2010.

Jensen, Adolf E. *Das religiöse Weltbild einer frühen Kultur.* Leipzig, 1939.

____. *Mythos und Kult bei den Naturvölkern*. Wiesbaden, 1951. English Translation: *Myth and Cult among Primitive Peoples*. Chicago, 1963.

Jensen, Adolf E. and Heinrich Niggemeyer. *Hainuwele: Volks-Erzählungen von der Molukken Insel Ceram*. Klostermann Verlag, Frankfurt, 1939.

____. *Die Drei Ströme: Züge aus dem geistigen und religiösen Leben der Wemale*. Leipzig, 1948.

Johnson, Buffie. *Lady of the Beasts, Ancient Images of the Goddess and her Sacred Animals*. San Francisco: Harper and Row Publ., 1981.

Joseph, Frank. *The Destruction of Atlantis*. Rochester, Vermont: Bear and Company, 2004.

Keightley, David N. *Sources of Shang History; the Oracle Bone Inscriptions of Bronze Age China*. Berkely. U of California Press. 1978.

____. *The Ancestral Landscape; Time, Space, and Community in Late Shang China (ca. 1200-1045 B.C.)*. Berkely. U of California. 2000.

____. "The Making of the Ancestor; Late Shang Religion and its Legacy," in John Lagerwey, ed. *Religion in Chinese Society, vol. 1*. Shatin, N.T, Hong Kong, (2004) 2006.

Kramer, Samuel Noah, ed. *Mythologies of the Ancient World*. Garden City, New York: Anchor Books, Doubleday, 1961.

____. *Cradle of Civilization*. New York: Time Inc., 1967.

Krickeberg, Walter. *Altmexikanische Kulturen*. Berlin. Safari Verlag. 1975. Layard, John. "Maze Dances and the Ritual of the Labyrinth in Malekula." *Folklore XLVII*. Folklore Society Great Britain. 1936.

____. *Stone Men of Malekula*. Chatto and Windus. London. 1942.

Levine Marsha A., "Domestication, Breed Diversification and Early History of the Horse," McDonald Institute for Archaeological Research, Cambridge, UK. Http://research.vet.upenn. edu/HavermeyerEsquireBehaviorLabHomePage/Reference.

Lévy-Brühl. *How Natives Think*. (1912). Translated by Lilian A. Clare, London, 1926.

Levy, Mark. *Technicians of Ecstasy: Shamanism and the Modern Artist.* Ruth-Inge Heinze Books, 1993.

Lewis, Mark Edward. *Sanctioned Violence in Early China.* Albany. State University of New York Press, 1990.

Li, Shujiang and Karl W. Luckert. *Mythology and Folklore of the Hui, a Muslim Chinese People.* Albany: SUNY Press, 1994.

Luckert, Karl W. *The Navajo Hunter Tradition.* U of Arizona Press, Tucson, 1975.

____. *Olmec Religion, a Key to Middle America and Beyond.* Civilization of the American Indian Series, Vol. 137. U of Oklahoma Press. Norman. 1976.

____. *Navajo Mountain and Rainbow Bridge Religion.* Flagstaff. Museum of Northern Arizona Press. 1976.

____. *A Navajo Bringing-Home Ceremony; the Claus Chee Sonny Version of Deerway Ajilee.* Flagstaff. Museum of Northern Arizona Press. 1978.

____. *Coyoteway, a Navajo Holyway Healing Ceremonial.* Johnny C. Cooke Navajo Interpreter. Tucson & Flagstaff. Univ. of Arizona Press and Museum of Northern Arizona Press, co-publishers. 1979.

____. *Egyptian Light and Hebrew Fire; Theological and Philosophical Roots of Christendom in Evolutionary Perspective.* Albany. SUNY Press. 1991.

____. *Dragon over America, Religion from Olmec to Aztec,* a downloadable video-script, 2000. <www.historyofreligions.com/dragon.htm>

____. *Out of Egypt an Other Son,* a downloadable video-script, 2002. <www.historyofreligions.com/outofe.htm>

Malotki, Ekkehart and Michael Lomatuway'ma. *Stories of Maasaw, a Hopi God.* ATR series vol. 10. Karl W. Luckert general editor. University of Nebraska Press. 1987.

Mann, Charles C. "The Birth of Religion: The World's first Temple," in *National Geographic*, Washington D.C. June, 2011.

Mauss, Marcel. *The Gift.* Transl. by W. D. Halls. New York, London. W. W. Norton Co. 1990.

Milankovitch, Milutin. "Glacial and Interglacial Scale, NOAA Paleoclimatology ," http://www.ncdc.noaagov/paleo.

Mithen, Steven. *After the Ice; a Global Human History 20,000 to 5,000 B.C.*, Cambridge, Mass.: Harvard University Press, 2003.

Morgan, Lewis Henry. *Ancient Society, or Researches in the Line of Human Progress from Savagery, through Barbarism to Civilization.* 1877.

Paproth, Hans-Joachim. *Studien über das Bärenzeremoniell.* München. KIaus Renner Verlag. 1976.

Peeples, Lynne. "Did Lactose Tolerance First Evolve in Central, Rather Than Northern Europe?" in *Scientific American.* August 28, 2009.

Herbert Plutschow. "Archaic Chinese Sacrificial Practices in the Light of Generative Anthropology," *Anthropoetics I,* no. 2, p. 5. University of Los Angeles, CA, 1995.

____. "Xunzi and the Ancient Chinese Philosophical Debate about Human Nature." *Anthropoetics 8, no. 1* (Spring / Summer 2002).

____. "Ancient Human Sacrifice on China's Periphery," in *Anthropoetics 14,* no. 1. 2008.

Pritchard, James B. ed. *Ancient Near Eastern Texts Relating to the Old Testament,* 3rd ed. Princeton, N.J., Princeton University Press, 1969.

Radin, Paul. *Primitive Religion, its Nature and Origin.* New York. Dover Publications. 1957.

Rasmussen, Knud. *Intellectual Culture of the Iglulik Eskimos.* (Report of the Fifth Thule Expedition 1921-1924. Vol. VII, Nr. 1.) Copenhagen, 1929.

Reichholf, Josef H. *Warum die Menschen sesshaft wurden….* Fischer Taschenbuch Verlag. Frankfurt a. M. 2010.

Renfrew, Colin. *Archaeology and Language: The Puzzle of Indo-European Origins.* New York: Cambridge University Press, 1987.

Richey, Jeffrey. "Confucius (551-479 BCE)." Internet Encyclopedia of Philosophy. Http://www.iep.utm.edu/confucius/.

Riegel, Jeffrey. "Confucius," 2006. Http://plato.stanford.edu/entries/confucius.

Rudolph, Ebermut. *Schulderlebnis und Entschuldung im Bereich säkularer Tiertötung. Religionsgeschichtliche Untersuchung.* Peter Lang Verlag. Frankfurt a. M. 1972.

Sakellarakis, Yannis and Efi Sapouna-Sakellarakis. *National Geographic Magazine.* Washington D.C. February, 1981.

Sayce, Archibald Henry and Edward Gibbon. *Ancient Empires of the East, 1.* Philadelphia: J. D. Morris. 1906.

Schärer, Hans. *Ngaju Religion.* The Hague: Martinus Nijhoff, 1963.

____. *Der Totenkult der Ngaju Dajak in Süd-Borneo.* S'Gravenhage: Martinus Nijhoff, 1966.

Schmidt, Klaus. "The 2003 Campaign at Göbekli Tepe (Southeastern Turkey)." *Neo-Lithics 2/03.* Berlin.

____. *Sie bauten die ersten Tempel; das rätselhafte Heiligtum der Steinzeitjäger.* C. H. Beck, München (2006), dtv edition 2008.

____. *Göbekli Tepe—a Stone Age Sanctuary in Southeastern Anatolia.* Exortiente—www. exoriente.org. English edition of the 2008 German volume, expected publication date Dec. 2012.

____. "Göbekli Tepe—the Stone Age Sanctuaries. New results of ongoing excavations with a special focus on sculptures and high reliefs." UDK 903.6(560.8)"633/634":636.01. *Documenta Praehistorica XXXVII* (2010).

Smith, Jonathan Z. "A Pearl of Great Price and a Cargo of Yams: A Study of Situational Incongruity." *History of Religions 16*, no. 1 (1976): 1-11.

Spencer, A. J. *Death In Ancient Egypt.* Great Britain: Penguin Books Ltd, 1982.

Turnbull, Colin M. *The Forest People; a Study of the Pygmies of the Congo.* New York. Simon and Schuster. 1961.

Ucko, Peter J. and G. W. Dimbleby. *The Domestication and Exploitation of Plants and Animals.* Aldine Publishing Co.. Chicago, New York. 1969.

Vajda, Edward J. "The Dene–Yeniseian Connection," (February 2008 Symposium) in *Anthropological Papers of the University of Alaska,* edited by James Kari and Ben Potter. June 2010.

____. "Ket Shamanism" in *Shaman*, Vol. 18. NOS. 1-2. Spring/Atumn, 2010.

Van Seters, John. *The Hyksos, a New Investigation.* New Haven, Conn.: Yale University Press, 1966.

Waley, Arthur, transl. *The Analects of Confucius.* Vintage Book. George Allen & Unwin. 1938.

Wei, Cuiyi and Karl W. Luckert. *Uighur Stories from Along the Silk Road.* Lanham: University Press of America, 1998.

Wild, E. M. et al. "Neolithic massacres: Local skirmishes or general warfare in Europe?" *International Radiocarbon Conf.* 18, Wellington, NZ. 2004.

Wilkins, Jayne, Benjamin J. Schoville, Kyle S. Brown, Michael Chazan. "Evidence for Early Hafted Hunting Technology." *Science Magazine.* Vol. 338 no. 6109 pp. 942-946. 16 Nov. 2012.

Wilford, John Noble. "With Escorts to the Afterlife, Pharaohs Proved Their Power." *New York Times* 16 Mar. 2004.

Wlosok, Antonie. *Römischer Kaiserkult.* Darmstadt: Wissenschaftliche Buchgesellschaft, 1978.

Index

ISBN 978-0-9839072-2-0 paperback

www.ingramcontent.com/pod-product-compliance
Lightning Source LLC
Chambersburg PA
CBHW032147080426
42735CB00008B/617
* 9 7 8 0 9 8 3 9 0 7 2 2 0 *